OTHER BOOKS

Bunty's War: A young girl's diary tells her story of survival as she grows from schoolgirl to woman in World War Two England.

Bunty's New World: A young woman's diary records wonder, hilarity, despair and success in her new world, America, after surviving her ordeal in World War Two England.

BUNTY'S BEGINNINGS

BUNTY'S
BEGINNINGS

—A Lion on our Doorstep—

IDA GREENE

ISBN: 9798642219904

In loving memory of my parents, Jack and Ida Amiss, without whose lives and mine this book could never have been written.

CONTENTS

PREFACE .XIII
INTRODUCTION XV

EARLY DAYS
The Edwardian Ditchfields 1
"The Oojahs" 3
The Amisses 4
The Tape Recorder 5
Dad the Daredevil 6
A Sailor's Heritage 10
Attraction of Opposites—Wedding Bells 13
Opportunity Knocks 17

BEGINNING THE ADVENTURE
Dad Goes First 23
Destination Kenya 26
Preparations 27
Port Outward 31
Portuguese Men 'o War 33
The Blue Mediterranean 34
The Canal. 39
King Neptune's Court: 42

KENYA
Mombasa Reunion 47
The Lunatic Express, Train to Nowhere 55
Flora, Fauna and Massacres 61
The Great Rift Valley 78
Effie and Kisumu 81
The Cover-Up 99
Nature's Beauty—and Jiggers 107

LIVING THE ADVENTURE

Sightseeing in Paradise 118

Social Circles and the Happy Valley Set 126

The Black Mamba 137

Malaria! 140

Brain Teasers 144

A Walk in the Sun 146

Mother Nature's Fury 150

Christmas and Hogmanay 152

EXPECT THE UNEXPECTED

A Welcome Surprise! 161

An Unwelcome Shock 163

Our World Turns Upside Down 167

UGANDA, HERE WE COME!

Namasagali 175

First Impressions 180

Life on the African Frontier 191

A New Friend, New Challenges 201

A Call from on High 206

GREAT EXPECTATIONS

Greasing the Ways 213

Doctor Singh 217

We Taste Uganda! 221

Tribes in our Household 228

UGANDA THE BEAUTIFUL

The Mountains of the Moon 237

A Furry Present 249

Ripon Falls 251

Obonyo's Cow 256

Christmas with the "Commish" 261

NOW WE ARE THREE

Doctor Singh to the Rescue 269

Namirembe Cathedral 289

Ayisha—Crisis in Paradise 297

The Enchanted Forest 303

Joey 313

DANGER IN PARADISE

Terror of the Nile .321

Lion on our Doorstep 326

Little Ida 330

A Hideous Tragedy 338

ENGLAND BECKONS

Pack Up Your Troubles! 345

Standing on the Equator. 349

Starboard, Home .355

Bunty Gets Her Nickname 361

HOME TO STAY

Doctor's Verdict 367

A Home of our Own 372

Polly 377

Polly the Prankster .381

Moving South 389

EPILOGUE

REFERENCES

Preface

IDA AMISS JOLTED awake; it was barely daylight on a cold Sunday morning in the north of England. "Jack, wake up! What's that noise?" She tapped her sleeping husband urgently on the shoulder, catching him in mid-snore.

"Oh no, what time is it?" he grumbled, opening one eye. He had been enjoying the warmth of a comfortable bed and was looking forward to what he called an extra 'forty winks'. Ida shook his shoulder. "What noise, anyway?" he demanded.

"There's someone moving about in the house, Jack; I heard them. You know we've had some break-ins lately in the neighborhood. Please get up and see."

Jack groaned and sat up. He had just put one foot down on the cold bedroom floor when a timid knock came on the closed door. A little voice asked, "May I come in and snuggle?"

"Oh, Jack, it's alright—it's only our little Bunty," said Ida, with a sigh of relief. She addressed the closed door, "Of course, dear, just reach up and turn the doorknob to come in." She moved over in the bed, making room between Jack and herself, a warm spot that I climbed into clutching my favorite toy—'Jock' the knitted monkey—by one leg. Soon, we were all rearranged under the double-bed blankets and soft eiderdown (down comforter). By now, both parents realized that all thoughts of the luxury of sleeping late were out of the question, so Dad went into his usual performance to keep his feet warm. He lifted both legs to raise the blankets a few inches, sending a cold draft up through the bed. The exaggerated sounds of chattering teeth from Mom and me fell on deaf ears, as usual. When the blankets were high enough, Dad pulled his legs back and lowered them, creating a shelf folded into the blankets with his feet tucked warmly into it. Once this was done to his satisfaction, we knew we could proceed.

I came straight to the point with my usual topic on such occasions. "Tell me a story about when you were in Africa, please," I begged my sleepy parents—adding proudly, even if a bit redundantly—"that's where I was born, you know!" My parents laughed at the earnest expression on my face; I usually added this fact as the persuasive clincher. Knowing that further sleep would be out of the question, they settled back on the pillows and took turns to repeat one of the stories that I loved to hear over and over again throughout my childhood.

As my life passed into adulthood and I came to live in America, I remembered many of these stories of my parents' extraordinary life on the East African frontier in the 1920s. I thought to myself, "It's a shame to let those stories be forgotten; I'll have Mom and Dad tell them on my tape recorder, and maybe one day I'll write them up. Who knows, they might make a good book! And because my life *began* when Mom and Dad were in Africa, I'll call it *Bunty's Beginnings*."

It's many years and almost a whole lifetime later, but here's the book; now completing a trilogy—a legacy to leave for my family and to anyone else who may be interested.

I have always believed that writing is merely speech written down. This is how I wrote *Bunty's Beginnings,* also *Bunty's War* and *Bunty's New World* . Mom and Dad spoke "*English* English"; here and there you may find the "American English" translation in parentheses.

So now, come with me as we uncover the story of their event-filled early lives, told by Mom and Dad in their own words. I hope you will enjoy reading this book as much as I have enjoyed writing it.

Introduction

"LONG AGO AND far away, I dreamed a dream one day . . ." The old 1940s song kept haunting me as I dreamed about writing this book.

Although I was too young at the time to remember anything about my first two years spent in Africa and our subsequent return to live in England, I grew up remembering my parents' stories, repeated many times as family stories usually are. Their voices on my tape recordings re-told these tales as they happened when they lived almost on the equator in the 1920s. As I began to write from the tape recordings, I sometimes found myself substituting my own edits and writing style in some of the notes that Mom and Dad had read into the microphone about their incredible experiences. In some places, their notes were sketchy, to say the least, and I took the liberty of expanding them from my research. I hope I am forgiven. But first, let me fill you in on what I learned by researching the background of the continent that my parents would call home for four remarkable years.

I was amazed to discover that Africa is so big! It is the second-largest continent in the world, next to Asia. Statistics show that it is bigger than all of China, India, the continental United States and most of Europe, combined! I didn't know that the Sahara Desert in northern Africa is larger than the United States! At this writing, there are 54 different countries in Africa, each with its own native language and traditions. And topping all the other facts, Africa has the dubious distinction of being called the hottest continent in the world.

Now to explore the historical background of the place on this great continent where my parents found themselves in 1924, which was then called British East Africa:

A "traveler's handbook" written by a Roman traveler around 40-70 AD, recorded that goods were traded by merchants at ports on the East African coast. It is thought that these traders were Arabs. They came in successive waves, bringing with them the teachings of Islam, which, with the archeological discovery of remains of their wooden mosques, are thought to have been established as early as the 900s AD. However, there is no record of these Arab traders having ventured inland from the coast at that time.

The modern recorded history of East Africa began when Portuguese explorer Vasco da Gama landed at Mombasa on the east coast of what is now Kenya, in 1498. The Portuguese eventually took over in the area. Fast-forward to 1729, when the Arabs ousted the Portuguese and the region came under the rule of the Sultan of Zanzibar, who profited handsomely by the trade in ivory and also in the human slave trade (much to the consternation of the British).

Traders from India were already entrenched in the area when Christian missionaries arrived from Europe, teaching and giving medical help wherever the natives trusted them. In some places, they were persecuted and even killed by natives fearing new ideas that threatened their belief in traditional superstitions and witch doctors. The missionaries contrived to practice up-to-date medical techniques by encouraging the local witch doctors to add their age-old magical chants, thereby building trust and keeping the peace for all concerned. Their Christian faith gave the missionaries strength to persevere. They slowly established schools and translated the Bible into local tribal languages. Through the efforts of those missionaries over the years, it has been recorded that many previously rival tribal members became united in their conversion to the doctrine of Christianity.

In the mid-1800s, British explorers were searching for the source of the River Nile. Doctor David Livingstone influenced the explorations of Burton, Speke, Grant, Cameron and Stanley, resolved by the expedition of Speke and Grant in 1892 which established the source of the White Nile to be at Lake Victoria.

In 1873, the British succeeded in pressuring the Sultan of Zanzibar to give up his slave trade. By the mid-1880s, Africa was being divided up by the European nations. British influence was challenged by the Germans, who, in 1884, persuaded some of the East African tribal chiefs to switch their allegiance from the Sultan of Zanzibar to the Kaiser of Germany. They followed up by establishing the German East Africa Company. When this news leaked out to the British, they were shocked into establishing the rival British East Africa Company in 1888, claiming the territory of Kenya and also neighboring Uganda. The company was poorly financed, however, and went bankrupt. In 1895, The British Government took over the bankrupt company and the territories of Kenya and Uganda became British Protectorates.

In the face of more threats by European rivals, it was realized that Britain needed a means of transporting (if necessary) men and materiel to defend its East African territories. The British Parliament was eventually persuaded that it would be politically and financially to its advantage to finance a British East African Railway, which was completed in 1906 (more about this later).

Fast-forward again to World War One: Britain defended its territories against the Germans who had settled in eastern Africa. After war's end in 1918, the Treaty of Versailles awarded the defeated Germans' territory Tanganyika (now called Tanzania) to the British. Tanganyika joined Kenya and Uganda to become British East Africa.

In the years following World War One, Kenya and Uganda began to attract a variety of British and other European settlers. British cattle-farmers imported cattle to cross with the skinny African ones, resulting in a better breed which could withstand the climate and improve the production of the local variety. Sheep farmers followed suit, crossing British sheep with the hairy, non-wool-producing African ones that looked more like goats than sheep! Other settlers carved out farms and plantations on the fertile land in the Highlands, whose altitude made its climate favorable despite its proximity to the equator (it was recorded that exposure to the direct rays of the sun at the equator could kill a person). In the 1920s, people came privately or were sent by the British Government to develop the natural resources of the area and to open up trade and commerce.

On my trips back to England after I came to live in America, I took a small tape recorder with me and asked Mom and Dad to record the stories that I had heard during my childhood. These include accounts of their early lives which were destined to result in their chance meeting, their marriage, and their adventures in Africa where I came into their lives: Bunty's beginnings!

There were no diary entries to guide me in writing *Bunty's Beginnings* as there had been for *Bunty's War* and *Bunty's New World*, so I used the tape recordings which had been made by Mom and Dad as a framework around which to build this book. I added the many characters' personalities as I envisioned them and conversations as they may have taken place. The names of some of these people have been created from what I thought they may have been. Much research has been needed to verify, expand and add to the facts spoken into the tape recorder, but I have been fascinated to learn more about my own "roots" than I never dreamed existed.

Periodically, when I was growing up in England, I would hear my parents speak a string of Swahili words and phrases—no doubt when they didn't want me to know what they were saying! Never having seen the words written, I only remembered them phonetically, but thanks to the miracle of today's electronic language translation on the computer I was able to put together some of them to use in this book.

It's time now to set the stage for our journey to what used to be called The Dark Continent, but first let me introduce the two main characters and their very diverse backgrounds: Mom and Dad Amiss, a.k.a. Ida ("Sunshine") and Jack.

The story begins . . .

EARLY DAYS

The Edwardian Ditchfields

BUNTY: Both my parents were born in Sunderland, which was then a thriving seaport and shipbuilding town on the River Wear where it emptied out on the cold and windy northeast coast of England, across the North Sea from Denmark. With its 670 years of shipbuilding history and its 400 registered shipyards, Sunderland had become known as the shipbuilding capital of the world. But let's begin our story with Mom and her family.

High-spirited, fun- loving, with dancing green eyes and auburn highlights in her long, brown hair, Ida Ditchfield was the fifth child in a family of seven. Tragically, her younger brother Enoch was killed in the final days of World War One. Her four older sisters had arrived in quick succession: Lily, Mildred, Hilda and Eleanor. Ida enjoyed the luxury of being the youngest girl and her father's favorite. Her younger brother, Bryan, was a surprise for his parents after his mother had thought she was beyond child-bearing age; today he would be labeled a menopause baby.

The Ditchfield parents, Enoch and Eleanor (fondly known to family and friends as Nock and Nell) ran their busy family life in a large Victorian house in Sunderland with the help of a scullery maid to do the heavy cleaning, the laundry and some of the cooking. A live-in relative, Auntie Annie, doubled with the housework and as a nanny for the children. Somewhere along the line, two cousins came to live with the Ditchfields; the house must have been bulging with children!

Supporting all of them was Enoch Ditchfield who had inherited from his father a successful tailoring business, together with three flourishing tailor shops and a thorough mastery of his trade.

The Edwardian Ditchfield household was a lively one, full of activity and laughter, and father Enoch saw to it that his children were encouraged to think for themselves. By the time the girls were grown up, they had bowed to the new fashions and stopped wearing long dresses that covered their ankles—a bold departure that was considered quite scandalous in those days. Mother Eleanor wouldn't have thought of doing such a thing, and the neighbors were shocked when her daughters appeared in public with their above-the-ankle skirts.

Father Enoch was determined that each of his children would be competent in playing at least one musical instrument, also that they would be trained to be financially independent as adults. Lily played the mandolin and became a schoolteacher. Mildred played the piano and became a milliner with her own hat shop. She was the stylish "lady of the family" and married a wealthy man. Hilda married young and quickly produced a son, but found time to combine her beautiful singing voice with her husband's tenor in duets at family gatherings and church concerts. Eleanor didn't join in the family concerts. Her instrument (if she had one) remains a mystery. She became a good cook and a confectioner with her own little sweet shop (candy store). Eleanor loved children. Although she never married and had children of her own, she was a favorite with the grandchildren when they came along; her patience was never-ending in teaching them rowdy card games as she sat with them on the soft drawing-room carpet. Last, but not least, young Ida could play the piano by ear, read music for the more serious pieces, paint, recite poetry and act.

With her green thumb and love of growing flowers, Ida dreamed of training as a horticulturalist to work in a Ditchfield uncle's greenhouses, but her father said that was a man's job and no place for a woman. She was artistically inclined and loved to entertain, so father Enoch sent her to art and elocution lessons instead. With her professional horticultural hopes in tatters, she contented herself by planting every square inch of available soil with flowers, wherever she went and as long as she lived. Although she was inclined to show her emotions and was easily moved to tears, she never allowed life's disappointments to defeat her; she made the most of what was left! As a result, she became proficient in what she learned in her elocution classes, entering local and national competitions called (in Welsh) "eisteddfods" which were held regularly all over England and Wales among competitors from several counties within each region of Britain. The eisteddfods in the north of England attracted men and women who excelled in art, music, poetry and drama from Sunderland and the surrounding cities, towns and villages. Ida's talents led her to win prizes at eisteddfods for her memorized dramatic renderings of the long, classical poems which were plentiful in those days. Some of her paintings were hung in the Sunderland Art Gallery. She also put her artistic talent to practical use as a window dresser for her father's tailor shops.

"The Oojahs"

The local brick church had been erected by workmen of another Ditchfield uncle, a building contractor. Before radio, television or other present-day means of family entertainment, the church people used the attached recreation hall—equipped with a large stage—as a "home- away from home." As well as being filled with church-school classes on Sundays, during the rest of the week Saint Gabriel's church hall was used for dinners, concerts, recitals, meetings, lectures and discussions. It also provided a perfect proving ground for father Ditchfield and his children's talents—with a few cousins, aunts and uncles recruited to help!

This multi-talented group was known as The "Oojahs Concert Party" (nowadays it would be called a variety show). Consisting of extended Ditchfield family comedians, singers, dramatic actors, magicians, dancers and musical instrumentalists, the Oojahs raised money for their church by traveling a circuit of other local church halls costumed as clowns, providing the variety of entertainment which was so popular in that era. An old photo of the Oojahs, seventeen members strong, shows a young Ida Ditchfield in her clown's costume, playfully stretched out on the floor in front of the group and posing propped up on one elbow.

In addition to being an Oojah, Ida was active also in a local drama group. She appears in another old photo costumed as Maria in Shakespeare's play "Twelfth Night". With all of her talents, she became quite well-known locally. Life, for her, was what the old song calls "A Bowl of Cherries".

The Amisses

BUNTY: My Dad, John (Jack) Heywood Amiss, was born (no doubt, with the help of a midwife) in a small house within walking distance of the Sunderland docks; an area across town from the more fashionable surroundings of Mom's home. He was the second of seven children in a family of five boys and two girls. His parents, Luke and Jane Amiss, were devout Quakers (also called Friends). Mother Jane put her religion into practice by her devotion to the poor and needy. She spent endless time and her spare money caring for less fortunate families in the neighborhood. Young Jack would often help himself to a piece of her oven-bottom cake (cooked slowly in a huge baking tin in the bottom of the coal-stoked oven, hence its name) which was destined for a needy neighbor's supper. He was impatient with the silence at the Quaker meeting house, and more often than not he arranged to disappear with his friends on some escapade when the rest of the family went to church.

Jack was endowed with a strong singing voice and he loved to sing. When he was still a boy soprano, one of his pals invited him to sing in the choir at his church, a neighborhood branch of the Church of England (Episcopal). Here, young Jack found his niche; much to the consternation of his parents he became a Church of England choirboy! He began to attend the church regularly, eventually growing up to become a full member and by then singing in a well-developed baritone voice. His singing wouldn't be confined to the church choir, however. He also sang in the school chorus, and he would become locally famous as he grew up for his repertoire of sea shanties.

Dad spoke very little of his father Luke and mother Jane. Unlike my recollections of the Ditchfields, I have only a dim remembrance of my grandfather Amiss. I have no recollection of ever having met my grandmother Amiss, and I knew only three of Dad's siblings, Lillian, Stanley and Arthur.

I have a feeling that the Amisses were not readily accepted by the Ditchfields.

***

The Tape Recorder

BUNTY: Fast-forward to 1945. At the end of World War Two, I married an American soldier and came to America; one of the approximately seventy thousand G.I. Brides from Britain. After the compulsory three-year waiting period, I studied the requirements diligently and was granted American citizenship. Having visited me in America the year after I arrived, my parents sent me a round-trip ticket to visit England the following year. I had been given a little tape recorder as a Christmas gift, so I took it with me along with a supply of tapes. Setting the machine down in front of my parents, I asked them to talk about their life experiences.

Dad was a born engineer; everything mechanical had interested him since his early childhood. The recorder intrigued him. He was also a good talker! I had no trouble persuading him to speak into the microphone about his boyhood in Sunderland, although he complained, "Well, it's a bit short notice, you know, Bunty. I'd have liked more time to think it over and prepare, but I'll do me best. As you know, I've some good yarns to tell! "

Mom was content to sit and listen—she seemed in awe of the tape recorder—but Dad was in his element. He switched it on and picked up the microphone. Knowing his love of singing, I wasn't too surprised when he started his commentary with a song; a somewhat garbled version of a little ditty from Gilbert and Sullivan's '*H.M.S. Pinafore*'. He had obviously forgotten the sequence and most of the words, but he didn't pay attention to such details!

Clearing his throat, he announced, "Hello, this is John Heywood Amiss speakin'. I've been asked by me daughter to talk about me boyhood, so here's the introduction:

'When I was a boy I went to sea, and now I'm a captain in the King's Navee.
    I cleaned the windows and I swept the floor, and I polished the handle on the big front door,
    I polished that handle so care-ful-ee, and now I'm a captain in the King's Navee.'

Dad the Daredevil

The tape kept running, and Dad's confident speaking voice began with the remains of a Sunderland accent; also, he was in the habit of throwing in a few nautical expressions as he went along:

"As a boy, I lived with me family down by the Sunderland docks, in a neighborhood close enough to the shipyards so that the dock workers could walk to work. Blow me down, not only did Sunderland *make* ships, it also produced men to *take* them out to sea and sail them. In the local Sunderland accent, the sayin' was: 'We makkem and takkem.' Sunderland natives are still known in the area by the nickname, the 'Makkems' and 'Takkems'.

"Me Dad went to sea whenever he could; he was never out of work because he filled in the time between voyages by workin' in the shipyards as a steam fitter. Oh aye, we were a seafarin' family, alright. I recall one large family get-together where there were a lot of old 'sea dogs': among 'em, no fewer than *twenty* Masters (captains)—active and retired! Me grandfather owned his own sailin' ship, and sailed in international trade between England and the Far East. On these long voyages, he took me grandmother with him—he often took his two boys (me Dad and his brother) to sea with him, too. Seafarin' has been in me blood for generations.

"Oh aye, I've had an adventurous life, alright! I believe me first adventure took place when I was scarcely three or four years old. It must have been a good 'un, to be impressed that deeply on me memory from so many years back! I can remember bein' lost. When me poor, frantic Mam found me, I was in custody at the local police station! I don't remember where I'd wandered off to, or what she said to me. She probably didn't report it to me Dad, or he'd have given me a good wallopin' and I'd have remembered that! I must've had the wanderlust, even at that young age. Me parents always said I was born with an itchy foot!

"Growin' up, we were an adventuresome lot of daredevils, me pals and me. After school and on weekends our playground was the Sunderland docks where we made our own adventures. One time, we built a raft out of scrap lumber and poled it down the River Wear. The tide was goin' out and we began to panic when we could hardly control the raft; the current had started to carry it toward the river's estuary. With all of our strength and by the skin of our teeth we managed to steer the raft to the riverbank before the current could sweep us out to sea on the recedin' tide. It was almost dark when we hopped off the raft, left it there, and made our way back home. I never dared to tell me Mam what took us so long or where we'd been!

"Oh aye, and I'll never forget that miserable owner of the local pork shop. No wonder he wasn't pleasant with us; we boys tormented him, alright—poor sod. He'd had a rail put up inside his shop window, and hangin' from it was a row of pig carcasses on hooks, ready to be cut up. Me pals and I dared one another to sneak through the shop door when the 'pork man' wasn't lookin' and give the nearest carcass a good shove, which made the whole row slide across the rail and fall off it at the other end. Once they began to move, we would run away as fast as we could, all the way home to safety. One day, it was *my* turn to be dared. I gave the nearest carcass a good shove, then when they all began to move I ran for me life with the furious shopkeeper in hot pursuit. He carried a 'steel' in his belt for butcherin' the pigs; I could hardly bear to think how terrible it would be if he caught me and hit me with it. I tried to run faster, but his legs were a lot longer than mine and I knew he was gainin' on me. I realized I could never get away in time and I panicked as I thought of the terrifyin' consequences."

Dad paused dramatically:

"I ran down the street as fast as I could. When I came to a house with a front porch, I quickly dived into the space under it, terrified that the 'pork man' had seen me hidin' place. I lay there shakin' with me heart poundin', expectin' him at any minute to arrive and drag me out feet first. He stopped right in front of the porch. I held me breath. At last I heard his footsteps dyin' away as he retreated, empty-handed, then I knew he thought he'd lost me. Before the homeowner could come out and ask me what I was doin' under his porch, I picked meself up and ran like hell for home. Luckily, me Mam didn't ask me why I was all out of breath! I never told me Dad, either. I thought to meself, 'Eee, man! If ever that butcher found out 'oo I was, and told me Dad, I'd never sit down again for a week!' Me Dad always told me, 'Jack, lad, now remember: *gan canny* (be careful)', but more often than not I forgot about his warnin'! I didn't try that again; those pork carcasses had lost all their attraction for me. Me Mam couldn't understand why I didn't want to eat pork after that, either!"

"I first became aware that education was really important, one day when I was growin' up and I saw laborers in the docks emptyin' the hold of a ship filled with iron ore. They were stripped to the waist as they shoveled the red iron ore into barrels to be transported. Their skin was covered with red dust from the ore, and there was nowhere to wash it off when they were finished, so they waded into the river and washed themselves in the murky water before they went home. Sunderland was also in a coal-minin' region. I went to a coal mine one day and watched some of the miners come up from the coal seams in an open-sided cage (coal mine elevator), stripped to the waist after diggin' in the mine all day. Black coal dust covered their faces, arms and upper bodies. It stuck to their skin and had to be scrubbed off. In those days, the mine owners provided no facilities for them to wash; they had to go home to get scrubbed clean. I thought to meself, 'That's not the life for you, Jack.' I knew then and there that I'd have to do well in school to escape such misery."

BUNTY: Jack Amiss grew up tough. He was medium height and muscular; good-looking, with hazel eyes and a thick mop of dark brown hair framing his weather-bronzed face. He was quick-witted, pro-active, and what they call in America an "A" student. He had an almost photographic memory. A compulsive reader and talented writer, he graduated from school with honors at age fourteen. He had won several prizes for excellence in mathematics in his school years. The awards were usually books: classic tales and poems full of adventures and daring deeds written by famous authors, which were "right up his alley". When he left school, he went to work as an apprentice in one of the shipyards. He soon became fascinated with the workings of ships' turbines in their engine rooms, prompting him to begin to study for qualifications as a marine engineer.

A Sailor's Heritage

Dad enjoyed talking about his early life so much that he didn't even pause for a cup of tea!

"When I was old enough to go to sea, I was footloose and fancy free, so I spent the early years seein' the world and takin' exams, workin' me way up to higher qualifications as an engineer. My first rung on the ladder was when I signed on as ship's fifth engineer with the British Merchant Navy, makin' transatlantic runs on oil tankers to and from America.

"Years later, In World War One, I signed up for duty in the Royal Naval Volunteer Reserve. With me qualifications by that time, the Royal Navy granted me a commission as a sub-lieutenant RNVR, when I was called to active duty toward the end of the war. I entered the service in 1917 as an engineer-officer and continued to sail on oil tankers.

"I was on me favorite ship, the *San Zeferino,* an oil tanker owned by Eagle Oil Transport Company which named its freighters after Christian saints. We were on the Atlantic, on our way to take on oil at Tampico, Mexico, when she was torpedoed by a German submarine. She began to take on water, and I quickly escaped up the ladder from the engine room onto the deck. It was obvious that she would sink. Another ship in our convoy came up alongside and took all the men off her except five who lost their lives. On the rescue ship from a distance, we sadly watched the *San Zeferino* sink slowly into the sea. One of our crew had a camera and took a photo of her goin' down by the bow before she made her final plunge into the Atlantic. I have a copy of that photo in me album. Aye, she was a gallant ship, alright; I'll never forget her."

BUNTY: It may be appropriate here to say that I remember from earliest childhood a singing game; a special favorite of mine that Mom, Dad and I used to play whenever Dad came home from the sea. The three of us would form a little circle with our arms around each other, and slowly rotate while we sang:

> "Three times round goes our gallant ship,
> Three times round goes she,
> Three times round goes our gallant ship,
> And she sinks to the bottom of the sea."

As the verse ended, we all flopped down in a giggling heap onto the floor. I can close my eyes, see us in my mind's eye and hear us in my mind's ear, to this day! Looking back, I think that in his own way this was Dad's lasting tribute to the *San Zeferino,* with a light touch added!

***

But let's go back to Dad's tape recording of his nautical career:

> "Before the war ended, I sailed on oil tankers to England with desperately-needed oil from Galveston, Texas; New Orleans, Louisiana; and Philadelphia, Pennsylvania. We were torpedoed twice more after the *San Zeferino,* losin' all three ships. Luckily, I was picked up and brought to safety each time to join another ship.
> "After the war, I volunteered to stay in the Royal Navy for an extra year on a minesweeper, clearin' mines from the English Channel to make it safe for post-war commercial shippin'. For this extremely dangerous job, I was awarded a special medal by the British Government—one of the very few that were minted for this particular work. I was proud of that medal,

and someday I hope to pass it on to me grandson, now that I'm lucky enough to have one. (BUNTY: This medal is now his grandson's most precious tangible reminder of his Grandpa).

"In 1920, I used some of me savin's to pay for the college courses I would need to take in Sunderland to earn me a Chief Engineer's Ticket (Certificate.) I also took courses as a Deck Officer, which included navigation studies and others that would eventually qualify me as a ship's Master.

"It was while I was takin' these college courses that I met Ida Ditchfield."

***

BUNTY: I was just a gleam in Dad's eye when he met Mom in 1920. On Saturday mornings, when her classes were in recess for the week-end, Ida indulged her love of outdoor sports playing field hockey with a team of girls called The Shamrocks. She carried a reminder of her hockey days for the rest of her life; she was hit on the forehead just above her left eye by a stray hockey ball. Fortunately, it missed her eye and there was no serious damage. However, a bruise with a lump appeared above her eyebrow. The lump didn't subside, but it eventually calcified and there it remained—an obstinate, unwanted decoration. After the accident, she wore her hair combed down over that side of her forehead for the rest of her life to hide the permanent reminder of her hockey days!

One fateful Saturday morning, the Shamrocks played against the men's hockey team that Jack Amiss had joined while he was attending his college classes.

***

BUNTY: It was on my next trip to England that Mom decided to try out the tape recorder. Envying Dad's pleasure in using the machine and seeing him reading from notes he had made, she had decided to make some notes of her own to give her confidence and avoid awkward pauses when she spoke.

Mom began to read in her well-trained voice (the result of those elocution classes):

Attraction of Opposites—Wedding Bells

"It was half-time in the hockey game and I had gone over to the stand where they served water with lemon slices to cool us off after dashing about the field. Instead of squeezing the lemon into my glass of water, I drank the water and ate the lemon slice, as I usually did! As I did so, I had the uneasy feeling that someone was watching me. Turning, I saw a handsome, dark- haired, athletic-looking man, leaning on his hockey stick and staring at me curiously."

Dad broke in, with his Sunderland accent:

"Oh aye, I thought to meself when I first saw Ida, 'Aye, now there's a nice-lookin' lass, and she's certainly got a fine pair of legs!' But watchin' her suckin' on that lemon slice without so much as a sour face, I blurted out, 'What are you doin' that for?' "

Mom interrupted:

"I felt annoyed at this silly question. I snapped, 'Oh, because I like the taste of sour lemons at half-time, of course. I always eat the lemon and drink the water!' Then I thought, 'Well, *that* got his attention! Oh, but I shouldn't have snapped at him and sounded so sarcastic; now he'll never speak to me again. He'll think I'm very cheeky (impertinent)—and he's so attractive, I don't want to risk losing him!' "

Dad was becoming impatient with Mom:

"Now, Ida, don't interrupt; this is *my* story," he complained. He went back to his notes:

"I'd never had a steady girlfriend yet—never had time for one, really—and I couldn't help thinkin', 'Well, this one's not only good lookin', she's got spirit, too! But these days a nice young girl doesn't go out alone with a man without a chaperone! Hell's bells! But oh, wait; come to think of it, I believe me pal Bobby goes out with her friend, Flo. I really do want to get to know Ida better. I've got it! If Flo will per-suade *her,* and I can persuade *Bobby,* maybe we can all go on a date together.'

"In the followin' weeks, I met Ida again regularly at the lemonade stand. It was gettin' near the end of hockey season. I thought to meself, 'Well, Jack me lad, it's now or niver!' So I got up me courage and said, 'Ida, I've been wonderin' if you and Flo would go with Bobby and me for a day out on the beach next week with another couple, some friends of Bobby's? Please say you will.' I held me breath. To me surprise, she nodded and—just like her—she said, 'I thought you'd never ask me, Jack! The answer is yes, I would love to go!' "

BUNTY: Flo and Ida probably chattered excitedly while they packed a picnic lunch for the occasion. On this part of the northeast coast at Sunderland, its wide beaches of yellow sand are punctured by outcrops of rock and separated from the concrete path on the prom-enade above them by a lofty sea wall. At high tide in the savage winter storms, North Sea breakers dash furiously against the sea wall after rolling in to cover the rocks dotting the beach below. In summer, the storms disappear, allowing tall, rectangular beach-tents made of striped canvas to be rented and erected on the beach. They give would-be bathers a place to change their wet bathing suits and provide shelter for picnics from the cold wind blowing across from Denmark.

I closed my eyes and envisioned the six friends; the men erecting the tent in a convenient space and pegging it down on the soft yellow sand, followed by the giggling chase down the beach and into the water for a quick, chilly swim. After everyone had changed into dry clothes, a portable spirit stove would be set up outside the tent for making hot tea to accompany the picnic lunch. An old photo shows the laughing couples grouped on the sand in front of the striped tent, radiating the joy of their day out together.

Two personalities more opposite than Jack's and Ida's could never have been imagined, but after an appropriate time of courtship, Jack proposed to Ida.

***

Mom consulted her notes and took up the story:

"Jack fascinated me. He was well-mannered, and he treated me like royalty! He was very handsome but a bit rough in his speech—in an attractive sort of way—and he enjoyed telling me exciting tales about his boyhood exploits and his life on the sea. He was so different from any of the boys I'd met. We were becoming very fond of each other. Jack loved to see the sun shining on my long, dark hair with its golden glints; it inspired him to invent his own private nickname for me, 'Sunshine '.

"I had begun to think I would *never* get married; two of my sisters already had husbands and I was determined not to be left on the shelf. My fiancé had been killed in the First World War. My parents had loved him almost as much as I did and it took a couple of years for us all to get over his death. Then I met Jack. Mother and Father weren't too keen on Jack Amiss.

As far as they were concerned he came from what is called in America the wrong side of the tracks—and his conversational manner was serious, without the lighthearted touch of my family's chatter. But I found him fascinatingly different, and I hoped he found me fascinating, too!

"After what seemed like ages, Jack asked me if I would marry him. I'd been expecting (and hoping) to hear this for weeks, and I accepted his proposal. Now we were about to ask my parents for their blessing. We went into the drawing-room with them and closed the door. Father said to Jack, rather bluntly, 'Well, young man, our Ida's used to having a good life, and I want to know what your prospects are.' "

Dad interrupted before Mom could get any further:

"Oh aye, it was quite an ordeal for me when I asked father Ditchfield's permission to marry his favorite daughter. Strictly speakin', it was just a traditional formality because she was over twenty-one and legally she was free to marry me if he refused. But I didn't want to put her through her decision to marry me without his blessin', knowin' how close she always was to her Dad. I squared me shoulders, looked her father in the eye, and said, 'Well, Mr. Ditchfield, I'm almost at the end of my college courses to gain a first class certificate as Chief Engineer and earn enough money to make a comfortable life for Ida and myself. I want to tell you that when I asked her to marry me, she looked surprised—but not too much so—and she said, 'Yes.' "Father Ditchfield stood up. He looked even taller than his full six-foot height. I was a bit nervous wond'rin' what his verdict would be. To me relief, he smiled and said, 'Well, Jack, it looks as if Ida has already made up her mind, and she's always been a sensible lass, so how can I refuse?' He held out his hand to me and I felt his firm grip as I shook it. That was reassurin'; not exactly words of welcome, but blow me down, they were good enough for meself and me Sunshine. We set the date for our weddin', after a suitable period of bein' engaged. Marryin' too soon after becoming engaged in those days implied that there was to be a 'happy event', and I didn't want the family or the neighbors thinkin' that I had got Ida into trouble!"

BUNTY: They were married early in 1922; a smiling bride in a tailored suit and a serious-faced groom clutching her arm possessively, flanked by the Ditchfield family. The only person representing the Amiss family in the photo was Dad's father.

After a break for lunch, Dad was ready to talk about the next chapter in his life:

***

Opportunity Knocks

"I had always fancied working for the P&O (Pacific and Orient) Line. With me new qualifications I was offered a job with them to sail as Chief Engineer. The income was excellent and Ida was comfortable livin' with her family in Sunderland, but there was one giant problem: I was often away for weeks at a time on voyages to the Far East—not a good recipe for a healthy marriage!

"From one of me voyages to Japan, I brought Ida a delicate, egg-shell-china tea and dinner service. Another time, it was a beautifully-crafted Joss Man figurine depictin' a traditional 'god of plenty'—hand-painted over white porcelain—to bring good luck to our home when we had one to call our own. Sunshine was thrilled with the beauty and thoughtfulness of the gifts. However, they were no compensation for the strain on our marriage imposed by me long absences when I had to leave her to be a 'grass widow' so frequently.

"Both of us realized that our married life could be damaged by the long stretches of time apart. The constant farewells and reunions with weeks in between were particularly stressful for Ida, so I decided to look for a different job. Out went me résumés. Although by now me credentials were excellent, shore jobs for a sea-goin' engineer were few and far between. I realized that I wouldn't have anywhere near the income I was used to when I went to sea. I tried one job as a hospital engineer for six months which I hated, and I resigned. When me next batch of résumés were sent out, they were requests for openin's overseas where I could take Ida with me. I wasn't too optimistic—in addition to a good salary, I was also lookin' for the promise of job security for the future.

"A classic example of job security—or lack of it—came in the shape of an offer from the Union Cold Storage Company in Manchuria, China, which yielded a hefty income, and I could bring me wife with me. However, before I could accept, a letter arrived from the company statin' that, due to the danger from recent raids by bandits in Manchuria, the job had been transferred to Nanking for safety and was no longer available! I was a bit disappointed, but I could almost hear the sigh of relief from Ida to be spared from attacks by bandits halfway across the world! I decided to try a different approach.

"After the 1914-1918 war, the Crown Agents for the Colonies began a period of expansion in the British Empire, includin' the openin' up of trade in central Africa. Me itchy foot had already decided me to apply for a job overseas where I could earn a good income and take Ida with me. It seemed like a tall order, but this time me résumé went out to the Crown Agents for the Colonies. To me surprise, they offered me a job with the Board of Trade as the ship's captain of a passenger and cargo vessel based at Kisumu port, Kenya, in what was then British East Africa. A job like this one boggled me mind (and that took a lot of bogglin'!) It was more than I ever dreamed of! It promised good money and security—in fact more than I could ever hope for if I stayed in England—and I could take Ida out there, too! I'd have a ship under me again, but instead of sailin' on the open ocean I'd be on an inland sea, Lake Victoria, stoppin' at the ports around the lake to take on and discharge passengers and cargo. We would also carry the Royal Mail. I was told to expect to stay in Africa for at least several years. It sounded like a dream come true! I decided that if I could persuade Sunshine, I would accept the offer. She thought about it, saw how anxious I was for the job, and said 'yes'. A letter confirmin' me appointment came from the Board of Trade soon afterward."

***

BUNTY:I could almost hear Mom thinking privately, while digesting this news, "What did I get myself into? What have I done, marrying a man who wants to take me away from the only family and hometown I've ever known, and plant me in the wilds of central Africa? I'm scared to death." Aloud, she probably said, "But, Jack, I've never left home or my family—or Sunderland—even for a short time, let alone for years! And what would my parents say?" Then, with a smile, she would have added something positive to please him, "But on the other hand, Jack, what an adventure it would be!"

I wonder if Mom privately rationalized, tongue in cheek, "Oh well, at our wedding, I *did* promise God to love, honor and obey my husband until death do us part! Maybe I'm being tested?"

Jack and Ida Amiss

The Oojahs (Mom in front)

Beach party

BEGINNING THE ADVENTURE

Dad Goes First

BUNTY: Dad was accustomed to writing reports for a ship's log and later to keep track of his water purification work, so it was instinctive for him to chronicle copious notes to read into the tape recorder. He began with eagerness:

"Oh aye, and so here I was, early in 1924, packin' me big cabin trunk and hand luggage for the journey to Africa. A list of suggestions had been sent to me ahead of time by the British Board of Trade, so I had ordered a topee (pith helmet) and a pair of mosquito boots, and into the trunk they went. I rolled up me shorts, short sleeved shirts and underwear and stuffed them in wherever there was an empty space. Me formal evenin' wear (carefully folded and includin' that blasted cummerbund) was saved to go in on top, after the rest was packed. In went me black patent leather dress shoes, some favorite books, a tennis racquet, a box of tennis balls and a deflated soccer ball. There was still room in the trunk, so in went a few handy tools: a level, pliers, plane, wrench, small saw, hammer, drill, brace and bit, chisel and screwdrivers, also a small supply of nails, screws and sandpaper. I put aside me 'whites' (officer's dress uniform) to wear aboard me ship and folded them to be put in on top with the evenin' wear. With all those heavy tools in the trunk, I wasn't surprised when it took two strong men from Carter Paterson movers to carry it downstairs for shipment to Africa!

"In those days, the only protection against malaria was quinine, so into a suitcase went the supply of tablets that I'd ordered, along with a first-aid kit, aspirin tablets and a box of Epsom salts (a handy item to have on hand). I'd hand-carry the breakables in me overnight bag: a sealed bottle of iodine, mouthwash, shavin' kit with a small mirror and a bottle of castor oil. I double-checked to make sure that me binoculars and sunglasses were packed in the hand luggage too, for me to use on the outward voyage.

"Ida and I exchanged tears and hugs as she stood on the Sunderland station platform with the Ditchfields and me Dad to see the train off to London. I leaned out of the open train window, shakin' me handkerchief to the little group wavin' at the station until we couldn't see one another any longer. After the long train journey to London, I made me way to the docks where I boarded a ship for the voyage to Mombasa on the east coast of Africa.

"I met a chap on the ship who was a medical officer workin' for the British Government. He was obviously a veteran traveler with his crinkled, suntanned face and nonchalant manner. He held out a slender, brown-backed hand as we sat down to our first dinner on the ship, and said, 'I'm Doctor Ralph Weekes, how d'you do?'

"We shook hands and I said, 'Jack Amiss here, outward bound from Sunderland. Glad to meet you.' We chatted many times over dinner—trivialities that we could share with our fellow passengers at the table—but I never really knew much about Ralph until one day he came and joined me while I was on deck, leanin' on the rail lazily watchin' waves from the empty miles of ocean lappin' around the ship.

" 'I say, Jack,' he began, 'I've been meaning to ask you where you are headed. Are you going as far as Mombasa? You look like an old hand at being on the sea, and probably an old hand at being out in Africa, too. I'm coming back to Africa after a six months leave in England. I never married, so I'm footloose and fancy-free to go my own way. Every time I go home to England, I tell myself I should stay there and settle down, but there is such a desperate need for professional medical people in Africa that I keep finding myself on the ship going back just one more time. I'm currently contracted to the British Colonial Government in Nairobi as a medical officer.'

"I turned to him and said, 'Well, as a matter of fact, Ralph, I've been goin' to sea for years, first as an engineer in the British Merchant Service on oil tankers, back and forth between North America and England before and durin' the Great War, and then to the Orient on the P&O Line. I'm goin' to Kisumu port in Kenya as captain of a ship on Lake Victoria. This will be me first tour of duty in Africa. Best of all, it's a job where me wife will come out and join me as soon as I've found us a place to live.'

"Doctor Weekes gave me a long look. 'Jack,' he said, 'I have some advice for you. Go to Kisumu, have a good look around, then *go home!* It's no good—it's no place for you to live, out there. Among other things, Kisumu is noted for malaria!'

"I didn't take his advice. After the sea voyage, I took the train from Mombasa to Kisumu to get settled into me job and find us a house before sendin' for Ida. In the meantime, she had been busy gettin' ready for the journey to join me."

***

Destination Kenya

BUNTY: Let me share a few researched facts about my parents' destination, Kenya:

Sometimes referred to as "Magical Kenya", this country has become a favorite present-day tourist destination. Kenya is the 47th largest country in the world—about the size of the American state of Texas—although it has twice the population. Kenya extends inland from the Red Sea coast of east Africa to the centre of the continent. It has an amazing diversity of climates and geographical features: a warm, humid coastline, temperate savannah grasslands and tropical forests, equatorial heat during the day. It also hosts part of the Great Rift Valley containing a chain of fresh-water lakes and high, snow-capped mountains with glaciers. Last, but not least, it borders 20 percent of the shoreline of Lake Victoria, the second-largest fresh-water lake in the world after America's Lake Superior.

Kenya has been inhabited since the evolution of the first humans on earth; it has rightly been called "the cradle of humanity" by anthropologists. It has many tribal cultures and languages, as well as flora and fauna. But I doubt if Mom or Dad had known much, if anything, about these things before setting out for their new home in Africa—and there was so much for them to discover, as we shall see!

Up to this time, Dad had been the one to use the tape recorder. Mom had been content to let him monopolize the machine, but I suspected *that* wouldn't last long! Sure enough, by the time I made my next visit to England, she produced a notebook already filling up with reminiscences. It was the first time I had ever seen her with a notebook—she had a habit of scribbling notes on the backs of envelopes—but I think Dad must have advised her otherwise!

***

Preparations

Mom oozed self-confidence when she began to read into the micro-phone from her notebook:

> "Meantime, back in Sunderland I had begun to make prepara-tions ahead of time for my own journey to Kenya. I sent a letter to a tropical outfitter's store in London to ask for a list of things they recommended that a woman needed for life in East Africa. Following Jack's example, I ordered two items on the list that I thought I shouldn't be without: a topee and a pair of mosquito boots. I could hardly wait to try them on when they arrived. I unpacked them as the family watched; an audience full of curiosity, dying to see me try on such unknown articles. First to be unpacked was the topee: a lightweight, beige-colored helmet with a wide brim made of thick, molded pith. Over it was stretched a white cloth cover that could be removed for washing. I went into acting mode when I tried it on, modeling it with an exaggerated air of importance while I mischievously mimicked an aristocratic accent, 'Ewww, I saaay, don't ai look grend?'"

BUNTY: I can imagine that the audience obligingly laughed and clapped. Mom was wound up now, as she continued:

> "The mosquito boots came out next. They were made of soft leather; knee-length brown suede. I put them on and pulled them up on my legs. At the tops of the boots were drawstrings, enabling them to be drawn tightly around each leg. The ac-companying directions said that that they were designed to avoid snake bites and also to prevent insects from getting into the boots. For the first time, it struck me that I was going to a country where there would be a two-way threat: the sun and the local wild life!
>
> "The topee and boots joined other items in my new cabin trunk: my poetry books, a volume called *The Complete Works of*

William Shakespeare, an aging bible (a long-ago gift from my Sunday school teacher), several favorite classical novels, my tennis racquet and some tennis balls. I also packed my treasured set of silver 'apostle spoons', given to us as a wedding present by my sisters. Sets of new underwear and summer clothes cushioning a few framed photographs of my family helped to fill up the trunk.

"Sunglasses were going to be indispensable; I left them out to put in my handbag. I dutifully ordered a supply of quinine tablets to have in my suitcase so that I would be ready to begin taking a daily preventive five-grain tablet—hopefully to protect me from malaria—beginning each day on shipboard the week before I arrived at Mombasa.

"Thanks to my sewing machine, I had developed a talent for sewing! My list told me that I would need some evening clothes, so I bought some black taffeta and made a swishy, floor-length skirt to wear with each of the three lacy, 'mix and match' blouses that I bought. After I had made the black taffeta skirt, the sewing machine was put to work making several long, loose-fitting cotton dresses to wear in the daytime heat. The sewing machine was then wrapped and crated, ready to be sent with my trunk to the ship. Another wedding present, given to Jack and me from the Ditchfields, was a wind-up gramophone (phonograph), so I wrapped it up tenderly and had it crated ready to be sent, too. The few records we had collected for it were stowed in my trunk, wrapped in soft clothing to cushion them (I hoped) from heavy handling.

"I had reserved my 'good' jewelry to carry in my hand luggage: a cameo brooch set in gold which had been my grandmother's, the little garnet ring given to me by my parents on my twenty-first birthday and two sets of earrings and necklaces—one fashioned out of shiny black jet and the other with sparkly, iridescent crystal beads. I would wear my wide gold wedding band and the engagement ring with its tiny (but perfect) blue-white diamond.

"Watching these preparations, Mother was overcome by the unthinkable departure of her youngest daughter. The tight little grey bun on top of her head wobbled slightly as she wailed, 'Oh, Ida my dear, how can I stand losing my baby daughter? And you're going to live in that awful, hot, smelly place so far away, too!'

"For the first time, my excitement was dampened by conflicting emotions; sadness for leaving everything familiar and gladness for looking ahead to sharing a new kind of life with Jack. I stifled a sniffle and tried to sound positive as I put my arms around Mother's shoulders, trying to comfort her. With what (I hoped) sounded like a cheerful voice, I gulped and said, 'Oh, Mother, you're making Africa sound just like the description of Hell that I heard about in Sunday school! I expect I'll be homesick sometimes, but I'll be with the man I love, and it's going to be wonderful having new experiences that we can share. I'm going to be just fine. Please don't worry.' I wished that I felt as confident as I sounded!

"Refusing to be comforted, Mother wailed all the louder, but as the days went by and she saw how resolute I was, she gave up and accepted the inevitable. One day, the letter came from Jack that I had been waiting for; it was time to buy my ticket and prepare to board ship for Mombasa."

***

BUNTY: I have to intrude here for a minute or two. Neither Mom nor Dad mentioned anything about having studied beforehand about Africa to prepare them for this new life, so everything about it would be a fresh shock or delight in its own way (which may be the best way to prepare for such an adventure, in any case!)

Mom was enjoying herself. She addressed the tape recorder:

"I was really getting used to feeling the spirit of adventure. Jack's letters were full of humor about his new experiences and his ups and downs as he adapted to a new way of life in a new country. The weeks flew by; it seemed like no time at all until I had my passport and sailing ticket. And then the day came for me to leave Sunderland.

"All the Ditchfields were on the platform at Sunderland railway station; I had a sudden feeling of fright as I leaned out of the train window and waved goodbye to them. I fluttered my handkerchief until I couldn't see them any longer; it was soon wet with tears as I asked myself, 'What am I doing? Have I made a terrible mistake? But I mopped the tears dry when I thought of Jack waiting for me at Mombasa. He said he would meet me off the ship and then we would travel inland to Kisumu together by train. My emotions see-sawed back again into uncertainty, 'But,' I reminded myself uneasily, 'before that, I've never been on a ship and I have a long sea journey to make, all alone!'"

BUNTY: Mom was *not* a good sailor! I often heard her say, jokingly, "All I have to do is *look* at a ship, and I'm seasick!" On cue, her affliction began when she boarded the passenger liner as it pulled away from the London docks, leaving behind all that was familiar on her way to a new and uncertain destiny.

We stopped here for a cup of tea.

***

Mom resumed her story with renewed enthusiasm:

Port Outward

"I followed the steward carrying my suitcase to my designated home for the voyage. It was on the port (left) side of the ship. He opened the door, and what a pleasant surprise I had when I looked inside! The picture I had in my mind of what a passenger's cabin would look like was a tiny cubbyhole like the one depicted in an old, sea-saga movie I had seen, where I would be imprisoned for the length of the trip. Instead, the description that popped in to my mind was the word 'posh' that I always used in England to refer to something (or someone) "upper-class" and elegant. I looked it up in the ship's library, later in the voyage after I recovered from my inevitable siege of seasickness. It was a bit vague, to say the least:

'Although unsubstantiated, the story goes that *posh* is an acronym, P.O.S.H., attributed (rightly or wrongly) to the supposed fact that in the early days of the British Empire, well-to-do English travelers on ships sailing to India from England created it to stand for **P**ort, **O**utward—**S**tarboard, **H**ome, meaning that the best accommodations on a ship were on the left (port) side sailing from England to India and on the right (starboard) side returning from India to England. The acronym, with its expanded meaning as a word, caught on world-wide and we hear it to this day.'

"My stateroom was quite roomy, and I wasn't too surprised to see that the furniture was either attached to the wall or bolted to the floor, or both. There was a nice wardrobe (a piece of furniture for hanging clothes) equipped with a full-length mirror and a row of clothes hangers waiting to be filled. There was an elegant dressing table (vanity) with a mirror and plenty of room in the drawers. The sleeping arrangement was a bit disappointing, however: a rather narrow bunk-bed attached to the wall. It hadn't entered my head that I might fall out of a wider one that wasn't attached to anything, if the weather turned stormy! Unpacking my suitcase with familiar clothes and toiletries made me feel more settled, but the rolling of the ship—even on its relatively smooth trip out of the London docks into the English Channel—was a foreign sensation to my stomach that made it feel queasy.

"Determined not to give in, I washed and went to the dining room. I saw an empty chair at a table for four where a pleasant-looking man and woman were already ordering their meal. They smiled at me and waved to me to join them. A waiter was hovering, so I ordered dinner—sparingly, not wanting to upset my already uneasy stomach. I turned to my traveling companions and introduced myself. The motherly, round-faced woman held out her hand, 'Ach, Ida, I am zo happy to meet you; vee are Eva and Heinrich Eichmann'. Her husband smiled at me and held out his hand (I could imagine him clicking his heels under the table).

"Never having met any Germans before, and with the wariness of meeting a recent wartime enemy, I wondered if they felt the same way about me! However, the Eichmanns—who spoke English with a heavy German accent—literally took me under their wing, turning out to be my figurative anchor as they showed me overwhelming kindnesses that I hadn't expected. I thought of the war; my brother and beloved fiancé had been killed by Germans in World War One. I mused to myself, 'I didn't know how kind and thoughtful ordinary German people are. It just goes to show—in a war, it's the politicians who teach ordinary people to hate one another and to be cruel.'

"The ship was soon well underway. Approaching the coast of Portugal and the notoriously choppy Bay of Biscay, I was already seasick. Eva Eichmann attended to my every need, and I felt blessed to have found such a friend."

Portuguese Men 'o War

"When the ship slowed down to make its first stop at Lisbon in Portugal, I felt well enough to go up on deck, taking in the fresh air in big, grateful gulps after the stuffiness of my stateroom. I found my new friends with a lot of other passengers looking intently over the rail at something in the bay. Joining Eva and Heinrich, I asked, 'What do you see down there in the bay?'

"Eva replied, 'Yoo must focus on zee surface over there, Ida, and you vill see zee famous Portugueez Men of Var.'

"I had brought with me a small pair of opera glasses; not as good as Jack's powerful binoculars, but I thought they might be handy to have on the voyage and they could fit nicely into my pocket. I'd heard about the Portuguese Men o' War, but I wasn't prepared for the scene in front of me as I looked at the ruffled surface of the water. Floating in the bay were churning islands of jelly-like masses as far as the eye could see, with pretty pink, blue, mauve and purple sail-like structures showing above the water. What I couldn't see were the long tentacles extending beneath the water, whose venom could paralyze or kill anything that brushed up against them. I remembered the message that had been broadcast over the ship's loudspeakers, warning passengers not to swim in the bay or go on the beaches during the short stopover in case they brushed up against one of these Men o' War and were stung (even washed up on the beach , they could still sting). The ship pulled into its berth at Lisbon port. I was so relieved not to have to endure the heaving and rolling, that I was only too happy to stay on board during our brief stop and get a good night's rest.

"I began to feel a lot better up on deck as we left the unpredictable waters of the Atlantic behind and the ship hugged the Portuguese coast toward the calmer Mediterranean Sea.

Free of seasickness, I found a deck chair and enjoyed sunning myself for the first time. It wasn't long before a lively young couple flung themselves into the two deck chairs next to me and introduced themselves. The vivacious little blonde bubbled breathlessly, 'Hello, there! We're Dorothy and Oliver Holly. Hope you don't mind us, plonking down next to you. Please call me Dolly. This is my husband.' The attractive young man in his blue blazer and white flannel trousers grinned as he nodded at me, 'My name's really Oliver, but we think it's fun to be 'Dolly and Ollie Holly,' so just call me Ollie'

"We all laughed and I said, 'I'm Ida Amiss. Glad to meet some fellow Brits. Where are you headed?'

'Well, we're on our honeymoon,' bubbled Dolly, blushing. 'We're going all the way to Mombasa, stay awhile, then go on inland to explore what it's like up around Nairobi—how about you?'

"'I'm going to Mombasa, too,' I replied, 'and then on to my new home in Kisumu by train with my husband; he's meeting me off the ship.'

"The 'Jolly Hollys' remained my good friends for the rest of the voyage."

***

Mom needed a break from all this talking, so we turned off the tape recorder and spent the next hour relaxing over lunch. She was determined to continue her account of her voyage, so she began again:

The Blue Mediterranean

"We had left the choppy English Channel and the ship sailed along smoothly now. With no more seasickness, I was really beginning to enjoy being on shipboard. We entered the Straits of Gibraltar off the coast of Spain, and I made my way to the ship's rail just in time for us to pass quite close to the highly strategic, towering Rock of Gibraltar guarding the entrance to the Mediterranean. I searched with my little opera glasses to see if I could see some of the famous early inhabitants I had read about once in a newspaper article. I had cut the article out and put it in a scrapbook. Knowing that we would be passing through the Straits of Gibraltar, I brought the article with me on the voyage. I still have that article, and here's a quotation:

'Inhabited for centuries by humans, The Rock still retains descendants of its original settlers: the Barbary Apes, macaque monkeys thought to be the remnants of their ape ancestors from time immemorial. . . The British occupied Gibraltar in 1704. In 1782, a British historian wrote about the Barbary Apes : '. . . neither the Moors, Spanish nor English, nor cannons, nor bombs, have been able to dislodge them.'

"I learned something more from reading that article: In modern times, the Barbary Apes have become the top visitor attraction in Gibraltar, crowding boldly among tourists for handouts, but there is a penalty against people feeding them—in fact, they are so important to the Gibraltar economy that there is an item in the government's budget for their food allowance, and in the event of illness or injury they are eligible to be treated in Gibraltar's Royal Naval Hospital!

"I had heard the expression *The Blue Mediterranean,* but I wasn't prepared for the sight of it when the ship sailed past The Rock and into an unbelievably beautiful world. My words seem inadequate to describe the exact color of this calm, land-sheltered sea, but I'll try! The color of the water was a dark, cobalt blue where our ship was sailing, fanning out into a true azure as it mirrored the cloudless, blue sky. As we sailed nearer to the shoreline and the water became shallower, the color changed into a transparent blue-green, finally rolling gently to shore as fussy, frothy, white breakers onto the waiting sand of the beaches.

"The next stop was at Marseilles on the south coast of France. Here, Eva and Heinrich disembarked to spend their vacation on the French Riviera. Eva hugged me and handed me a piece of paper. 'Ach, Ida liebling, here is our address; and you be sure you write to uz.'

"We had become such close friends on the voyage that I felt a pang of sadness. I thought of the words that Jack said so often about those who come closely into our lives, but who quickly go out again. Jack called them *ships that pass in the night.* The Eichmanns were friends such as these, to be treasured while we were together but then to be released for us to go our separate ways.

"Now completely over my seasickness, I let my mind drift as I lay lazily in my deck chair, absorbing the welcome sunshine on deck and marveling at the magnificence of the Mediterranean scene around me, especially that beautiful blue of the sea. There was one brief stop at Genoa in Italy before the ship reached the Suez Canal. As we approached the coastline of Egypt, I saw a shore lined with tall, graceful palm trees—me, Ida Amiss, who had never seen a palm tree in her life! It was like viewing an exotic photograph. This was the continent of Africa!

"The rails on the ship's deck were crowded with passengers as we slowly approached the entrance to the Suez Canal at Port Said, where we would stay overnight. Swimming in the water around the ship as it slowed down near the dock, dozens of young boys waved their hands in the air to catch coins that the passengers threw down to them. When they missed a catch, they disappeared under the surface to retrieve the coins they had missed, bobbing up again to the surface like human corks and triumphantly holding up their catch for all to see. As we pulled into the dock, a flotilla of vendors in rowboats appeared and began to surround the ship. Their boats were filled with giftware of all kinds: copper and brassware, trinkets, fabrics, embroidered cushions, costume jewelry. The vendors juggled for strategic places, outdoing one another to shout at the passengers lining the rails and holding up samples for them to see.

"Dominating all this pandemonium was a little man in a long white robe with a red fez on his head. Word spread around the deck that he was called The Gully-Gully Man. He was standing up in a boat, chattering away, telling jokes and laughing as he performed magic tricks. Many of the passengers threw money down to him. We were told that he had been invited to come aboard after dinner to entertain the passengers.

"The ship's engines stopped; we had arrived at Port Said. I was leaning on the ship's rail, wondering how the vendors could hope to sell anything from their boats with such a distance between them and the ship, when Dolly Holly bounced up to me and said breathlessly, 'I say, Ida, we're going ashore to Simon Arts; how about coming with us?'

"In England we had heard about that fabulous, world-famous shop at Port Said called *Simon Arzt;* Dolly pronounced it 'Simon Arts'. I had looked forward to visiting it but I didn't want to go ashore alone, so I was happy to accept the offer to tag along with the Hollys. The store lived up to its legendary reputation. There were lots of tempting things to buy, but what caught my eye was the display of Egyptian cigarettes. I'd never smoked in my life, but I thought Jack might enjoy a packet or two, so I splurged and bought a carton in their highly decorated box with Simon Arzt's picture and name on it.

"The Simon Arzt store was a wonder! Designed for customers who were well-heeled tourists, it had class with a capital 'C' and steep prices to match. Sales attendants wore white gloves and white uniforms, topped with red fez hats. The art deco building sprawled for an entire city block. I read its history in the little pamphlet that was slipped into the bag when I bought the cigarettes:

'Simon Arzt was a Jewish tobacco merchant who had originated his own brand of Egyptian cigarettes, elliptical in shape instead of the customary round, with gold-colored paper tips and filled with tobacco that has a distinctive, sweet smell. As the years went by, his store expanded as Arzt imported a variety of attractive, fine-quality merchandise: lace from Malta, porcelain from China, silver from Damascus, to name several. Arzt then expanded his merchandise to include all types of tropical clothing for incoming tourists. In addition to becoming an irresistible tourist stop, the store became one of the world's largest department stores of its time.' "

***

Mom turned off the tape recorder, stood up and stretched her legs. She must have decided to finish her tale of the stop at Port Said, so she began to record again:

"That evening after dinner on board, we were entertained by the Gully-Gully Man. He set up his magic table, and with a theatrical flourish he placed a set of brass cups on it, turning them upside down. He chose a 'volunteer assistant' (planted in the audience beforehand) who specialized in leading the applause while he continued his performance. Among his magic tricks were some old favorites. First, the assistant put a thimble under one of the brass cups, where it always re-appeared unexpectedly under a different cup from the one chosen by another (real) volunteer from the audience. I clearly remember another trick where he drew an egg from behind the assistant's ear, then produced a live chick from the egg. There was more 'magic' when he visited one of the ladies in the audience, pulled a bunch of fake flowers from the sleeve of her dress, kissed her hand and presented her with the bouquet.

"It had been a busy, tiring day, and I was almost falling asleep as the Gully-Gully Man went through his repertoire.

When the magic show was over, I was glad to I bid the Hollys 'Sweet Dreams'—too tired even to think about the narrowness of my bed."

***

The Canal

"Next morning, the ship steamed out of Port Said and into the Suez Canal. We were given an interesting lecture by the Purser about the canal (it must have been his 'party-piece', as Jack would say). He began by telling us that the present canal is 101 miles long and 673 feet wide. He didn't mention how deep, but I trusted that we would clear its bottom in our ship."

BUNTY: I also did a bit of research on the Suez Canal:

Back in the 1700s, French emperor Napoleon Bonaparte took an army on an expedition to Egypt. Among their other discoveries, they found the famous Rosetta Stone, which enabled the translation of ancient Egyptian hieroglyphics. Napoleon envisioned a canal that would join the Mediterranean to the Red Sea, giving access to the east coast of Africa. This, he reasoned correctly, would shortcut the existing trade route to East Africa, which at that time entailed sailing 4,300 miles all the way down the west coast of the continent, around its southern tip and northward up its eastern side. He also foresaw that France could benefit hugely from fees paid by Britain and other trading countries to use the canal.

But was it possible to build such a canal? What would it cost? And where would all the water come from to fill it? How could it cope with a difference in sea levels? These enormous problems laid the idea to rest until the 1800s, when French engineer Ferdinand de Lesseps founded a company to build the canal. Filled with water from the north-flowing River Nile, it was finally opened in 1869, at a cost equivalent to 100 million dollars; a tremendous fortune in those days. It revolutionized shipping routes to the East for posterity.

***

Mom was proud of the notes she had taken. She read flawlessly from them into the tape recorder in her best elocution-trained voice, as her story unfolded:

"When we entered the smooth waters of the canal, I noticed how hot and humid the air was becoming, so I limited my time on deck to early morning before the sun began its assault on my unprepared skin. In those days, sun blockers were unknown. People slathered themselves with 'suntan oil' in the hope that it would prevent sunburn while still producing a suntan (in reality, it was more likely to cook them a little and leave them with painfully red skin). The Hollys offered to give me some of their oil, but I hated the feeling of its slippery stickiness on my skin so I decided that if I sat in whatever shade I could find, that would be the best thing to do. There was a warm breeze blowing, caught by the ship as we moved along, but it didn't make the heat feel much less. My long hair was beginning to be a nuisance, continually soaked with perspiration despite the fact that I piled it up into a bun at the back of my neck. I seemed always to be washing it, but at least it dried fairly quickly in the hot sun! In desperation, but not wanting to shock Jack when he met me at Mombasa, I resolved to have it cut into a currently stylish 'bob' as soon as I was settled in Kisumu and could find a good hairdresser.

"The first thing I saw when I went up on deck in the canal was another ship coming toward us. I was puzzled to think how on earth the two ships could pass each other in such a narrow space. I was soon to know: they couldn't! Our ship pulled into a little passing-bay at the side of the canal and waited until the other ship's stern was disappearing into the distance before starting up again. Needless to say, several of these stops slowed us down a lot and it took us a seemingly endless 40 hours to pass through the canal. It could have taken us longer if there had been locks on the canal. We were told that they weren't necessary because the level of the water in the Mediterranean at the northern end of the canal is just about the same as it is in the Gulf of Aden at its southern end, where it flows into the Red Sea.

"When our ship came to the end of the canal, it stopped at the port of Aden. Dolly was with me at the rail when we pulled into port. We were in for a surprise: a small replica of London's famous Big Ben clock tower stood overlooking the harbor! Dolly gazed at it and exclaimed, 'I say, Ida, I just heard someone say that its name is Little Ben—appropriate, eh? It's making me homesick, just looking at it!' She darted away to tell Ollie.

"Underway once more, the ship sailed into the blue-green waters of the Indian Ocean and on southward down the east coast of Africa toward our destination: Mombasa."

***

Mom took a break while we had a cup of tea. After its restorative magic, she picked up the microphone again, chuckling as she began to tell the saga that she called the most memorable part of the voyage:

King Neptune's Court:

"What an unforgettable experience came next! It seems just like yesterday in my memory. We were on course for Mombasa, but before we reached our destination the ship first had to sail across the invisible equator line.

"Little did I guess that I was soon going to experience the ceremony which I'm sure has remained indelibly printed in the memory of all who have 'crossed the *line*' (i.e., the equator, zero degrees latitude) for the first time. These unfortunates are known as 'Pollywogs' (unseasoned, novice sailors) and they have to earn the title 'Shellbacks' (veteran sailors) by crossing the line. The day before we reached the equator, a note signed *King Neptune* was delivered to my stateroom. It said:

'Pollywog Ida Amiss, you are hereby summoned to the Court of King Neptune. Wear your clothes inside out and back to front, and report to the sun deck tomorrow morning at eight of the clock.'

"I had just finished reading it when a knock on the door announced the arrival of a breathless Dolly. She must have run all the way to see me in her excitement. 'I say, Ida,' she puffed, 'just think—we're going to cross the line tomorrow! But did you get this funny note from King Neptune? And what on earth is a Pollywog? And look how we have to wear our clothes! Let's be sure to stick together, whatever it means.'

"Jack had told me what 'crossing the line' meant to novice sailors, but I didn't spoil the surprise for Dolly. 'Yes,' I said, innocently, 'I've just finished reading the note. But why would we have to put our clothes on inside out and back to front? Won't it be fun to find out?' Dolly didn't look convinced.

"At 7 o'clock breakfast, snickers and raised eyebrows followed us as the Hollys and I walked through the dining room to our table, laughing at one another and at some of our fellow Pollywog passengers with their equally bizarre appearance. Full of curiosity, we climbed up the stairs to the sun deck where several rows of seats had been set up around the swimming pool. We sat down expectantly.

"A wooden armchair had been set up near the edge of the pool. Sitting in it, disguised as King Neptune, was the barely recognizable ship's Purser. I knew him as a suave-looking individual in a meticulously-tailored uniform whom I'd already met on several occasions earlier in the voyage. This morning, he looked a bit scruffy. He'd grown a beard and was wearing a gold-painted cardboard crown on his head, from which dangled strands of wet seaweed. In one hand he held a large, gold-painted cardboard trident attached to a long pole, and in the other he clutched a bullhorn. He was flanked by several of the ship's officers (also wearing beards) who were dressed in green-dyed underwear over which they wore flowing capes draped with more strands of wet seaweed. A strange figure wearing a white baby-bonnet sat with them, his naked body covered below the waist by what looked like a large white diaper. He held a baby's rattle in his hand, which he occasionally shook to prove his identity.

"Probably attracted by all the activity, a small crowd of curious onlookers added to the general hubbub as they joined the rows of Pollywogs waiting nervously for the proceedings to begin. Suddenly, King Neptune stood up and struck the deck three times with his trident. Everyone was silent.

"'Welcome, Shellbacks and Pollywogs,' he roared through his bullhorn, 'the Court will now come to order. It has come to my royal attention that you 'Wogs have committed crimes for which you will have to pay forthwith.' He must have been going in alphabetical order, as my name was called first! 'Pollywog Ida Amiss, come forward,' he cried. I began to walk toward him. 'Down on your hands and knees, woman,' he commanded. I got down on my hands and knees and made my way across the deck to end up in front of the towering figure. King Neptune looked down on me and announced, 'Pollywog

Amiss, you have committed the crime of wearing your clothes inside out and back to front. You must pay for this; you must kiss the Royal Baby.'

"Two of King Neptune's attendants ran forward and helped me up; they marched me over to the figure in the bonnet and diaper. He didn't say a word, but shaking his rattle he pointed to his bare, hairy chest. To my horror I saw that it was smeared with what looked like a thick glob of Vaseline. Gathering my courage and my dramatic inclinations, I rose to the occasion. Turning to look at the audience I held my nose and rolled my eyes, creating a wave of laughter from the watching crowd. King Neptune frowned and struck his trident furiously three times on the deck. I decided I'd better obey his command to kiss the Royal Baby or suffer a fate worse than death, so I planted a kiss on the greasy mess, which almost made me sick. The attendants handed me a paper napkin and escorted me back to my seat as I wiped my mouth. They lashed me harmlessly with limp strands of wet seaweed on the way, and rescued me when I almost collapsed on the deck from laughing so hard. My audience of fellow 'Wogs clapped and cheered.

"Dolly and Ollie went through similar treatment when their turn came. Ollie was spared from having to kiss the Royal Baby, but he was tossed unceremoniously into the swimming pool before being released. He pulled himself out of the water with a smile of relief and dripping clothes. Having seen a few 'punishments' handed out by King Neptune before he got to the 'H's', I think he was probably expecting much worse!

"Next day, a steward delivered a large white envelope to my cabin. It contained a fancy certificate stating: 'Pollywog Ida Amiss, having successfully paid her penalty for her grave crime to His Majesty King Neptune, is now officially a Shellback.' Nautically speaking, I had arrived! I kept that certificate stored in the cabin trunk for the rest of my life.

"After another 280 miles, the ship reached Mombasa, Kenya."

Mom and the Jolly Hollys

KENYA

Mombasa Reunion

BUNTY: Before we go any further, let me fill in a bit of research about Mombasa, which was—and still is—the port of entry for Kenya; it has long been called *the gate to East Africa.* Its Swahili name derives from the words for *Island of War*, due to its violent history:

When Mom and Dad arrived at Mombasa in 1924, Kenya was part of the British Empire—a large tract of territory known then as the Kenya Colony. Brits didn't come on the scene much before the 1800s, when British explorers began to travel to the interior from Mombasa. The famous Scotsman and doctor, David Livingstone, originally went to Africa as an explorer, joined by other British explorers such as Speke and Burton, whose mission was to find the source of the River Nile. Also in the 1800s, Christian missionaries braved the climate, insects, diseases, animals and hostile tribes, in obedience to the biblical commission: "Go, therefore, and make disciples of all nations", bringing the first schools and non-tribal medical help that the natives had ever experienced.

Mombasa is Kenya's second-largest city and largest port. The port of Mombasa is situated on Mombasa Island, on an inlet off the Indian Ocean coast. The city of Mombasa extends across the inlet onto the mainland; the two were connected in the early days by an iron bridge.

Nowadays, Mombasa is the world's main tourist destination for Central East Africa and is growing by leaps and bounds. With its pleasant climate, as early as Mom and Dad's arrival it was already a flourishing vacation area with its own Simon Arzt store! The city's population is still growing; research shows that in 1920 its population had numbered only 750. By 1925, this had grown to 1,077. The latest count I could find is 939,370!

The history of Mombasa shows that it has had a checkered succession of inhabitants. Tradition says that it was founded by a native Swahili tribe between the first and second centuries AD. (The word "Swahili" means "coast" in Arabic.) Mombasa's earliest recorded history shows that in the early 1300s it was visited by Ibn Mattuta, an Arab explorer and traveler from Morocco, and that in 1331 he built a mosque there (the early mosques and other buildings were built of wood, so there are none left intact, but archeological remains tell the story). The town became prosperous, trading with traveling caravans in spices, gold and ivory.

In 1498, Portuguese explorer Vasco da Gama sailed into the port. He must have liked what he saw, judging from the reports he took back to Portugal. It took awhile, but in 1529 Portuguese conquerors occupied Mombasa.

In 1631, the Portuguese were ousted by the Turks. Battles waged between them for several decades, and occupancy seesawed back and forth. The Muslim Turks finally took over from the Christian Portuguese in 1661, although their occupation was complicated by periodic violent uprisings led by the incumbent African native chiefs.

In 1887, Mombasa was leased to the British. It became the first capital of the British East Africa Protectorate, but this designation was later moved to Nairobi around 1906, and there it has remained since Kenya gained its independence from Britain after World War Two. Today, Mombasa's population is still predominantly Muslim.

Important in its history, in 1901 Mombasa became officially the eastern terminus of the famous (or infamous) Uganda Railway—more about that later.

Another fact of interest is that (at this writing) Roanoke, Virginia and Boulder, Colorado are Mombasa's twin cities in the U.S.

***

Mom took a well-earned rest from the tape recorder until the next day, when she was ready to record her arrival in Africa:

"After being on shipboard for almost a month and having traveled 6,834 nautical miles, I had finally arrived at my destination, Mombasa. The night before we docked, I was too excited to sleep very long. I had my suitcase packed and locked before daybreak and went down to the dining room for an early breakfast, making sure that my customs declaration form was securely tucked into my handbag.

"Suitcase in hand, ready to disembark, I went up on deck so as not to miss my first glimpse of this new country. I gasped in surprise at what met my eyes: as far as I could see were miles of stunning white, sandy beaches and undulating palm trees lining the shore. I breathed deeply in the fresh air which carried the faint perfume of flowers and spices. The ship slowly nosed into the harbor, carefully maneuvering into its berth at the dockside. I heard and felt the engines stop. An odd sensation; it was as if my ears suddenly stopped working and my feet craved the pulsing of the ship's movement under them again. A crane swung deeply into the ship's hold, bringing up a huge net piled with large pieces of luggage marked 'Not Wanted on Voyage'—trunks, boxes and crates of all shapes and sizes, golf clubs, folded tents, mountain-climbing gear. The full net was lowered onto the pier's concrete floor, to be opened by a crowd of waiting porters who loaded their carts and sped away to distribute the contents under the appropriate letters of the alphabet in the customs shed. I leaned over the rail, searching for Jack's face among the crowd waiting on the pier below. Suddenly seeing him, I felt tears of relief splash on my cheeks as I waved to him. He spotted me and waved back deliriously. Dolly and Ollie appeared at the rail next to me. We hugged and exchanged hastily scribbled addresses with promises to write. I moved to the head of the gangplank with my suitcase to wait my turn in the crowd of people disembarking from the ship.

"On the pier, I could see Jack take a pipe out of his mouth and tap it on a nearby pillar to shake the unburned tobacco out of it, after which he put the pipe away in his pocket. 'Oh, bother,' I muttered under my breath, 'now he's smoking a pipe! Oh well, I can always keep those Egyptian cigarettes from Simon Arzt's and take them back to England as gifts— if we ever go back!' But I soon forgot about the cigarettes when I saw Jack struggle through the waiting mob at the foot of the gangplank to greet me. My favorite film star couldn't have looked more handsome; he was a picture of masculine good health enhanced by his sun-tanned face, dancing eyes and welcoming grin. The next moment we were in each other's arms. After what must have been the longest hug and kiss on record, Jack reluctantly let go of me and regained his composure.

"'I've brought someone I want you to meet, Sunshine,' he said, turning to two young native men standing nearby. Each was wearing the customary formal native dress: an ankle-length, white-cotton robe called a *kanzu.* The taller of the two stepped forward. Jack introduced him, 'This is Obonyo. He's my personal boy—he looks after me—and he'll be our head houseboy.' I tried not to show my surprise; I had never seen skin so dark. My hand disappeared into an extended big one as the magnificently-built young man bowed his head to me and said, '*Hujambo, Memsahib Amiss',* (Greetings, Mrs. Amiss). Jack took the arm of the smaller boy, 'And this is Omolo. He will be *your* personal boy, Sunshine, and he'll be an invaluable help to you—just you wait and see.'

"I guessed that the young lad was only about 12 or 13 years old. He stepped forward, and I took his hand, '*Hujambo, Omolo'* (Hello, Omolo), I said, proud of the one word of greeting in Swahili that I knew. The little fellow beamed, his white teeth appearing to be even whiter in his shiny black face. '*Hujambo, Memthahib Amith*', he said shyly with downcast eyes. His broad smile of welcome revealed that several of his lower front teeth were missing, which explained why he spoke with a lisp! I thought, 'He's really too young to have had all that tooth decay in his permanent teeth; I wonder what happened to knock those teeth out—maybe it was an accident, or maybe someone punched him in the mouth?' Satisfied with these possibilities, I forgot about finding out. He stepped back quickly to pick up my suitcase, placing it nonchalantly up on top of his head.

"We found my trunk and boxes at the customs shed under the letter A. I produced my customs declaration which said I had nothing to declare. The uniformed customs inspector surprised me by merely glancing over it and my luggage. Marking each with piece with a large cross in white chalk, he waved me off, and said, '*Sante sana, memsahib*' (Thank you very much, ma'am).

"Obonyo swung my cabin trunk across his muscular shoulders as if it were as light as a feather, and started off down the pier. Little Omolo trotted behind him, balancing my suitcase on his head. A porter followed with the rest of the luggage. Puzzling over their greeting, I asked Jack, 'Well, Jack, I know that the word '*hujambo,*' or just '*jambo*', is the Swahili word for 'hello', but why did Obonyo and Omolo call me *memsahib*? Sounds like an Indian word to me.'"Jack had the answer; he had evidently asked the same question when he first heard Indian words mixed with the Swahili, 'Well, Sunshine', he said, 'there were Asians here in Africa long before other nations came. Also, I was told that in the late 1800s they were recruited from India by the thousands to build the railway, bringin' their native language with them. Many of them opted to stay on in Africa after the railway was built. Over the years, some of their Hindi and Punjabi words crept into the Swahili language, usually to fill in where there were no Swahili words for them;

'*memsahib*' is one. Swahili is now spoken by most of the natives, in addition to their own tribal language and some English. The generations of '*muhindis*' (Indians) that have called East Africa their home, have by now become well-educated. Some own shops, businesses, small hotels—others have become doctors, lawyers, accountants—and some even work at clerical jobs in the British Civil Service—they are British subjects just as all people in the Empire are, you know.'

"Changing the subject, Jack said, 'By the way, love, I decided to arrive in Mombasa a day before your ship docked, to book us in at a good hotel and also to let the lads have a chance to look around. They were thrilled enough with the train trip, but seein' a city for the first time was even more of a thrill, so I gave 'em each an extra bit of pocket money to enjoy 'emselves. I bet they'll have some rare tales to tell, next time they see their families!

'Oh, and Sunshine, I have wonderful news,' he continued, 'the British Board of Trade representative says that there's a vacant house in Kisumu for us to move into right away! The house isn't far away from me pal, Ted McTavish, who is the stationmaster at Kisumu. Oh aye, Sunshine, you'll like the McTavishes. Ted and his wife, Effie, have offered to meet our train and take us home with them for the night; what a relief! I had visions of both of us havin' to stay at that miserable Kisumu hotel where I've been livin' all these weeks. Obonyo and Omolo will be with us every day in our own home. Don't underestimate them; they can understand more English than they can speak. You'll pick up a lot of Swahili from them and they'll enjoy tryin' out their English on you. In the short time I've been here, I've learned quite a few Swahili phrases from bein' on the ship and havin' to make meself understood. I'll pass them on to you, me love, as time goes by.'

"He looked at my weary face. 'Poor Sunshine,' he exclaimed, 'so many things for you to learn about your new home in such a short time. I'm sure Effie will be a big help to you. One last item, I promise: we call the African natives that are our household help *boys*. This isn't a derogatory term at all—most of them *are* very young—and they don't take offense at bein' called *boys*.

"Jack must have noticed how uncomfortable and flushed I looked. He tried to comfort me, 'We'll soon be at the hotel for the night, old girl, and you can get a meal and some rest. You'll feel better when it gets cooler after the sun goes down. Tomorrow, you'll have a chance to get your land-legs back. You'll miss havin' those sea-legs you developed with the motion of the ship under you durin' those weeks on board! After all, you've traveled more than 6,000 sea miles on a movin' vehicle!!'

"Still feeling very tired, with my head throbbing from Jack's well-meant torrent of information, I was in no mood for a joke. I'm sure he meant to tease me when he added, with a wicked smile, 'Just think, Sunshine, tomorrow you'll start on a beautiful ride on the train to Kisumu. We're almost home, you know—only another 600 or so miles to go!' Another 600 miles—that was *not* funny! It made me feel sick at the thought of so much more traveling to reach the end of my journey; and he was making a joke of it! My temper flared. I was hot, sticky and worn-out from a night's sleep shortened by the exciting prospect of seeing him again. I could have swatted him, if I'd had the energy! Instead, as I wallowed in self-pity, I snapped sarcastically, '*Thanks for telling me, Jack, that's just what I didn't need to hear!*' When he saw his bride looking like a hot, sticky thundercloud, Jack gave me an apologetic hug and a long kiss that made up for everything!

"We caught up with Obonyo and Omolo outside the pier where rickshaws were waiting. There was also a row of *boda bodas* (motorcycle taxis equipped with extra-large pillion seats.) Some of these took off groaning under the weight of as many as three passengers and/or freight ranging from small packages to sacks of grain and even lengths of pipe! We chose our rickshaw, and Omolo carefully put my suitcase into it. He and Obonyo loaded my trunk and boxes into a larger rickshaw and jumped in beside them. I can't remember when I'd been so glad to sit down! Jack had given Obonyo some money to pay for both rickshaws. While I watched him haggle in Swahili with the owner over the price, I noticed that our rickshaw was operated by four natives smartly attired in long white *kanzus* and red fez hats. It took three to push it from the back (giving it the name *pousse, pousse)* while the owner ran in front, steering it from his position in the shaft. Jack had told me that for long distances, a crew like this one could operate a rickshaw for 8 miles, after which they would be relieved by a new team; good information to know, but happily not needed for the trip to our hotel.

"After the crew assembled, the leader raised the shaft and began to sing. I was to discover that the natives usually sang as they worked; more of a chant than a melodic song. They usually made up these 'songs', reciting the events of the day. In the case of the Mombasa rickshaw boys, we were told that sometimes the songs were about their impressions of the passengers—where they were going and what they were going to do. The three men pushing our rickshaw joined in the song with their leader, on one note in the minor key.

"The rickshaw bumped away from the dock and across the iron bridge into the city of Mombasa. The singing of the rickshaw boys was soon drowned out by the noise in the street. We heard the owner shout '*poli-poli*' (slowly, gently) as together they expertly inserted us into the street traffic to join the dozens of other rickshaws (some of them pulled by men on bicycles) struggling along among countless hand carts. The torrent of vehicles included *tongas* (carts drawn by oxen or donkeys) and *tuk-tuks* (three-wheeled taxis), together with a few sputtering *garis* and *piki-pikis* (cars and motorbikes). In this general confusion there were also natives on bicycles or on foot, taking their lives in their hands amidst the crush of moving wheels but apparently unaware of any danger. Above it all were shouts and yells as drivers and pedestrians shrieked at one another to get out of their way. As we approached the hotel, the traffic thinned out and we heard the rickshaw boys still singing. Since then, I have often wondered what they sang about and what their opinions were of us! Maybe it's just as well that we didn't know!

"The streets of Mombasa were bordered with beautiful frangipani blossoms, but on that heart-stopping trip through the traffic to the hotel I was too close to a state of paralysis to appreciate them. I was also too numb to cringe when a little lizard climbed up the wall behind the hotel clerk's desk as Jack signed us in! The hotel room was warm and stuffy; the shutters were still closed tightly against the equatorial sun. The air in the room gradually cooled when we switched on the ceiling fan which stirred it around, and the electric light worked when we turned on the switch. After my narrow bunk on the ship, what a relief it was to enjoy the luxury of a wide double bed, even though Jack got a bit tangled up in the mosquito netting hanging over it from the ceiling! He finally broke loose and tucked the edges of the netting carefully in under the mattress. Our second honeymoon had begun.

***

The Lunatic Express, Train to Nowhere

BUNTY: I decided to research the history of the Uganda Railway, and was captivated by the story which has become the topic of many accounts:

Although it had already been referred to as a *lunatic line,* the Uganda Railway's train service was later dubbed by an even more descriptive name: *The Lunatic Express.* This name was not officially coined in print until Charles Miller published his book in 1971: *The Lunatic Express; an Entertainment in Imperialism.* I'll call it the *Lunatic Express* because it was the only East African railway in existence at that time. Without any competition, the locomotives could treat its schedule as a mere suggestion, go as fast or slowly as they pleased and still eventually get to their destination—which was how the train was behaving when Mom and Dad rode on it!

When the proposal for the railway was first introduced in the British Parliament in the 1800s, it was officially referred to as the *Uganda Railway,* although its 660 miles of track and 1,200 bridges—stretching from Mombasa on the coast to Lake Victoria in the interior—were all in Kenya! Years of controversy followed the original idea proposed to the British Parliament. It was considered to be absurd—'*a gigantic folly*'—to construct a railway through hundreds of miles of undeveloped wilderness at an astronomically-high cost estimate. Doubting members of Parliament dubbed it *The Lunatic Line.* A protesting statesman of the time, Henry Labouchere, wrote:

"Where it is going to, nobody knows,
 What is the use of it, none can conjecture;
  What it will carry, there's none can define,
  It surely is naught but a lunatic line."

At last, after five years of debate, opposition was overcome by the realization that such a strategy was needed not only for trade but also for military use, in case Britain had to protect her territories in the interior of East Africa from attempted annexation by other countries. Construction was finally begun in 1896. The 657-mile long, single-track, 3 foot 6 inch gauge railway took five grueling years to complete. In 1901, equipped with 22 outdated locomotives from India, the cost of the completed railway is estimated by one source as 5.5 million pounds sterling, an unthinkable amount in those days (the equivalent of about 650 million pounds in British money in 2016).

When it was completed and in operation, the value of *The Lunatic Line* was endorsed by Charles Eliot, Commissioner of British East Africa from 1900 to 1904, who said, "It is not uncommon for a country to create a railway, but this Line actually created a country."

In 1907, when Winston Churchill was 33 years old and serving as British Under-Secretary of State for the Colonies, he traveled to the heart of Africa on the *Lunatic Line*. Based on his journals, he published a book in 1908 called *My African Journey,* and in it he wrote this about the Uganda Railway:

"The British art of 'muddling through,' here is seen in one of its finest expositions. Through everything: through the forests, through the ravines, through troops of marauding lions, through famine, through war, through five years of excoriating Parliamentary debate, muddled and marched the Railway."

The Uganda Railway was constructed with an incredible number of difficulties, setbacks and tragedies. The first problem had been to recruit reliable laborers to construct the railway who could tolerate the equatorial climate, diseases and insects better than Europeans. Providence provided the answer: approximately ten thousand laborers were brought in from neighboring India (already the "jewel in the crown" of the British Empire). In addition, about two thousand native Africans were also recruited. It is estimated that 25 hundred laborers died during construction: from tropical diseases, drought and attacks by animals and hostile natives—to name just a few of the causes—while 65 hundred more were badly wounded in accidents. It was said that building the railway took four lives for every mile. Of those Indians who had survived, about sixty thousand remained and settled in Africa.

Parts for the railway (including the locomotives) had to be built, numbered, disassembled and the pieces imported by ship from India. They were then reassembled at Mombasa. Once put together again, the reassembled locomotives could go to work on the waiting track, transporting crucial materials needed to build the railway as it progressed, in order to keep construction continuous.

In 1907, Winston Churchill rode the *Lunatic Express* along its entire length, from Mombasa to Kisumu. A wooden park bench was attached to the front of the cowcatcher as an observation platform, so that four travelers could be strapped onto it and observe the scenery as they traveled. The same bench was subsequently used by American President Theodore Roosevelt in 1909, who wrote, "On this, except at mealtime, I spent most of the hours of daylight." The story goes that Roosevelt also brought with him a bathtub and library, both of which traveled with him on safari, having to be carried on foot by paid native bearers. After having had two such distinguished rear-ends sitting on it, the observation bench from the train is now on display in Nairobi's Railway Museum.

The intended benefits of the railway were realized to the advantage of all concerned. At its astronomical cost, it initially lost money, but in a few years it became profitable and remained so until its eventual decline due to improved roads and faster means of transportation.

Britain had already condemned slavery and the practice of humans being forced to transport goods by foot over long distances. Research provided the interesting information that one of the advantages cited to justify the railway's construction was that by enabling the export of raw materials and the import of manufactured commodities, this aspect of slavery had been suppressed. But could Winston Churchill have been wearing rose-colored glasses when he romanticized by calling it, ". . . one of the most romantic and most wonderful railways in the world"?

On his famous safari in 1909, Theodore Roosevelt appeared somewhat cynical when he wrote this rather blunt observation: "The railroad, the embodiment of the eager, masterful, materialistic civilization of today, was pushed through a region in which nature, both as regards wild men and wild beast, does not differ materially from what it was in the Pleistocene Era!"

As time went by, tales were told of *Lunatic Express* locomotives periodically falling off the rails, with the breakdowns causing disruption of service and untold damage to the single track. Another disturbing story emerged, of sparks from the trains' steam boilers causing wildfires across the tinder-dry, sun-scorched grass of the savannah in the dry season.

It was not uncommon in the early days of the *Lunatic Express* for it to be delayed when it stopped to let a herd of wild animals cross the track. Another delay was justified by stopping to allow important hunters on board to get off and take potshots at the wildlife that was in such abundance on the grassland of the savannah. Apparently, the hunters would come back sooner or later (usually empty-handed) and the train would continue on its journey. (I couldn't help but think of the wounded animals left behind them to die a slow and agonizing death.) In Kenya in the1920s, there was wholesale slaughter of game, usually killed on safaris merely to exhibit the heads of the animals as trophies mounted on walls in the hunters' homes. Neither Mom nor Dad mentioned experiencing such delays on their journey, for which I'm grateful!

Time marches on, and the *Lunatic Express* is no more. Its last train ran on April 28, 2017, to be replaced by modern trains with more than a single track!

But let's go back to 1924, to find my parents as they prepared to board the train at Mombasa:

***

Mom began to read her notes, now thoroughly enjoying her experience with the tape recorder:

"We were up at crack of dawn next morning. After an early breakfast at our hotel in Mombasa, Jack and the boys gathered up the luggage again. Rickshaws were lined up on the street outside the hotel, waiting for customers. Jack and I climbed into one of them with our hand luggage, while Obonyo loaded my trunk and the boxes into another. After a brief haggle between Jack and the owner about the fare, our rickshaw joined the suicidal traffic flow once more. Amazingly, we arrived intact at Mombasa railway station, and all our luggage was soon resting in a pile on the platform waiting to be loaded onto the train.

"Having seen the big steam engines on the long-distance trains in Sunderland, this one looked to me like a toy replica with a dozen or so carriages, a dining car and a luggage car lined up behind it on the track. The train was the pride of the Uganda Railway, and it was to be our home for almost three days. Instead of the *Lunatic Express,* Jack referred to it as the *Honeymoon Express,* because we had never actually had a real honeymoon! He produced our tickets and we were escorted to our first-class compartment. Obonyo and Omolo waited until the luggage had been safely loaded, and then they quickly disappeared to their own accommodations on the train. Our compartment was equipped with a hat rack, overhead luggage rack, sink and toilet (a lid in the floor, covering a round hole through which the train track could be seen). There were two berths with mosquito nets, and two leather-covered armchairs near the window. A more conventional toilet was down the corridor, but having our own private one (such as it was) would be good for emergencies! A complete absence of toilet paper in both places made us glad that we had remembered to bring our own supply from the hotel!

"We sat expectantly at the scheduled time for departure— but nothing happened! We waited, getting up to ease our cramped legs periodically as the time stretched into hours. At lunchtime, Jack bought us some fresh fruit and bottles of lemonade from a vendor on the platform. He had become progressively angry. He looked at me and saw that I was begin- ning to wilt from the tropical air stagnating in the motionless train. There were fans in the ceiling of the corridor outside our compartment, but not one of them was working while the train stood still. Jack's patience (never his best attribute) was wearing very thin. 'Damn it all, don't they know what a timetable is, here?' he stormed, 'Nobody seems to be at bit concerned—passengers keep wanderin' in and out of the train—and I saw those blasted porters all sittin' there on the platform eatin' their lunch.'

"We were already several hours later than the scheduled time for departure when we heard a lot of shouting on the platform. The engine began to let out clouds of smoky steam, as if to say, 'Come on, you lot; I'm ready to go, why aren't you?' Another half-hour went by. At last, after a series of loud puffs and clanks, we felt the carriage jerk. Several jerks later, the engine laboriously pulled the train out of the station. We were on our way!"

Mom ran out of breath and put down the microphone. After a stiff cup of tea, she picked up her notes again:

"You know how I got seasick when I even *looked* at a ship? Although I had my 'sea legs' with no more seasickness after the first part of the voyage, I wondered if my problem with motion sickness would continue on the train. It didn't help when we had a briefly-worded notice issued with our tickets. It declared, 'Passengers who are prone to motion sickness are advised to take out their false teeth at the beginning of the journey!' After conquering seasickness with my sea legs, now I had to get my train legs! Luckily, although my stomach was unreliable for traveling, I didn't get sick on the whole train trip; and fortunately, I didn't have false teeth, either!"

***

Flora, Fauna and Massacres

"We gazed out of our compartment window as we left Mombasa with its red, corrugated iron roofs and with its beaches and elegant palms, delicate frangipani bushes, trumpeting hibiscus blossoms and cascades of purple bougainvillea. Leaving behind its humid, swampy outskirts, we journeyed through lush green orchards of mango and papaya trees. These alternated with banana and coconut groves introduced to Africa by ancient Asians centuries before— as were orange, lemon and lime trees. Through the train window, we glimpsed beautiful birds and butterflies. Vividly-colored flowers were growing alongside the track. Next, we skirted a tropical forest, its towering green trees garlanded with flowering vines, knit together with trailing ropes of lianas climbing from tree to tree.

"The train left the tangle of tropical forest as it headed north and west toward Nairobi. High elephant grass, rippling from gusts of the hot, dry wind, gradually gave way to vast stretches of flat savannah grassland that seemed to quiver in the heat. It stretched as far as the eye could see, interrupted here and there by a stream, muddy river, lone acacia or wild fig tree. A forlorn cluster of acacia trees, accompanied by a scrawny palm tree or towering baobab, indicated a water hole.

"I remember that one time the train came close enough for us to see a gathering of big black birds on a treetop. They were vultures: scavengers, hopefully scanning the ground to spot a likely meal (probably the remains of a small creature killed by a larger one). I'd heard that vultures were noted for their persistence. They returned time and time again after being chased away by the owner of the carcass, staying long enough to pick the remains off the bones before retiring back to their treetops to sleep it off and wait for the next opportunity. Maybe the sound of our train scared them. As we watched, they rose in a cloud from the treetop on their great black wings. They flapped in ungainly flight to wheel around in circles before settling back again, wings folded. They were close enough to the train for Jack's binoculars to show us their murderous-looking heads and beaks. I complained to Jack, "Oh, what ugly, disgusting things they are!' He replied, in his matter-of-fact engineer's voice, 'Yes, Sunshine darlin', but they *do* keep the place clean!'

"The natives believed that most of the trees found on the savannah were planted by elephants! This isn't as strange as it sounds, because elephants love to eat acacia leaves and their seed pods, carefully tearing them off to avoid the tree's huge thorns before popping them into their mouths. History tells us that elephants have traveled across the savannah for centuries on their migration routes. As they came across an acacia and enjoyed a favorite treat, some of its seeds were probably dropped in their dung along the way, taking root and over time growing into acacia trees.

"Giraffes are fond of acacia leaves, too. I learned that giraffes need to eat 60 pounds of leaves per day—they avoid the acacia's thorns by negotiating around them with their long tongues to tear the leaves off the branches, and when they find an acacia they gorge themselves. You can imagine what a strain this must be on the poor acacia, but it has a plan to retaliate! It can release tannins which are not only so bitter that the giraffes can't stand the taste, but they generate something else which makes it a one-two punch: an ingredient that upsets their digestion! With this secret weapon, the acacia gets its revenge, as if to say, 'ENOUGH-GET LOST!' The giraffes move on to find an acacia growing in a neighborhood where news of the secret weapon hasn't yet been heard, where they proceed to gobble up the leaves while the gobbling is good!

"As well as the acacia, there were other trees on the savannah that I had never seen or heard of before. After we were settled in Kisumu, I visited the public library and looked up the trees of the savannah. I found some fascinating information. I read that another tree I had wondered about is called the sweet-scented tamarind. Its short trunk is crowned with many horizontal branches, each with pretty, ferny leaves and clusters of bright, orange-colored flowers. I read that after the flowers die, their fruit develops into fat, curved seed-pods that hang down from the branches looking like bunches of brown sausages. The tamarind yields fruit with sharp-tasting, edible pulp—an ingredient in Worcestershire Sauce that is used in cuisines around the world! The natives add sugar to make it into sweetmeats (candy) and they dry the fruit and use its sweet smell as potpourri to disguise cooking and other odors!

"I was particularly interested to read about the baobab tree, known as the 'Tree of Life', and possibly the most important tree in Africa. I copied the article and put it in my trunk to read to my family when we returned to England some day:

'A giant with an amazing life-expectancy, the baobab can live for thousands of years. It is often referred to as the icon of African bush land, a rather strange-looking affair growing up to 60 feet high, with an extremely wide, straight, shiny trunk, branching into sub-trunks. These are topped with weird-ly-bent, leaf-covered branches clawing out in all directions. The natives nicknamed it the 'upside- down tree', and they believed it had magic qualities. This belief was based on a legend that the gods were angry with the baobab tree and threw it down to earth where it landed upside down, with its roots sticking up in the air. Magically, it still produced fruit. The baobab's branches, which are bare for most of the year, look like tangled roots to this day.

'The baobab is called the 'Tree of Life' because it provides life-sustaining products to benefit humans and animals alike. It can grow to be as wide around as a grain silo! Its huge trunk is hollow enough to fill with water in the rainy season which remains fresh and pure for months; invaluable for sustaining life on the dry savannah. The leaves of the baobab are packed with nutrition and vitamins, and they can be cooked like spin-ach. Its fruit (nicknamed 'monkey bread') is edible and very nutritious; although rather bitter-tasting. It is packed with vi-tamin C, used as a health-booster and a healing medicine. The pulp is also used with sugar to make fruit drinksand to thicken jams. Huge, sturdy, oval seed pods hang from its branches; the natives scrape out the pods, dry them and use them as scoops for the water stored in the baobab's hollow trunk!'

"Fascinated, I read more about the baobab, provided by nature for such importance to life in Africa:

'This Tree of Life also provides shelter for animals. Birds build nests in wide crevices in the tree bark. Although it sounds cruel, this is one way that nature helps chameleons, lizards and snakes to survive by preying on eggs or helpless baby birds in the nests, which are easily accessible to them in the baobab tree. Even the bark and roots of the baobab are useful: the bark is used to make rope, cloth and paper; the roots are used to make red dye. Both bark and roots also have medicinal purposes and are an antidote to poisons.'

Mom was apologetic:

"Oh, dear, I've gone on talking rather long, haven't I? Well, that's enough about the baobab. Sorry to have been carried away by all that information, but you know me and my addiction to horticulture! And it shows you how dependent the natives were, upon nature and her gifts."

We took a break to have lunch. Dad trotted off for his 'forty winks'. Mom wasn't about to relinquish the microphone. She continued, "Now I'll get back to our journey on the good old *Lunatic Express:*"

"For hours, the train carried us through the savannah which stretched in all directions. We began to detect in the far distance what looked like trees with a hazy ridge of hills behind them. Daylight wouldn't be here much longer, so we unpacked our night clothes. An attendant walked through the corridor, shouting above the noise of the train wheels on the track that dinner would be served at seven o'clock that evening, and breakfast next morning would be served at seven-thirty. We washed and changed, then swayed our way down to the dining car. I was astounded by the opulence that greeted us: upholstered red leather seats at our table for two, and a white linen tablecloth meticulously set with highly-polished silver-ware and sparkling crystal glasses. I exclaimed, 'Goodness me, Jack, what a nice surprise! After some of the disappointments we've had in this train, I'd begun to wonder if we would eat with our fingers!' I can't remember what was served for dinner, but it must have been good. If it hadn't been, I would surely have remembered it!"

***

Mom had run out of breath and also notes (both temporarily), so Dad took over, reading from a fat notebook of lined paper, which in his methodical way he had dedicated to be used exclusively for his tape-recordings:

"Oh aye, we had an excellent view of the vast country passin' outside our train window. I was glad I had brought me binoc-ulars along with us. Havin' had the experience of using 'em when I first traveled on this railway from Mombasa to Kisumu. I knew they would come in handy to give us a look at the scenery close up.

"Much to Ida's relief, the train stopped overnight. She was just about done in by the motion and noise of its swayin', bumpin', clangin' and clatterin' over the iron rails, to say nothin' of the oppressive heat. Those were the days before air condi-tionin' and the compartment fan in the ceiling only worked when it felt like it. When the blasted thing wasn't workin', it was downright suffocatin'. We had tried openin' the window when the train first started up, but a hot wind blew in, carryin' with it flies and a shower of rusty red dust from the side of the track that got into our mouths and stuck all over our hot skin. You can bet yer boots we didn't try *that* again! But what a difference when the sun went down; it became unbeliev-ably cool. When the train stopped for the night we opened the window just a crack, hopin' that none of the local flyin' wildlife could get in and start buzzin' around the mosquito nettin' on our bunks, but enough to feel the coolness of the night air. Believe it or not, we were actually glad to pull the nice warm blankets up around our chins, and we both had a good night's rest.

"It was first light next mornin' when the train started up again. I've always been an early riser, but Ida was still snoozin', so I closed the window and sat in one of the comfortable chairs in our compartment to look out and see what was goin' on outside.

"At the equator, just before daylight there's a 'false dawn': a soft, white light on the horizon where the sun will come up. The light gets clear and bright; then it shrinks and fades, leavin' darkness again before the true dawn breaks. I looked out on the first faint light of true dawn that separated the twelve hours of tropical night from the twelve hours of day. The first blush of sunrise began to spread pink and gold streaks over the horizon in the blue mornin'sky. I was wishin' I could share the sight with Sunshine, and as if she heard me thinkin' she suddenly awoke and sat up in her bunk. She looked surprised to see I was already up. She said, 'Hello, my love. I'm so glad I woke up in time to see this spectacular sky—in fact, with so many new things to see it's almost a waste of time to spend it in bed!' I thought it best not to answer that remark! We sat awhile longer, holdin' hands and just enjoyin' the beauty of the sunrise.

"We put on our clothes from the day before; there was no use puttin' on clean ones, they'd have been dusty and soaked with sweat almost as soon as we'd done up the buttons! In the dinin' car, an appetizin' breakfast was served: scrambled eggs, sausages, baked beans, toast with marmalade, topped off with delicious Kenya coffee (its flavor was already famous in England). After all that breakfast, we welcomed the idea of goin' back to our compartment to recover, relax and enjoy the scenery. While we were havin' breakfast, the attendants had made up our berths with clean sheets and neatly-folded blankets. We settled into our chairs to watch what was happenin' outside the window."

***

All talked out, (at least for awhile) Dad handed the microphone over to Mom, who picked up her notebook to resume describing that momentous train journey:

"We could see white settlers' farms spread out here and there as the daylight strengthened. There were little clusters of thatched huts a distance away from them; homes of the farm workers. Native women were already working in the fields—some with babies strapped to their backs—before the heat of the sun would make it too unbearable. The lives of these native women in the countryside were filled with hard work. We saw some of them carrying huge bundles of tree branches on their heads, to be used as fuel for the cooking fires outside their huts—I wondered how their necks could bear such a weight! I remember how annoyed I had been to overhear one train passenger say, condescendingly, 'All they seem to do is carry things on their heads, grind corn and have babies.' But I realized that she hadn't been far from the truth, and my heart ached for those women.

"While the mothers were away from the huts, young girls were put to work caring for small children. One could be seen carrying a baby on her hip while clutching the hand of a toddler. In some places, they brought the children toward the edge of the track to see the train and wave to the passengers as we passed by. Sometimes, it seemed as if a whole village had turned out to greet us. Once in awhile, a small group of little boys ran alongside the slowing train with arms outstretched in the hope of catching coins thrown to them by the passengers.

"Farmland gradually gave way to another stretch of scrubby,

savannah-type grassland, with small bushes and a solitary tree here and there. The train rattled over an occasional bridge when a small river appeared. For hours we watched the wild animals: baboons, water buffaloes and elephants, grazing or wallowing at a stray waterhole. Other animals—a group of loping ostriches, some giraffes and a solitary rhinoceros, moved along at a leisurely pace. I could hardly believe my eyes when the binoculars showed us a pride of lions sleeping in the sun on a little hilltop in the distance.

"The monotony of the flat ground was regularly interrupted by humps and hillocks. Here and there, huge mounds of earth formed lofty cones, some as high as the small trees and thorny bushes growing on the plain. We later found out that these were ant hills, or 'termite mounds' which can get to be 30 feet high and 80 feet across! We learned that some of the mounds could house as many as 3 million ants in a working colony, while others had been abandoned and were simply standing empty. There are one or more egg-laying queen ants per colony (a queen has been known to lay up to six thousand eggs!) The mound contains huge numbers of sterile male and female worker ants and others that can mate. The underground life cycle of a colony is supervised by worker ants that tend the eggs, feed the larvae, and care for the pupae until the new ants emerge. At the rainy season in late summer, swarms of termites that have developed wings leave the colony.

"There's more to follow about my experience with termites, but let's get back to our train journey:

"There were innumerable little railway stations along the line. It was said jokingly that every time the railway builders came to a habitable piece of land, they built a railway station! There were usually no more than 30 miles between them along the track, each with its metal place-name hanging above the tiny platform. The name signs were made of metal because wooden ones would provide good meals for the local white ants and eventually fall apart! Surrounding each station were carefully cultivated, tree-shaded flower beds whose blossoms dazzled us with their variety of bright colors. Behind every station house, there were European and Indian settlers' homes, nestled together as if for mutual protection. At some of the stations, enterprising Indian merchants had set up *dukas* (thatched, open-fronted booths) at the edge of the platform, to sell their wares to locals and train passengers. As time passed, this collection of buildings would become the beginning of one of the towns that grew up around train stations all across Africa.

"Our train stopped at some of the stations to take on and discharge passengers as well as to collect water and logs of wood to feed the endless appetite of the engine. Bundles of wood were also scattered alongside the railway line at intervals, to be picked up and fed to the locomotive if its supply ran short. When another train approached from the opposite direction on the one-track line, one of them would take refuge in a 'lay-by'—a short, parallel railway siding made for the purpose—until the other had passed.

"The track needed constant attention, to prevent it from becoming clogged with fast-growing grass and weeds that were dangerous enough to clog the trains' wheels and cause a derailment. As we traveled along the line, laborers leaned on their long-handled hoes just long enough to let us go by before resuming their endless weed-hacking.

"Traveling north on the plains near Tsavo, we passed more herds of elephants, giraffes, impalas and wildebeest, and even spotted lions, leopards and cheetahs. Here, history records a terrible tragedy that took place when the railway was being built."

***

Dad was excited when he found his place in his notebook and took the microphone:

> "Oh aye, there's a story about Tsavo. What a tragic event it was
> that happened there! I hope you won't mind hearin' it again,
> Sunshine. I remember how terribly upset you were when I
> told you about that incident, but I'll tell the story again and
> I promise to make it short:
>
> "In 1895, laborers buildin' the Uganda Railway track pitched
> their tents alongside it for the night. Exhausted from the day's
> heavy work, they fell sound asleep. Before they knew what
> was happenin', a night-huntin' pride of lions suddenly attacked
> 'em, draggin' 'em out of their tents, tearin' 'em apart and eatin'
> the poor lads alive. It happened so fast that they had no time
> to defend themselves or even to cry out for help. It's said
> that more than a hundred laborers were killed that night. The
> name Tsavo means *slaughter*—the incident was called 'The
> Tsavo Massacre'.

Dad was visibly upset after re-telling this story, but Mom was ready
with her notes. Quickly changing the gruesome subject, she found
the place she had marked in her notebook and began:

> "There was more grassland to see as we chugged north and west.
> It was getting much cooler on the train now. We had traveled
> about 300 miles from Mombasa. It was dark by the time we
> arrived at Nairobi, so we could see nothing of this large town
> which is the capital of Kenya. We were told that the train had
> slowly climbed to 5,500 feet above sea level—no wonder the air
> felt cooler! The train pulled into a siding for the night. My bunk-
> bed was surprisingly comfortable and so was our compartment;
> the heat had dispersed as evening came, helped along by the
> elevation. I pulled the blankets up around my neck to get warm
> and didn't hear a thing until daylight seeped through into the
> compartment and woke us next morning. "
>
> "Untidy piles of luggage were on the station platform at

Nairobi. A crowd left the train as a mixed, international collection of passengers waited to take their places. There were soldiers in their uniforms and Indian women decked out in elegant, silk *saris* draped with jewelry, standing with their turbaned menfolk. Native men in *kanzus* stood with urban African women dressed in floor-length, brightly printed cotton dresses in a variety of styles and colors, with ropes of shiny, glass beads decorating their bare shoulders. Standing next to them was a group of European tourists with the inevitable topees, sunglasses and cameras.

"Men shouted at porters to follow them to first and second class carriages. Crowds of natives—some only in loin cloths—jostled one another as they rushed noisily to find the third class carriages already packed, then tried to find a place with many others hanging out of windows and standing in the narrow corridors.

"Once everyone was on board, the engine emitted a few high-pitched whistles, protested a few times, then seemed to shrug its shoulders as it left the station as if saying to itself, 'Thank goodness that's over; now I can get on with my job'. It pulled the train slowly after it at first, reminding me of the little engine in the children's story *The Little Engine That Could*. As it gathered speed and continued to climb higher, the rhythmic sound of the wheels had me imagining that our engine was saying (like the one in the story), 'I think I can, I think I can.' *I hoped it could!*"

***

BUNTY: Before we leave Nairobi, capital of Kenya and its largest city, let's pause here for a bit of its history:

The name Nairobi came from the Maasai tribal language, and it means *place of cool waters*. Three hundred miles inland from Mombasa, at an elevation over 5,000 feet above sea level, Nairobi has a cool, pleasant climate: mid-70 degrees Fahrenheit in the daytime, dropping to the mid-50s at night. And the Maasai were correct with its name: Nairobi does have a good supply of cool water! However, the land was uninhabited until the building of the *Lunatic Express* when the Uganda Railway created a supply depot there in 1899. In 1900, a committee was formed to plan the town. This coincided with the formation of the Nairobi Club and the building of a racecourse (first things first?). By the end of 1901, Nairobi had become the first stopping-off place for explorers and settlers on their way from the coast to central Africa.

By 1903, the railway was in use to transport imported and exported goods, supplies and equipment. Nairobi was flourishing. That year, its first post office was opened. Creation of a police force, bazaar, and a lighting system followed. Hotels and banks proliferated. In 1905, Nairobi became an administrative centre, taking the place of Mombasa as capital of the British Protectorate of Kenya. It also became the jumping-off place used by the tourist industry for big-game hunting and photography safaris; nowadays Nairobi is dubbed "Safari Capital of the World."

In 1927, the township covered 30 miles, and in 1950 Nairobi was declared a city; the population had exploded from 10,500 in 1906 to 350,000 by the time Kenya became independent in I963. At this writing, its inhabitants number over 3 million!

Changing the subject, it is recorded that in 1979, 3 million dollars' worth of illegal elephant tusks (10 tons of ivory) were burned at Nairobi by the authorities, to underline Kenya's commitment to conservation of wildlife.

***

Back at the tape recorder, there was no stopping Mom now as she continued her story of the train's progress:

"When the train left Nairobi, we made our way down to the

dining car and enjoyed a well-cooked English-style breakfast; always a satisfying meal. When we returned to our compartment, again our beds had been made up with fresh linens.

"Once more, I was awed by the vastness of the passing scene as we continued on our journey. The train rattled over shaky trestles bridging yawning ravines and soggy swamps to emerge among more miles of sun-scorched, brownish savannah dotted with occasional stunted trees. Sometimes, when the train slowed down, impalas and zebras were apparently so unafraid that they would run alongside it as if they didn't know it was there.

"Periodically, out on the vast savannah was a small water hole; a stubborn, cool spot in the unforgiving heat, ringed with thirsty animals. It was like watching an outdoor zoo. I never dreamed I'd see such a variety of animals; some peacefully grazing, stopping only momentarily to look up when the train whistle blew, then continuing to munch on the sparse grass. Only the giraffes and the ostriches seemed to panic when we passed too close to them. We came upon a group of warthogs with curved tusks, galloping along. Their little tails stood straight up in the air as they ran. I couldn't understand why they were there one minute and when I looked again they had disappeared into thin air. Then I spied a straggler, who—quick as a flash—dived backwards into a burrow in the ground. I noticed other holes, and then I knew how the others had done their disappearing act!

"As the train slowly climbed away from the plains, more trees appeared and we could see what looked like an unending ridge of high cliffs coming closer, announcing our approach to the Great Rift Valley. A few miles out of Nairobi, I had fancied I could see Mount Kilimanjaro looming faintly in the distance. At 19,000 feet, it is the highest mountain in Africa. I also thought I spied Mount Kenya on the horizon (second in height only to Kilimanjaro) with its snow-covered peak rising to 17,000 feet. Were they the mountains, or were they both only clouds above the trees? I'll never be sure!

"When the train stopped one time to take on wood and water for the engine, a small herd of zebras wandered casually across the track. Next, a troop of baboons appeared. It looked like a huge family: grandfathers, grandmothers, fathers, adolescents, and mothers with babies riding on their backs. I'd read an article which called baboons opportunistic omnivores! They'll eat *anything,* given the chance; they were also known to become scavengers and eat the leftovers of a kill after it had been abandoned by another animal. The article said that an adult baboon can weigh from 22 to 82 pounds and can stand as high as 2 feet tall. Now that they were close enough, I could see that they had big teeth, too. I had read that they have a reputation for being bad-tempered, so after seeing those teeth, I made a mental note to stay away from baboons! They came boldly up to the train windows, peering in at the passengers with curiosity and chattering to one another in little shrieks as if to say, 'What could those strange creatures be, in that big, funny cage?' I actually felt like a prize specimen on display!

"Jack was snoozing and missing all the action, so I shook his arm and said, 'Wake up, Jack, see what you're missing!' He woke up and said petulantly, 'Oh, I wasn't asleep, Sunshine—I was just.*'restin' me eyes!'* He always had boundless energy, keeping it fueled with frequent naps which he would never admit taking. I decided that he must view napping as an insult to the strong work ethic inherited from his Quaker parents! *'Resting his eyes'* became a family joke which he always enjoyed with unabashed good humor. But let's go back to the *Lunatic Express* and the baboons:

"Some of the passengers threw food out of the train windows, setting off a general scramble as the baboons lunged toward it to pick it up. Shrill, angry screams and squabbles broke out all over the place. They fought to hang on to the food they had caught, while others tried to grab away a mouthful for themselves. The big alpha male seemed to take charge and bring peace, and the females and older baboons meekly obeyed and stopped fighting. When the engine sounded its whistle and started up again, the baboons scattered in panic, disappearing into the bushes. The memory of that baboon family troop will always be with me—it was like watching human nature in the raw!"

***

It was Dad's turn again He was wide awake and eagerly waiting to take over the tape recorder from Mom:

"Oh aye, as the train chugged on, mile after mile north and west of Nairobi, we came to the ancestral lands of rival tribes, the Kikuyu and the Maasai. These two tribes feared and opposed the buildin' of the railway. They shared an ancient tribal prophecy of evil that said, 'An iron snake with as many legs as *monyongoro* (a centipede) will cross our lands as it spits fire—from the lake of salt (Indian Ocean) to the lands of the great lake (Lake Victoria).' They interpreted this to refer to the railway, and they reasoned that the 'evil iron snake' should be stopped.

"So, in 1895 the construction of the *Lunatic Express* met with another tragedy; this time at Nakuru, about 100 miles out of Nairobi. A relief caravan had set out on foot to replenish food and other supplies for the Uganda Railway's advanced survey team workin' to map out where to build the track and carry on with the construction. It was a huge caravan, with over a thousand porters carryin' the supplies, escorted by armed *ascaris* (native police). Fifty of the *ascaris* had rifles. The caravan's destination happened to be in the territory of the Maasai tribe, near one of their villages.

"The caravan's journey to reach Nakuru was uneventful;

the survey team was replenished without incident. But, unfortunately, the story doesn't end there. Havin' successfully delivered the supplies to the survey team, the porters got ready to begin their caravan's return journey. That evenin', some of them went to a Maasai village and stole some milk. They also tried to entice some young Maasai women to join them at their camp. A Maasai messenger was sent to the encampment to warn the leader of the caravan to control his men. Next mornin', some of the porters were said to have armed themselves with rifles and entered the Maasai village, seizin' the girls by force. Accordin' to the story, two of the girls were raped, and rifle shots were fired. In fury and revenge, the Maasai descended upon the caravan. They speared and slashed at the porters, killin' more than six hundred of 'em.

"Ida was devastated when she heard me tell her this story. 'Oh, Jack,' she quavered, what kind of a place are we going to?'

"I put me arm around her to reassure her. I said, 'Come on, Sunshine, cheer up! Remember, me darlin', *that* terrible event happened back in the 1800s. After all these years, conditions have improved a lot; I've not heard of anythin' like that happenin' since then.' Ida didn't look very convinced, so I thought I'd better drop the subject. Lunch on the train was a good break to give her a chance to regain her usual good humor."

Mom had been depressed to hear that story again. After a substantial lunch, she took up her notes, back to her own happy self. She was soon reminiscing:

***

The Great Rift Valley

"The flat land gradually gave way to gently rolling, forested hills. Soon we would be approaching the Great Rift Valley—an enormous swath of land cutting across East Africa—a valley so wide that it would strain our eyes trying to see the steep, craggy cliffs on its opposite side. We passed a few native villages near the railway track. Again, whole families came out of their thatched huts to watch the train go by. Jack smiled at them and said something cheerful for a change, 'Oh aye! After all these years they're convinced that the iron snake means them no harm! Would you believe, they actually come out and wave to it?'

Mom was on a roll. With a smile for Dad, she went on again with her description of the train journey:

"We were now about 30 miles out of Nairobi. Tired as we were from the long train journey, we couldn't take our eyes off the emerging magnificence of the scenery that we were seeing out of our carriage window. We were nearing the East African Highlands area of the Great Rift Valley. The engine huffed laboriously as it climbed the steep track through the uplands. Rolling green grass had given way to forests of tall trees as we reached an ear-popping 6,000 feet. Climbing even higher, the train seemed to perch perilously at the top of the escarpment at 8,290 feet above sea level.

"I was reminded of Winston Churchill's book *My African Journey,* when he wrote, '. . . you climb up a railway instead of a beanstalk, and *there* is a wonderful world.' He was right! From this vantage point, the beauty of the view was overwhelming.

"From our perch at the top of the escarpment, we saw the 40-mile wide Great Rift Valley, spread out below us. The sight took our breath away (almost literally) as we made the descent. Glowing in the sun, the craggy escarpment gave way to dark, semi-evergreen forest as it stretched down toward the valley, smoothing out into green, grassy slopes that reminded us of England. From our bird's eye view, the towering, 150-foot trees looked like miniature shrubs; it must have been like viewing them from an airplane. Straining my eyes to see the escarpment at the other side, I swallowed, to clear my ears! I felt my hands clutch the seat as the train zigzagged on the track to descend almost two thousand feet to the valley below.

"It took what seemed like ages to inch down the escarpment. As the train moved lower, there were wildflowers growing by the side of the track with great swarms of beautiful butterflies busily feeding on their nectar. By some miracle, we arrived at the bottom to begin traveling across the valley floor; a flat tract of land stretching for miles across. In some places it had fertile soil with settlers' farms watered by streams meandering through; in others were dry patches of grassland populated by occasional wild animals and dotted with single trees standing to attention. Here and there were small clumps of trees. Flocks of brilliant-colored birds flew from their branches as the train puffed along, disturbing them. I thought to myself, 'What a breathtaking country this is, giving us visions of beauty that I never knew existed!' When we had reached the flat expanse of the valley, the train picked up momentum to speed across it. Once it reached the other side, the engine reduced speed once more to a crawl, as it climbed up the second escarpment. From the top, we had a glimpse of Lake Naivasha—and maybe it was my imagination, but I thought I saw Lake Victoria in the distance, looking like a huge, blue-grey, inland sea."

BUNTY: Before we leave the Great Rift Valley, it deserves some more fascinating information:

For 'starters', I was astonished to read that it is so immense—it can be seen from outer space! I continued to read that the Great Rift

Valley dates back to early in the earth's formation (about 35 million years ago) caused by the collision of tectonic plates which tore an enormous, six-thousand-mile crack in its surface, extending from southern Russia through the centre of the African continent all the way down to what is now South Africa. This created a huge valley, with high, craggy sides—50 miles wide in some places—bordered by mountain ranges with their own valleys. Ancient volcanoes in the Great Rift Valley left behind them a chain of craters which filled up with water over time to create shallow, alkaline, fresh-water lakes. The eastern and western mountain ranges that were created in the upheaval then gave way to the rain forests of the central plateau located in Kenya and Uganda.

Archaeologists have been digging in the Valley for many decades. History was made in recent years by a discovery in its steep-sided ravine, the Olduvai Gorge. Anthropologists Louis Leakey and his wife Mary found the famous 2.5 million-year-old fossilized female remains of what scientists believed to be the earliest form of a human being. "Lucy" became an instant hit, world-wide! The Great Rift Valley was rightly dubbed as the site of the cradle of mankind. And all of the accounts agree with the same observation: The Great Rift Valley has to be seen to be believed!

From the train on top of the escarpment, Mom and Dad could probably have seen Kenya's Lake Naivasha glittering in the distance—a magical gathering-place for wild birds that we'll hear about later. In about another hour, they arrived at Kisumu—their first hometown in Africa.

***

It was time again for Mom to bring her notes to the tape recorder:

Effie and Kisumu

"The Kisumu railway station was a neat little corrugated iron building, surrounded by well-kept flower borders vibrant with blossoms of all colors. Our train was slow at coming to a stop as if unwinding from all it labors, giving us a chance to see the crowd of people waiting on the small station platform. As we had seen at Nairobi station, Europeans stood in one little group, Indians in their turbans and saris gathered in another, natives in another. Wandering among them were a few other natives; some of them naked with the exception of a scanty loincloth—which hid very little and left plenty to the imagination! In embarrassment, I tried not to stare! Jack took our suitcases, and we staggered onto the open-air platform on our cramped legs. Effie and Ted McTavish were there, waiting for us.

"Effie was attractive: slightly-built, medium height and very well groomed, with hazel eyes that sparkled as if they had just seen something very funny. She always spoke excitedly as if she were rushing off somewhere (in a high-pitched, feminine voice that might have starred her as an operatic soprano) sometimes followed by an apologetic little laugh. She was inclined to get carried away, once she began to speak. Later, when we were alone, Jack (who has always been suspicious of talkative women) confided to me in a whisper, 'Sunshine, this one is a champion—she can talk the hind leg off a donkey!'

"Ted was tall and athletic, with sandy-colored hair that was already beginning to thin on top. His pale blue eyes were framed in a long, thoughtful face, and he hadn't lost any of his Scottish burr. He was the stationmaster at Kisumu train station; he and Jack had become good friends before I arrived. Effie and Ted rushed to greet us and we all shook hands. I felt hot, disheveled and nervous. I thought, 'Oh well, now they've seen me at my worst—anything from here on has got to be an improvement! All I want is a nice cool wash—and I'll ask Effie where I can get my long hair cut off!'

"Effie looked at my flushed face and gushed, 'Oh, Ida Dear, let's get you home as soon as we can.' (Effie always called me Ida Dear after that) 'Here's my fan—it will help you feel cooler.' She plucked a folded fan from her handbag, shook it out to open it, and handed it to me. I accepted it gratefully, and made it flap as fast as I could to stir the hot air around my crimson face. Effie went on in a soothing voice, 'It's going to be nice and cool soon; after the sun goes down it will be even better. Oh, by gosh, Ida Dear, you *do* look done in!'

"Although she meant well, this did nothing for my discomfort, although the fan helped stir up the hot air and I felt that I could at least begin to breathe deeply again! I forced a weak smile, and thought silently (and rather ungraciously), 'I see you noticed.'

"Obonyo and Omolo had shepherded our luggage off the train, and Ted shouted to them: 'Och, me lads, we'll tak the big stuff to the left-luggage office for the neet. Then the two of ye go on home, and we'll all hie over to the Amisses' new hoose tomorrow mornin'. Now, Jack, ye jist foller me.' He led us to his shiny new touring car that had recently been imported from England and we piled in, with the hand luggage stowed in the boot (trunk.) Ted arrived back after supervising Obonyo and Omolo with the large pieces, which they left to be picked up from the Left Luggage Office the following day. He then drove us through the centre of Kisumu town with its cluster of white municipal buildings and nice-looking stores. On the outskirts, we came to the residential district where Europeans employed by the British Government were supplied with furnished houses. We stopped in front of a pretty, white bungalow (ranch house) standing on a manicured lawn surrounded by flower borders in full bloom. Effie ushered us into her guest bedroom. She addressed us brightly in her high soprano, 'Well, here we are, my dears, courtesy of the British

Board of Trade! Get a good wash, and change of clothes if you like, and we'll have sundowners and dinner. As I washed and changed, I wondered what a sundowner could be.

"Jack perked up, 'Oh, that sounds grand, Effie. After this long day, I could use a good snifter; we'll be ready before you can say '*Jack Robinson!*'"

"The cool water in the washbasin standing near the bed felt wonderful on my hot face, and after a quick wash I felt more like myself. I changed into the long skirt and clean blouse that I found rolled up in my suitcase. Feeling more presentable for going in to dinner, Jack and I soon began to recover from our lengthy train journey and I looked forward to getting to know our host and hostess. We found Ted and Effie sprawled in wicker chairs on the verandah. Their feet rested on beautifully carved wooden footstools which I was quick to admire. Effie chirped, 'Make yourselves comfortable, you two. Would you fancy a footstool each to relax you? We bought ourselves several more of these when we knew how comfy they are. They're hand-carved by the natives out of one single piece of wood—clever, don't you think?' I sank thankfully into my chair, enjoying the extra comfort of putting my feet up on the footstool and making a mental note to ask Effie where we could order some for ourselves.

"No sooner had we had sat down when a tall, distinguished-looking houseboy in a long, white robe glided in on his bare feet. He set a tray with glasses and several bottles on the little table next to Ted. 'Och, this is Joshua, our head houseboy,' Ted said proudly. Joshua nodded to Jack and me with a polite smile and a greeting, '*Hjambo, bwana, hjambo, memsahib.*' (Hello sir, hello ma'am) He turned and left as quietly as he had arrived.

"Effie, the perfect hostess, spoke with a little giggle, 'I say, the sun will be going down any time now; we can set our watches by it. We call these drinks *sundowners*. We always toast the sunset with a sundowner. I like to think it's to celebrate the coolness after sunset. Isn't that fun?'

"Ted, the perfect host, added, 'Och, I've got some Tusker beer for you and meself, Jack. Turning to me, he said, 'Now, Ida, can I suggest a wee gin and tonic? Or wud ye preferr a wee gin and lime?'

"Jack said, 'Oh aye! Thanks, Ted, me lad; I'm ready for a snifter!' He relished the local Tusker beer (one of his first dis-coveries shortly after arriving in Kenya) and had already found a source to buy it in the market before I arrived. On my part, I wondered what to say. Growing up in Sunderland, I'd been used to drinking a glass of wine on special occasions—usually with a meal—but the women I knew in my day in England didn't drink beer or spirits (liquor); both were considered a man's drink and most un-ladylike! There was no sign of any wine on Ted's tray, and besides, I was very thirsty! I didn't want him to think that I had no idea what a gin and tonic was, but I knew that I hated tonic water, so I said bravely, 'I'll have a small gin and lime, please, Ted'".

***

BUNTY: When Ted had mentioned Tusker beer to Jack, I knew we would hear its name before long, so here's a brief history of this famous brew:

Wherever they went in the world, the Brits couldn't have survived long without their beer! It would have cost a fortune to have it ex-ported in the quantities that would be required by them in Central East Africa, so an enterprising family decided to start a brewery in Kenya. They were undecided about what to name their lager beer. Around that time, the founder of the company was unfortunately killed in an accident with an elephant. To honor his memory, his brother decided to name the beer Tusker, which was what British hunters called large bull elephants with huge tusks. The first Tusker beer was introduced in 1922, made with imported malt extract. But later, locally grown barley was malted and used, which increased quantities, improved its taste, and reduced costs.

On a personal note: I remember that Dad always called his false teeth his 'tuskers'! I don't believe he was thinking of beer—maybe elephants ? His false teeth may have been rather large; who knows?

***

Now back to Mom's hilarious story:

"Ted poured the drinks. I was very thirsty, and I took an exploratory sip of my gin and lime. Surprised at how much I liked the taste of the lime juice, I said, 'Oh, this is so refreshing' and swallowed a large mouthful. I began to feel a pleasant inner warmth, and didn't protest when Ted, the attentive host, filled up my glass again. Spread out comfortably in the wicker armchair with my feet up, I took a few more generous sips. My legs, imprisoned in my mosquito boots, felt rather hot under my long skirt. I suppressed a sudden urge to toss the boots off onto the floor and hitch up my skirt, but etiquette prevailed over impulse.

"Effie shrilled, 'Ida Dear, you'll be needing a few a few pointers, so I'll come over tomorrow with Ted to help you get settled in your new house. Living out here takes a bit of getting used to, you know, but you'll be just fine. You'll be ready for bed tonight—one that isn't moving—after being on the boat so long and then on the train. Oh yes, and if you need more than the chamber pot tonight, there's an outdoor lavatory (toilet) a little way from the back door; we call it a 'choo'. You'll need to take a flashlight—there's one on the washstand—and if you use the choo, be sure to look under the seat before you sit down out there in case there's a visitor or two; the local spiders love that outhouse!'"

BUNTY: I must butt in here to say that neither Mom nor Dad ever mentioned an encounter with any daunting African spiders:

Research told me that there are more than 35 thousand spider species world-wide, of which there are a few thousand in Kenya, many of them with a poisonous bite! Eye-opening statistics show that some African spiders can grow to measure a leg span of 8 inches across. Ugh! Spider control was a source of concern to the British authorities in those days before the invention of effective insecticides. However, I took comfort in reading that they are reclusive creatures and are seldom seen. Even more comforting, was the added comment that there are some birds in Africa that feast on spiders, keeping their numbers down to a minimum, but I had the somewhat depressing thought that it was highly unlikely for any birds to go hunting in a latrine!

***

Mom continued her story, giggling as she re-lived the tale of her encounter with the gin and lime, so let's join her with her sundowner:

"Joshua padded in to bring lighted oil lamps for the windows at each corner of the verandah, and then quietly padded away.

"Enjoying my gin and lime to the hilt, I looked at Effie a bit unsteadily, but by now I was feeling sure that nothing could possibly go wrong with my rosy world; I didn't even shudder at the thought of the local spider club having a reunion in Effie's *choo*. Out of the corner of my eye, I could see that the sun had headed toward the horizon: a bright golden globe sinking lower as if in a hurry to go to bed. It set the sky on fire with pink and gold light as it disappeared, replaced in minutes by blackness sprinkled with stars. Conversation had died temporarily; words didn't belong in watching the magnificent sight of the sunset. The warm darkness that followed made me feel even more comfortable, and the sound of tree-frogs and crickets was music to my relaxed ears. Ted broke our silence. He lifted his glass of Tusker.

'Och aye—to the sunset,' he sang out.

'To the sunset,' we echoed.

Ted filled up my glass again."

BUNTY: And what would explain the rapid sunset at the equator? Mom and Dad had mentioned this African phenomenon to me from time to time as I grew up, but they never explained how or why darkness arrived so suddenly after such a short twilight (usually a scant 25 minutes; so different from the long period of twilight in the north of England):

The closest non-technical explanation I could find was this: "At the equator, the sun sets with its rays perpendicular to the horizon, shortening them. The further away it is from zero degrees latitude, the longer the rays become, enabling their slanted light to stay closer to the horizon for a longer period of time, thus creating a longer twilight."

I'm still not sure that understand it, but it sounds plausible!

***

Mom continued:

"Our eyes slowly adjusted to the light from the lanterns on the verandah. Ted's voice was matter-of-fact, 'We put yon leets there all neet to keep any wild animals wandering aboot outseed from cummin' any closer; ye canna' be too careful oot here ye know!'

"After another gulp of gin and lime, even the mention of wild animals wandering around at night didn't strike terror into my rosy state (although I did wonder, rather fuzzily, what had happened to the electricity). As if he heard my thoughts, Ted explained, 'Och, we don't need to run yon wee generator to keep the fans goin' all day and all neet. It gets nice and cool when yon sun goes doon, so we keep the oil lamps handy when yon current goes off. Well, now, you've seen the sun goin' doon yonder, so let's awa' and have a wee bite o' dinner.' He rang a little bell, and Joshua silently collected the tray and bottles. I tottered slightly as I hung onto Jack's arm to follow Effie and Ted into the dining room lit with mellow candlelight; a romantic background for the meal. The candlelight glowed around the centrepiece of fresh flowers, casting a splash of their color on the white linen tablecloth and the beautifully-appointed dinnerware. Jack thoughtfully held my chair steady for me as I sat down rather heavily. Through a pleasant haze, I noticed that each of the dining room table legs stood in a kerosene can. Not sure that I was seeing things, I asked, 'Do I see your table legs standing in kerosene cans, Ted?'

"In response, Ted launched into his findings about safari ants: 'Och aye, we have to dee that as a precaution. Ye have to stand the table legs in the middle of empty kerosene cans with some water and kerosene in the bottom. This stops safari ants from crawling up the legs to join ye at mealtimes! Jist mak' sure yon table legs don't tooch the sides of the can, or the nasty little beesties will climb reet up them and onto the table. As many as 50 million of yon safari ants can be on the move tagither. They're unstoppable if anything's in their way; they just climb oop and over it! Now, if that dining table weren't standing in yon cans, and if it was in their leen of march, those ants would dash along in formation—four or more abreast—up yon table legs, then they wud poor across t'table, munchin' awa' at any and all food they came across, including yours! They'll bite ye, too, if ye git in their way! Now listen, Jack, ye will have to do the same thing for y're own dining table, as soon as ye have one! I'll give ye some kerosene cans to git ye started. Thank hiven we've niver had safari ants; and I hope to God ye don't either!'

"My reaction was somewhat clouded, but I remember feeling what a relief it was to get through dinner without any sign of a safari ant! I can't remember what I ate that night, but by the time I had finished drinking that last gin and lime I didn't much care, and getting into bed in record time, I slept under the mosquito net like a log until morning!"

BUNTY: My mind was full of questions, so I read an article on safari ants (*saifu,* in Swahili):

The article stated that *saifu* are one of the insect scourges of East Africa and many other tropical countries. I read that safari ants don't build permanent ant hills, but sometimes just live in holes in the ground. Usually after has rained, as many as 50 million of them will form a column, a couple of inches wide, and go on the march in search of a food supply. While on the march, they leave behind them on the ground little white 'mushrooms' shaped like small umbrellas, the signal to a new ant column when it arrives that they won't be coming back. We heard that the natives collect these and serve them in a sauce or soup as a delicacy, which made me wonder if Mom and Dad may have unwittingly eaten some! To set my mind to rest, I rationalized that if they had, the 'mushrooms' would have been sterilized by the cooking!

I found more fascinating information. Marching along its flanks, the column of *saifu* is guarded by soldier ants. Much larger than the other ants, the head of each soldier ant is equipped with a lethal set of pincers, capable of killing any other insect that threatens or attacks the column. I also learned an interesting sidelight: in the absence of medical aid, the natives used these soldier ants as emergency surgical sutures, holding them over a wound to allow the ants to use their pincers to bite and close the flesh on each side of it. Enough ants were used this way to close the entire extent of the wound. Their heads were then twisted off, leaving the pincers in the wound to allow it to heal before removing them. They say: 'Necessity is the mother of invention'; I think the natives had heard this saying before we did!

***

Mom went on with her story:

"Next morning bright and early, Effie knocked on our door. 'Time to get up, you two,' she warbled, 'we'll take you to your new home after breakfast, before it gets too hot for you to move in.'

"Jack stretched and yawned. He reminded me, 'Oh aye, Sunshine, before you put your mosquito boots on, don't forget to shake 'em well; you never know what might have decided to sleep in 'em all night! I didn't tell you this, love, so as not to upset you before you came to Africa, but on my first mornin' at the hotel in Kisumu town I shook me boots and a scorpion fell out. It had its tail up, too, ready to sting me. That taught me a lesson alright! I bought a boot rack the same day! It'll be the first thing that I'll unpack when we move into our new home. We should both remember the drill: hang our boots up on it at bedtime, and before we put 'em on next day always turn 'em upside down and shake 'em, then look inside just to make sure there's nothin' still lurkin' in there! We'd better both remember, too, to wear our moccasins around the house at all times, day or night. We should never go barefoot, no matter how good it would make our tootsies feel when they're hot. You never know what's strollin' around on the bare floor. And darlin', you'll be glad to learn that I've become tidy, too! I've learned not to leave me clothes in a heap on the floor for anythin' to hide in, so I hang 'em up as soon as I take 'em off. And I've also learned to make sure to close the drawers tight after they've been opened.'

"I shuddered, 'I'm glad you didn't tell me about that scorpion and the creepy-crawlies before now, Jack—I might never have packed my trunk to come here!'

"After a delicious breakfast, the men stowed our suitcases in the boot of the car. Effie was already sitting on the front seat, eager to get started. Ted drove us to a little street with a few well-spaced houses on it and stopped the car in front of one of them. Obonyo and Omolo, who had caught up to us on the *piki-piki*, dragged our suitcases out from the boot and carried them into the house, then hopped into the car to go with him to the railway station, to collect the rest of my luggage from the Left Luggage Office and to bring it into the house to be unpacked. Ted announced their arrival, rather unnecessarily, 'Och aye, here we are.' Looking around appreciatively, he continued, 'So this is yew'r new hame? Very nice! Now mind ye, if ye need anythin', be shuer to send a boy to us to ask for't; we'll be that pleased to help ye any way we can.' He turned to Effie, 'I'll be back in an hour or two to pick ye up, loov.'

"I could hardly wait to see the inside of the furnished house that we would occupy, courtesy of the British Board of Trade. It looked trim and inviting from the outside: a whitewashed, one-storey structure with dark green-painted doors and shutters, encircled by a verandah with windows around all four sides. It was topped by a flat corrugated iron roof. I walked down the path in front of the house, envisioning myself planting flowers to create an explosion of colors in freshly-dug flower borders. I thought, 'I can't wait to get my hands in the soil and make these flowerbeds bloom. I can see that a lot of gardening is needed around here to brighten things up.' Little did I know that I would have company—the heat, the insects and maybe a snake or two!

"I heard Jack calling to me. He had gone round to the back of the house and there was excitement in his voice, 'Come here, Sunshine—come and look! To my amazement, down the backyard there was a tennis court! I thought, 'It's a good thing we brought our tennis racquets, after almost leaving them behind—I thought we'd never need them. Playing tennis practically at the equator sounded totally impossible! But the packing list said to bring tennis racquets if we had them.' I soon found out the reason: the elevation made the temperature quite comfortable, except in the middle of the day. However, there was a catch: for a practical game of tennis, players had to be on the court in the morning at daybreak, to avoid drowning in a pool of perspiration from the heat and humidity by the end of the game.

"I was impressed by our new surroundings. The house next to ours was a convenient distance away; we would never be overlooked. Behind the tennis court was a stretch of grass, bordered by low bushes. On this clear day, a line of purple hills was visible in the distance: the Maragoli Hills, bordering the Nandi Escarpment in the Great Rift Valley. Growing in the lawn on one side of the house was a beautiful young acacia tree with delicate leaves on its branches. It was in full bloom with lovely little yellow flowers whose fragrance filled the air. On its lower branches hopped several yellow weaver birds, whose nests hung from the tree looking like knitted bags.

"Jack, Effie and I eagerly mounted the flight of steps to the front door. There must have been a couple with children living in the house; here and there were remnants of comic books on the verandah floor. The inside of the wide verandah was pretty and cheerful, with a newly-painted, white wicker swinging sofa and several comfortable-looking chairs. Standing against the inside wall of the verandah, the small table with four white wicker chairs would be perfect for informal meals. Scattered around the verandah were several planters containing wilted plants that would need gallons of water to get them to stand up straight again (I made a mental note to give them my earliest attention). The house had a dining room, lounge (living room), tiny kitchen and two large bedrooms separated from two smaller ones by a long hall. We decided to offer the use of the two small bedrooms to Obonyo and Omolo. The other large bedroom would be useful as a guest room, if we had overnight visitors. All were furnished with plain but well-kept furniture, with serviceable carpets on the wooden floors. I took my suitcase into one of the large bedrooms, deposited it on the double bed, and distributed the contents into two piles, one to be washed and the other to be hung up in the standing wardrobe. This very English piece of furniture had hangers and drawers ready to be occupied. Against the wall, there was a washbasin stand, with a large washbasin and a jug (pitcher) already filled with water. Thank you, British Board of Trade!

"Jack went off to make his own inspection while Effie and I examined the small kitchen. I opened some of the drawers and found polished cutlery ready for our use. In the cabinets above, there were enough dishes to feed a small army, all nice and clean. In those days before refrigeration, there was a thick wooden food cabinet, on legs that stood in the inevitable oil cans—an uneasy reminder of its contents being protected from hungry safari ants. It also had a cover of mosquito netting around it! Effie explained that this was a meat safe, and that it could survive the heat to keep meat, butter, milk and other perishables fresh for a day or two. She sounded like a teacher in a classroom as she continued: 'If you want a change from meat, there's always fresh fish available, right after it's been caught in the lake. Jeremiah, our cook, sometimes smokes fish to preserve it. This gives it a whole different flavor. If you've never tried any, do so—it's delicious!. All your milk should be boiled while it's still fresh. Also, your cook will have to boil all your water, even what you use in the washbasin. It has parasites in it that will play havoc with your insides if you accidentally swallow any!'

"There was no cooking apparatus in the kitchen, no apparent indoor plumbing or a kitchen sink. I blurted, 'But, Effie, there's nothing here to cook with! And I've noticed that there's no bathroom either! Effie's voice dripped with her own brand of good-hearted patience, 'Oh, yes, Ida Dear, you're right to be puzzled, but look outside the back door. Your cook will prepare your meals down the backyard. There's a skillet and a little cast-iron stove down there, sitting on the charcoal brazier.' She tittered, 'Don't worry, dear, it's far enough away so there won't be any danger of the house catching fire! Your cook will use that little oven out there for baking, and he'll bring the food in and serve it whenever you tell him to have it ready. Oh, and if you don't go yourself, I think it's a good idea to send a houseboy down to the market once a week with a grocery list from your cook. Oh, and don't forget to ask him to get you some of that fresh fish from Lake Victoria. Your cook will be able to do wonders with it—and wait 'til you've tried it smoked!'

"Effie drew a deep breath and continued her lecture, 'As far as a bathroom is concerned, there's a washbasin with a large jug of water and a towel rack in each bedroom. You'll have a *choo* down the backyard like we do, and emergency pots for under the beds. Ted and I take our baths in a portable tin bathtub in the kitchen, because it's easier for the boys to carry it out the back door to empty it. You can use either a tin bathtub or a collapsible canvas tub like the ones they take on safari, but they are really messy. If you use the bathtub in the kitchen, it's easier to clean up any spills off the kitchen floor, but if you absolutely don't want to take a bath in the kitchen, you can take a bath anywhere you like in the house! Just ask one of the boys to bring the bathtub in and warm up some water to fill it, wherever you want it to be. It's lovely to soak as long as you feel like it!' She giggled as she added, 'Ted is a great soaker—he looks like a white prune when he gets out of the tub! When you're finished, just tell the houseboys. They will come and take the bathtub outside to empty it and probably use the water on the flowerbeds!'

"My new friend and mentor seemed to have found her second wind. She burbled on, 'Oh, Ida Dear, your house-boys will probably be arriving today. You'll find them to be cheerful, willing and helpful. Just be cheerful and thoughtful toward them yourself, and everything will be alright. Now remember, Ida Dear, I go into town regularly—just to get out of the house—so you can come with me whenever you like. Just send one of your boys, and I'll let him know what time I'll drive over and pick you up. Kisumu town has some good shops and a market that's pretty well stocked with everything you'll need, and I've a favorite English tearoom where we can have lunch! In addition to local produce in the market, you can get quite a lot of imported goods and canned food from the stores. If I were you, Ida Dear, I'd start making a list of things you need as soon as you can.'

"Effie had one last gem of advice: 'Don't fret about language problems; you'll be surprised how much English the natives know. You'll pick up a lot of Swahili from them; they'll be very willing to help you. Don't worry, Ida Dear, you'll get along just fine. Well, I'll be going along home. As long as I have a ride, I won't have to bother Ted to bring the car.' She headed for the verandah door, leaving me with my head bursting with all this new information to store.

"I followed her out, grateful for her eagerness to help me. I said, 'Thanks, Effie for all this good advice! I may not remember it all, but you've made me aware of some of the things I can expect! 'Oh, and Effie, I have a favor to ask.' (my long hair had reached the point of no return; I had noticed Effie's stylish, short haircut with envy.) 'Where will I find a good hairdresser? I can't stand this long hair of mine another minute.' She assured me, 'Don't worry, Ida Dear, we'll get you a nice bob. I can take you into Kisumu town tomorrow morning, how's that?. I'll stop by for you about 9 o'clock. You won't see much long hair on the ladies out here in Africa!'

"I wondered why Effie had said she had a ride home. Where would she get a ride, without Ted coming to pick her up? I soon found out.

"I followed Effie round the corner of the house. She called to Obonyo, who was usually within hearing distance. They talked for a minute or two, and then walked over to where he had parked his motorbike. Effie pointed to it and then to him and to herself. He grinned, nodded and said, proudly, '*N'deo, memsahib—piki-piki.*' (Yes, ma'am, it's a motorbike') He obviously thought she was admiring his *piki-piki*. Effie shook her head impatiently and pointede obviously to herself then to the motorbike. Obonyo's face reflected surprise, but he nodded, and stood astride the vehicle while Effie took a few steps back and hitched up her long skirt. Making a running leap, she landed squarely on the pillion seat. I heard her squeak, '*Sante sana, Obonyo, quenda, quenda*' (Thanks a lot, Obonyo, let's go, let's go,). After gaily waving her hand to me she shrilled, 'Toodleoo, Ida Dear' and clasped Obonyo firmly around his middle. Off they went, roaring around the house and down the road, quickly disappearing out of sight.

"I discovered that Effie had a reputation in the neighborhood for being a bit of a free spirit, sometimes shocking the Edwardian neighbors when she did things that simply were 'not done' by self-respecting Englishwomen, but I adored her for who she was, and hoped she would never change.

"Effie didn't forget about my hair; she was as good as her word. The following day, the hairdresser in Kisumu town lopped off the offending long strands. I heaved a sigh of relief mixed with some regret. I had been proud of my hair and the envy of my friends in Sunderland; when I was younger it had grown so long that I could actually sit on it! Not wanting to shock poor Jack at Mombasa by getting off the ship with my hair cut off, I endured it as best as I could on the voyage. By the time I had reached Kisumu I'd had enough; I decided that the hair had to go! After he finished cutting, the hairdresser wrapped my hair up into a newspaper-covered bundle and gave it to me to take home. Out of sheer sentimentality, I accepted it and thanked him. When I arrived back at the house, I stowed it away at the bottom of my cabin trunk.

"Next time Jack came home, he took his first look at my new haircut. It must have been a big shock to him, because he exploded into his nautical vernacular, 'Well shiver me timbers, what's been goin' on here? Blow me down Sunshine, is that really you?' I patted my new bob and said defensively, 'Oh, Jack, it wasn't easy, deciding to have my lovely long hair cut off, but I couldn't stand it any longer—it had to go!' He gave me a critical glance and said rather petulantly, 'I loved that long hair of yours, you know, Sunshine.' Then he added, grudgingly, 'Oh, well, at least they gave you a good, even haircut. When I'm on the ship, I have to hack away at me hair with a razor blade to keep it trimmed until I have time to see the barber at one of the ports!' He cocked his head to one side and examined my bobbed hair closely. He had one more comment, 'Oh well, I suppose I'll get used to it.' Then, with all the generosity he could muster, 'Actually, darlin', it makes you look younger!' I didn't know whether to laugh or cry! Had I really begun to look old to him with my long hair? Maybe I got my new haircut in the nick of time!

"My anguish over Jack's reaction to my new bob was easily overcome the next time I washed it—the freedom was such a relief that I couldn't have cared less about his opinion!

"Luckily, no insects invaded the neat little package from the hairdresser. I eventually took my discarded 'crowning glory' back to Sunderland in my trunk, not daring to declare it in case the customs inspector decided to confiscate it. Jack had a comment for this, too, 'Good for you, Sunshine; if it had moved when he saw it, he'd probably have shot it!' "

***

BUNTY: Now that Mom and Dad had become residents, it's time to research some interesting facts about Kisumu Here's some of what I found:

Although Kenya occupies only a comparatively small shoreline on Lake Victoria, Kisumu is an important port on the lake. It is only a few miles south of the equator, but being located at 3,711 feet above sea level gives it a livable, year-round daytime temperature of between 80 and 87 degrees Fahrenheit. It is hot and humid during the day, cooling off into the 60 degree range at night to make it more pleasant for sleeping, but still with some humidity in the air.

Kisumu is one of the oldest settlements in Africa; its first inhabitants were probably hunter-gatherers, dating back to the first millennium BC. It has always been a centre for trade, and for centuries it was the location of a trading place for local tribes. Its name *Kisumu* in the JaLuo language meant "place to look for food and barter." Over the ages, it became absorbed into the territory of Bantu tribes followed later by Asian Indians who settled the coast of Lake Victoria and built mosques, introducing the religion of Islam to the region.

Kisumu's original location on swampy ground was poorly suited to allow it to develop into a town with heavy, permanent buildings. In the early 1800s, when its site was moved to a rocky outcrop at the head of Lake Victoria's Winam Gulf, the town began to develop on firm foundations. It rapidly evolved from a village into small city, to become a government headquarters for the surrounding provinces.

In 1888, the British East Africa Company arrived in Africa and the battle to build the Uganda Railway (a.k.a. t*he Lunatic Express*) raged in the British parliament. After the decision was made to build the railway, Kisumu was chosen as its terminus because through its port it could link rail and lake traffic, thereby expediting transportation and trade from central Africa to the coast at Mombasa. Upon completion of the railway, Kisumu was re-named *Port Florence*, for the wife of the chief engineer who had been given the honor of driving in the last stake. However, it reverted back to its original name, Kisumu, in a matter of months.

The first "knock-down" lake steamers to reach Lake Victoria were manufactured in the early 1900s in Scotland. Their parts were transported by ship to Mombasa and then by railway to Kisumu's dockyard, where they were reassembled and launched. On his visit to Kenya in

1907, Winston Churchill called Kisumu (with its high elevation above sea level) "the highest dockyard in the world." Eventually, a fleet of cargo vessels and lake steamers was operating on the lake.

By the 1920s, the British had established farming in the foothills of the Aberdare Mountains of Kenya, nicknaming them "The White Highlands'. The farmers became wealthy from their coffee and tea plantations. Kisumu was the obvious terminus for these and other agricultural products, also for the thriving trade in ivory (before public attention became focused upon the need for—and value of—wild-life conservation). Over the following years, export and import trade flourished, to make Kisumu's port a close second in significance to Mombasa. British-organized plans for building the town began to be carried out: paved roads, government offices, and shops with store fronts to replace the original dilapidated two rows of *dukas,* new hotels and many other Western conveniences. Kisumu town fast became the epicentre for business in Kenya. Now the third-largest city in Kenya, Kisumu has become one of the fastest growing cities in Africa.

Comment: I was intrigued to read that (at this writing) Kisumu has two sister cities in the U.S.A.: Roanoke, Virginia and Boulder, Colorado.

***

The Cover-Up

Dad had been "resting his eyes" while Mom had been reading her lengthy notes to the tape recorder. She gave herself a needed break by making sandwiches for lunch. Now fully awake, Dad laughed, recalling the incident that happened on the day after they moved into their house. He asked Mom, "Well, blow me down, Sunshine, do you remember when you first saw the lineup of our new houseboys at Kisumu?"

Mom giggled, rather sheepishly, "Oh, will I ever forget it? But it's your turn to talk, dear. You tell about it!"

Dad lost no time in re-telling one of his favorite stories:

"By our second mornin' in Kisumu, Obonyo had recruited the houseboys as if by magic. He came to find us and take us to meet them. In the kitchen, Abraham, the cook, was the first to be introduced to us, with his helper—appropriately named *Isaac*. Next, Obonyo took us out to the verandah to meet the others. Omolo had helped him to assemble them: two neat rows of assorted black, muscular bodies standin' to attention. 'Here they are, *memsahib*', Obonyo declared proudly to Ida, 'I get you best houseboys in Kisumu.' There was a water boy to fetch water from the nearest supply point, with a helper; a laundry boy to do the washing and *his* helper to do the ironin'; a *m'toto*' (young child or pre-teen) to clean the *choo* and empty the chamber pot when necessary; a *shamba* boy to do the gardenin', with one helper to cut the lawns and another to sweep the front path; a boy to supervise the housecleanin' and *his* helper to polish shoes and the cutlery. There was also one to do the shoppin' and *his* helper to carry it for him.

"Ida wasn't prepared for what she saw when we were ushered in to inspect the houseboys. I hid a smile when I looked at her face and saw her jaw drop open. All of them (except Obonyo and Omolo in their *kanzus)* were stark naked except for a skimpy loincloth, each one of which had a large bulge betrayin' the fact that it obviously had somethin' to hide! I had to control meself from laughin' when I saw me Sunshine concentratin' hard to look each one straight in the eye as he was introduced, to keep her glance from wanderin' any further down! After we had greeted all the new houseboys, she took me aside and whispered, 'Oh, Jack, I'm so thankful that Mother isn't here to see them—what a jolt *that* would have been to her Victorian upbringing; she would have swooned on the spot and then I'll bet she would have packed up and gone back to England! I don't know if she would ever have recovered from the shock.'

"Me Sunshine paused for a minute, and then she muttered under her breath, 'Oh, Jack, I can't have them running all over the house like that, in their birthday suits! We've got to cover them up! Please tell Obonyo to get them some shorts— it's better to have them *half* naked than *totally* naked! Thank goodness you had my sewing machine sent to Kisumu station after I had it crated back in England. It was on its way to Africa before I even set foot on the ship! We can have it delivered now that we have an address. As soon as it arrives, I'll take it out of its crate and start on some kanzus! In the meantime, I'll send Omolo and Obonyo to the market or one of the department stores for enough white cotton material to make the boys each a *kanzu*. And I'll ask them to get at least 20 yards of 2-inch wide, red satin ribbon.' "

Dad took an after-lunch "rest for his eyes" while Mom continued the tale:

"With my sewing machine back on duty, I used Obonyo's spare *kanzu* as a pattern, and eventually I'd produced numerous flowing white garments in various sizes, each adorned with a sash of red satin ribbon. Obonyo was delighted that there was enough red satin ribbon for me to make sashes for him and Omolo, too, who was thrilled with how his sash looked, and lisped admiringly, 'N*zuri thana, Memthahib Amith*' (very pretty, Mrs. Amiss).

"Jack had become fairly proficient in what was called 'kitchen Swahili' in the time he'd already been in Africa, and he kept enlarging his vocabulary from the natives on the ship, so he translated for me the gist what Obonyo told him next. He said that the boys were so proud of their 'uniforms' and so impressed by the magic of their new *memsahib*'s machine, that they had worn their kanzus with the red sashes to show friends who worked at other European households, making them gratifyingly jealous. The boys passed gossip from household to household, so evidently the news traveled around! *Memsahib Amiss* and her *kanzus* with red sashes had become famous!"

***

BUNTY: I learned that in the 1920s there were more than 40 native tribes in Kenya, each speaking a tribal dialect and with differing tribal traditions and regulations! Gradually, however, some of these traditions were already dying out—especially among the natives who lived and worked in the larger towns and developing areas—and Swahili was becoming the universal native language that they chose to adopt.

Research showed me that the Kavirondo tribe had been longest in Kenya, but gradually natives had arrived from Kikuyu, JaLuo and Maasai tribes, seeking work in the growing towns and cities. Some of our houseboys were from these tribes. By the 1920s, some of their customs were being replaced by European ones. However, those Kavirondos living away from urban areas were still noted for their pride in displaying their nakedness with the belief that wearing clothing led to immorality.

According to one source in my research, in some Kavirondo villages women could lose their good reputation by wearing clothing, or could even be ostracized or expelled from their village due to a tribal superstition that if a woman wore a loincloth she would have no children. After they had been married a few months, women wore a "tail" suspended at the back from a string around their waist. My research showed pictures of both men and women totally bare from the waist up, with the men wearing only a string-held loincloth. I was surprised to see some photos of Maasai tribal men and women wearing chains of bright beads wound around their foreheads and wrists; also hanging from their necks and waists—which partially covered their nakedness. (I read that glass beads—a proud possession—were imported from Europe by Arab traders in Africa as far back as the twelfth century!)

I speculated that the rural Kavirondos in those days may have considered that the use of clothing by other tribes or by Europeans was ornamentation rather than for protection; they probably regarded it as impractical for everyday use, since they spent most of their waking hours outdoors in the equatorial heat. I could just hear Dad saying, 'Good thinkin'!

Sexual misconduct didn't seem to tempt the Kavirondos as a result of nudity; they were known for their lack of promiscuity—in fact, they were said to be the most moral tribe in the area! I guess that's what happens when nothing is left to the imagination! It reminds me of the famous quote of Winston Churchill, when he received a visitor while taking a bath in his bathtub. When the visitor knocked on his bathroom door, he shouted, "Come in; I have nothing to hide!"

But, getting back to Mom's story, evidently our Kavirondo house-boys had been so enamored with their new *kanzus* with the red sashes that they had thrown their tribal custom of nudity to the winds and wore them proudly (at least in our house). If they were challenged in their village, I'll bet that they blamed their *kanzus* on the inhibitions of the crazy English! Anyway, my research revealed that by the end of the 1920s the custom of nudity was fast dying out.

Pondering all of this information, I thought facetiously to myself, "You know, Bunty, maybe they've got something there—I'm so glad Michelangelo didn't put clothes on his iconic statue of David, nor on his fresco painting of the Creation of Adam on the Sistene Chapel ceiling, nor on his fresco mural of the Last Judgment—look what the world would have missed!

***

In their new home, once everyone had settled into a routine, domestic life began to take on some semblance of order. Mom again took up the story where she had left off:

"At first, living in Kisumu was a sudden, rude awakening for me to the many challenges in everyday life that were waiting to pounce on me in East Africa! Without the help of the houseboys, life would have been a constantly exhausting affair.

Battling the enervating heat and humidity was bad enough, but ground water was inclined to rise into some of the houses during the rainy season (it left a damp smell of mildew in the house which lingered for days—or weeks—after the rains subsided). Indoors, no running water was piped in; it had to be hand-carried by houseboys from the nearest source: a river, stream, pond or well—and always had to be boiled before it could be used. In addition, there was no electric service—we had to provide our own power for lighting and for the ceiling fans with a small, oil-powered generator which had a tendency to break down at regular intervals.

"There was no telephone service to private homes in the suburbs of Kisumu town at that time. The wireless (radio) was still in its infancy. The commonest form of local communication was by word-of-mouth. Native drums and the telegraph were the fastest and most reliable source for passing news. The nearest telegraph was at the railway office in Kisumu, but stringing telegraph wires from place to place on rows of poles was a risky business. Cutting down and making the poles provided a problem; there were no machines or facilities for stripping trees of their bark and making them into poles as we know them today. In many cases, the telegraph 'poles' were actually live trees with the branches trimmed off to allow the wires to be strung. After awhile, the branches would begin to sprout again and entangle the wires in them as they grew, so the repair crews had to be expert tree-trimmers, too!

"The crews were constantly being advised that a pole was down; one of the reasons would have been hilarious for my family in England to read in my letters, but certainly not funny to the telegraph repairmen. Reports of wires and poles being down were most common in elephant country. Apparently, the elephants found the poles to be just as convenient as the local trees—they had a habit of leaning their enormously heavy bulk against them to rub their sensitive, itching hides. The 'itching posts' either broke off or fell over from this treatment, bringing the telegraph wires down with them. But if one could be found, there was a 'silver lining' to that problem: the men on the telegraph repair crews were never out of work!

"The local water had to be boiled and strained before it could be used. Purified, bottled water was available, but not in the large quantities that were needed for the household. Pessimistically, I thought, 'No wonder there's a lot of alcoholism out here with all these setbacks, but I suppose booze *is* safer to drink than the local water! However, I wasn't tempted to submit to booze; I decided to stick to boiled water and the soda pop we could buy in sealed bottles!

"Washing our clothes was another challenge. Water for washing them had to be hauled up in buckets by hand to the backyard. The buckets were emptied into a 44-gallon drum which was perched over an open charcoal fire to heat the water. Keeping the clothes clean was quite a trick; they got stained with the red dust in the air which wanted to stay embedded in the fabric. White garments were a special challenge; anything that was accidentally washed with the dust-stained ones usually turned pink! I found out that the famous English dye, 'Reckitt's Blue', was available in the market, so I had to make sure that the laundry boy used it to tint the water pale blue for the white clothes, and wash them in it separately to keep them looking reasonably presentable. Obonyo rigged an outside clothesline for the laundry boy and his helper to use, and unless it was rainy season the clothes dried in record time. The helper who did the ironing got plenty of exercise, running in and out to collect the items to be ironed as soon as they dried on the line.

"In Kisumu town, the roads which extended out into the residential areas had drains, but there was still no sanitation in the houses. The little wooden outhouses were put together with wooden pegs—metal nails for the purpose being 'scarce as hen's teeth'. Voracious white ants (termites) loved to eat the pegs, so the *choo* was in constant need of repair. This happened regularly, when whatever part of the structure the pegs had been holding together was sufficiently weakened to fall apart!

"My first visit to our *choo* down the backyard was worse than I had expected. Inside the door, extending from one side of the *choo* to the other at sitting-height, was a wooden plank with two holes in it. Under each hole was a large bucket (I never had the courage to look into one!). I presumed that there were two holes in case one of the buckets became filled before its contents could be collected. The only other possible reason for two holes, I decided, was so that nobody needed to be lonely in the *choo*! We were never exactly alone, either. Lingering inside the *choo,* there were sometimes insects or small creatures to keep us company. Flashlight batteries had to be checked regularly to make sure they were always working, in case an emergency nocturnal trip was needed to the outhouse with its smelly contents. The buckets were emptied into containers on a *tonga*, an ox-drawn cart that (usually) came by early every morning. I never found out where the stuff ended up and I never asked! I finally got used to using the chamber pot under the bed at night for emergencies, after I recovered from my first embarrassing moments with the little *m'toto* who came to empty it every day. The houseboys had their own *choo,* at quite a distance somewhere down the backyard. I never ventured down there to look!

"Although I could almost hear my family giggling hysterically when I described these things in my letters, I was still recovering from the unanticipated shock of dealing with them in my new life! However, in all fairness, I must say that there were compensations for all of the living hazards and discomforts. Among our blessings were: the willingness and helpfulness of the houseboys; the golden sunshine that was so scarce in northern England; the beauty of the sunsets and sunrises; the amazing variety of flowering shrubs and trees; the magnificence of the vast landscape all around us. With my passion for horticulture, I began to make a scrapbook of pressed wild-flowers. Thanks to the help from the encyclopedias in Kisumu town's traveling library, within a year I had found names for no less than eighty of them!

"Winston Churchill put into words his admiration for the African flora. Gazing out to see Lake Victoria from the grounds of his hotel in Kisumu town, he had written in his diary: 'The most beautiful plants and trees grow in profusion on all sides. Beyond a blaze of violet, purple, yellow and crimson blossoms and an expanse of green lawns, the great blue Lake lies in all its beauty'.

***

Nature's Beauty—and Jiggers

"Echoing Churchill on the topic of beautiful Lake Victoria, within about a week of our moving in and when Jack had gone off to join his ship, Effie obviously thought that I was already feeling lonely. She twittered, 'Oh, you know, Ida Dear, we are practically *sitting* on beautiful Lake Victoria; you simply *must* let us take you to see the sunset on the water. It's a sight that tourists flock to watch, and here we are in Kisumu, within a stone's throw! I'm sure Jack will have seen it so many times from his ship that it doesn't thrill him any longer, but while he's away and you're alone, Ted and I thought it would be nice to offer you a quick trip down to the lake to watch it. Coming back we'll be in the dark, but the roads are fairly reliable down there, and it's only a hop, skip and jump from home!' Little did she realize that I would have given my eye-teeth for her invitation! I probably sounded as eager as I felt when I practically yelled, 'Oh yes, Effie, *please!*'

"Late next afternoon, the three of us were in the car on our way to the lake. Ted jostled for a good viewing position among dozens of other cars and sightseers. Their numbers convinced me that this sunset must indeed be a sight not to be missed. Within minutes of our arrival, the bright yellow globe began to sink in the sky. Ted closed the car windows tight. He warned, 'Och, after sundown is just the time yon hungry, flyin' pests come dashin' oot in their droves doon here at the lakefront—especially the mosquitoes. We dinna want to be a meal for yon unwelcome little beasties, nor be left with the diseases they carry!'

"We settled back in the car seats with silence all around us. A constantly-moving kaleidoscope of motion and color gradually unfolded before our eyes. As the sun sank lower in the sky over the blue lake, it developed a luminous white halo making it glow brighter than ever, creating a golden pathway of light on the water's quivering surface that stretched from the horizon all the way back to the shore. Horizontal layers of dark cloud above in the blue sky gradually became edged with the same white light.

"We watched, speechless. As the clouds changed color, now they became tinted with pink. Hesitating momentarily, the sun paused before sinking lower on the horizon, to turn a row of green hills into black silhouettes at the far side of the lake. In front of us, the white sand on the beach darkened into grey, under clouds now edged with streaks of pink and gold. Fish eagles swooped on the water's surface for their last meal of the day, and fishermen in small boats stopped casting their nets and headed for the shore to beat the approaching darkness. The sun seemed to hesitate, pausing momentarily on the horizon as if wondering where to go, then it abruptly disappeared out of sight. Left behind, a sky streaked with horizontal lines of gold, orange and red lingered for a moment before a curtain of darkness fell on the whole scene, giving way to a star-studded, night sky of black velvet. Minutes later, the moon appeared, shedding its pale glow to complete the entire event.

"Ted broke the spell of our silence, 'Well, lassies, we'd better be gettin' back while I can still see yon road with me head-lichts.' He deftly backed out of the tightly packed vehicles and was among the first in line to make a dash for the unlit road. I was quite relieved when he pulled safely into our driveway. I thanked both he and Effie for such a description-defying experience and headed for bed. I remember that when I tried to put the picture into words in my next letter home, the family wouldn't realize how I groped for adjectives eloquent enough to do it justice.

"In the weeks that followed, Effie grew as close to me as any sister could have done. I was grateful for her help; in fact she became my anchor: a friend to rely on (especially when Jack was away) who gave unstintingly of her time, helping me to adjust not only to my new marriage but to the daunting task of being in charge of a household in this unfamiliar country.

"I had overcome the near-nudity of the houseboys success-fully with their *kanzu* uniforms, but they still padded around barefoot. I was glad that I'd been able to cover up as much of them as I had already, so I decided not to mention their feet.

"Jack had already warned me not to go barefoot—ever! I even wore my moccasins to walk from bed to wash basin! Until I read about it, I wasn't aware of how susceptible bare feet in Africa are to disease, including jiggers (not to be confused with 'chiggers'). The article explained how these tiny sand-flea parasites burrow under the toe-nails and into the soles of bare feet so deeply that they are difficult to remove. The whole process is revolting! The female feeds off the blood of her human host and lays innumerable eggs, after which she dies. Before doing so, she burrows back out through the skin, leaving a tiny hole, which can (and usually does) become in-fected. Horrifying pictures in the article showed me the foot of a victim, with black, infected scars covering almost all of the toes and soles of the feet. Meanwhile, the eggs left behind develop into larvae, which develop into jiggers and lay more eggs, and so the terrible cycle continues. The infestation is very painful to the victim, and if it becomes rampant it makes walking without pain impossible, disabling the sufferer."

BUNTY: The infestation of jiggers and its disastrous consequences qualify it as one of Africa's most neglected diseases:

In my research, it was documented that recently the government of Kenya had officially acknowledged an estimated two million people to be suffering from jiggers, and ten million more are at risk of infestation. A campaign has been started to fight this scourge. At this writing, there is still no vaccine. Treatment (where available) consists of bathing the infested areas of entry with potassium permanganate solution, followed by a thick application of Vaseline to cut off the oxygen supply to the jiggers which then suffocate and die. Treatment centres have now sprung up and "National Jiggers Day" was instituted to encourage sufferers to seek relief.

It is written that little attention has been paid to another devastating disease in Kenya. Its name is bilharzia. It has been named one of the eighteen neglected tropical diseases in the world, and although it has been estimated that millions of people world-wide are currently infected, it is said to cause more disabilities than deaths.

Living in the reeds at the edge of Kenya's rivers and lakes are tiny snails, hosts to parasitic blood flukes. The snails deposit these parasites into water used by humans who wade out through the reeds in order to bathe or to do their washing, sometimes defecating into the water and adding to the pollution on which the snails thrive. The parasites released into the water carry bilharzia. They enter the blood of their victims through the skin, where they multiply to cause infection and damage in organs such as the bladder, intestines, spinal cord and brain.

Sufferers are often unaware of what is causing their disease and simply live with it without seeking treatment. If the parasites attack the bladder, however, the urine turns blood red, which is so alarming that it sends the victim running to seek medical help (if it is available). Bilharzia can cause nerve damage resulting in seizures or paralysis. Particularly in children, it causes anemia and malnutrition; when it attacks their brain they suffer learning difficulties. In girls, the infection-filled organ can be the uterus, causing great pain and often necessitating surgery for its removal. In this instance, for a girl it could also mean social disaster; if it makes her infertile she may be ostracized from her village or considered unsuitable for marriage. Bilharzia is rampant in Africa largely because of ignorance of its existence, lack of medicines to treat it, and doctors who have trouble with its diagnosis.

My research also uncovered other diseases found in Central East Africa, such as tick fever, carried by the bite of a tick, and sleeping sickness, carried by the tsetse fly—a biting fly about the size of a housefly. The first organ to be affected by sleeping sickness is the brain. Mom and Dad never mentioned any of these diseases in their commentary, so I didn't dig any further. However, I did discover that the reason why the little islands in Lake Victoria became uninhabited: their populations were wiped out by sleeping sickness. Most are still uninhabited, but much has been done since then to eradicate the tsetse fly, so one disease is hopefully on its way out and the islands' populations may be on their way back!

***

Mom dusted off her glasses and picked up her notes:

"Jack was usually away sailing on Lake Victoria for seven to ten days at a time, but sometimes he was gone longer if they ran into one of the violent storms that periodically ravaged the lake. His ship had to call in at each of the ports around the lake with its mission to discharge and take on passengers, cargo and the Royal Mail, which was a different experience each time it happened. He was happy doing the work he knew well and enjoyed; no two voyages were alike, so life on board was never dull.

"Although his passengers were few, Jack made sure that their voyage ran smoothly. They enjoyed hot baths, as well as electricity and hot and cold running water in their comfortable cabins. They dined on good food in a well-appointed dining room with nicely polished cutlery and attractive china. The crew wore uniforms; Jack wore his 'dress whites' in his position as captain when he was on duty on the bridge and also when he presided over the captain's table at dinner. He literally lived on the ship during the voyage, but thankfully he was replaced by another captain when it returned to Kisumu port. He could then hop on a river steamer and come home to Namasagali for some relaxation before it was time to join his ship again at Kisumu port. With a new load of passengers, cargo and mail, the ship would take on oil for its engines and begin its trek around the lake once more.

"At first, I fretted about being left all alone in the house for a week or more at a time with no human activity other than Effie's visits and the presence of the houseboys. When I felt sorry for myself, I often relied on the gramophone for company. Listening to it meant quite a bit of work! First of all, I had to wind it up by cranking a handle that fitted into an opening on its side. Once this was done, I placed a record on the turntable. Next, I carefully swung the arm holding the gramophone needle to the outermost edge of the record and lowered it, turning the switch on to start it playing. Only then could I sit down, put my feet up and relax. When the needle had successfully traveled around and around the entire record in concentric circles and the music had ended, I walked over to the gramophone and turned it off, or played another record. Often, when going through the few records we had, the gramophone ran down and needed to be cranked to wind it up again. When I had exhausted the supply of records or had played all I wanted, I got up again and turned the gramophone off, lifting the arm holding the needle and securing it in its resting place on the edge of the turntable. Then the records had to be carefully inserted into their paper jackets and stored until the next time I had the energy to play them again! Looking back on it all in this day and age, I was amazed at how that entire performance has been replaced by one touch of a button!

"When he first watched this routine and heard music coming from the gramophone, Omolo reacted with fright until he realized that the contraption was harmless. Later, when he heard me playing the gramophone, I could always be sure he would find an excuse to linger near the machine. He gave it his full attention, watching it and listening incredulously to the music, no doubt wondering how its tinny sound came out through the big black horn that was the speaker. As for me, once I got the hang of operating it, I became so addicted that I began to wonder which would wear out first: the gramophone, the records, or me!

"Omolo sensed my loneliness. He showed his concern by offering to do things for me and by bringing me little presents ('I bring you prethent, *Memthahib Amith* '): a flower that had just opened, a new fruit for me to taste. But I had to grit my teeth and try not to shudder when he presented me with the discarded skin of a snake! He had found it outside somewhere on the ground where it had become too small and the snake had wriggled out of it to make room for the new, larger one underneath. Omolo said, 'Nith prethent, *memthahib,* bring good luck!' He obviously thought I would welcome it as the rare and precious 'good luck' token that it was considered to be by the natives. I tried not to think about its ex-tenant, still alive and slithering around somewhere in the neighborhood in its new skin. I thanked Omolo for his thoughtfulness, and—not to hurt his feelings—-asked him to put the snakeskin high on a on a window sill out in the verandah (so I wouldn't have to look at it!) Omolo seemed surprised at my distressed reaction to this prized token of his regard for me, but at least this way he could be sure it was in a place where it could work its magic. I must confess that some days I could use all the good luck I could get!

"Omolo was always cheerful, and eager to comply with anything I asked him to do. One of the first times I enlisted his help was when I discovered something mysterious going on in my bedroom. I knew that he tidied the room up every morning after I was 'up and doing', and I asked him how it was that this morning I'd noticed a strand of knitting wool (yarn) trailing across the floor, originating in the drawer where I kept my knitting and ending at the closed bedroom door. I was sure I had wound it up and put it away in the lowest drawer of the chest of drawers. I checked out the drawer again, and there was the ball of wool, still in the drawer where I had put it, but mysteriously it had become unwound. The knitting and other balls of wool that I had brought with me from England were untouched. Then I remembered my bad habit of not closing drawers completely, but how that strand of wool could have magically escaped during the night and found its way across the floor was a complete mystery to me. I called to Omolo, '*kuja hapa, Omolo, shari gani?*' (Come here, Omolo, what's going on?). I felt quite proud to be trying out my Swahili on him, and looked anxiously at him hoping not to see a vacant stare! He grinned and said, '*Omolo funga, memthahib.*' (Omolo will fix it, ma'm.) I wondered what he had in mind—it wasn't long to wait.

"A few minutes later, he knocked on the bedroom door. I called out, '*Kuja hapa,*' (come in). Omolo came into the room. '*Habari tha athubuhi, memthahib*' (Good morning, ma'am) he said, holding out something in the palm of his hand. I gazed in horror at what I saw. There, curled up and obviously quite dead, was an enormous, formidable-looking, shiny, black beetle with an evil little head and long, curved feelers—the ugliest thing I ever hope to see. I recognized it as a scarab beetle, one type of which is the dung beetle (probably the ugliest of the lot.)

"Omolo grinned from ear to ear, 'Omolo *queetha koofa ca-beetha dudu, memthahib* (Omolo made the insect very dead, ma'am) he announced triumphantly, adding in his halting

English, 'Now he never learn how to do knitting!' I laughed
and replied, '*Sante sana, Omolo*' (I was proud that I could say,
'Thank you very much, Omolo,' in Swahili.)

   "I had once read an article about scarab beetles in my
encyclopedia back home in England, but I never thought I
would ever actually see one of their relatives! Dung beetles are
named because they gather dung and roll it up into a ball to
lay their eggs in it as food for the grubs after they hatch. Ugh!
Evidently, this dung beetle thought my knitting wool would
make a good addition to its ball of dung which presumably
was somewhere outside the house! The drawer was open far
enough for it to get in and seize its prize, but, to its dismay, it
wasn't able to drag the strand of wool under the small space
at the bottom of the bedroom door through which it had been
barely able to squeeze its own body. The frustrated insect must
have given up in disgust and left the strand of wool there,
emerging from under the door in time to encounter Omolo
on the other side. The thought that my knitting wool might
have ended up rolled up in a ball of dung made me feel sick!
Weakly, I waved my hand at Omolo to take the dead beetle
away, followed by a thorough session at the washbasin to
clear my memory of the incident. Afterwards, I had no trouble
remembering to keep that drawer tightly closed!"

                              ***

BUNTY: I was curious enough—after hearing Mom's experience—to
find out more about the dung beetle's family, the scarabs:

   Scarab beetles were made famous by the ancient Egyptians, who
believed that they brought good luck and had magical qualities.
Historical records show that the ancient Egyptians also associated
some of their trees, plants, animals and insects with magical and
divine powers. These beliefs are still held by some of the African tribes.

The ancient Egyptian sun-god, Ra, was often depicted with the head of a scarab to associate him with magical qualities. They believed that the inexhaustible Ra rolled the sun over the horizon at sunrise, after which he rolled it across the earth all day until sunset. He must not have needed any sleep, because he rolled it all night through the underworld to reach the earth's horizon again in time for the next sunrise. Symbolically, the scarab rolling its dung ball was a reminder—if a somewhat smelly one—of Ra's superhuman energy!

Traditionally, the scarab has always been a symbol of good luck. The ancient Egyptians often wore charms in the image of scarabs, based on the belief that the beetle had magical power to protect them in the same way that it fiercely protects its eggs. Nowadays, people buy ornaments and jewelry in the form of scarabs, both for themselves and also to give them to their favorite people as good-luck gifts.

I'm quite sure that even if Mom had known any of this, she still wouldn't have been convinced to love her scarab visitor!

LIVING THE ADVENTURE

BUNTY: Mom was having a great time reading from her pages of hand-written notes. She was ready to relate the story of the first 'side trip' that she and Dad took to Lake Naivasha, but first I'll insert results of my research about this unique body of water:

Huge Lake Naivasha is one of the chain of soda lakes created 6,000 feet above sea level by volcanic eruptions in primeval times, when the earth's tectonic plates were pulling the African continent apart to form the Great Rift Valley. The name Naivasha means, in the Masaii language, "rough water," because of the sudden storms that arise over it. The lakes were formed by water filling up the craters of extinct volcanoes, and are kept supplied from the deluges in rainy seasons and thunderstorms. Eight miles in length, Lake Naivasha is also supplied by fresh-water springs. There is no visible outlet from the lake, but it is thought to have an underground outflow. Because of its high mineral content, it contains only a few species of fresh-water fish (mostly, common carp) but it supports a wealth of microscopic algae which in turn feed the enormous flocks of flamingoes that come to feast and roost there. It has been established that the fossil remains of flamingo ancestors date their existence back to between 30 and 50 million years ago, so Lake Naivasha must have been a favorite of theirs even way back then!

Now let's go back to Mom and Dad's invitation to visit Lake Naivasha. Mom tells the story:

***

Sightseeing in Paradise

"'Coo-ee, Ida Dear,' was Effie's way of announcing that she had arrived on one of her visits. She sounded excited as she gushed, 'I say, Ida Dear, it's time you and Jack began to look around and visit some of the beautiful places there are to see in Kenya. Ted and I went out to Lake Naivasha last year. Oh, Ida Dear, that's a place you really *must* visit. It's a nice ride on the train, too. What do you think about all four of us going there one weekend? Would you and Jack come with us? We know a lovely little place there to stay overnight called the Bell Inn.

"I was thrilled. I remembered seeing a glimpse of that spectacular lake when the train teetered at the top of the escarpment on our way to Kisumu. Even Jack, who enjoyed staying put at home on his days off after a week or more of steady traveling on Lake Victoria, was enthusiastic. Overnight reservations were made at the Bell Inn, near the lake shore. After Jack had time to relax for a day or two at the beginning of his next few days of leisure, the four of us set off for Naivasha on the first morning train out of Kisumu railway station. Effie and I had packed our lunch which was now stowed in her wicker picnic basket for us to enjoy on the train journey.

"As always, the vastness and variety of the scenery were breathtaking. We left the marshy lowlands around Kisumu and crossed miles of grassy plains quivering in the heat, bordered in the distance by a misty range of mountains. On the plains, small herds of game grazed or galloped: zebras, elephants, giraffes, antelopes, and a couple of rhinos, but nowhere near the numbers of animals we had seen from the train window on our journey inland from Mombasa—it already felt like ages ago.

"This time, as luck would have it, the fans in this train's ceiling were working, making the journey very comfortable. We had the pleasure of chatting with Effie and Ted and getting to know them better as we exchanged the usual funny stories about growing up in Britain. In addition, there was always local news and gossip to exchange and laugh about. We stretched our legs on a walk to the dining car. There, we eagerly enjoyed the sandwich lunch from Effie's picnic hamper, topped off with a pie that Effie had baked in her small, kerosene-powered oven. I had contributed vacuum flasks of 'limeade' made with cool boiled water and freshly-squeezed limes from the tree outside our back door. When I took the first gulp, this time I didn't have to worry about any gin!

"Outside the train window, the grassland began to sprout acacia and baobab trees that gradually multiplied into forests. Hills appeared in the background. Behind them arose the range of Aberdare Mountains emerging, majestic and purple, from their misty shroud at the far edge of the Great Rift Valley. Effie said, 'You know, Ida Dear, over there by the foothills is Happy Valley. I must tell you *that* story someday!' She was interrupted by the awesome sight that had just come into view from the train window.

"Ahead of us we could now clearly see a huge lake cradled in the valley, with sun and clouds making patterns on its bright blue surface. Looking through the binoculars, we saw farms and ranches spread out on the slopes rising above the lake. Minutes later, the train pulled into a station with the letters NAIVASHA on a sign hanging above the narrow platform. We joined the crowd of passengers leaving the train—mostly tourists like ourselves—and found rickshaws. Hopping into them with our suitcases, we bumped all the way to the Bell Inn overlooking the lake. This little privately-owned hotel was one of many which had begun to appear in the area.

"If there hadn't been a nice hotel available, I don't think the McTavishes would have suggested a trip to the lake, and for good reason. In those early days of travel in East Africa, overnight accommodation was primitive, to say the least. It was in what they called a dak bungalow, a monstrosity of a building, described by one traveler as 'about as handsome as a stack of hay'. The closest thing to one of these is now known as a hostel, and we would have had to bring our own bedding! At Naivasha, one of these sub-standard accommodations still existed as 'The Royal Hotel' behind the railway station, built in the early days of the Lunatic Express. I was wondering what *our* hotel would be like. I was pleasantly surprised.

"We arrived at the charming little white-painted Bell Inn well ahead of dinner hour, welcomed by the hotel staff with cool drinks of lemonade. Hot, sweaty and weary from our cramped train journey, we all decided that it would be a good idea to take advantage of a rest in our rooms. Jack and I fell asleep almost as soon as our heads hit the bed pillows. After a refreshing nap followed by a cool wash and change of clothes, we joined Effie and Ted in the hotel's lounge.

"Ted said, 'Och, I made inquiries while the two of ye were snoozin' and found out that there's a bus trip doon to yon lake to see the sunset. I booked our seats in the wee bus that taks the tourists doon . It's a sight we should na' miss!'

"The little bus came to pick us up with a dozen other passengers as the day's heat was beginning to cool. Shimmering in the late afternoon sun, ahead of us stretched the big, blue lake edged with papyrus reeds. Jutting up near its centre was the ragged tip of the original volcano which had erupted, its crater becoming submerged over the centuries as it filled with water. On the opposite shore was a short stretch of grassy plain with grazing animals, which sloped upwards to become clumps of trees backed by a mountain range.

"We arrived at the lake, where the bus stopped at the shore and the driver turned off the motor. Near the papyrus at the edge of the lapping water, dozens of marsh birds had congregated: herons, pelicans, egrets and stately marabou storks whose long, elegant feathers were selling at a premium in Europe to decorate ladies' hats.

"Suddenly, before our startled eyes, a pink cloud came into sight high above the lake. Magically, as it arrived over the water, its reflection colored the surface pink! The cloud was now near enough for us to see that it was an enormous flock of pink flamingoes flying with long necks and legs outstretched to streamline their bodies as they flew. The sound of squawks and whirring wings grew deafening in the quiet air as they approached. Moving in perfect formation, the mass of birds swirled around, circling the lake, and came in to land on the water. We now knew why the sight before our eyes has been called 'the greatest phenomenon of nature in the world;' it was something we would never forget! The flamingoes landed on the lake, covering it like a great pink blanket. After landing, many stood ankle-deep around the lake in the shallows to begin a slow, deliberate walk on their long legs. Their heavy, black beaks dangling from long, pink-feathered necks trolled the shallow water, greedily shoveling up and swallowing large numbers of nutritious microorganisms and the tiny crustaceans that give them their pink color.

"Ted had brought along a small bottle of wine and four paper cups. He was determined that we should have a sundowner, wherever we were! 'Och aye,' he said, 'We canna' let the sun go doon without a sundowner!' Remembering the saying, *'forewarned is forearmed'*, I didn't let him put more than an inch of wine in my paper cup! Some of the other tourists on the bus had brought sundowners, too, and we all solemnly raised a toast to the sunset, its dying rays casting red, orange and yellow reflections in the blue sky above and silhouetting the great blanket of pink flamingoes floating on the water. All conversation in the bus stopped as we watched this incredibly beautiful sight of a lifetime unfolding before our eyes, until it disappeared with the sun when darkness took over.

"The blackness became overarched by a galaxy of stars, so bright in the clear night sky that they looked close enough for us to touch. Ted observed dryly, 'Och, 'tis glad I am that I'm not driving—we'd niver have found our way back to yon hotel in the darrk!'

"But we did find our way back—the bus driver probably made this little excursion with the tourists routinely. He switched on his headlights and announced, 'Before we go back to the hotel, ladies and gents, we'll just go on a small detour; I have something more to show you.' With headlights lighting the trail, he inched his way along the lake shore to a small bay. Here, the reeds near the water's edge seemed to be boiling with activity. Our eyes gradually adjusted to the dimly-lit scene. Amidst the turbulence, the ugly heads of dozens of hippos could be seen splashing and thrashing about as they came to life after their daytime nap. We could see their huge mouths gaping open to expose large, strong teeth.

"Our bus driver suddenly became a tour guide: 'Hippos are considered to be the most dangerous animals in Africa, folks. Those rows of teeth are growing in 20 inches of jawbone, and when a hippo's mouth snaps shut, the force is enough to bite a human in two! Oh, yes, they have been known to attack and kill humans!' You could almost hear the gasp go through the bus!

" 'As if this wasn't enough bad news,' he continued, 'they're a menace to the people who live near the lake; they get into *shambas* and plantations during the night, trampling the growing crops while they forage. Believe it or not, a hippo needs to eat an average of 88 pounds of food a night. It sounds like a lot, but actually it's less than the average daily requirement of a dairy cow! Although they prefer to feed on plants and grass, hippos have been known to attack and kill animals (including each other) and they've even been known to scavenge and eat a kill left by another animal.'

"Watching these creatures from the safety of the bus, we could hear their grunting and growling filling the air as the hippos cavorted about in the water like children let out early from school. Our driver didn't stay long. He cautioned, 'The hippos sleep most of the day in those papyrus reeds, but they come out at night to eat. They'll soon be coming up from the water to graze on the grass near where we're parked, and it's dangerous to tussle with a hippo. They've been known to charge a vehicle that gets in their way. It's time for us to go!'

"There was a hush in the bus while the driver turned it around and headed back to the Bell Inn. Dinner was waiting, and the four of us ate as if we hadn't seen a square meal for a week! We all slept well that night, but we were up again at sunrise with renewed energy, to take a stroll together in the hotel grounds before breakfast. I admired the abundance of beautiful flowers in the hotel gardens overlooking the lake. In addition to other flowering bushes, I was in awe of the magnificent red poinsettia bush in full bloom by the door of the hotel. From this vantage point, with our ever-present binoculars we focused our eyes to try to see snow-capped Mount Kenya. There she was in the distance, in the clear morning air—all 17,000 feet of her—with her snow-capped peak shining white, reflecting the sunshine.

"Bringing our attention back to the lake in front of us, we gazed at the amazing variety of birds. In addition to the flamingoes, there were ducks, geese and pelicans sailing on the water. Fish eagles—white, with big black wings—swooped down to catch fish in their talons. The morning sun flashed on brightly colored kingfishers as they dived to catch their breakfast, while cormorants took time out from their fishing to perch on rocks with wings outspread to dry. At the water's edge, foraging along the edge of the lake, cranes, egrets, herons and storks waded in the shallows as if to cool their feet, their eyes searching for any stray fish that might swim within catching distance. They were joined by spoonbills and flamingoes walking slowly along with their heads down and beaks open to scoop up a meal. I learned later that central Africa is a bird-watchers paradise, with more than 10 per cent of the world's bird species living in Kenya and Uganda.

"Time stood still as we stared at the ever-changing picture. We lingered at the lake until hunger overtook us, then headed

back to the hotel dining room for a hearty early English breakfast before catching the train back to Kisumu. The long journey
brought us back as darkness was fast approaching, and we
were too weary to eat much before bedtime. Feeling romantic, I murmured to Jack, 'Well, dear, this weekend we've had
enough experiences to dream about for the rest of our lives.'

"Always the practical engineer, Jack burst my poetic bubble
when he quipped, 'Oh aye, Sunshine, the stories about those
hippos have left me with a permanent nightmare!'

***

BUNTY: A social note about Kisumu:

When Mom and Dad arrived, Kisumu town was growing by
leaps and bounds, having been previously mapped out by British
Government planners to keep its development well-organized. By
1924, it had grown from a small, crude pioneer town into one with
imposing government buildings in British colonial-style architecture
at its centre and attractive suburbs on its outskirts. Kisumu's growth
rate soon exceeded itself by a whopping 264 per cent!

In the early years, Kenya's society was divided into three factions:
settlers, colonial employees and traders. In the 1920s, the new immi-
grants in Kisumu were young and predominantly British; only 7 per
cent were "foreigners" from other European countries. Each group
found its own social level. The caste system left behind in Britain
followed them to Kenya, and there was quite a snobbish social code
in East Africa. The first batch or two of British men to arrive were
largely wealthy would-be plantation owners, or appointees to gov-
ernment-type, executive positions in local affairs. These were the
upper class who circulated socially with their own kind as they would
have done in Britain. The political practice of name-dropping was
common. As they used to say, "To 'get on' in society in Kisumu, it
isn't *what* you know, it's *who* you know!"

Wives were frowned upon at first by the authorities who felt that having a wife underfoot would distract the attention of the husband from his job. Also, it was reasoned that a trailing wife would disrupt the tranquility of the community by causing unwanted problems for him while she adjusted to the climate and living conditions. History suggests that the local British Commissioner had even threatened to transfer the men if they brought their wives with them, but he finally relented and accepted the inevitable!

Women had to be tough in order to adapt to the environment and to handle domestic problems, including houseboys with differing customs and tribal taboos. But, as time went by, more of the ladies began to follow in their husbands' footsteps and migrate to the Dark Continent. Ironically, women had the vote in Kenya prior to those in Britain, and employment was readily available for them as nurses, teachers, and typists in government offices.

Private clubs began to spring up in Kisumu, becoming the focal point for social group relaxation with sports, parties, dances, dinners, card- playing, and other entertainment. At first, the members of upper-class clubs "looked down their noses" and made sly digs at the new, middle class clubs available to workers who had begun to arrive. After the railway was completed, there was an influx of more of the middle classes, including railway employees who staffed the many station stops along the route. Kisumu's Scottish stationmaster, Ted McTavish, was one of these. The railway personnel were inclined to be clannish, and tended to stay in a group isolated from other British ex-pats. This gradually changed, and the lower echelon of British civil servants and farmers were included—at first being invited to friendly competition in sports events and later rising to full club membership.

Initially, about the only exercise available to white people in Kisumu was walking, but by the time Mom and Dad arrived there was already a nine-hole golf course and tennis courts had sprung up, many of them for their club members. As the clubs multiplied, more competitive sports were added such as cricket and soccer. Although play was confined to the cooler hours in early morning or late afternoon, it was still a sweaty business. After the games, players and outdoor spectators usually went into the clubhouse for a sponge-down to revive them (as yet, showers were not common as a way to bathe). Conversation consisted of grumbles mixed with an exchange of jokes, local gossip and discussion of the news in the month-old letters and newspapers from England. The wives soon had bridge and mahjong groups established; those who didn't wish to watch their husbands' outdoor sports could while away the time in the clubhouse playing indoor games, reading or chatting, cooled by ceiling fans while the men sweated out of doors.

During the Christmas holidays, in the cool of the mornings the British population gathered to hold a traditional "sports day"—a family affair which included hurdles, foot races, high and long jumps. Then there were the age-old contests: tug of war, sack race, egg-and-spoon race, wheelbarrow race and three-legged race, with silly prizes awarded such as a transparent mini *kanzu;* a fez dyed purple with a feather in it; a hairnet; a false moustache; false Santa Claus whiskers; a Santa hat; a pair of lady's underpants; a bunch of balloons or a funny false nose. This was a great occasion for Brits from all over the area to meet and greet one another, and many bonds of friendship resulted that would last a lifetime

***

Mom was all geared up with enough notes to continue her story:

Social Circles and the Happy Valley Set

"At some point in his early life, Jack had joined the Church of England, or—as it was known in Africa—the Anglican Church. We attended church services when he was home, in the little corrugated iron Anglican Church in Kisumu. It would soon be replaced by a larger one built of stone, as it was filled to overflowing by the British population. There was no church hall attached to the original church in which to hold social activities, as there was back home in Sunderland.

"In addition to the need for a larger church, the middle-class British and European arrivals in our Kisumu neighborhood felt the need for a local meeting place where they could regularly stay in touch with one another to socialize and exchange news, opinions, complaints and suggestions. By the time we arrived, a neighborhood clubhouse had been built. About a month after our arrival, Effie and Ted took us with them and introduced us around to the club members. The building had recently been enlarged to include a big, multi-purpose meeting room with a stage at one end, along with a well-equipped kitchen to make food service possible. There was no bar, but there were lockers for keeping one's own drinking requirements.

"The new meeting room at the club had been built to be versatile. Before long, we were invited to a favorite event: a dinner party followed by a nostalgic sing-along. Nobody ever tired of the popular songs we had left behind in the 'old country'. I often described my mediocre singing as 'a noise that usually comes out of my mouth on key'. But with Jack's forceful baritone, Ted's bass that sounded like a foghorn and Effie's piercing soprano, we often led the singing. Someone had donated an old, upright piano that needed tuning but otherwise served its purpose. I was certainly no concert pianist, but I knew enough about playing the piano to thump out chords to accompany the songs in the absence of Ian McNab, our accomplished pianist. Jack's loud voice was well-suited to leading the sea shanties that everyone knew, and he usually closed by singing what he referred to as his 'party piece', a famous north-country ditty called *On Ilkley Moor Bar T'at*. In almost incomprehensible dialect, it told the story of a man who found himself on the desolate, freezing moorland of Ilkley in Yorkshire, after going to court his lady love *bar t'at* (without a hat) to protect his head from the frigid air on the moor. The song told of the dire things that would happen to him if he caught his 'death of cold'. The chorus was belted out lustily by the audience after each of the almost endless string of verses warning the hero of the consequences he could expect without wearing his hat. The song ends with a series of horrific warnings about what will befall him after his demise as the final consequence of his carelessness. However gruesome, the words never seemed to lose their comedic effect on the audience, who joyfully roared out chorus after chorus. Jack's performance was received with clapping and cheers, but it always struck me how funny and incongruous the song sounded, so close to the equator!"

***

Dad opened his eyes. Mom handed over the microphone to him. He must have been listening with his eyes closed, because without hesitation, he began:

"Oh aye, everyone enjoyed *On Ilkley Moor Bar T'at* alright! I had a good life in Kisumu. In spite of a couple of bouts of malaria, otherwise it was social and happy. Ida made new friends who helped to relieve some of her homesickness and loneliness while I was away. Our club was fun, but it was also conservative. Some of the members of the upper-class clubs in Kenya were notorious for the excesses in their lifestyle, but (thank goodness) we had none of that nonsense to contend with. With me strictly moral Quaker upbrin'in', I'd developed a healthy aversion to the carryin's-on of promiscuous snobs like them.

"Along with our close friendship with Effie and Ted, our club in Kisumu provided our main source of social life. By and large, we made our own entertainment. Sunshine enjoyed playin' mahjong with Effie and some of the other women. When they played, they all smoked cigarettes—in those days we hadn't heard about the ill effects of tobacco on health—so Ida began to smoke, too. She dug out that carton of Egyptian cigarettes she'd bought for me at Port Said, which she never gave to me when she discovered that I'd switched to pipe smokin'. When she tried her first cigarette, to her surprise she found it to be quite mild and pleasant, so she stuck to the Simon Arzt brand with its gold paper tips from then on. She was now quite happily attached to her gin and lime sundowner, after she learned how to make one drink last all evenin'! What a sophisticated lass she was becomin' compared with the one I'd married in Sunderland!

"Our circle of friends grew quickly, thanks to Effie and Ted's shepherdin' us around durin' those early weeks in Kisumu. Ida was gettin' used to the idea of livin' in a totally different world from the one she knew in Sunderland. It was comfortin' for her to be with people who were all in the same boat, bein' up against livin' without the conveniences we had taken for granted back home.

"Ida was concerned about what to do with our rubbish (garbage) and cast-off clothin', so she asked Effie who said—little knowin' that her advice would soon come full circle—'Oh, just give it to one of the houseboys, Ida Dear, he will dispose of it for you'."

Mom broke in, "Oh, Jack, please let me tell the rest of this story!" Dad reluctantly gave up the microphone and she chuckled as she began the tale of another favorite experience:

"I shall never forget the first of Effie's formal dinner parties that we attended, a few weeks after we arrived. Ahead of time, she had counseled me with information that she felt I should know: 'Ida Dear, 'I've invited another two couples to have dinner with us. We all wear evening dress to my formal dinners, and we gather on the verandah beforehand for a sundowner.

Ted will come to pick up you and Jack about six-ish, and we'll have dinner at seven.'

"I thanked her and began to plan which clothes I would wear. I chose one of my white, lacy, long-sleeved blouses and my one long, black taffeta skirt. I wondered if my crystal necklace and earrings would be too dressy, but I said to myself, 'Don't be so silly, Ida, you didn't bring them all this way to sit in the drawer', so I laid them out with the blouse and skirt. I gave myself a cool sponge-down in the bedroom. The long sleeves and skirt felt very confining after the comfortable, loose dresses I had become accustomed to wearing in the heat. Jack grumbled, 'I'm almost sorry I brought me evenin' togs with me—it's like buttonin' meself into some kind of torture instrument!' But out came his black evening suit, and I was soon tying his black bow tie for him under the stiff white collar of his shirt. He balked (as usual) at the cummerbund, 'I'll be damned if I'll wear one of those; I don't care if the other men *are* wearin' the blasted things. I don't think I can get it round me waist anyway; our Abraham's cookin' is just too good for me waistline! As it is, I'm goin' to have to let out me braces (suspenders) to lower me trousers a bit!'

"Jack wasn't the only one making adjustments. This time, with that first gin and lime in mind and its effect on my empty stomach, I made sure to eat a little snack before we left home! Ted's car whisked us to the McTavishes', and we were relaxing on their verandah by the time the other guests arrived. Two couples came to the front door. Jack and I stood up to be introduced. Ted turned to the nearest couple and said, 'Och aye, Ida and Jack Amiss, meet the Pinkingtons—Victoria and George.'

"Victoria—a tall, elegant blonde—looking stunning in a low-cut, black velvet evening gown with a necklace of dia-monds at her throat—shook our hands with her rather limp one and said in her English upper-class accent, 'I'm so-oo-oo gled to meet you, Jeck and Ida. Jest call me Vickie, dahlings. I jest love nicknames, don't yew? Yew *are* lucky, Ida, you dewn't need to abbreeviate yours!'

"I was thinking, 'Oh, dear, I'll be darned if I'll tell her that my nickname is Sunshine! Heaven knows what she would do with *that* information,' adding to the thought somewhat defensively, 'and my sparkly crystal necklace looks just as nice as her diamond one!'

"George wasn't quite as tall as Vickie and obviously less dominant; he spoke with a stutter and was addicted to teasing people, especially his classy wife. With a wry smile, he stammered, 'V-Vickie loves royalty and their n-nicknames, you knew. Wud yew b-believe, s-she looked all over for a m-man to m-marry whose name was Albert or Edward like the royal p-princes of England, so that she c-could c-call him by his nickname, B-B-Bertie or Teddy, but she found me, instead: George. H-however, that n-name must have pleased her—I *am* n-named ahfter a king of England—but she almost didn't m-marry me, because n-nobody has heard of a n-nickname for George, eh what?' He gave a self-conscious chuckle and quickly sat down.

"Ted rapidly introduced the other couple, the Porters. Isabella Porter was plump and jolly; she looked as if she'd had a struggle to wriggle into her rather snug-fitting evening dress. She gushed, 'Oh, welcome to Kisumu, my dears; loverly to meet you both.' She pumped our hands energetically.

"Dennis, her husband, wore a look of perpetual gloom. He intoned, 'Hope the climate hasn't got you down, yet. You'll get used to it, but it's a dashed nuisance, damn it all.' He moved our hands up and down with a tired motion, 'It's nice to meet you, anyway.'

"Sundowners were served in time for us to toast the sunset. We raised our glasses as the great golden ball lowered rapidly into the horizon, leaving clouds tinted with amber and crimson streaming across the sky. Soon afterwards, total darkness enveloped the verandah, relieved only by the light from the oil lamps burning at its corners, until the stars popped out to shine brightly in the still air. But, best of all, the sun's disappearance brought with it coolness which stayed with us all evening. I felt pleasantly relaxed with my gin and lime whose stronger effects had been avoided with the little snack before I left home. I sipped my drink slowly under the watchful eye of Ted, who was probably wondering if he dared to offer me a refill. When Effie invited us all to go into the dining room, I took Jack's arm—this time graciously and not in desperation as I had done on the previous occasion.

"In the unaccustomed humidity, coupled with some warmth from the gin and lime, my body felt at is if it would melt inside my blouse and trickle down under my heavy skirt into my mosquito boots that seemed to get tighter and tighter. I longed to shake off the offending clothes and change back into my comfortable, loose house dress. Wishing that Effie had said we needn't dress up, I was hoping that my flushed face hadn't betrayed my discomfort. Minutes later, I realized that I wasn't suffering alone. When we sat down at the dining table, I noticed that all the ladies were politely perspiring, too. The toes of their tight, hot mosquito boots were peeking out from under their skirts, looking so incongruous with the elegant evening clothes that—in my relaxed state with the gin and lime—I was tempted to giggle. I decided against it for the sake of decorum.

"Everything was perfect in the dining room, lit by the twinkling candles on Effie's beautifully-set table: the white linen tablecloth; the bouquet of fresh flowers as a centre-piece; the immaculate silverware, glassware and bone-china plates; not a thing out of place. I suppressed another giggle when I saw the table legs standing inelegantly in their kerosene cans and thought of all of us in our evening clothes wearing mosquito boots instead of the dress shoes that would have been the case in England. Ted poured the wine; Effie rang her little bell. Their cook, Jeremiah, came out of the small kitchen in a white *kanzu*, holding a tureen of steaming soup in his hands. I thought I saw something pink around his waist, and as he came closer I realized, to my surprise, that it was a lady's pink corset! It was very much the worse for wear; one suspender (garter) dangling forlornly at the front and another from one hip; the remaining two were missing completely. The apparition advanced and prepared to serve the soup.

"Conversation stopped abruptly and we all gasped in astonishment. Effie's face blushed crimson as she sprang to her feet and snatched up her linen table napkin, swatting poor Jeremiah with it as she chased him around the table, squeaking, 'Oh, oh, oh!' as she ran. They both ended up in the kitchen, and we heard Effie's muffled voice shrilling before she came back and sat down. We were all silent—what was there to say? In a minute or two, Jeremiah reappeared, minus the corset, holding the soup tureen from which he hadn't spilled one drop. In the silence, he ceremoniously served the soup which was still warm and delicious.

"Slowly, the conversation resumed, turning to the goings-on in the community. I was rather shocked and disgusted at the tales about who was arrested for drunk driving, whose wife which man had seduced lately and which two couples had switched husbands and wives. With her composure regained, Effie said, 'Gosh, Kisumu sounds almost as bad as Happy Valley'! (I made a mental note to ask her to tell me about that place sometime.)

"Victoria was in her element. A born social climber, she bragged about being invited to a cocktail party at the magnificent house of the local 'DC', as she called the resident British Crown Colony District Commissioner, 'My deahs,' she gushed, 'just think of us among all thews VIPs! The DC made me feel reahly included like one of them, too! End he ectually winked at me! I expect we'll be invited again—just you weyt and see.'

"I would remember to avoid Vickie in future; she gossiped about so many people! I had no intention of letting Jack and me be among them, innocent as we were of any of the out-landish behavior of her targets. Jack and I helped the rest of us to turn the conversation to less offensive topics, and that finally shut her up.

"Nothing was mentioned about Effie's corset. Jeremiah had obviously been given the offending garment by Effie for dis-posal. He had probably never seen such a thing before, so he didn't recognize that—with its suspenders missing—it was to be discarded, so he had worn it in her honor to thank her for such a nice gift. I was told later that in those early days of the Empire, cast-off European items such as trousers and jackets, sun helmets and broken umbrellas were also prized novelties, particularly among the native chiefs!

"Effie would have realized all of this if she had known, or even if she'd had the time to think it over. However, all her reflexes at that moment had pointed to her open-mouthed guests staring at the apparition with his corset and his soup bowl, and she had reacted accordingly. She apologized to Jeremiah afterwards for her behavior. I had learned another lesson in understanding the thinking and customs of the na-tives. There would be much more to learn."

***

BUNTY: Famous German writer and philosopher Johann Goethe wrote, "The best thing we derive from history is the enthusiasm it arises in us." My curiosity couldn't be contained until I had researched the infamous Happy Valley Set; it had now been mentioned by both Effie and Vickie, Effie's snobbish dinner guest:

It took very little digging on my part to realize that this has been the subject of an enormous amount of repetition and exploitation! I was surprised to read that the history of the Happy Valley Set came about as one of the results of the building of the *Lunatic Express*.

To help offset the huge cost-overrun of the railway, the British Government promoted a scheme to encourage a large-scale settlement of adventurous Brits in Kenya, providing them with a subsidy to set up farms and produce cash crops for export; cotton being the prime crop needed for manufacture in British mills. The soil was also good for growing coffee and tea; both products were much in demand for export. The resulting income would defray the cost of the subsidy and make the farmers wealthy, as well as helping the government to defray the cost of the railway. A production agreement was put in the hands of the local native tribes to avoid their opposition.

The first area to be settled by the British was in the beautiful foothills of the Aberdare Mountains, just north of Nairobi. The first colonial farmer in the area gave his location the nickname "Happy Valley." It was soon apparent that the British government's subsidy scheme had been *too* successful! It attracted so many settlers at such a great cost that the British colonial administration decided it soon had to end it! Bringing not only would-be farmers, it also had attracted a number of wealthy young aristocrats who used the scheme to emigrate from Britain to East Africa professing their desire "to escape high taxes, overcrowding, the miserable British climate, and to have fun." Some of them formed a clique which came to be called The Happy Valley Set. They had building materials brought in to construct palatial country mansions reminiscent of those on the hereditary estates they had left behind in Britain. Water was piped in from huge tanks outside; lighting was supplied from large generators. Some had brought their servants from Britain to live in the servants' quarters, but it was rumored that their native houseboys lived outside in huts, bitterly described as "in near-slavery, at the mercy of their white masters."

The members of the Set were not only a favorite topic of conversation in East Africa in the 1920s, but their fame has been immortalized in newspapers and magazines, books and movies ever since. Many of the men had no intention of becoming farmers; they hunted, partied and played polo. The women were wealthy 'hangers-on'. The Set established what they considered to be an aristocratic, safe haven away from the confines of Victorian and Edwardian moral behavior in England. They seemed to consider "fun" to be more important than work. One critic dubbed their lifestyle, "The three A's: Altitude, Alcoholism and Adultery". Others described it, "Weapons-Grade Hedonism". In the 1920s, tales of their sexual perversion and promiscuity, orgies and part-ner-swapping, leaked out and became publicized. Stories revealed their alcoholism and drug-taking (cocaine was a favored drug). There were even accounts of lovers shooting each other and themselves, in fits of depression induced by both uncontrolled habits.

Time stood still in Happy Valley. It was an idyllic location com-manding breathtaking views, where its bored, hedonistic inhabitants lived in the fairytale, "fast lane" life of the very idle and very rich. They conducted frequent dinners and parties. The story was told of one hostess who routinely received her guests in her bath. Sitting naked in a beautiful onyx bathtub, she greeted them as they arrived and invited them in for cocktails. Other accounts described the nature of the house parties, some of which required the guests to dress in nightgowns and pajamas for dinner. Especially outlandish were the sexually explicit party games. One story tells about the tradition that when dinner was over, each woman blew a feather across the table to where the men were sitting. The "lucky" man on whom her feather landed would be her sleeping partner for the night. The party couldn't end until everyone had a partner other than the one with whom they came!

Lurid accounts of promiscuity, booze and dope leading to bizarre behavior kept emerging over the years. With repetition, some of the stories began to resemble the game "Whispers" in which the beginning whisper is passed around a circle of people from one to the next, so many times that it loses all resemblance to the original one. Obscene stories about the Set kept the local European society supplied with gossip for years. Some of the accounts that I read—about the party games in particular—were just too disgusting to include in this book!

As those scandalous years went by, the great Happy Valley estates gradually became deserted, fading into decay and obscurity like their former inhabitants. Sadly, some of the elegant houses were taken over by negligent squatters with barefoot children who grazed their goats and sheep on the overgrown lawns. An occasional mansion was salvaged to become a school, hotel or museum, but most were abandoned. The equatorial climate claimed its own, in some places engulfing the once carefully-tended lawns and flowerbeds with waist-high elephant grass and weeds. Graceful open porches and their wooden supports fell apart with the persistence of termites and climate, each of which seemed jealous to reclaim its original ownership. However, with the growth of the tourist trade by the early 2000s, a government project was initiated to rehabilitate eighteen of these houses for a tourist visiting circuit.

***

But let's go back to the 1920s, and life in Kisumu with Mom and Dad. Mom was primed to read into the microphone about the next unexpected event:

The Black Mamba

"When we had been in the house a few days, I took time from my unpacking and rearranging, to satisfy my curiosity about how our tennis court looked close-up. It was a little distance from the back of the house, with a path leading to it which was shaded by overhanging tree branches. In preparation for our arrival, the elephant grass that had sprung up across the path since the departure of the previous tenants had been cleared away, but I didn't fancy wandering down there alone, so I asked Omolo to go with me. He unfurled a sun umbrella and held it protectively over my head. I noticed he had picked up a *panga* (a thick, curved knife, or machete) in his hand, and in his halting English he lisped, 'I go firtht, *memthahib*, thnakes in trees.' The natives were terrified of snakes; without prompt medical attention, many of them died from snakebite. Omolo had only walked ahead of me for a short way when he stopped in his tracks, visibly shaken as he looked down at something on the path in front of him. He dropped the sun umbrella, raised the *panga* and stood very still. He gestured to me to stop. Whispering, he lisped, '*Quenda, quenda, memthahib, black mamba, kali thana, quenda pethi pethi!* ("Go, ma'am, go away; black mamba very fierce, go quickly, quickly").

"I turned and fled toward the house, bumping into Obonyo and several houseboys who had come running out to see what was wrong. Each one had snatched up a thick stick, and when they saw Omolo they silently tiptoed up to where he was standing, finger on lips, gazing down at the coiled snake which was still snoozing on the warm path ahead of him. The boys were able to get to Omolo before the snake could slither rapidly away. Once they were near enough to strike it, they shouted, '*Mamba baya sana, kwesha kufa, mara moja.*' (the mamba is very evil, let's kill it right now). Quickly raising their sticks before it had time to escape, they pounded the snake until it was dead. How I got back to the house I'll never remember, but I do remember that after I was safely through the back door the horror stuck me. I trembled all over with the realization that I might have stepped on that snake if Omolo hadn't been there to protect me. I said a quick prayer of thanks that none of us had been hurt in the scramble—or worse—bitten by the snake."

BUNTY: Snakes! I learned a lot about them in my research. Well-equipped for survival, they have a keen sense of smell and sight. They are deaf, but extremely sensitive to vibrations in the ground to warn them of approaching danger (luckily, that black mamba must have been a sound sleeper). Africa has its share of venomous snakes, some of which are routinely captured and "milked" to make anti-venom serum. If you're bitten, the trick is to find a source of anti-venom quickly enough!

The black mamba is normally shy and reclusive, but when cornered, startled or hunting, it is one of the deadliest snakes in the world. A tree-dweller by day and sometimes sleeping in a vacant burrow in the ground at night, it preys on birds and small mammals such as hyrax, rats, mice and bush babies. Its skin isn't black, but either grey or brown. When it opens its mouth to strike, it reveals the reason for its name: the entire inside of its mouth is black. It has been documented as the largest venomous snake in Africa, measuring an average of 8 feet. It is also known for its bad temper, *keli sana* (very bad-tempered). The black mamba moves with lightning speed, and is so dangerous that it has very few predators. A bite from a black mamba is usually repeated rapidly five or six times, carrying enough venom to cause the onset of symptoms almost immediately, which makes its strike nearly always fatal. It is estimated that only two drops of its venom can kill a man. No wonder the houseboys were galvanized into action—double-quick!

Mom went on with her narrative:

"Several of the houseboys came back to the house, leaving the ones who had no tribal taboo against touching anything dead to dispose of the snake's body. I was reluctant to go out again after all the commotion was over and the snake's body had been removed, but I knew now that I could rely totally on Omolo's watchfulness, so we went on down the path and looked at the tennis court. It was a grass court—rather the worse for wear, but still in flat enough condition to support a game of tennis. I made a mental note to ask Jack to get a new net, but in the meantime the tattered old relic strung across the court would do the job. When I played tennis with Jack or Effie, Omolo always escorted us. With unlimited patience, he he squatted down to wait while we played then escorted us back to the house again. Effie was an excellent tennis player. She often came over for a tennis match but we both had to be up and ready at daybreak, because by the time the match was over it was too hot outdoors to continue. I can still hear her voice in my 'mind's ear' trilling, 'Forty love, forty love, Ida Dear—Oh, hard luck, but you made a good try!' "

***

Malaria!

"It was after one of our tennis matches that I began to feel dizzy as Effie and I walked back with Omolo to the house. I also felt very hot, but I blamed this on the fury of the tennis match and the beginning of another hot day in Kisumu. A cool drink of boiled water didn't help, and I had begun to shake with chills. My body ached all over. I developed a headache and began to feel nauseous. Effie ordered me to take off my clothes and get into bed, while she told Obonyo to gather up as many blankets as he could find. They piled these on top of me, tucking them under my chin. I felt alternately cold and hot, shaking and feverish, in spite of frequent sips of cool, boiled water. Effie told Obonyo to get in touch quickly with Bwana Amiss, and tell him to come home. He ran out to his piki-piki and roared off to the railway station where there was a telegraph to contact the ship. Effie went over to the washbasin and poured out cool water to soak washcloths and wring them out. She peeled off the bedclothes long enough to sponge my entire body with the cold compresses to keep the fever down. I suppose I must have lost consciousness, because I didn't remember any more until late afternoon.

"Jack hitched a ride to Kisumu port on a lake steamer, and arrived late that afternoon to find me drifting in and out of consciousness and poor Effie exhausted from having no lunch and working so hard to reduce my fever. I vaguely heard him say, 'I can't thank you enough, Effie. Please let the boys get you a bite to eat, then Obonyo will take you home on his *piki-piki.* Go on home now, there's a good lass; be sure to get some rest for yourself.'

"I expect Effie wearily slung one leg over the pillion seat behind Obonyo, and off they went.

"In the following days, Jack was wonderful. He'd had training in first aid back in England, and he used all his knowledge to keep my fever from boiling over! In about two weeks, I was well enough to get up and about again, but not ready yet for another beating by Effie on the tennis court."

Dad interrupted with his side of the story:

"When I arrived home, I found Ida swelterin' under her blankets with a high fever, but I continued Effie's work by applyin' cool compresses all over her body, keepin' up the treatment all night long so that her temperature wouldn't get out of hand. Eventually, thank God, her fever broke and she soaked the whole bed through with perspiration. There were clean, dry sheets in the chest of drawers, so I changed the bed to make her more comfortable. That was the turnin' point, and by mornin' her temperature was almost normal again so we didn't need the doctor. That fever had knocked the stuffin' out of her, makin' her as weak as a kitten, but with good care she slowly improved—a gradual introduction to liquid foods, then to whole foods again, and plenty of boiled water to drink. She was terribly tired for more than a month afterwards. Young Omolo was greatly concerned. Every day he would ask me, *'Habari memthahib, Bwana Amith?'* (How is your wife, Mr. Amiss?'). When she was well enough, I let him greet her in person and satisfy himself that she was on the mend.

"I was terrified before the fever broke, and I wondered if I should ever have brought her out to Africa. But me Sunshine was tougher than I'd realized! In a week she was 'sittin'up and takin' notice', as they would say in Sunderland, and in a couple o' weeks she was well enough for me to go back to work. Little Omolo watched her like a hawk and waited on her hand and foot, treatin' her like a respected close relative or even a child of his.

"Luckily, Ida had an uncomplicated case of malaria. I like to think that our daily doses of quinine had helped to keep it so. She began to think more clearly after the fever broke. I remember bendin' over her and sayin', 'Hello there, Sunshine— welcome back among us again.' She smiled and said, 'Oh, Jack, I'm so glad to see you; now I know I'll get better!' She was just about back to normal by the time I had to leave. Between little Omolo's attention and Effie's faithful visits—nearly always with a bunch of flowers for Ida to cheer her up—I felt confident enough to go back to work, knowin' she was in good hands."

BUNTY: Malaria! The information I found was horrifying:

A hundred years ago, it was confirmed that the disease is caused by the bite of a female anopheles mosquito, carrying microscopic quantities of the disease from biting a human or an animal already infected. She sinks her eager little proboscis into the skin of her new victim, depositing the disease into his or her bloodstream with her bite. I learned that almost half the world's population is at risk to contract malaria. It is a life-threatening, flu-like disease of varying intensity, established to be the third largest killer of children in the world. Shocking statistics estimate that world-wide a child dies every two minutes from it. It occurs in epidemic proportions in some countries, including Africa, where to this day the disease remains one of the greatest causes of death, mostly in children under the age of five. It is recorded that in the twentieth century alone, half of the population in tropical Africa became infected, playing havoc with the economy and family development. Mosquitoes are scarce in the daytime (they are most active at night) but I learned that only areas in Africa above four thousand feet are mosquito-free. At this writing, malaria is by far the leading cause of death in the country of Uganda.

The complication from a series of repeated, untreated attacks of malaria—the dreaded blackwater fever—is often a death sentence. Unfortunately, a method of complete prevention or cure has yet to be discovered. I have a hazy remembrance from my early childhood of seeing a bottle of quinine tablets in our bathroom medicine cabinet; Mom and Dad took them regularly for years after their return from Africa, as a preventative for this disease, which can recur for years without a bite from its host. Fortunately, neither one of them ever had malaria again.

In recent times, the use of insecticides and the mechanics for draining and spraying mosquito breeding grounds have become effective means of reducing the numbers of these deadly insects. Among the rural native population in Africa, the use of mosquito bed nets has become an effective weapon against malaria and these are gradually being introduced in villages where none previously existed.

On a somber note, research reveals that malaria was believed to be the greatest health hazard to Allied troops serving in World War Two in countries where it is prevalent; history estimates that about five hundred thousand men in uniform were infected on war fronts in Africa and the Far East. J.P. Byrne, editor of *The Encyclopedia of Pestilence, Pandemics and Plagues,* wrote: "In World War Two, sixty thousand American soldiers alone died from malaria in Africa and the South Pacific."

***

Mom changed the subject:

Brain Teasers

"Another challenge was that '*choo*', our outdoor toilet! I discovered that a strong liquid disinfectant, Jeyes Fluid, had been imported from England and was available in one of the *dukas*, so we bought some for the houseboys to use in the latrine. It had a strong smell, but a more tolerable one than carbolic acid, which I remembered as the usual antiseptic disinfectant used in British hospitals in those days. Jeyes Fluid also had antiseptic qualities. As well as acting as a great cover-up for the offensive odors, it also seemed to be a deterrent for the resident blowflies and spiders—one whiff and they disappeared!

To my dismay, when I gave the first bottle of Jeyes to the *choo* boy, he promptly emptied the entire contents into the *choo*, necessitating an emergency trip to the market to replenish the supply. Envisioning gallons of the stuff being poured down the *choo* every day, and the resulting constant trips to the market to buy more bottles, I found an old cup without a handle and used some indelible black ink to draw a line around it, a short way up on the inside. Obonyo brought the *choo* boy to me, and I used sign language to point to my handiwork, pouring a small amount of Jeyes Fluid into the cup, as far up as the line. I pointed to it again; he smiled and nodded. I congratulated myself on solving the problem so easily without attempting to explain in words—my Swahili was far too limited for that! However, on the following day the contents of the entire bottle of Jeyes had disappeared again down the *choo*. In desperation, I asked Obonyo to explain to the *choo* boy in a language he could understand. He happily obliged with an unintelligible (to me) string of Swahili. I just had to trust that he was instructing the *choo* boy to use the measuring cup *before* pouring any disinfectant down the *choo*. My admiration for him knew no bounds when, as an extra precaution, he wrote the instructions in Swahili on a label and stuck it on the bottle! After personally demonstrating to the boy how to measure out a small quantity of Jeyes up to the level of the black line in the cup, Obonyo bowed to me and left the *choo* boy standing there with his mouth open. I need not have worried; Obonyo's help did the trick, and although we must have used innumerable gallons of Jeyes Fluid while we were in Africa, I no longer had to order a new bottle of it every day!

"Our ingenuity was constantly being challenged. Jack rescued two empty vinegar bottles and pounded a series of small holes in their screw-on bottle caps. Voilà! Two sprinklers! 'Jack the Engineer' had now become 'Jack the Inventor'! For some unknown reason, I had brought a small funnel with me from England. I was glad to have this to funnel some Jeyes Fluid into one vinegar bottle for the *choo* boy to sprinkle around in our *choo* and also in the one used by the houseboys, when the 'perfume' from either one (or both) became too strong. Omolo was delighted with his own new toy: the other bottle, given to him filled with water to sprinkle our clothes before the helper did the ironing.

"Another brain teaser was never resolved, and I still wonder about it. The corrugated iron roof had enough space between it and the ceiling of the house to accommodate some kind of strange, nocturnal creature. Very often, if they couldn't find a Swahili word for it, the natives would invent a word that described a texture, smell or sound, like '*piki-piki*' that sounded like a motorbike. They invented a name for the inhabitant in our roof that sounded like 'squash-squash'.

"What it was that 'squashed' things in the roof, we never did find out! Sometimes, in the equatorial night, I would be awakened by 'kathump, kathump, kathump'—some kind of animal bounding across the planking above the bedroom ceiling. Then came a 'whoosh' as it pounced and slid to a halt, followed by a 'crunch, crunch, crunch' as it relished eating whatever it was that it had caught, bones and all. The boys weren't at all concerned; the creature never seemed to leave the attic (no

holes were ever found for it, or its prey, to get in and out.)
After awhile, I didn't even hear it, sleeping all through the
night while the '*squash-squash*' pursued its hunting activities.
Maybe we had it to thank for the reason why the house was
rat-and mouse-free!"

BUNTY: A prolonged search for more information followed, as I frantically tried many links on the Internet to identify what kind of animal
the "squash-squash" could have been, but all my efforts came up
empty! I finally decided that it must have been a ferret or some such
animal, chasing and eating rats and mice. But how it was possible
for the "squash-squash" or its prey to have found a way into the attic
will always remain a mystery.

***

A few years went by between my visits to England. As he grew older,
Dad was more frequently 'resting his eyes'. Mom's voice was beginning to dominate the sound waves on the tape recordings. She readily
picked up the microphone:

"Here's Ida Amiss, on Bunty's current visit to England. I'm taking
up the story of our lives in Africa again on this new tape with a lot
more notes from what I remember about this beautiful—but cruel—
country, so 'here goes':

A Walk in the Sun

"While we were in Kisumu, Effie, Ted, Jack and I had many
outings together, but some stood out above the others, leaving lasting memories. Effie acted as a self-appointed travel
agent; on her frequent visits she was quick to propose trips

that we could take to explore special places in the surrounding area. On one of her visits, she put down her coffee cup and squeaked, 'Ida Dear, how would you and Jack like a trip to the Nandi Escarpment? On your journey from Mombasa, you probably saw it from the train when you had almost reached Kisumu—it overlooks the Great Rift Valley. It's only a short drive to get there, and we can do a bit of hiking to enjoy the scenery.' For a minute I was too surprised to say a word, but before she could change her mind I blurted, 'Oh, Effie, I'd love it!'

"I was excited. The Nandi Escarpment is now referred to as one of the fifty treasures of Kenya. During our journey from Mombasa to Kisumu on the *Lunatic Express*, we had experienced the strain on the train's engine as it climbed up the escarpment, followed by its heart-stopping descent on the other side, but I had never dreamed of actually setting foot on its lower slopes with their views of the Great Rift Valley.

"So it was, that one beautiful, sunny Saturday morning the four of us climbed into Ted's car and went off to the Nandi Escarpment. Ted parked with other cars on the hillside by a chalet used by hikers and climbers as a starting spot for their activities. All around us, other tourists were already in various stages of preparation for a hiking and climbing weekend.

"I consulted my guidebook, which told me that an escarpment is a long line of cliffs and steep slopes with an area of flat land forming a valley below. A matching escarpment was on the opposite side of the valley. Escarpments were common on the sides of the Great Rift Valley, and this one was the nearest within visiting distance. It was named for the Nandi tribe, who were the inhabitants when white settlers invaded to set up farms and plantations throughout the late 1800s and early 1900s. The Nandis were ferociously opposed to the building of the Uganda Railway (a.k.a. the *Lunatic Express)* and the resulting influx of white colonialists, but as the years went by, they realized the value of putting their land to work, particularly to grow tea. Nowadays, they own much of the tea business in the area."

BUNTY: An interesting comment: Some of the world's top runners have emerged from the Nandis (a division of the Kalenjin tribe) since Kenya began to send native competitors to today's international sports events. But let's go back to Mom and her story:

"We were prepared for our hike, dressed in durable shoes, long pants, shirts and hats. With the sandwiches and flasks of lemonade we had packed, we set off to see the wonders of the area. We were not disappointed! Words can't describe the scenery adequately—but I'll try!

"Stretching along the trail before us as far as the eye could see were miles of rolling, green hillsides—some with outcrops of rock, others with terraced plantations—overlooking the immensely wide valley below. The escarpment itself rose above our heads to about 6,000 feet above sea level, but we were at a considerably lower altitude, comfortable for walking in the golden sunshine. There was a cool breeze, laden with fragrance from a nearby tea plantation grafted into the hillside. Several white clouds drifted lazily in the blue sky above as if taking their time to enjoy the view below them. Far from being the first hikers here, we followed the trail already worn by many feet over the years—travelers like ourselves who had come to marvel at the panorama. There was no need for conversation in the presence of this unspoiled paradise.

"At lunchtime, we walked just far enough away from the trail to sit on the grassy hillside, choosing a spot near some bushes for some privacy to unpack and eat our picnic lunch. We munched contentedly as our eyes lingered over the magnificent views. Our sandwiches disappeared fast; I wonder why food always seems to taste better when it's eaten out of doors? We hadn't realized how much the unaccustomed exercise and bracing air had worked up our appetites! Some of Abraham's favorite pastry desserts went well with our lemonade, and soon all the food and lemonade we had brought with us had vanished, down to the last crumb and drop.

"Like true hikers in the wilderness, we ended our lunch break by using the privacy of the bushes for a comfort stop before walking back to the trail. After more walking, Jack looked at his watch. The practical engineer in him came up with a common-sense observation: 'You know, I was thinkin' we'd better remind ourselves that however far we've walked, we'll have the same distance to walk back to the car!' Jack's words were a wake-up call; we had been so anxious to see what new vista was waiting for us as we rounded every bend in the trail, that thinking about the distance back had escaped us. Our lemonade was all gone; Effie and I felt thirsty and decidedly weary by the time we had even retraced half of our steps! Ted looked at our tired faces, 'Och, lassies, dinna' get wilted on Jack and me, now! Up yon hill a bit there's a wee plantation hoose, let's go oop and see if they have some tea to serve us.'

"We dragged ourselves another few yards up the hillside. Sure enough, there was a sign on the path: 'Mrs. Brown's Tearoom' with an arrow pointing to the plantation house. Staggering into the tearoom, we sank gratefully into comfortable chairs at a little table by a window. Effie and I agreed later that we couldn't remember ever enjoying a cup of tea as much as that one! Seeing the view of the valley from the window felt much more comfortable sitting on a chair than on the bare ground; we all had a second cup of tea and felt obligated to buy packages of it to take home. I saved one package to bring back to England and give to the family. They would never dream that there could be anything as civilized as an English tearoom in the wilds of East Africa!

"When we arrived home in the late afternoon, Jack and I didn't even take time for a ritual bath in the tin bathtub, making do with a quick wash at the washbasin before hungrily attacking Abraham's welcome supper. After eating, we were hardly able to keep our eyes open before falling into bed. However, we both agreed it was well worth the physical exhaustion to see firsthand the grandeur of the Great Rift Valley; a memory that we would re-live for the rest of our lives."

***

It was lunchtime, so Mom paused after describing her trip to the Nandi Escarpment. A quick sandwich did the trick to renew her energy for her next session with the tape recorder. Dad sank sleepily into a comfortable armchair for his 'forty winks' while Mom took out her notebook:

Mother Nature's Fury

"Although, for the most part, we enjoyed comfortably calm weather in Kisumu, it was interrupted from time to time by ferocious storms like none I'd ever known in England. The first time I experienced one of these storms at close quarters, I'll never forget how unprepared for it and how frightened I was. Jack was away; there I was, alone in the house except for Obonyo and Omolo.

"In the ground around the house were rocky outcrops streaked with iron and copper ore, coloring them a rusty red. We had just experienced a stretch of hot, dry weather. The wind blew in off the lake, collecting red dust from the rocks and covering everything in its path with a thick, red film. It suddenly began to blow harder. I didn't know it at the time, but this was usually the sign announcing that a storm was approaching. I went out onto the verandah to see what was happening. Obonyo padded behind me and silently closed all the window shutters except one, which I had asked him to leave open so I could see out.

"The storm came up quickly in the late afternoon. As I watched, the sun faded as the sky got darker and darker, soon to be jarred by blinding blue shafts of jagged lightning. They were attracted by the ore in the rocks, and in front of my startled eyes lightning zipped from one outcrop of rock to another all the way around the front and back of the house, followed by ear-splitting cracks of thunder, then torrential rain. I felt a lot less poetic than Shakespeare, but he was right when he called thunder 'heaven's artillery'. I heard later that after a storm there were always reports of people who had happened to be outdoors and were killed by lightning bolts. Another report said that in one storm there had been hailstones big enough to knock down a native's hut!

"The storm lasted all night; it seemed to go on forever. I became terrified at the sudden flashing brightness of the lightning and the deafening booms of thunder that followed (Shakespeare called it 'a deep and dreadful organ pipe'). I remember running from the verandah into the bedroom, diving head first into the bed and cowering under the mosquito bed-net, pulling the bedclothes up over my head. Omolo saw me running into the bedroom. He knocked on the door and asked anxiously, '*Thari gani, memthahib?*' (what's the matter, ma'am?) Feeling a bit self-conscious, I poked my head up out of the bedclothes and said, 'Oh, Omolo, *asante sana, nishapoa* (thank you so much, I'm alright).

"Omolo quietly padded away. It was so good to know that he and Obonyo were always within reach!

***

Christmas and Hogmanay

BUNTY: When Mom and Dad looked out of their verandah windows on December 25 that year, Kisumu must not have looked (or felt) at all like the snowy Christmases they knew in Sunderland. Flowers were in full bloom, leaves were on all the trees, and it was 85 degrees Fahrenheit outside! With its proximity to Lake Victoria, the humidity made it feel hotter and even more uncomfortable. I expected to hear that a quiet dinner at home would have been the extent of their holiday festivities. But then I had reckoned without the club.

Mom polished off a quick cup of tea to prepare herself to read from the voluminous notes which were fast filling up her notebook:

"I had already helped to organize a concert party at our club, like the 'Oojahs' at our church in Sunderland who performed variety shows in our own church hall and also in many others around town. At the club in Kisumu, 'Kisumu's Klowns' had attracted would-be theatrical stars who were delighted to lend their acting, singing, instrumental and dancing talents to perform for an otherwise entertainment-starved audience of club members.

"That summer, we decided to begin rehearsals for some entertainment followed by a Christmas party. Faintly hopeful of some amateur theatrical opportunities in Kisumu, I had brought with me to Africa a copy of a short musical comedy skit that the 'Oojahs' had performed successfully. I thought I might try it out with the K.K.'s. It was amazing how many volunteers were keen as mustard to take part in the show, to help design and construct scenery and to concoct costumes. A normally reticent couple surprised everyone by offering to take care of opening and closing the curtains! There was a cast of twelve; in no time each character was bagged by an eager, would-be star! To my surprise, I was elected to be the producer!

"It was decided to have our show and Christmas party on Boxing Day (the day after Christmas) which was the national holiday back home in England when Christmas presents were exchanged by the family. An ancient English tradition, its origin goes back to medieval times. The King or a rich local official rode in a carriage through the poor areas of towns on the day after Christmas—no matter what the weather—tossing out 'Christmas Boxes' of money as gifts to the needy folks lining the streets. Although we weren't poor, my family always referred to our Boxing Day presents as Christmas Boxes.

"Meantime, here in Kisumu, the closer it came to performing our play, the more nervous I became. Jack woke me from a nightmare one night when I was moaning in distress, demanding, 'Wake up, Sunshine, what's the matter?' I clung to him and said, 'Oh, Jack, I dreamed that the audience booed us off the stage!' His reassuring reply soothed me back to sleep, 'Don't worry, Sunshine, everything's going to be alright.' I wished I'd had his confidence!

"Boxing Day dawned with bright, 80-degree sunshine under a blue sky to greet the performance of our play after months of diligent rehearsals. When the time came for our performance, I joined in the age-old custom for good luck of wishing the performers to 'break a leg' (secretly praying that they wouldn't). Effie ducked down into the prompter's box in front of the stage with her copy of the play in hand, making us all feel a lot more confident. We needn't have worried; there were gratifying ripples of laughter from the audience at all the right places in our play. By some miracle, none of us forgot our lines (or, if we did, we covered them up like true troupers and adlibbed the bits we forgot).

"It just shows how starved the audience must have been for 'live' theatre! When the performance was over, the players forgot their nervous exhaustion, basking happily in applause from an audience clapping, cheering and calling for curtain call after curtain call. I was totally unprepared when people stood up clapping with cries of 'Producer, Producer,' and tears of joy ran down my cheeks as when, to my surprise, Ted came forward as I took my last bow and presented me with a bunch of beautiful tropical flowers. The fragrance of the frangipani blossoms in it stayed with us all the way home later in his car, as a reminder. After the play, everybody danced for awhile to the records played on a borrowed gramophone until we were called to the buffet table. Set out with English-style Christmas fare contributed by the club members, the table fairly groaned with the weight of the holiday spread. There were slices of cold roast beef and chicken with newly-baked bread to make sandwiches, also salads and a platter of sliced tomatoes (a real treat). Garnishes included imported English pickled onions, piccalilli and chutney, and for dessert there were mince pies, fresh fruit salad, home-made Christmas fruit cake and Kenya coffee.

"Wine flowed, and the party went on into the wee hours. Everyone agreed that it had been well worth the effort, including the entertainment. Effie whiffled, 'Oh just think, in another few weeks we'll have to start planning our next Christmas show'. Ted gave her a tipsy look and insisted, 'Och, but no' until we've celebrated Hogmanay, me loov.'

"Jack raised his glass of Tusker and shouted, 'Oh aye, here's to Bonnie Scotland and first-footin' at Hogmanay to welcome in the New Year!'

"We raised our glasses. 'To Hogmanay', was the roaring reply. Tired but happy, club members went home that night to rest up for the next celebration."

***

Mom went off to put the kettle on for tea. Dad had awakened from his 'forty winks', refreshed and ready for the tape recorder. Opening his notebook, he began to talk into the microphone:

"Oh aye, before we leave the Christmas season in Africa, let me tell you that I was curious to find out what our houseboys did (or didn't do), to celebrate the occasion. I hadn't wanted to ask Obonyo in case he rattled off a long string of Swahili words that I couldn't interpret. I'd forgotten that both he and Omolo had been sent to mission'ry schools as children, and that they might be Christians! The schools gave the natives a pretty good knowledge of English, which they understood better than they could speak. Anyway, I asked Obonyo if he and the boys were goin' to need a day or two off to celebrate Christmas. I hoped he would remember enough English to spare me a flood of Swahili that would leave me high and dry! He came through magnificently! I can't remember all of what he said, but I've made notes of me recollections of how he would have answered me inquiry:

"'Obonyo, tell me how you spend Christmas; I'm very interested, but not in Swahili, please.'

"Obonyo would have nodded his head and smiled, '*Deo, Bwana*, *santé sana, i takuambia*'. (Yes, Boss, thank you very much, I will tell you.) His reply in his broken English could have been like this:

'Day before Christmas, relatives come from Nairobi to village where my family live. They help us make pretty the huts. Then we go to church for midnight service. Might as well not go to bed, because Christmas party begin at village after church. So much to talk about and we sing, too. We have plenty *urwagwa* (native beer, made with fermented bananas and maize.) Party last all night. When sky get bright next mornin' we put on new clothes. We save money for Christmas and buy new clothes long time before because so many buy, it make tailors sell all and close shops in November! When Christmas here, we say each other, '*Heri ya krismasi* (Merry Christmas) and answer is, '*We-we pia*' (and to you, also.)

'If not sleeping, we go to church again, sing and dance at service to welcome Baby Jesus. Children act out Baby Jesus coming to Africa. Some people tired; sleep through service. At home, family always have big doings. My father, he have *mbuzi* (goat), made fat in *boma* (enclosure for livestock) nice and big, ready for family feast. Women get *mbuzi* ready and begin make *nyama choma* (roast meat). Women make lovely feast. Lots of food. They make *ugali* (cornmeal porridge), *wali wa nazi* (coconut rice), *sukuma wiki* (vegetable stew: green cabbage, onions and tomatoes), *chapati* (flat bread), *katchumbari (*tomato salad), *mabuyu* (a candy—baobab seeds coated with sugar.) Plenty fresh fruit. Have big picnic outside. We eat and eat until no more room in *tumbo,* (stomach) and drink *urwagwa.* Laugh and talk. Sing, too, all day long. People fall asleep after eat, or if drink too much *urwagwa* . We invite poor people in village to come to feast. Next day public holiday, English Boxing Day. We give small gifts. Spend most of day sleeping. When we not too tired we visit friends. Sometimes party go on many days.'

"Well! After all that, I thanked Obonyo and told him that he could have some days off for Christmas! But I told him to be sure to get plenty of rest before he came back on his *piki-piki,* because I didn't want him fallin' asleep over the handle bars!"

***

Re-energized by another cup of steaming, hot tea, Mom was eager to get started again:

"At the club, the McDougals, McNabs and Camerons got together to organize the ancient Scottish custom of celebrating the New Year or Hogmanay (the Scottish name for the New Year's celebration which includes first-footing). Ian McNab said, 'Och, we must have a wee party at Hogmanay. Eeven if it's an aity degrees ootside in Africa and withoot any blanket of snoo, it still might be a braw bricht moonlicht nicht (fine, bright, moonlight night) for the first-foot!'

"I was feeling quite homesick when I listened to their plans for New Year's Eve. I couldn't help having a nostalgic sniffle when I remembered myself as a young girl at one of those traditional Ditchfield family gatherings to celebrate the coming of the New Year. My mind temporarily left my surroundings in Africa, and I was back again at the New Year's celebration in my family home in Sunderland on New Year's Eve:

"We spent all evening playing party games and singing around the piano. At about five minutes to twelve, the men and boys left the warmth of the drawing-room fireplace. They began to mill around in the front hall, struggling into their overcoats, gloves, hats, scarves and boots. Among them was my Uncle Harry McKenzie, the family's traditional first-foot, who was required to be a tall, dark-haired man. He was still tall, as required of a first-foot, but as the years went by his dark hair had grown a hint of grey at each temple. But Uncle Hal wasn't going to give up his place of honor easily. Grey temples notwithstanding, he led the family males out into the snowy night, to wait for Sunderland's church bells to announce the arrival of the New Year on the stroke of midnight. Mother, the lady of the house, lined up the family females (old and young) behind her in the front hall, facing the closed door. I remember tingling with excitement when the clock on the drawing-room mantelpiece struck twelve, followed by a loud knock on the front door.

"Mother opened the door, and we heard Sunderland's church bells pealing joyously from all over town, symbolically ringing out the old year and ringing in the new. Uncle Hal put his foot across the threshold; the first foot to enter in the New Year, bringing good luck for the house and all those in it. In one hand, he carried a piece of coal to symbolize enough warmth for the house in the coming year (all fireplaces were coal-fed, no central heating in those days!) Uncle Hal always made the piece of coal look like a miniature Father Christmas (Santa Claus), wrapping it in bright red crepe paper and adding a white beard of fluffy cotton wool. In the other hand was a piece of rock salt wrapped in white tissue paper. This was symbolic of plenty to eat in the New Year. Tucked under his arm was a bottle of wine to symbolize plenty to drink in the coming year. Putting them into Mother's hands, he kissed her and wished her a happy New Year. He then passed down the waiting feminine line with a hug for each and a wish for good luck and happiness in the year to come.

"Meantime, one by one, each of the men and boys stomped his feet outside to shake the snow off his boots before stepping into the house. Following Uncle Hal, they crossed the threshold, breathing out little puffs of vapor into the cold night air as they came. Shrugging out of their overcoats, they passed down the waiting welcome line of ladies and girls, causing an outbreak of kisses, hugs and good wishes for the New Year. The front door was closed, and pandemonium reigned. When at last it died down, everyone went into the dining room where the sideboard (buffet) was laden with a plentiful supper, to be followed by one of Mother's special fruit cakes served with plenty of good, red wine. After the feast, we stood in a circle around the table, crossed our arms and held hands, pumping them up and down in true Scottish tradition as we sang 'Auld Lang Syne' (literally, 'Old Long Since', or 'For Old Times' Sake'). More hugging and kissing followed, with cries of "Happy New Year" reverberating around the house. In the wee hours of the morning, drowsy folk made their way home or upstairs to climb into bed, weary but very happy to have been together for the promise of a good year to come.

"I dragged my mind back to the present. Our New Year's Eve in Kisumu was totally different: no family or snow, but the company of good friends and the bright moonlit night that Ian McNab had wished for, accompanied by a background chorus of tree frogs and cicadas.

"The McNabs, McDougals and Camerons had recruited Effie and Ted McTavish to join them on a committee to plan this traditional Scottish New Year's Hogmanay celebration. The ladies provided a mouth-watering buffet supper, for which the club members were invited to bring contributions. The men rehearsed their midnight exit and re-entrance after voting for tall, dark-haired Ian McNab to be the first-foot. The men had decided not to come into the house from outdoors, so as to avoid the hordes of mosquitoes waiting to pounce on them with their little stingers quivering in anticipation of a tasty meal. Instead, the men lined up on the club's mosquito-netted verandah a few minutes before midnight. At the stroke of twelve, Ian McNab knocked on the door of the club room. The frustrated mosquitoes were left safely out of doors, buzzing hungrily around in the velvety darkness which was brightened by galaxies of stars, an almost-full moon, and little twinkles of light from thousands of darting fireflies.

"Effie acted as hostess of the 'house', and the ladies lined up behind her inside the clubroom to greet the first-foot and his followers. Ian McNab handed her a bottle of wine and piece of rock salt, wishing her a Happy New Year with plenty to eat and drink (no coal needed for warmth, so near the equator!). Hugs, kisses and Happy New Year's wishes were exchanged with the waiting ladies as the men came in. When the noise and laughter from the greetings subsided, everyone headed for the buffet table where there were freshly made sandwiches, English pickles, home-made mince tarts, cheeses, fresh fruit and the left-over remains of the fruit cakes we had enjoyed at our Christmas party a few days before. There was plenty of wine, Tusker beer and coffee to wash it all down.

"Fully stuffed, we sang around the piano for awhile until we felt comfortable enough to walk to the dance floor at the end of the hall. Lights were dimmed, and we danced to an assortment of loaned gramophone records. When the time came to say goodnight, we stood in a large circle around the hall, crossing our arms to hold hands and pumping them up and down as we sang 'Auld Lang Syne' played with gusto by Ian McNab on the old upright piano. We sang so lustily that we almost lifted the corrugated iron roof off the clubhouse; the volume made greater, I'm sure, by the pangs of homesickness.

"I thought to myself, 'My next letter home about our Hogmanay will be a surprise to the family; I bet they'll share it with the neighbors.'

"And they did!"

EXPECT THE UNEXPECTED

A Welcome Surprise!

BUNTY: Mom was becoming established in Kisumu society, taking her turn at giving dinner parties, sharing picnics, playing mahjong and enjoying with Dad the companionship of friends for sundowners. She soon earned admiration at the club for her entertaining talent, and decided that she had adapted (as much as possible) to the new challenge of living on the African frontier of the British Empire. However, nothing in life is known to run uneventfully for long, and she was to experience no exception to the rule.

***

Mom continued the story on the tape recorder:

"I became a bit suspicious when I began to feel rather queasy in the mornings instead of looking forward to a hearty breakfast as I usually did. I blamed it on the heat, but after missing two periods I thought it was time for a visit to the doctor. Jack and I were thrilled by the confirmation of my pregnancy. At the time, we could think only of the glowing prospect of having a child of our own and not about the hazards that lay ahead. My breakfast-time appetite soon returned and I began to let the waistbands out on my clothes.

"Tennis matches with Effie were forgotten with my confirmed pregnancy, and the treadle on my sewing machine began working steadily to make the first baby clothes. I think Effie was more excited than I was! Anxious letters began to arrive from Mother, worrying about my health and offering all kinds of what she thought was useful advice. I wished she had given me some helpful pointers on what to expect, but childbirth information in her day was handled a lot differently from the more modern 1920s, and her advice was very general, in fact, something I could do without! She meant well, however, and I kept her posted on developments as they came along.

"When the midday heat could be avoided, the summer weather was pleasant and dry enough to keep the mosquitoes away in the daytime, so picnics were all the rage—a good way to socialize with our neighbors who weren't members of the club. Neighborhood wives proudly contributed delicacies taught to their native cooks with recipes brought from home. The houseboys were kept busy setting up folding tables and chairs in the shade at the edge of the forest bordering our backyard lawns. Colorful tablecloths were added to make a cheerful, festive atmosphere. Experts at outdoor cooking, the cooks dug a long, shallow pit well ahead of time and built a charcoal fire in it; they were soon presiding over a row of chickens roasting on a spit they had erected over the fire. For dessert, they brought an array of English pies and cakes, baked in their little ovens on backyard braziers.

"Picnics were arranged as a late lunch, so that husbands could put in half a day at work and be in time to join the party. We feasted on the picnic food, followed (for those who had the energy) by games of badminton and quoits (tossing a heavy ring of rope to encircle a peg in the ground) played in the shade of the towering trees by the picnic tables. Sundowners were celebrated early enough so that we could make our way home before darkness came. The houseboys raced to clear away the remnants of the picnic and pack up before the sun had time to disappear, mosquitoes made their appearance, and oil lamps would be needed to show the way home.

"Jack was fully occupied with his job, satisfying his love of the sea and making a lot of friends among the Europeans he met on his voyages around Victoria Nyanza, as he always called the great lake. Having become involved in Kisumu society, I didn't have time now to get homesick, and (thanks to Effie) my bouts of loneliness tapered off to last for much shorter periods. The days sped by.

"England seemed to exist in another world of memory. Letters arrived with the Royal Mail, but usually so long since they were written that their news was very much outdated. I presumed that the same time-lag applied to my own letters in return. News from the family sounded pretty humdrum compared with all of my new experiences, but there were disturbing rumbles in sister Lily's' letters that times were changing in Sunderland—for the worse, as far as the Ditchfields were concerned."

***

An Unwelcome Shock

BUNTY: Mom paused. A stray tear made its way to the corner of her eye and splashed onto her notebook. She quickly excused herself and went out into the kitchen. I'll take over here while Mom regains her composure:

History tells us that after the first flush of the economic upturn following World War One, Sunderland had experienced a gradual decline in its industries; some of the dockyards stood empty, coal miners and factory workers were unemployed, and prices had risen. In some places in the northeast of England there was 70 per cent unemployment. Poverty among the unemployed grew worse.

Trade in cheap, "ready-made" clothing had flourished since the war, taking the place of higher priced, tailor-made clothes. With the advent of "ready-mades", men and women with tailoring skills were being employed in clothing factories rather than in tailor shops. All of these factors began to affect Enoch Ditchfield's tailoring business. He had become stubbornly unwilling to invest in a stock of "off the rack" clothing, maintaining that the shift to "ready-mades" was just a fad which would die out and restore the tailoring business to reign over the clothing industry as always. Enoch still refused to change his mind and his business began to fall off alarmingly. He had to close one shop, then another. Clinging to his remaining shop, he was still adamant that better times for custom tailoring were just around the corner—but that didn't happen. Finally, he was in danger of losing not only the one shop left, but also the stately old Victorian house that had been the Ditchfields' family home for so many years.

Mom had regained her composure after shedding private tears of memory about the tragic news of her proud father's financial downfall. Back from the kitchen, she picked up the microphone:

"Next time Jack came home, I showed him the letter I'd received from my sister Lily. It described this financial disaster and how she had become the support that Father needed.

"Having taught for several years, Lily was now an established schoolteacher with a steady income, enabling her to move out of the family homestead to live independently in an apartment closer to the school. Her letter said that, faced with this new calamity, she gathered up her courage and confronted Father. She told him she had been thinking over what was happening, and announced that she had decided to take out a mortgage on the house in her own name. She said that she was sure she could manage the payments on her teaching salary (they were about the same amount as she was currently paying for rent) if she moved back home and lived there rent-free. She added that if Father's cousin (Uncle John Walker, the building contractor) and his workmen were to add a little kitchen on the upper floor of the house, those rooms would make a good apartment which she could then rent out to supplement her income. She mentioned that, as a matter of fact, one of her teacher friends had been looking for an apartment; she was sure that the woman would be glad to move into it.

. "Lily said that initially Father was outraged, but he had eventually swallowed his pride and allowed her to carry out her plan. The beautiful old house was saved by the new mortgage; the newly-created apartment was almost immediately occupied by one of Lily's schoolteacher friends and the monthly rent from it helped to cover the mortgage payments. With this solution, Mother, Father and Lily would also have enough money left over to live on.

"Jack's first reaction was to say that we should offer to help financially, and we did make the offer in our next letter home. However, I worried privately that this would put a dent in the savings we needed when we returned to England to buy a house and furnishings for ourselves. And now, in addition, in a few months we would have the added expense in our budget for a much-longed-for third family member. I needn't have worried. Lily responded to our offer by saying that If she had needed financial help, she would have asked us for it. It was good news that she had things well in hand—she had saved the day, for Father and for us.

"I thought to myself, 'I am so glad that the whole family had kept this unsettling story to themselves in their letters while it was developing; I would have been worried to death. Half a world away, we already had enough to cope with in daily living; we certainly didn't need any more challenges! Anyway, we couldn't have helped Lily to get around Father's stubbornness; Jack might have lost his temper and made things worse!'

"I decided that in future I'd be careful to make the letters I sent home to the family as interesting and entertaining as possible for them to read, and that I'd be careful to avoid complaining about the lack of amenities and other hardships of living in Africa. I said to myself, 'It may help to lift their spirits if I make jokes out of my stories in future. At least it will give them something cheerful to tell the neighbors!'"

***

Dad awoke from "resting his eyes" and consulted the pages of notes he had prepared for telling the next chapter in their story. Mom handed him the microphone:

"Oh aye, we had a very happy life in Kisumu, in spite of the climate and havin' to dodge the insects, livin' without indoor sanitation, runnin' water, cookin' or bathroom facilities, adequate electricity, good roads, local public transport and all the other conveniences we were used to havin' back home. I resented needin' to accept such things in order to live fairly comfortably, but everyone out there was in the same boat, you see. They say that when things are bad, misery loves company, so we had grumblin' sessions periodically to let off steam on "men's night".. I don't think it made anythin' easier, but at least we could get our frustrations off our chests!"

"Oh aye, to be sure, the greatest antidote to life's challenges in Kisumu was the activity associated with our club. There were travelin' bands and a travelin' cinema which stopped at some of the new hotels in Kisumu town to play for a dance or to show films sent out from England. Quite often, they'd let our club see one of the latest silent films. Ian McNab did a great job playin' an accompaniment for the old 'silents', sittin' at the piano with his eyes glued on the screen. He pounded loudly on the bass notes for the dramatic scenes and tinkled them on the higher ones durin' the romantic interludes. I particularly remember those first Charlie Chaplin films. Oh, blow me down, what a clever, funny man he was—a genius in his time, by gum! Ian McNab thoroughly enjoyed playin' happy music for the background in Charlie's films! The clubhouse fairly rocked with our laughter, and sometimes I thought we'd raise the corrugated iron roof, we laughed so hard.

"Ida had settled in at Kisumu just grand. She was lucky to have Effie as a friend and she made many more friends as we met people at the club. She even persuaded them to put on a variety show like the ones she and her family used to do in Sunderland. This gave more people a chance to show off their talent for singin', dancin' and tellin' jokes. Ida had me bustin' with pride; I didn't call her 'Sunshine' for nothin', she charmed everybody! At Christmas, she produced a seam-splittin' skit that was just as good as when the 'Oojah's used to do it. She did a champion job of that, too, which showed what a talented lass she was.

"Meantime, I was enjoyin' me own job on the lake as captain of me ship, makin' valuable acquaintances among the railway stationmasters and supervisors on the loadin' piers at the ports. Life for us was lookin' rosy. I never missed a day's work, except when I came down with a couple of bouts of malaria. Nasty bastards, those mosquitoes! But nothin' prepared us for the next shock!"

Our World Turns Upside Down

"I was home one weekend and we were relaxin' on the verandah when we heard a familiar noise outside. I said to Ida, 'Here comes Obonyo on his *piki-piki*—I wonder what he's been up to?' And as he came closer I shouted, 'Oh, come and look, Sunshine, he must have saved up enough money from his wages to buy a new *piki-piki* with a sidecar!'

"Ida looked happy. She grinned and said, 'Oh that's wonderful news, Jack! Now I won't have my insides shaken up like

I did when I had to ride on that uncomfortable pillion seat of his. It'll be much more comfortable in the sidecar when he takes me to the market or sometimes over to Effie's for a visit.'

"Obonyo came rushin' into the house. We expected him to be excited to show us his new *piki-piki,* but he wasn't smilin'. The expression on his face looked as if he'd been slapped with a dead fish! 'Oh, *bwana*,' he wailed, in his haltin' English, 'you and *memsahib* goin' away.' The dialogue between us went somethin' like this:

'*O, bwana,*you and memsahib goin' away!'

'What *are you* talkin' about, Obonyo? We aren't goin' anywhere.'

'Oh, yes, *bwana,* you and *memsahib* goin' to Namasagali in Uganda! I hear this from one of boys who tell me he get news on drums from friend in Nairobi.'

'Oh get away with you, Obonyo. That can't be true.'

"But—blow me down—it was! The followin' week, a formal letter arrived on the stationery of the Agent for the Crown Colonies in Nairobi:

'Captain John H. Amiss is hereby transferred to Namasagali, Uganda, at the junction of the branch railway line and the enlarged port terminus for river traffic.'

"Needless to say, I was flabbergasted! Ida dissolved into tears. 'Oh, Jack,' she moaned, 'Namasagali is almost 200 miles away, in the middle of nowhere! And we're just getting nicely settled here in Kisumu, with lots of new friends. *How could they do such a thing?'*

'Well, Sunshine,' I said, as gently as I could, 'I'm afraid there's no alternative! Let's look on the bright side. It's goin' to be a promotion for me with a nice increase in salary for us, and now that Namasagali has just recently become the new junction for railway and river traffic between Lake Victoria and the River Nile, we'll be 'in on the ground floor' as it grows.'

"I knew that Ida was very resilient. She never complained for long, and I was sure that when she got over the shock, she would accept this new turn of events with her usual good spirits and determination to make the best of it. I'd been used to travelin' for so many years that movin' didn't bother me, but havin' to leave Kisumu behind would be a real wrench for Ida, who wasn't used to movin'. She had spent all of her life in the same house in Sunderland before comin' to Africa, and here was the second move in a little more than a year. Poor lass!

"Our friends at the club gave us a gala farewell party and Sunshine wept all through it! There was packin' to do, however, so she had to busy herself to keep her mind off movin' to another strange place and makin' new friends, if there were any there to make! I had heard of Namasagali as a lonely outpost with only one house—the railway stationmaster's. But I didn't mention any of this to her; she had enough to think about. And maybe things had improved since then; I certainly hoped so, for both our sakes!

"Ida had been quiet for awhile. Suddenly, she cried, 'Whatever are we going to do without Obonyo and Omolo, Jack?'

"Before I could I reply, Obonyo—who had been standin' quietly in the doorway—said, 'No worry, *Memsahib Amiss*; Obonyo and Omolo comin' with you! I get new *piki-piki*, so I bring him in sidecar.'

"Ida was overcome; tears of relief poured down her cheeks. She sobbed, 'Oh, Obonyo, *santé sana, santé sana, nzuri sana, nzuri sana* (thank you so much, that's very good!)"

UGANDA, HERE WE COME!

BUNTY: Let's take a break here for research on some facts about Uganda—a small country but a beautiful one—the country that is Kenya's next-door-neighbor.

In the Introduction to this book, I wrote about the early history of East Africa for as far back as it is known. When Mom and Dad arrived in 1924, Uganda was still a British Protectorate, but it gained independence in 1962 and has suffered disastrous internal conflicts ever since.

Uganda derives its name from the ancient kingdom of Buganda, which then encompassed most of the country. Straddling the equator, it is about equal to Great Britain in size (the United States is almost forty-one times larger). Surprisingly, Uganda rates as the second most densely populated country in the world for its size, after Ethiopia. The people are diverse, culturally and ethnically, with at least thirty native languages spoken. The common language is Swahili, and even back in the 1920s, many native Ugandans could speak their tribal language, also Swahili and English.

Most of Uganda is on a high plateau, which accounts for the pleasant, year-round climate called moderate tropical, with an average temperature of 80 degrees Fahrenheit in the daytime and 65 degrees at night. There are two short rainy seasons in spring and autumn, and two dry seasons in winter and summer. Blessed with abundant fertile ground, Uganda produces lucrative crops for export including cotton, bananas, cocoa and tobacco, to name just a few.

Uganda abounds in natural wonders, with miles of savannah teeming with wildlife whose numbers and variety defy description. It is also home to the world's only remaining, endangered mountain gorillas; safaris with people from all over the world go each year to observe them. Its bird population numbers over a thousand species; half of the entire bird species in Africa. Situated in the Great Lakes Region of Africa, Uganda contains a section of the Great Rift Valley with its chain of fresh-water lakes. Also, it boasts extinct volcanoes, snow-covered mountains with glaciers, huge waterfalls, vast acres of virgin tropical forest, and it includes a substantial amount of Lake Victoria's shoreline.

At 4,000 feet above sea level, Lake Victoria was once described as being at "a height above the highest rooftop in England". Fairly young (geologically speaking) Lake Victoria is estimated to be 400 million years old, created at the same time as the other Great Rift Valley lakes. In 1858, famous British explorer John Hanning Speke wrote of his and fellow explorer Richard Burton's amazement at what they found in Uganda, with its natural beauty and cultured people. Speke, the explorer, was the first European to see the huge lake and to document this vast, 27 thousand square miles of water. Not surprisingly, he named it Lake Victoria in honor of British Queen Victoria. In Lake Victoria, Speke was convinced that he had found the source of the great River Nile.

The Welsh-born explorer and journalist, Henry Stanley (of Stanley and Livingstone fame) who accompanied Speke in 1871 on another expedition to search for the true source of the River Nile, is credited with creating the widely-acclaimed name for Uganda, "The Pearl of Africa". Many years later, Winston Churchill must have had this in mind when he described Uganda in his book *My African Journey:*

"For magnificence, for variety of form and colour, for profusion of brilliant life—bird, insect, reptile, beast—for vast scale, Uganda is truly 'The Pearl of Africa'." He also wrote: "Uganda, from end to end, is a beautiful garden where simple food of the people grows almost without labour. Does it not sound like a paradise on earth?" He continued, "Uganda is a fairy tale. The scenery is different, and most of all, the people are different from anything else here to be seen in the whole range of Africa. The land is rich; the people peaceful and industrious with no great differences between class and class."

With an abundance of food which is easy to grow for its population, Uganda is considered to be self-sufficient. Even its trees provide sustenance and protection: a plentiful variety of fruit, shade for protection from the direct rays of the equatorial sun; firewood and charcoal to cook food and heat homes (also the smoke is effective in warding off insects), "butter" for cooking. There is even an oil tree that produces the base for a best-selling skin cream world-wide! But the star performer is the amazing baobab tree. In addition to its other attributes, the baobab collects supplies of pure drinking water and has bark with medicinal properties.

Although times have changed radically in Uganda since Churchill's visit in 1908, he included a rebuke with his advice for the British government. Bemoaning an insufficient amount of investment in this country where he saw its great potential compared with that in other colonies, he begged Parliament for an investment of ten thousand pounds sterling per year. He wrote:

". . . Scarcely any money has been spent on Uganda for European roads, extensive railways; no waterfalls harnessed; no public works of any serious description have been undertaken . . . But, it is alive by itself; it is vital . . . in spite of its insects and disease, it should in the course of time become the most prosperous of all East Africa and the driving wheel of all this part of the world! Nowhere else will a little money go so far, nor the results be more brilliant, nor substantial, nor more rapidly realized."

Churchill wasn't finished with his admonitions, and his vision for Uganda:

". . . Cotton, rubber, fiber, cinnamon, cocoa, coffee and sugar should be cultivated on a large scale. A settler's country it can never be; it is a planter's land where, under supervision, the native population should be organized and directed to prosperity . . . for the good of its people."

Churchill was on a roll; he advocated the extension of the *Lunatic Express* into Uganda (the railway line had ended in Kenya). He even mapped out a nautical route down the Nile to Egypt for transportation and commerce, so that someday: ". . . by rail and river, an uninterrupted stream of communication will prevail."

But Churchill wasn't the only one to see the unexplored possibilities for the development of Uganda. Another early English visitor observed, "Most of Uganda is rich and fertile: hills and dales, rolling, grassy downs, pastures, mountain slopes and steep ridges—a land of infinite possibilities. But as yet the British public is comparatively ignorant of these excellent possibilities."

The name that explorer Stanley had coined for Uganda, "The Pearl of Africa", has stuck, and it is quoted in many of the travel agency itineraries today. "The jewel in the crown of East Africa" is also the description given to Uganda in the written accounts of many who have been there. At this writing, the well-known book publisher *Lonely Planet* named Uganda the best country for tourists to visit, and world-famous *National Geographic Magazine* joined its fan club, heaping praises upon its natural marvels.

In his 1908 book, Churchill rhapsodized about the Ugandans, admiring the fact that the tribes were so well- organized in the native kingdom of Buganda. He praised the people of the Buganda nation, calling them "eager and reliable, polite and intelligent." He wrote that most were able to read and write, and added that many were Christians (a complimentary plug for the diligence of British missionaries who worked together, regardless of their varying denominations, to bring education, medical care and spiritual assurance). As the missionary schools progressed from the 1800s into the twentieth century, they were well attended, and by the 1920s future native leaders and teachers were being trained. After their sons successfully completed the level of education necessary for admission, tribal chieftains began to send them to Oxford and Cambridge Universities in England for a higher education. In addition to academics, European-type organized competitive-sports events were gradually becoming popular in Uganda among the natives.

However! There is always another side to every coin! In addition to the admiration he expressed about Uganda, Churchill was frank in acknowledging some of the drawbacks in that 1900s paradise. He wrote: ". . . cuts do not heal; scratches fester; even small wounds become running sores. Malaria is rampant, starting suddenly as deadly blackwater fever from a third or fourth attack . . . Uganda is defended by its insects!" After his 1907 visit (with no antibiotics, insecticides or effective preventive inoculations yet available) he even admitted that this was no place for the white man to live—just as Dad was told on the ship on his way to East Africa, almost two decades later!

So, in 1925, Mom and Dad were about to leave Kenya for the next phase of their lives. They probably hadn't read any of the foregoing description of their new country, but while they were there they explored whatever they could, with the means they had available. Mom, for sure, fell in love with—and in awe of—Uganda.

Dad put in his "two cents" about their next move, but first, let me share my research on Namasagali, their new African hometown, which, in another few months, would also become mine.

Namasagali

It was disappointing that despite all my digging, I could find very little information about Namasagali's early history. Mom and Dad had been no help for this in their notes, probably because they were so consumed with the task of everyday living under 1920's conditions that it didn't even enter their heads to explore what was in the past. In my search for information, I found one resource that dryly defined Namasagali as "an old colonial town with a well-functioning railway transport system." No doubt this was written in its "glory days" in the 1920s and 1930s when it was part of the British East Africa colony. The town certainly had a good economy back then!

Namasagali is about 85 miles north of the equator. It has an elevation of almost 3,500 feet above sea level, which gives it a relatively comfortable year-round temperature ranging from 70 to 85 degrees Fahrenheit. With a bearable 40 to 75 per cent humidity, its climate is described as being like springtime all year. The town is on the eastern bank of the Victoria Nile (or White Nile, one of the two main tributaries of the River Nile). It is about 55 miles north of Jinja on Lake Victoria, the location of the established source of the River Nile. The river flows north for 2,700 miles as the White Nile until it joins with the other main tributary, the Blue Nile, and together they flow to complete the 4,132 mile journey northward to Egypt as the great River Nile itself.

In its colonial period, Namasagali was surrounded by cotton farms established and controlled by the British government to feed the factories of the textile-manufacturing industry in Britain's midlands. Cotton farming gave employment to local natives as farm laborers and also as laborers at its rail junction, loading bales of raw cotton onto the train wagons. Other natives earned their living as fishermen in their boats on the river. Those with more education worked as houseboys and as clerks documenting goods being transported on the railroad. Others had jobs in the developing factories or learning to become ironsmiths, a skill imported from Kenya.

In those days, on the farms surrounding Namasagali, many of the native men worked from dawn to dusk, as they had done around Kisumu. The women sometimes worked as farm laborers, but were primarily responsible for the welfare of their family: doing household chores, raising children, tending the domestic animals and growing fruit and vegetables. In addition, they were adept at handcrafts, using any spare time they had to make articles to sell in the market, including beaded jewelry. They kept some of this for themselves, to wear on special occasions as multicolored strands of glass beads (in some tribes, a woman's standing in the community was measured by the amount of jewelry she owned). From the clay soil, they made hand-painted pottery baked in an outdoor kiln. As soon as they were old enough, girls helped their mothers to collect reeds from the river-bank, dry them, dye them and weave them into a variety of colorful baskets of all sizes and shapes; most of them to sell in the market, but with some left over for use in their own village.

Beginning at quite a young age, children were expected to help with many of the chores around the house, in addition to succeeding in school. They had to learn to fit in their studies with their work, and to do well at both.

But it wasn't all work and no play. Villages held gatherings for special occasions, including periodic *ngomas*—festivals for socializing and feasting, also dancing and singing accompanied by tom-toms, flutes and other native instruments. A *ngoma* could go on all night. Keeping time with the music there was a lot of hand-clapping, foot stomping and chanting to cheer on the dancers who sometimes wore outlandish costumes. Every now and then, a traveling native musi-cal group might come to perform in small towns and at ngomas in some of the villages. The *ngoma* could include one village or a group of villages with entire families participating to celebrate a puberty ritual, a wedding or a funeral. "War dances" were popular: the men painted their bodies and pretended to attack one another with sticks and *pangas* as they danced, while the audience clapped its hands, beat tin cans and stomped its feet in joyful rhythm, egging them on.

Shortly before 1924 when Mom and Dad arrived on the *Lunatic Express,* Kisumu in Kenya had been its original terminus, but a new branch of the main railway line was built, extending into Uganda. This branch went north from the Lake Victoria port, Jinja, to Namasagali. At the newly-expanded port of Namasagali on the Victoria Nile, it was now possible for giant, shallow-draft, stern-wheeler steamers to anchor and discharge their cargo from Lake Victoria. In reverse, an incoming load would be taken on at the Namasagali junction, to be transported south to Jinja and the lake. One report states that from 1920 to 1925 the tonnage of cargo handled at Namasagali jumped from 18,600 tons to 46,703 tons! Extensive marshaling yards were built for the assembling and transfer of imports and exports, enabling a flow of trade to and from the interior of Africa to connect by rail with the distant east-coast port of Mombasa on the Indian Ocean: gateway to Europe and the Far East.

Namasagali's river traffic thrived and expanded for more than a decade, until the advent of paved roads and modern transport vehicles intruded to introduce more efficient commercial routes.

Comment: Stern-wheeler ferries were not only an important part of commercial lake and river transportation. As early as the 1920s, it became popular for travel companies to hire them to take rich tourists for pleasure cruises on the lake and river, generating yet more lucrative income for the area.

Sad to say, as more modern transportation became available, Namasagali's ferry and railway links eventually fell into disuse. To quote one recent comment, ". . . the pier at Namasagali lies in waste and stands like a betrayed martyr." The once-booming marshaling yards and sheds at the junction of river and rail sank into dereliction and abandonment. As another commentary phrased it, "Namasagali became a lonely ghost".

Embracing a more cheerful aspect of Namasagali's history, Christian missionaries had brought education to that part of East Africa, establishing the first official school in the region. In 1895, classes had begun in the home of one of the English missionaries in Namasagali to teach the natives how to read and write English. The first elementary school in Uganda was born, and in 1905, the expanding school was divided into two schools for elementary and senior classes, housed in buildings with walls of reeds and roofs of grass.

In the 1960s through the 1980s, education at Namsagali flourished. It became renowned for its excellent secondary school which blossomed into the most prestigious college in Uganda, built with sturdy, modern construction. However, with the decline of Namasagai over the years, its famous college sank into near-oblivion. The buildings fell into disrepair; the college became a shadow of its former self. At this writing, there is a movement to bring it back to its former glory, but it may not be achieved for years, if ever.

Let's shake off the gloom of Namasagali's eventual decline and go back to 1925 to hear about what it was like for Mom and Dad to be transferred to a town beginning its economic climb upward:

***

Dad took up the story. He polished his glasses, consulted his notes, and exclaimed triumphantly, 'Well blow me down, I've found where I left off!'

"Oh aye, by 1925, when we arrived there, Namasagali was expandin' by leaps and bounds as it grew in importance with the fast-developin' trade and commerce of Central East Africa. A revolution was goin' on with local means of transportation, too, to replace the natives' previous ways of movin' humans and goods. For centuries they had relied on Shank's Mare (the human foot), graduatin' over the years to ox-carts, donkeys, rickshaws and ramshackle bicycles. Then along came the railway, steamships and early motor vehicles for movin' from place to place, which was the stage at which we found ourselves.

"Employment and income gradually increased for the natives in Namasagali, but when we first arrived their feet and old bicycles were still their main way of gettin' locally from point A to point B. As employment and the economy grew, however, the bicycle trade flourished among the locals. Owners sold their old bikes to those who had been on foot, while shiny, new, imported bikes were appearin' on the dusty dirt roads for those who could afford them. For those who could afford even better, imported motorbikes were beginnin' to appear, and more affluent white folks ordered some of the early model motor cars from Europe and America for themselves. It was excitin' to see Namasagali become a thrivin' place for its inhabitants.

"I had a damn' enjoyable life in Namasagali, alright! Although I was still called upon to be Master of a ship, I spent some of my time now in the marshalin' yards supervisin' the loadin' and unloadin' of cargo. The number of big stern-wheeler steamers on the river had increased. With their shallow draft, they could easily make the run up the Victoria Nile from Lake Victoria to Namasagali and back, carryin' passengers, cargo and the Royal Mail for transfer to the railway. Namasagali's railway depot and river wharfs became busier and busier.

"What a stroke of luck it was, too, that our move meant that I was closer to home, where I could spend more time to give Ida a hand! I had noticed that she had become more dependent upon me in the house, especially now that she had found she was carryin' a child."

***

Dad went back to his chair to rest his eyes. Mom took up the microphone:

First Impressions

"When I first saw Namasagali, I began to cry. I was hot and tired; Jack and I had been traveling all day after leaving Kisumu, but I was getting used to the much slower pace here in Africa. First, there came the long, slow boat trip on Lake Victoria from Kisumu to Jinja port. There, we transferred to a meandering river steamer which stopped at a few villages along the Victoria Nile to pick up native passengers or discharge them from the tender being pushed in front of it.

Arriving at the Namasagali dock, we climbed with our suit-cases into one of the rickshaws hanging hopefully around, for a dusty ride to the town on the hard-packed, rutted, clay road. We slowed down behind an ox-drawn wagon as it bumped along. It reminded me of a picture in my geography book when I was in school. A man trudged alongside us for awhile with a large stalk of bananas balanced precariously on his head, probably the way he had always carried them. He was pushing an empty wheelbarrow. The two of us burst out laughing at the sight. Jack remarked, 'Now, that's what I call takin' tradition *too* far; why the hell is he carryin' those bananas on his head instead of puttin' 'em in the dam' wheel-barrow? That would've been a lot easier on the bananas *and* his head!' Jack was yet to learn that you don't interfere with tradition in Africa!

"Namasagali town, when I first saw it, was little more than a run-down village. The one main street with its red clay road sent up little swirls of red dust around the rickshaw, coating everything it touched. We passed through the market, where a few *dukas* were open. It was a noisy place, with everyone talking at once—merchants and customers bargaining over the prices. Indian men in *kanzus,* along with half-naked native men and women, squatted on the ground on both sides of the road in the market, shouting one another down in Indian or African dialects to advertise their fruit, vegetables and other goods piled on little carts or on the ground beside them. One of the *dukas* seemed to be selling food, so Jack told the rick-shaw man to stop. I was glad to climb down and stretch my legs. As good luck would have it, we were able to buy some bottles of soda pop and freshly-made sandwiches. To the de-light of the proprietor, we bought a large supply, as we didn't know how long it would be before we could get an entire meal when we arrived at our new home. When the rickshaw started up again, we enjoyed a snack as we bumped along the road. On our way out of the market, we passed firewood for sale; large bundles of thin, dried branches bound around by thick rope, to be hauled away balanced on the heads of native women customers.

"The main means of transporting goods in and around the town seemed to be on foot, by donkey cart or by the donkeys themselves with huge loads piled onto their little backs. Two men trudged alongside us on the road for awhile, bending their backs to support a pole on each shoulder. A length of canvas hung between the poles, sagging with some heavy, unseen load. How different all of this was from Kisumu! I was soon to discover that life out here 'in the wild' was never like that in the Kisumu suburbs. A sense of depression washed over me.

"Jack paid off the rickshaw man, and I brightened up when I saw our new home, one of several large, sprawling bungalows spaced out along the top of a steep bank overlooking the river. Elevated on its cement-block foundation, it really looked beautiful: a white, single-storey house with green-painted wooden shutters at the verandah windows and a red-painted, flat, corrugated iron roof. Jack was nowhere in sight, presumably off to look at something behind the house, so I climbed up the twelve cement steps and turned the handle on the unlocked front door, stepping into a sunny verandah surrounding all four sides of the house. It had wide wooden floorboards and wooden Venetian blinds at the windows to deflect the direct rays of the sun. Against the inside wall stood a little white wicker table and two white wicker chairs; perfect for informal meals. I closed my eyes and imagined a pram (baby carriage) parked in this cheerful place when our baby would be here. The previous occupants had left two dismal-looking paintings on the verandah walls, one showing a camel at a desert oasis bordered with palm trees and the other showing two camels with riders approaching some desert ruins. However, the newly-painted wicker furniture more than compensated, and the pictures looked refreshed after we had re-furbished the frames with gilt paint, a week or so later.

"There was a large bay window at each end of the verandah, and—best of all—in the ceiling were big, beautiful electric fans. I could hardly believe our good luck; there must be a generator somewhere in the house! There was a furnished lounge and dining room and a small kitchen lined with cabinets but with no stove or sink, two large bedrooms and two more small ones down the hall—the same layout as there had been in Kisumu. Each room was furnished, courtesy of the British Board of Trade, in about the same fashion as the one in Kisumu. It didn't really surprise me when I found no sign of a bathroom; I just felt grateful for the comfort of coming into a house already furnished..

"I set down my suitcase in the large bedroom and unpacked my night clothes and moccasins. Jack reappeared and went to the big double bed to let down the rolled-up mosquito net from the ceiling, where there was a welcome electric fan. He disappeared again, hopefully to find and start up the generator, and soon the blissful sound of the ceiling fans stirring the stagnant air in the house was music to my ears. Someone must have been in the house to make sure that the generator was in working order and to put clean linens on the bed. Under it was a white china chamber pot embellished with pink roses. I also noticed that there was fresh water in the jug standing next to the washbasin. Stripped down to my underwear, I splashed water on my flushed face, flopped onto the bed and just stayed there, falling asleep almost as soon as my head touched the pillow. We had been up at dawn to catch the steamer from Kisumu port; it had been a very long day. A short, deep nap took the edge off my weariness and I was soon up and about again, full of curiosity, to explore the rest of our new surroundings.

"Refreshed by my nap, curiosity propelled me to the verandah windows to see what was outside, while daylight lasted. I was pleased to notice that each of the windows and outer doors had been equipped with a fine wire mesh insert, enabling them to open for fresh air without letting in unwelcome insects (especially the mosquitoes). I picked up Jack's binoculars and looked through a window. What I could see took my breath away. I blinked in surprise and gasped out loud, 'Oh—it's simply beautiful!' I stood there, overcome by the vista in front of me.

"Perched on top of the hill, our roof was protected from the daytime heat of the sun by several large shade trees, spaced around the house in the expanse of green lawn. I recognized most of them, but there was one that I'd never seen before. It had a bare, straight trunk, at the top of which was a gathering of large branches growing straight up in one enormous bunch, looking like a fistful of huge fingers all trying to reach the sky simultaneously. It turned out to be called a spurge, appropriately nicknamed a candelabra tree, which could grow to be 25 to 30 feet high. I thought I could see a yellow mist across the tops of its branches, which the binoculars revealed to be small yellow-green flowers.

"I put the binoculars to work again to look beyond the candelabra tree, guiding my vision down the high riverbank. A short distance below the grassy incline of our backyard, I spotted a small grove of banana trees. The see-through fence that enclosed it revealed a cluster of neat, round, dried-rush huts with conical grass roofs. When Jack had first seen huts like these, he was curious to know why they were round and not rectangular and how they were constructed. He found out some interesting information: each hut can be erected in an hour or so, usually constructed by the native women with walls made of branches coated with clay or mud. The reason given for its round shape is so that there are no corners where evil spirits can hide! The roof is supported by upright tree branches and filled in with reeds woven with twigs or a framework of branches to support a thatch of elephant grass. Inside the hut, the floor is usually covered with woven grass mats. Bed mats, made from soft rushes or animal skins, are brought out and spread on the floor at bed time.

"We were learning more about native life. Back in Kisumu, Ted had told us that most of the men left their villages at dawn to work on the surrounding farms and that they ate only one meal a day after their work was over. By contrast, here in the growing community of Namasagali, work was available closer to home; some of the men were houseboys, others worked at the railway junction or local marshaling yards and dockyards that were rapidly expanding nearby.

What an improvement in working conditions! They were given a lunch break, and could be home in good time for supper!

"The piece of information that Jack enjoyed most was that if a man had more than one wife and if he could arrange it, each wife had a hut for herself and her own children! Tongue in cheek, he said to me, 'Well, Sunshine, I'll bet *that* saved a lot of family squabbles, and think of the fun that a husband could have decidin' which hut he would come home to for supper and to stay the night! He must have felt like a bloody Sultan!'

"I'm not sure I saw the all advantages. I retorted, 'Well, Jack, I hope that the husband would remember which wife had which of his kids when he called them by name. If not, he would be in trouble—or in the wrong hut!'

"Standing at the verandah windows that first day in Namasagali, I found it impossible to tear myself away. As I looked through the binoculars at the little native settlement down the hill from our backyard, I focused on young girls minding toddlers and babies outside the huts. Near them were older women sitting on the ground in a circle, using some kind of utensil to pound something inside a wooden receptacle that they held clasped between their knees to keep it steady. It looked like a hollowed-out log, closed at one end. I found out later that they were grinding maize (corn) to make *mahindi*, finely-ground cornmeal flour used for cooking and baking. When I mentioned this to Jack, he told me he had read that maize was introduced into Africa by the Portuguese in the

1500s, along with tomatoes and tobacco, and that (together with bananas) it had become a staple food in Africa. I was to discover later that bananas are the world's fourth most important crop, and that Uganda is reputed to be the world's second-largest producer, marketing them year-round all over the world. I thought to myself, 'Already I'm beginning to call this place '*Uganda, The Amazing!*'

"As I watched the women down the hill, one of them stood up and balanced her bowl full of *mahindi* on her head to transport it to her hut. For the first time, I noticed a baby strapped to her back by a strip of cloth wound tightly around her body. Outside another hut, a woman was kneeling on the ground using a 'fire stick' to start a cooking fire. Adjacent to the huts was a large *boma* where I spotted a few chickens and some goats. A much larger s*hamba* (fenced garden area) contained rows of growing vegetables. On the edge of the *shamba,* another pair of women knelt in the shade of the huge leaves of the banana trees, weeding around their precious staple food as it ripened like fat green fingers growing in rings around the branches. We heard that other fruits grown in Uganda include passion fruit, papayas, mangoes, pineapples and watermelons, to name just a few. No wonder a present-day travel company advertises Uganda as 'the tropical fruit basket of Africa'! In the neighboring vegetable patch, they grew okra, pumpkins, tomatoes, onions, sweet potatoes, peanuts and others that I couldn't name.

"I moved temporarily to the bay window at the end of the verandah where I could see the great river extending like a bright ribbon in both directions. A native *dhow* (sailboat) drifted lazily on the current, its sail catching whatever wind might stray across it. Returning to my original vantage place, I focused the binoculars past the *shamba*, down toward the rock-strewn slope of the riverbank. At its edge was the wide, glistening stretch of rippling water—the Victoria Nile—bordered with water lilies, papyrus reeds and grasses. Pulled up on the riverbank was a large wooden raft; evidently the natives ventured across to the other side of the river upon occasion. I spotted what looked like a large tree trunk lying near the raft; it had been laboriously hollowed out to make a canoe.

"Raising the binoculars higher, I looked across the river to the opposite bank. There was no sign of habitation, but a large pile of tree branches on the riverbank puzzled me. I was told later that some of the local native men earned their livelihood by cutting the wood and placing it at intervals along the riverbank, to supply fuel for the shallow-draft river steamers as they sailed to and from Namasagali's port. As the binoculars explored the other side of the river, its reedy edge gave way to a flat stretch of scrubby grass with brush-thicket and small trees, beyond which was a seemingly impenetrable tropical forest, stretching for miles before sloping up to a distant range of hills. These, in turn, faded into far-off mountain peaks on the horizon.

"I hadn't realized that it was almost time for sunset until I saw the radiant yellow ball that was the sun sinking lower across the river. I watched as it hovered for a few minutes on the horizon, casting a path of light across the water and illuminating gold and orange layers of cloud in the sky above it. Then it suddenly disappeared. Blackness took its place, quickly joined by points of light from tiny, darting fireflies. The moon was rising in the sky—a cold, white, almost-round globe. As if to keep it company, out popped thousands of twinkling stars in the black sky. Together, they shed a feeble light on the verandah. I walked carefully over again to a back window. It was comforting to be able to see the light from an oil lamp shining at the corner of our next-door neighbor's verandah, although it was quite a distance away along the dirt road that stretched between us.

"Later, I jotted down a little memoir of what I had just experienced, and it must have been in my trunk ever since! Quite unexpectedly, I found it—with the paper looking rather yellow—still in the bottom of that old cabin trunk! I fished it out to add to my notes for this tape recording. It brought tears to my eyes as I read it again, titled *The Day Thou Gavest, Lord, is Ended; a Memoir of Life in Uganda, by Ida Ditchfield Amiss.* I re-read my handwritten scrawl describing my first impression of my new home in Namasagali:

'Once, I lived in the jungle, surrounded by a land which reminded me of that first chapter of the Old Testament: *In the Beginning, God created the heavens and the earth.* This place, too, was still untouched by man; a Garden of Eden, with an abundance of fruit, birds and animals. There was glorious sun-shine all day, nearly every day! Silence prevailed all around outside the house, except for birds singing. One day, I watched the sun go down. It disappeared quickly below the horizon. No twilight, but a blanket of velvety darkness in place of the light. I was reminded of the old hymn we used to sing in school, at morning prayers. I sang it softly to myself:

> *Fear not the darkness;*
> *God keeps awake all night.*
> *To make our sleep more sweet and calm,*
> *He takes away the light.*

'It was like that in Africa. When darkness fell, silence pre-vailed. No birds sang. But then, suddenly, everything awoke: crickets cheeped, frogs croaked, jackals barked, hyenas laughed, hippos grunted, crocodiles yawned; each of them a part of the night's noises.

'Dawn came up—not . . .*up, like thunder. . .* as Kipling wrote—but as a quiet spreading of pale light across the blue sky. Peace prevailed, once more.

Written by Ida Ditchfield Amiss in 1925.'

"I had almost forgotten that I had put this little scribbled memoir in the trunk to take home with me to England some-day. Now I wish I'd kept a diary; it would have been much more useful!

"On that wonder-filled first evening on the verandah in Namasagali, I was startled when Jack materialized in the gloom, carrying a lighted oil lamp. He inquired rather im-patiently, 'Whatever are you doin' out here in the dark, lass, singin' to yourself? Come on, Sunshine, get a move on! Let's eat some of those sandwiches we bought at the market for a late snack; I don't know about you, but I'm still hungry—I could eat a horse!'

"We had dumped the bag of sandwiches and bottles of soda pop on the little table in the verandah (no refrigerator, back then). By the light of the lantern, I looked inside the bag, 'Oh, Jack, I'm pretty sure there are enough sandwiches and soda pop in here for us to eat now and tomorrow morning for break-fast, too! But we really need to stock up on some food. I wish we had some new houseboys to help us out, but where will we begin to find them? I wonder where Obonyo and Omolo could be? I hope they didn't get lost on their long trip from Kisumu to Namasagali on that *piki-piki*! . I miss them already, to say nothing of Abraham's cooking!' Jack ignored my last remark—he had a one-track mind where food was concerned. He said, 'Well, Sunshine, let's worry about tomorrow when it comes! I need somethin' in me stomach NOW to stop it from growlin', then I'll feel better. After that, bedtime won't be far off for this sailor.'

"I folded up the binoculars as we headed for the little table to eat our makeshift meal. Jack suddenly noticed the faint light shining from the next house, 'Oh, look, Sunshine, we have neighbors! That light must be on their verandah, but it looks like miles away!' Not wanting to spoil his discovery by telling him I had already seen the light, I nodded my head. I made a mental note to look more closely in the daylight to see if the neighbors were really so far away. Now that the sun had gone down, the verandah was nice and cool for us to eat our makeshift dinner by the light of Jack's lantern. The sandwiches were still fairly fresh, and it didn't seem to matter that the soft drinks were lukewarm.

"Before I went to bed, I couldn't resist the magic of one more trip out to the verandah. Jack had put a lighted oil lamp at each of its corners. Through an open window—mercifully protected from flying insects by its screen of wire netting—I felt the breeze that had sprung up from across the river, carrying on it the chorus of night noises that intruded upon the wall of silence around the house. 'Can I really hear hippos splashing and grunting in the river, or is it my imagination?' I asked myself.

"From the scrub and jungle across the river floated the muted, ghostly 'laughing' bark of hyenas. We were told that the sound of the 'laugh' carries for miles, and is actually a signal to alert the hyena pack to danger. These bold, nocturnal scavengers not only look very ugly, but they are savage and bad-tempered even with their own kind. When there is a meal to be had, they have been known to fight each other to the death over a carcass! Traveling in large groups, they will even attack lions and leopards busily eating their kill, and fight them for it. I can only imagine the bloodcurdling battle that must follow. If the hyenas win, they drag their prize out of reach of the losers in case they decide to challenge. With their heavy jaws and huge teeth, hyenas can eat every scrap of the carcass; they have the ability to crush its bones, devour and digest them, along with the skin! Hyenas are thought to have originated in Asia, although fossils have identified them as having been present in Europe a million years ago! We never saw a hyena, because they usually come out after dark (thank goodness), but we certainly could hear them, and once in awhile—with the wind in the right direction—I fancied that I heard the muted growl or roar of a lion drift across the river.

"For the first time in my life in this strange new world of wild animals, I felt that humans were merely an afterthought.

"Once more, my thoughts were interrupted by a somewhat petulant order from my husband: 'Come to bed, Sunshine! The scenery will still be there tomorrow.' He was right, of course, as usual! I hurried back into the bedroom."

***

Life on the African Frontier

It was Dad's turn for the microphone. He didn't have very much to say this time:

"When we disembarked from the river steamer at Namasagali, Ida has just described how we passed through the market and bought sandwiches and bottles of pop. We were both too tired to eat much that night, but me Sunshine found the view from the verandah so fascinatin' that she went back out to look at it again before finally comin' to bed. I was sleepin' like a log by the time she came back. We didn't budge until we were awakened next mornin' by the sun streamin' in through the verandah windows. Ida was mesmerized by the view, which—I must admit—was really quite breathtakin'. She could hardly wait to look out again on the beautiful scene from the verandah.

"Everything at Namasagali was quite different from what we were used to in Kisumu. Compared with our location here, *that* had been urban livin'! At Namasagali , we were literally on the frontier of the British Empire! At first, we were both a bit unnerved to find a little village of native huts at the end of our backyard, but this would be only one of the things that would demand adjustment to our new home.

"The trunks, boxes and crates that had been unloaded from the river steamer were brought up to the house by what looked like a safari of natives—some carryin' their loads on their heads. I stood at the front door and directed each one to be dumped in the appropriate room. As we had done in Kisumu, we reserved the two small bedrooms for Obonyo and Omolo, ready for them whenever they would arrive. *I hoped they WOULD arrive!*

"We'd just finished off the remains of the sandwiches and lemonade for breakfast, when a familiar sound could be heard in the distance. As it grew closer, our ears confirmed that it was a motorbike! Had Obonyo managed to get to Namasagali? Yes, he had! He staggered into the house on legs cramped by hours of drivin' the *piki-piki* for two days, but his white teeth flashed in a smile of greetin' that wiped away the lines of fatigue from his face. He cried out, '*Hujambo, Bwana Amiss; H'jambo, Memsahib Amiss*. Look, I bring you a present.' Another familiar figure darted out from the sidecar. Ida and I both shouted, '*Omolo, Omolo, 'jambo, 'jambo!*'

"It was almost like a family reunion! Blow me down, I was overcome by the loyalty of these lads when they decided to follow us to a different country that was not only unfamiliar to ourselves but to them, too. Admittedly we had been good to them; they knew we respected them and paid them good wages, but even so, for these lads to have traveled for so many miles on that buckin' *piki-piki* was truly an act of devotion, to say nothin' of bein' pretty hard on their hindquarters!"

Dad was beginning to look sleepy again, so Mom took up the story:

"Obonyo and Omolo inspected their new rooms with grunts of approval, obviously impressed by the British Board of Trade's taste in furnishings! After letting a couple of hours go by for them to get a little rest, I called to Obonyo. He emerged look-ing as fresh as a daisy, so I asked him for a ride in his sidecar into the village market.

"While Obonyo went off to do some of his own shopping in the market, I found one of the Indian *dukas* where the propri-etor had just finished making some curry, which looked and smelled delicious. Before it could be exposed to the possibility of insect visitors, I bought enough for or several meals, and at another *duka* I bought freshly baked bread which I had the proprietor make into sandwiches for our lunch. I also had him wrap up an extra loaf to accompany the curry later for dinner. When Obonyo found me again, we picked up more soda pop in sealed bottles, and I felt satisfied that we could now survive until he worked his magic to recruit a cook and some new houseboys. Shortly after he brought me back to the house, he roared off again on the *piki-piki* to look for some likely domestic candidates.

"That night, we experienced another tropical storm. This time, I was prepared for its fury, but in the raging of all the lightning and thunder (Shakespeare described it as 'a percus-sion of sounds') I was so glad that Jack was home to be with me. At bedtime, I was too tired from unpacking all day to listen to the drumming of rain on the corrugated iron roof—in fact I don't think I've ever slept so soundly, before or since!

"By the following morning, the storm had vanished. Jack was still sleeping when I got up and walked out onto the veran-dah. It was already daylight. I opened a window and smelled the sweet scent of the damp African earth. On the ground were puddles left over from the storm. Looking closer, I caught my breath at the dazzling sight before my eyes. Under the jac-aranda tree, heavy with its purple blossoms, was a huge puddle of water drying out from the torrential rain that had battered the house during the night. But something was different about this puddle—it was moving! As my eyes focused, it dawned on me that it was covered with a living, pulsating blanket of brightly-colored butterflies gathering to quench their thirst after the storm broke and the rain ended. I wondered if I could be fully awake or if the equatorial sun had damaged my eyes. After a few blinks, I took out Jack's binoculars to get a closer look. I could hardly believe the beauty and size of the butterflies; some of them looked as if they had a wingspan twice the size of the back of my hand! I learned later that Africa is on the migration routes of many butterfly species, either they are passing through or it is their destination at the end of a long journey.

"I took a look through the binoculars to see the butterflies close up. I recognized black-and-yellow tiger swallowtails and orange-and-black monarchs whose wings were edged with white spots. Most of the others I didn't recognize; they ranged in color from aquamarine to bright blue and white There were solid purples and yellows, brown ones with blue spots and black ones with white stripes! Lost in the amazement of the discovery, I couldn't take my eyes off the beauty I was witnessing. Once more, I marveled at the extravagant abundance and magnificence of nature in Africa.

"I was rudely shaken from my thoughts by Jack's voice, 'I don't know about you, Sunshine, but I'm ravenously hungry for some breakfast,' he boomed. I realized then just how hungry I was, too.

"I don't know how Jack thought that Obonyo could make anything for breakfast, but he told him we would eat breakfast out on the verandah. I was now convinced that he could work magic; he reappeared in minutes with two glasses of fresh orange juice, which he set down on the little table. It felt like being on holiday (vacation) at an exotic hotel as we sipped our juice, with a cool breeze coming through the verandah windows, the morning rays of the sun highlighting a cloudless sky above and the gorgeous view below it and dappling with sunshine the spanking new paint on our white wicker furniture.

"My daydreaming ended abruptly when Obonyo padded back out to the verandah on bare feet, followed closely by a well-built, handsome young fellow; his good looks marred by an overflowing paunch. Obonyo announced, '*Jambo, memsahib, bwana;* I bring Isaiah, chief *mpishi* (cook). I get you best cook in Namasagali!'

"By the look of him, Isaiah liked to sample his own cooking—a lot! His protruding middle almost oozed over his one item of clothing: a skimpy goatskin loincloth. I silently planned, 'M-m, maybe a nice white cooking apron would do the trick. And while I'm at it, I'll see that he gets a white chef's *kofia* (hat), as head (excuse the pun) of the kitchen.' The chubby houseboy flashed a delightful smile, showing off a perfect set of white teeth in his pleasant, glistening black face with its double chin. He bent forward as he bowed slightly. I looked away, instinctively dreading the effect that bending might have had on the rolls of flesh overflowing his loincloth. To my relief, the effect was nil; nothing was dislodged!

"Without any sign of embarrassment, Isaiah flashed a film star smile and said firmly, '*H'jambo, bwana, h'jambo, memsahib,* I will make you a beautiful English breakfast.' He spoke in a rich, bass voice. I could imagine him singing *Old Man River* equally as well as that other magnificent bass, Paul Robeson. Isaiah had obviously been educated at one of the missionary schools; he understood and could speak English perfectly. My relief knew no bounds; back in Kisumu I had struggled with my few Swahili words and woefully inadequate hand signals to give instructions to Abraham, our cook. I rejoiced to myself, 'Once I can cover him up, Isaiah will look like a perfect choice to be in charge of the kitchen.' I shook his hand, and he trotted off into the nether regions of the house to begin operations. After he disappeared, Jack shrugged. Like myself, he was wondering what the result would be.

"Obonyo said proudly: 'Isaiah one of my tribe, *JaLuo,* like Omolo. Like brother. Isaiah best cook in Namasagali, you see.

After breakfast, I bring other houseboys to meet.' And, as an afterthought, 'I lend Isaiah pair of my shorts, *memsahib*!' I wasn't sure how far Obonyo's shorts could possibly stretch to cover Isaiah's bulk, but I said, '*Asante sana,* Obonyo, *nzuri sana* (thank you very much, Obonyo, well done!).

"Isaiah was as good as his word. He set down before us a meal fit for a king (and queen). Without giving a thought to calorie or cholesterol content, we happily tucked in to an English breakfast of sautéed English pork sausages, fried tomato slices, fried eggs, ham and crisp fried potatoes, accompanied by toast and the famous Kenya coffee. Without a word with his mouth full, Jack gave a thumbs-up sign; we nodded to each other in happy approval. Isaiah beamed. He turned out to be a treasure.

"Before I left Sunderland, I had packed in my trunk one of the parting gifts that Mother had insisted I couldn't do without in Africa: a copy of *Mrs. Beeton's Cookery Book* (the current English cookery bible in those days). Once in awhile, I asked Isaiah to try an English recipe that I longed for. He followed my instructions as I read them out to him, measuring the ingredients and expertly putting them together. For Isaiah, cooking was his pride and joy; he always cooked everything to perfection. He was amazing: one try with a new recipe and he never forgot how to make it. He had memorized the names of English dishes and always filled my requests with a smile. He even let me help him bake scones! We usually shared one, hot and buttered, as soon as it came out of his little oven in the backyard.

"After the plates from Isaiah's first mouth-watering breakfast had been cleared away, Obonyo marched the new houseboys onto the verandah. I was glad to have been fortified with some good food, or I may have passed out there and then. Even though I had almost anticipated this from my experience in Kisumu, I still felt swamped to see the two rows of big, muscular young natives, clad only in their goatskin loincloths. At least, this time I knew what to do! After Jack and I had greeted each one separately, they all filed out again. I took Obonyo aside. Trying not to look as frantic as I felt, I croaked, 'Take me to the market on the *piki-piki* as soon as you can, please, Obonyo, so I can find some material in one of the *dukas* to make *kanzus for* them.'

"My sewing machine worked at full speed in the following days. The new *kanzus* were all made—complete with red ribbon sashes—and distributed to the houseboys. Isaiah was proud, not only of his new *kanzu*—which he wore on special occasions—but also of the new cook's apron and hat which he wore daily as his badge of authority in the kitchen.

"I decided to make slip covers to suit my own taste, to refresh the tired-looking furniture in the lounge. Thanks to my trusty sewing machine, before long there were also new, flowered covers for the cushions on the wicker chairs in the verandah, and a matching tablecloth was spread on the small table ready for 'outdoor' meals. I looked with satisfaction at them and at my new curtains with their pretty prints; made from the material I had found in the market at one of the Indian *dukas*. Already, the house was beginning to feel like our own home! Powered with current from our generator, the electric lamps we had inherited had drab parchment lampshades. I made covers for them out of material left over from the curtains, not being able to resist buying a few yards of fringe from the same *duka* to add a finishing touch around their edges.

"The houseboys didn't attempt to hide their astonishment at these home improvements. One day, Omolo came padding in to see me. Pointing to the lampshades he lisped, '*Memthahib Amith,* boy thay *bibith* (wives) in *thamba* (our backyard village) want come thee all the *maradadyth.*' (*maradadi* was a word used to describe something very fancy.) An appointment was duly made for the great event.

"Right on time, shepherded by Omolo, a group of six *bibis* arrived a few days later. At my advanced age of twenty-eight, they looked like young teenaged girls (they probably were; customarily, most were married at about twelve years old.) Omolo ushered them in through the back door. They wore their 'Sunday best' for the occasion; brightly colored, ankle-length, wrap-around skirts and long strands of glass beds. I was shocked to see that they were all naked from the waist up (even the beads didn't help!) Two of them had naked *m'totos* (babies) attached to their backs by a long strip of cloth, wound around their middles several times to bind the sleeping infants securely to them. Their visit was obviously a highlight in their lives; in those days they did heavy work with little respite. I admired the fitness and firmness of their bodies and their dignity in walking.

"I had already seen some of the native women in town when we lived in Kisumu, and had been impressed by their regal bearing as they walked, proudly erect and with grace, having learned from generations before them how to carry heavy objects on their heads. However, it disturbed me to see the price they paid in village life: to keep the fires burning, some of them carried heavy loads of wood to their village on their heads. These were held on securely by a leather strap that made deep, cruel clefts. I couldn't help contrasting this with how lightly my sisters and I got away with having to walk with only a book balanced on our heads, to teach us what Mother called 'deportment'.

"The *bibis* hesitated at the kitchen door, tittering shyly to one another. I went out to greet them, waving them on into the house. Their murmuring turned to cries of disbelief as they caught sight of the lampshades. Gingerly, one of the girls advanced toward the nearest lampshade and timidly stretched out a finger to touch the fringe. It obediently began to quiver and sway in response. She backed off as if it had bitten her! Seeing that she had come to no harm, a second girl approached the fringe and touched it. When it quivered into life, they all giggled and made "oohing" noises, nodding and declaring to one another, '*Maradadi, maradadi*' (beautifully fancy!).

"One of the infants stirred and began to make fussing noises, eyes opening wide—beautiful, dark brown eyes in a tiny black face that tugged at my heartstrings as I thought about my own baby yet to come. Without a sign of embarrassment, the young mother sat down on one of the dining room chairs and offered a breast to the baby, who sucked at it eagerly. When satisfied, the baby looked around in surprise at these surroundings which were so different from home. The young mother muttered, '*M'toto quenda lala mara moja*' (the baby will go to sleep pretty soon). As if hearing her, the beautiful eyes closed, sending her baby contentedly back to sleep.

"Each of the girls took a turn to finger the fringe on all of the lampshades in the room. They quietly looked at me, smiled shyly, and followed Omolo out through the kitchen to walk back to the *shamba* down the hill. I sat down and asked myself, 'I wonder what they will say to their husbands when they come home this evening?' Answering my own question, I thought, 'I'll bet their husbands will never believe hearing about the *living* fringes on those lampshade covers! ' Then, with a sudden wave of guilt came a terrible thought, 'I've heard those stories of wife-beating among the natives; I wonder if the husbands will think they were taking time out from their household duties without permission, and will beat them?' I called to Obonyo, 'Tell those husbands that I WANTED the girls to come and see me.' Obonyo did just that, and there was no trouble. I went to sleep that night with my conscience clear!"

"My love of gardening had taken me on an inspection tour around the foundation of the house when we first arrived. I had learned in Kisumu that, thanks to the comfort of the high elevation, I could putter around doing gardening in the early morning before the heat of the day set in. My hands itched to plant some flowers to brighten up the bare foundation walls. I was to discover that some of the flowers I had grown in England were also at home in East Africa. Here, they grew to be almost twice the size; I was told that some of them also bloomed more than once per season! With the help of our *shamba* boy (gardener), I planted gladioli, dahlias and fragrant roses alongside their tropical cousins: red hot pokers (torch lilies) and Barberton daisies in shades of bright red, yellow and white, filling the flower borders with color. Sweet-smelling white jasmine and cascading purple bougainvillea were already well established along the fence.

"When I was gardening, I almost forgot we were in central Africa, but overnight reminders of the wildlife kept me aware of it. Garbage had to be securely sealed in hyena-proof cans or in the morning it would be found strewn all over the place in their frantic search for tasty treats, the impala nibbled the grass and some of the plants, and occasionally wandering hippos trampled the lawn and flowers!

"There were several large trees shading the roof and others growing several feet away in the backyard, including the candelabra tree and a jacaranda with its short trunk and wide branches from which hung masses of purple, bell-shaped flowers before its leaves appeared. At the side of the house was a lofty, thorny acacia—the iconic, flat-topped tree seen in so many photographs and paintings of African scenery—with its umbrella branches, yellow bark, fragrant, yellow pom-pom flowers and huge thorns. The acacia is also known as 'The Devil's Thorn'; its four-inch thorns were said to be used to gouge tribal markings on the skin of young boys during their puberty rites. And at the front of the house was a beautiful delonix, otherwise known as 'Flame of the Forest' for its reddish-orange clusters of huge, lily-like flowers.

"This was really a new world of enchantment! I couldn't believe how lucky we were to have such a wealth of nature's beauty surrounding our new home. The trees weren't only beautiful; most of them were useful, too. Near the back door, there was a little avocado tree and also a lemon tree with huge oval lemons weighing it down. Keeping them company was a small tree bearing a crop of green limes and another with ripening oranges hanging from every branch. I couldn't help but think, 'Good gracious, how much better can it get? Now I know where Obonyo's orange juice came from—and I must ask Isaiah if he can make us some lemonade next time I see him. When the Ditchfields get my next letter to the family in Sunderland, they will never believe that to enhance a salad, make lemonade, cut lime slices for sundowners or squeeze fresh orange juice for breakfast, we just have to give the word to our cook and leave the rest to him! They're going to think we live like millionaires!'

"Easily available electricity, indoor sanitation and piped water were still abysmally absent, but I'd already had that experience in Kisumu, so I adjusted to coping without them at Namasagali. It was great having a little home generator sitting on the floor in the tiny kitchen, but, like our friend Ted McTavish back in Kisumu, we used it sparingly. The evening coolness up on our hilltop made it unnecessary to keep the ceiling fans going all night, and the glow from the oil lamps on the corners of the verandah gave us all the light we needed while we slept."

**

Mom was anxious to continue with her notes. Reinforced by a pause for lunch, she settled back in her chair to read into the microphone:

A New Friend, New Challenges

"About a week after we moved into our new home, I was re-laxing on the verandah with an old newspaper from England, when I thought I heard a bicycle bell tinkling outside. Curious, I put the paper down and started toward the verandah windows to have a look. Before I could do so, there was a knock on the verandah door. I opened it to find a plump little woman standing on the top step, smiling at me. Her topee was clamped on her head at a jaunty angle, topping her dark, curly hair. Her chunky body was dressed in an open-necked shirt and khaki-colored shorts, making her look as if she had just stepped away from a safari. Almost lost in the crinkling of her smile, her brown eyes were friendly but seemed to rest on me with curiosity as if making a quick assessment of this new stranger in town. She handed me a bouquet of brilliant tropical flowers and sang out cheerily, 'Good morning, Mrs. Amiss'. She pronounced the greeting with a lilting accent betraying her Welsh ancestry. She rushed on, 'Well now, we've heard you were coming to Namsagali, you know. I'm Megan Griffith, your next-door neighbor, look you, and I've just popped over on my bike to welcome you to Paradise!' Her voice broke into a throaty chuckle, 'Please call me Meg. My husband is David, but you can call him Davey, just like they do in Wales.'

"Davey Griffith was the British stationmaster at Namasagali; an important job since the town had become the only railway and river junction for traffic moving to and from Lake Victoria. His job was to keep this traffic flowing smoothly; his station now had an enlarged platform and was surrounded by wharves and storage sheds.

"Meg looked so trim and neat; I wished that I had been wearing something other than a voluminous housedress. I was dressed for comfort; even in these early days of pregnancy everything else was beginning to feel a bit tight around the middle, especially in the heat. I stammered, 'Oh, how nice of you, please come in. And thank you for these beautiful flowers.' I called to Omolo to bring some cool lemonade and asked him to put the flowers in a vase, waving my guest toward a wicker chair on the verandah near one of the windows with its spectacular views. Immediately feeling comfortable with her, I said, 'I'm Ida, Meg, so please drop the Mrs. Amiss. It's good of you to come. I'm so glad to meet you; I was already beginning to feel a bit isolated. I can just about see your house from here, and at night we can see the oil lamp on the corner of your verandah. Oh, Meg, it makes me feel less stranded to have you as a neighbor, even if you are so far away! That's something you can say about Namasagali: plenty of space! Our houses were much closer in Kisumu, but compared with the houses back home in Sunderland, they were pretty far apart, too.'

"When the lemonade arrived, we sipped our cool drinks companionably. Meg was easy to talk to, and I knew instinctively that we would be good friends. I missed Effie, who had been my lifeline when I first came to Africa. Our parting was a tearful one, but I remembered Mother's words when I left England, 'Remember, Ida, when one door closes in life, another one opens if we watch for it.' This had been the story of my life so far, and it looked as if it would continue. Here was Meg, the newly-opened door!

"Noting my baggy dress which now barely hid the beginning of a bulge, Meg observed, 'Now, Ida, I hope you don't mind my mentioning it, but indeed, am I right in thinking you're expecting a baby?' I nodded. Meg rushed on, her Welsh accent emerging in her excitement, 'Honest to goodness, I must tell you that it's envious I am! Davey and I haven't been so lucky, and we've just about given up trying to have a family. Indeed, it'll be wonderful to have a new baby living next door.'

"Meg and I spent a pleasant hour chatting, then she said, 'Indeed to goodness, hasn't the time simply flown? I must be getting back to make sure that a meal is ready when Davey comes home from the station.' Before she left, she said, 'I'll soon come back to see you, if you'd like me for another visit. Thanks for that lovely cool lemonade, Ida, and don't forget, now, if you need me for anything at all, just send one of your houseboys over to get me. I'm just a bicycle ride away.'

"I replied, 'Oh, Meg, please come any time, I'd love to have your company. And thank you for this beautiful bouquet of flowers. What a relief it is to have you for a neighbor.' I almost cried with thankfulness to have found another thoughtful friend. I had been apprehensive about the new neighbors in Namasagali; now I didn't have to worry.

"Meg climbed onto her dusty bicycle and rode off along the red dirt path that had been worn between our two houses. I thought to myself, 'She seems glad to have me for a neighbor! I wonder what they do out here for a social life? It doesn't look as if there's any club like the one we had in Kisumu.' In another few weeks, along came some social life, but a very different kind!

"I'd had some experience living in Central East Africa after living in Kisumu, but there were still new things to learn in Namasagali. At first, I felt uneasy at night when Jack was away but I soon became adjusted to living on this new frontier and I felt better knowing that Obonyo and Omolo were usually within calling distance. After I took off my mosquito boots each night, I carefully hung them upside down on the boot rack, to discourage any creepy-crawlies from getting in. Each morning I gave them a daily ritual shake and inspection to dislodge any possible lingering strangers before I put them on. I even sneaked a look under the bed every night, to make sure there were no unwelcome visitors lurking there!

"A large tank stood outside the back door with a cover to be opened in the rainy season to catch rain water. I couldn't imagine why rain water would be collected. I did remember that a rain barrel had stood outside Mother's back door to catch the rain water that ran off the roof. When I was a girl, the rain water had been used by Mother, my sisters and me to rinse our hair to soften it after washing it with the harsh, home-made soap we used in those days. Since my haircut in Kisumu, my bobbed hair was a joy to wash. I looked forward to trying out the rain-water-rinse treatment on it, next time the tank filled up again. Sure enough, my hair was silky and smooth when I rinsed it after the next rainstorm when the tank had caught its fill. Mother would be gratified to hear that her hair-rinse treatment worked in Africa, too. But was African rain water as safe as Sunderland's? I decided to take no chances and had it boiled.

"There was an unlimited source of water on hand in the river, but it had to go through a purification process before it was even fit to be boiled. The natives dug deep holes at the edge of the river until they hit water, which then filtered through the sand below the surface to begin the purifying process and form a well. The water looked clear by the time it was hauled out of the well into buckets to be carried up to the house and poured into a tank near Isaiah's brazier. 'But even if it did look clear,' I reasoned, 'it's probably still full of invisible microbes and heaven knows what else,' so we took no chances and boiled every drop! A charcoal fire was kept burning day and night in the backyard to insure a constant supply of usable, boiled water.

"Then, of course, there was a different outdoor *choo* from the one in Kisumu but not much of an improvement! Creepy-crawlies still found their way into it. I lost no time in buying a supply of Jeyes Fluid. Its strong smell and antiseptic qualities acted just as well in Namasagali to suppress the offensive odors and to deter the blowflies and spiders—one whiff and they disappeared—just like the ones in Kisumu! I'd brought the measuring cup with me, and I made sure that our new *choo* boy learned how to use it. Voila! We had no problem with the quantity of Jeyes that he poured down the *choo!*

"Having learned my lesson in Kisumu about the dung beetle, I made sure that all the drawers were tightly closed, so that a Namasagali dung beetle wouldn't be tempted to add my knitting wool to its ball of dung while rolling it along. Thanks to the *quesha kufa* skill of Omolo, that problem had been re-solved, and I felt confident that there would be no beetle in my bedroom in our new location. However, there would be many other experiences, good and not so good, waiting to surprise me".

***

Mom had more notes to read:

A Call from on High

"We had been in Namasagali only a few weeks when an official-looking envelope arrived from the office of the District Commissioner. It contained an engraved invitation:

'Dear Captain and Mrs. Amiss: The pleasure of your company is requested by the District Commissioner at a formal dinner to welcome newcomers to the area.'

"It was signed: 'Reginald Cornish, DC.' His signature was followed by the date and time, both of which I've forgotten.

"I said to Jack, 'Oh dear, I've only one decent dress I can still get into, and it's a bit too revealing, I'm afraid. My bump is just beginning to show.' Jack turned to me with an exasperated look; translated, it would have said, '*Women!*' Aloud, he said sweetly, 'Don't worry, Sunshine, just wear your best maternity dress; you'll have to be gettin' used to wearin' one from now on, you know, and you'll still look lovely.' As if he had just remembered what *he* would be expected to wear at a formal dinner, he grumbled, 'Well at least *you'll* be comfortable. Dammit, I'll have to wrestle with that bloody evenin' suit again. But I'll be damned if I'll wear that blasted cummerbund!'

"I didn't complain again!

"Feeling better, I decided to add a bit of lace trimming to the low neckline on my only maternity dress that didn't look like a tent, and let it go at that. I was delighted when Meg Griffith came to visit and said that they had received an invitation, too, and that they would drive us to the District Commissioner's dinner.

"On the day of the dinner, I couldn't hide the fact that I was nervous about meeting one of the British elite, but at least I would have Meg to bolster my courage. We bumped along in Davey's car on its hard rubber tires to our destination: the imposing, white-brick building that housed not only the local government offices but also facilities for entertaining guests. Feeling very important, I took Jack's arm and we mounted the cement steps to the front door. A doorman ushered us inside, where the District Commissioner and his wife were waiting to greet us. There we found quite a few other couples and a single man already seated in the large reception room. We all shook hands, and I can't for the life of me remember any of their names, except for the single man, Algernon Bloomsbury. He was probably an assistant to our host, whom Meg referred to affectionately as 'The DC', or 'The Commish'.

"The DC turned out to be a middle-aged man with balding hair, smiling blue eyes and a magnificent handle-bar moustache. He received us with outstretched hand. Jack took it and said, 'How do you do, Commissioner Cornish, sir. We're the Amisses, Ida and Jack.'

"The response was immediate and full of political enthusiasm, 'Ah, yes, Captain and Mrs. Amiss. So glad to meet you both and welcome you to the neighborhood (it's rather big, and very spread out, isn't it?)' Did he hold my hand just a little longer than necessary? I may have imagined it, but I could swear I saw his moustache quiver a little as he continued, 'I don't believe In putting on airs, so just call me Reggie, or if you'd rather, just 'Reg' will do. You don't mind if I call you Jack and Ida, eh? Welcome to Paradise, and if there's anything at all that I can do for you, please let me know!'

"Jack was overcome by this relaxation of the otherwise strict protocol of British upper-class snobbery, where working-class men were merely addressed by their surnames (last names). The Commish had what was known then in England as an Oxford accent, which identified him as one of the upper class, but he seemed happy to break the artificial barriers set by his peers and 'muck in' (associate) with the middle class—us. I took an immediate liking to him! Jack recovered from his surprise by saying, rather stiffly, 'Thank you, sir, we're so pleased to be invited to meet you.'

"Reggie beamed, making his moustache grow wider; "Now you can drop the *sir,* too, Jack.'

"After the introductions had been made, Meg and I sat down on a nearby sofa to join all those in the room being served with hors d'oeuvres and a sundowner. I had now mastered the art of lingering with my gin and lime. I sipped slowly, content to listen to Meg's animated conversation. After he first met her, Jack had observed to me, 'Well, here's another one, Sunshine! Just like Effie, Meg can talk the hind leg off a donkey! The climate must do somethin' to women after they've been here awhile!' He and Davey went off to look for some Tusker beer, and probably to use the men's room after all that jolting on the road. Meg had just begun another one of her stories when we were summoned to the dining room by a native member of Reggie's staff. His white-gloved hand beat politely on a small gong as he walked through the reception room in his butler's uniform topped with a little red fez hat (probably Reg's idea). Clearing his throat between gong beats, he announced, 'Dinner is served,' in a flawless English accent. We trooped into the impressive, mahogany-paneled dining room where the dinner table was set with Reg's official china. Well-spaced flower arrangements were centred down the length of the enormous white damask table cloth.

"At each place setting was a little white card engraved with the name of its intended occupant. Jack was seated across the table from me. Flanking each plate with its fearsome array of silverware, were crystal glasses in several different sizes and shapes. It was easy for me to identify the one for drinking water, but the others mystified me. I felt a twinge of uneasiness; which one was for what? I needn't have worried; the butler supervised two young boys in matching uniforms as they filled the appropriate glasses throughout the meal. It was a dinner such as I had never seen before. A mouth-watering course of locally-caught fresh fish paved the way for the main course which was typically English: roast beef with all the trimmings, followed by an English cream trifle for dessert. A fruit and cheese course brought the feast to a close, consisting of some luscious African fruits, followed by the inevitable serving of water biscuits (saltine crackers) and English cheeses. I don't know how, but I still had room for a sip or two of delicious Kenya coffee.

"I found myself seated next to an attractive man about Jack's age; his good looks were somewhat spoiled, however, by a receding chin. He had been introduced to me as Algernon Bloomsbury when we had first arrived. When we shook hands, he had had held mine a little longer than I expected, but I thought nothing of it. As we sat waiting for our first course, he turned to me with a suggestive leer on his face and breathed into my ear with a nauseatingly exaggerated upper-class accent, 'Ai sey, Ida, I feel as if I already neaw yew, my deah. I hope yew'll call me Algie.' He put his hand on mine under the table. I looked at Jack to see if he noticed Algie's familiarity, but he was absorbed in talking to the man sitting next to him. In a low, conspiratorial tone, Algie went on with a knowing wink, 'Yew neaw, my deah, you nevah need fear being lonely. I heah your hubby is away for long stretches of time on the lake, but remembah, yew can call on me if yew need me. I'm always available for yew, me dearie.'

"Feeling a bit alarmed, I looked at Jack again, but he was still engrossed in lively conversation with his neighbor and I couldn't catch his eye. Into my imagination popped those lurid stories I'd heard in Kenya about the Happy Valley Set! Algie would probably have fitted in with them very well. I couldn't believe what I was hearing, and I felt myself blushing, much to my consternation. I thought, 'Whatever can I say to him? He's obviously one of Reggie's staff, so I'd better not insult him by just ignoring him.' Aloud, I said, 'Oh, I may have felt a bit lonely at first but I've soon found plenty to keep me busy around the house, and also with my friends and neighbors.' Looking disappointed, Algie said, 'Oh, Ida deah, I'm sew glad for you, but just remember what I've said.'

"As dinner was served, course after course, I made as much empty conversation with Algie as possible about the climate, the beauty of the area, the blessing of our electric generator and other harmless topics. Luckily, Algie enlarged upon each one without any further suggestive remarks, although he had a habit of nudging me with his elbow as he talked. He definitely had a roving eye. It ranged around the table on the beautifully dressed women, and all through our meal I could feel his eyes on me from time to time. At one point he brushed his fork off the table, and as he bent down to retrieve it I felt his hand slide up my thigh. Instinctively, I pulled my leg away. Having thought it over, I decided not to involve Jack—I was afraid he would make a scene, or even take a punch at Algie after having a few Tusker beers. I thought to myself, 'Now, Ida, you'd better not say a word, just keep a stiff upper lip and let things take their course!'

"As the dinner wore on, I began to feel quite warm in spite of the puffs of cool air from ceiling fans whirring above the dining table. I was having trouble keeping my eyes open and a couple of times found myself nodding off. The wine served throughout the meal and that last glass with the fruit and cheese didn't help, nor did Algie's conversation which was conducted in an almost inaudible whisper.

"A reprieve from Algie's attentions came when the meal ended. Following British after-dinner procedure at such formal affairs, the men left to go for a smoke and glass of brandy in the adjacent smoking room, and we women were left to our own devices. I relaxed at last, enjoying chatter with the ladies left at the table. They all had funny stories to tell about their lives in Africa, prompting sympathetic giggles from their listeners. We could all identify with hilarious descriptions of their struggle with the ups and downs of frontier living, especially with the sanitation arrangements (or lack of!) In a more serious vein, they talked about their homes and families in England, which took my mind off my recent encounter with Algie but it made me feel homesick all over again. It would take a lot of memory work (and you know I'm not very good at that) to keep all their names straight, but I was happy to have found new acquaintances with whom to share our experiences and have a good laugh.

"The men came back from the smoking room in time for a serving of the local Kenya coffee, which has since become a favorite world-wide beverage. Its bracing effect kept me from dropping off to sleep until after we arrived back at the house. I couldn't wait to strip off all my clothes and dive into the waiting sheets under the mosquito netting. Jack came and kissed me. He never minced words. As he tucked in the netting around the mattress for an extra precaution, he inquired, 'By the way, Sunshine, who was that chinless wonder you were talkin' to at the dinner table? He acted as if he knew you *very* well. If he'd touched you I'd have knocked his block off—the cheeky sod!'

"I replied, sleepily, 'Oh, he just happened to have the seat next to mine at the table, dear. Quite nice, really, but not my type! *You're* the type I like best, my love.' I suddenly felt quite dizzy, and turned my face on the pillow to get comfortable. I thought, 'I'm glad Mother can't see me now, stripped naked and suffering from the effects of all that food and wine, to say nothing of the stress of Algie's advances!' Almost immediately, I was asleep."

GREAT EXPECTATIONS

BUNTY: Dad was becoming impatient with Mom, who had taken up what he thought was more than her share of time at the microphone, especially with the long-forgotten story of Algie. He motioned her to hand over the microphone, cleared his throat and began:

Greasing the Ways

"Oh aye, some odd things happened to me, too, while I was in Uganda. I remember one time when I'd taken over as captain of a large river steamer for a pal of mine; he needed a few days off to be with his wife who was down with malaria. The river steamers were shallow draft stern-wheelers, because of the unpredictable depth of the water in the Victoria Nile. As well as carryin' their own passengers and crew, they often pushed tenders ahead of them loaded with stacks of wood for fuel, as well as piles of bulky cargo. Natives were allowed to hitchhike on these tenders free of charge; as a result they were always packed with hitchhikin' humanity. All went well until a European crew member came dashin' up to the wheel-house and panted, 'Captain Amiss, you're needed down on the tender. There's a native woman there in labor, and she needs your help urgently. Will you please come?'

"I asked a deck officer to take over while I went to see what this was all about, quickly snatchin' up me first-aid kit, which

I always made sure was fully stocked (I replenished whatever had been used right away). There was a supply of bandages, large darnin' needles for removin' splinters, iodine, Vaseline, Epsom salts and that no-fail remedy, castor oil, with a large spoon to administer it. I remember how the natives came to rely on its magic powers; they lined up for a spoonful to cure ailments from headaches to constipation. With no medical facilities nearby, they had come to rely on my help, so I'd had quite a bit of experience in treatin' injuries like bruises and cuts. But a childbirth case was somethin' new to me.

"I followed the crew member down to the lower deck and we hopped across onto the tender. He led me to the small crowd of natives who had formed in a knot surroundin'a very young lass in labor (she was no more than a child herself). The crowd parted when I arrived, and I found the poor lass lyin' on the bare boards of the tender's deck, groanin' in agony, surrounded by chatterin' onlookers who were creatin' a lot of commotion but seemed unable to help her. Her husband stood by helplessly; this must have been their first child, because I didn't see any *m'totos* hangin' around. By the look of him, the young husband was sufferin' as much pain as his wife. I shouted to the crowd, '*kwacha kelele!*' (be quiet!). Turnin' to him, I said, 'S*hari gani*? *Shari gani*?' (what's the matter? what's the matter?) The young husband replied, '*M'toto bado kidogo, bwana*' (the baby hasn't come yet, sir.') I told my crew member to tell them to carry the girl up onto the steamer where I could attend to her. This would get the poor lass away from that howlin' mob and make her more comfortable. She was carried across onto the deck of the steamer and put down in the shade, where she continued to struggle and groan.

"Feelin' sure that I'd left the ship's wheel in the hands of an experienced European deck officer, I opened up me first-aid kit and scanned the contents. Seein' them reminded me of the last case I'd treated; a young boy who had a nasty wound in the skin on his leg that had required a few stitches. When the wound healed and I took out the stitches, the new scar tissue was pink! The boy reminded me that all Africans have pink skin and red blood under the black, and this was really the first time I'd thought of it. I realized then and there a simple truth: all of us humans are basically related 'under the skin', even when we act as though we're not. Oh aye, we're all connected!

"I'd had first-aid trainin' before I left England, but a child-birth case was a new problem and I was a bit scared, to tell you the truth. 'Now, Jack,' I said to meself, 'Now Jack, me lad, what can you think of that would help this poor lass deliver that baby? I'd never seen one be born, but I reasoned that it must get launched by slippin' out of her somehow! All I could think of, with me nautical heritage, was how they launched the ships on the River Wear at Sunderland. The ships were built on a structure called The Ways, a pair of rails which sloped downward at an angle toward the river. They had to be greased to allow the ship to slip easily down them into the water as it launched.

"I was lookin' glumly over the collection of things in me first-aid kit when I spotted the bottle of castor oil. 'Aha,' I thought to meself, 'well, Jack, it's worked successfully for lots of ailments since you've been out here in Africa, so *here goes!*' I took the bottle and the tablespoon out of the case. 'Any port in a storm, Jack,' I told meself, 'it might not do much good, but it can't do any harm, anyway!' And with that, I said a silent prayer and gave a spoonful for the lass, who swallowed it when she was in between groans.

"Just then, one of the crew came to tell me that I was needed to pilot the ship, so I packed up me first-aid kit and climbed the stairs to the bridge. For the next half hour I was kept busy sorting out a navigational problem on a tricky bend in the river on the way to Namasagali. When we were safely into smooth sailin' once more, the girl's husband came puffin' up the stairs to the bridge. He was grinnin' from ear to ear.

'*Bwana, bwana,*' he cried, in Swahili, "*m'toto wa kiume*!' (it's a male baby). He actually bowed to me in his excitement. I muttered to meself, 'I hope he doesn't think I had somethin' to do with *that,* too!' I shook his hand, clapped him on the back and said, 'Good news, good work, Dad!' He didn't have to understand; he knew I was happy for him, but he'd never have guessed how relieved I was for meself!

"When I could safely leave the wheelhouse again, I went down to see the new baby. There he was, at his mother's breast, and she was smilin' proudly down on him. I gently patted her on the shoulder and nodded my approval. She looked at me, smiled, and said wearily, "*Sante sana, bwana*" (thank you very much, sir).

"I told Ida the whole story when I got home. She said, 'Oh, Jack, I'm so proud of you!' Then she burst out laughin' when I couldn't resist sayin', 'But just think of it, Sunshine, that poor lass did all the hard work; all I did was to grease The Ways with a dose of cod liver oil when she was ready for the launch!" I can still hear Ida laughin'! This became a traditional tale in the family—it even made its way into the Ditchfields' parlor to tell their gossipy neighbors!"

BUNTY: The story was one of Dad's favorites; I'd heard it often when I was growing up. But I sometimes wondered if those in his audience who had never seen a ship launched into the Wear were fully appreciative of—or understood—what he meant by that punch line!

∗∗∗

After I had changed the tape, Mom added one of her own favorite stories:

Doctor Singh

"One of the first things that we knew we must do when we came to Namasagali was to find a doctor. My pregnancy was advancing and I was totally ignorant of what was happening or was going to happen. I was feeling fine, but Jack and I agreed that we must find a competent doctor soon. I broached the subject to Meg on one of her next visits. 'Oh, indeed', she said, 'the nearest doctor is over at the hospital at Jinja, about 50 or so miles away. He's Doctor Singh, from India, and he speaks English with a heavy accent. Davey and I think he's very competent. Jack can stop at Jinja hospital on his way back to Namasagali from the lake someday and make an appointment with him. He's at the hospital nearly all the time unless he's out on calls or has some emergency. He's quite a nice fellow; indeed to goodness, I think you'll like him, Ida.'

"Not many days later, Obonyo's drums told him some news that he relayed to me. '*Memsahib,*' he announced, '*Daktari* come see you tomorrow!'

"In due course, the doctor's dust-encrusted *gari* (car) labored up to the house, and I had my first encounter with him. Doctor Singh was short and heavy-set, with a prolific moustache and beard, and a well-fed, protruding middle. He wore a turban on his head. He spoke in a sing-song voice, with a strong Indian accent, 'Good day, Mrs. Amiss. I fear my English not too good,' In clipped phrases, he continued, 'It is my honor to meet you.' He had a firm handshake which gave me confidence in him immediately. He rushed on, 'How are you feeling?' Without waiting for an answer, he added, 'You look well; color good, eyes clear and all that.' He took out a tongue depressor and looked at my throat, then took my blood pressure. 'You know how many months you are? When was last menstruation?'

"I felt a bit embarrassed and told him when I had had my last period, then I blurted, 'Doctor, I must tell you that I don't really know anything about pregnancy or childbirth; my mother never broached the subject. In her day, it simply wasn't '*done*' to speak of such things, even to a daughter!' The doctor looked puzzled, and I imagined I could hear him thinking, 'These crazy English—not much sense—not savvy like Indian women.' But he said, 'Excuse me, please.' He disappeared outside. As I watched from the window, I saw him fumble around in his car and lift something heavy out of it. He arrived back in the house a little out of breath and sweating profusely. 'Here, Mrs. Amiss,' he said,' I will leave this book with you—it will tell you what to expect.' He dropped the large, leather-bound volume on the dining room table with a bang, 'Just lift up pages—this will give you good education.'

"He looked so uncomfortable that I wondered why he wore that turban in this hot climate; his head must have trapped a large amount of body heat! I learned later that the Sikh religion forbids the cutting of body hair."

BUNTY: Let me interrupt Mom's story to relate some interesting background about Doctor Singh that she didn't mention:

My research revealed that Sikhs constitute the fifth largest population in the world. At this writing, about twenty million live in India, most in the province of Punjab. There are estimated to be about five hundred thousand in the U.S.

Their religion forbids male Sikhs to cut hair on their bodies; to them it is a gift from God and therefore to be revered. Symbolizing respect for the Almighty, it is meticulously cared for: washed once a week and combed twice a day with a small wooden comb called a *kanga.* Men coil it into a bun and wear it on top of their head inside the turban. Women wear their hair long. I was also impressed to read that drinking intoxicants is, to them, as sinful as incest; drugs and tobacco are also forbidden.

Note: I remember that in World War Two, we in England had a high regard for the reputation of the Sikh regiments (from a then-unified India) who fought with such bravery and success for the British Empire; many of them were awarded war medals. As I was growing up, I remember seeing their regiments in the newsreels, marching proudly in military parades in their uniforms and turbans.

But, let's return to Mom's hilarious account of her meeting with Dr. Singh:

"I asked Omolo to bring some cool lemonade. Dr. Singh gulped it down gratefully, after which he seemed a bit more relaxed and chatted about the hospital at Jinja. 'That is where you will come to have baby, Mrs. Amiss,' he said, 'it is very nice staff and good food, too—European, you know—-run by your British Government. Now, before I go I must give small examination. Please lie down on your bed.'

"I fought to hoist the mosquito netting, which finally stayed up, about a foot above my head, and then I lay down obediently on the bed. I watched with satisfaction as Doctor Singh went to the washbasin and quickly washed his hands. He had me pull up my dress and pull down my knickers (underpants). He then slowly palpated my bare tummy. 'Oh, yes,' he muttered, 'doing very well. About another five months, then you will have lovely little one. I will come back to see you again, some weeks away. Now, you will eat plenty fresh fruit and vegetable. Fresh milk must be boiled, drink plenty. If no fresh milk, be sure you drink much of the tinned kind. Eat plenty cereals, too. Get a few hours daily rest; you will be just fine.'

"As he headed for the door, I stammered, 'Thank you, doctor, you've given me the reassurance I needed that all is well with me and the baby. I'll send you a message if there is a problem before your next visit.' He nodded briefly. In a minute or two, I heard his car's engine struggle to life with a sputter and he drove off over the rutted road of packed red earth, leaving behind a cloud of red dust.

"I looked with curiosity at the large, heavy book that Dr. Singh had left for me to read. Picking it up, I went out into the sunlit verandah and put it down on the table. I arranged a footstool at my feet and put them up on it, then opened the book. I was relieved to see that it was written in English! I quickly skipped over the introductory pages, which showed rather explicit colored pictures of the sex act, followed by another graphic drawing illustrating an army of tiny sperms making their way up a fallopian tube toward a rather large egg (in comparison with their size) waiting eagerly for a suitor, to lead him into a very large pink womb. Next, there was an illustrated account of how one victorious sperm gained entrance, fixed itself to an egg and began to divide. Eagerly, I flipped to the next page that had an illustration. It was the kind of thing we had at home in children's books: there were little flaps in the illustrated pages that could be lifted up to see what was underneath. I gingerly turned over to the next page. In glorious color, it showed a picture of a newly-pregnant woman whose abdomen was covered over by a flap of paper. Lifting it up, I was face to face with the large pink womb, looking like an over-ripe pear, covering another flap. Under this one, it showed the beginning of an embryo. I had to slow down to read the text, which explained the approximate timetable. I was so engrossed that I lost all sense of time, and it wasn't until I heard three toots, the signal from the river steamer bringing Jack home, that I realized how long I'd been sitting there! I closed the book and laid it aside for later in my pregnancy. I was glad I did. By that time, I was dreading the next pages!

"In my next letter to Mother, I mentioned that I would be going to Jinja hospital to have my baby. She wrote back in panic, 'Oh, Ida, do you mean to tell me that you won't be having a midwife? What's wrong, dear?' I had forgotten that back in those days in Sunderland a trip to the Infirmary (hospital) was only made under dire circumstances, sometimes foretelling a death sentence! Midwives were employed to deliver babies in the home, and even the doctor wasn't summoned unless there were some life-threatening complications."

***

BUNTY: The following afternoon, after a short break for a cup of tea, Mom was anxious to continue her reminiscences of Uganda; this time on her favorite topic: food.

We Taste Uganda!

"I was getting acquainted with the houseboys, who turned out to be an obliging lot. Our cook, Isaiah, was the star; a truly creative genius. Isaiah was always bringing me tasty tidbits to eat. With his vast knowledge of the local fruits and vegetables, he enjoyed every opportunity possible to try out something new on me, often bringing one of the delicious tropical fruits for me to taste which he had prepared to look like a flower on the plate. I learned to recognize and love the taste of pawpaw (papaya), passion fruit (how sexy!), red-ripe mangoes, and the sweet-tasting little red-skinned bananas; miniature versions of the big yellow ones, which Isaiah used in his delicious *ndisi* (banana pancakes.) Isaiah was a fabulous cook; favorites of his (and ours) were his roasted chicken or poached fresh fish, each of which he cooked to perfection. He was quite innovative with his meals, and introduced us to some of the local recipes:

Chapoti was a tasty flatbread; made with maize flour, it appeared regularly as an accompaniment to a meal.

Kikomando was Chapoti, cut into pieces and served with fried beans.

Ugali was often served for breakfast, a kind of porridge.

Isaiah served it with some of the local honey. Sometimes, white maize flour was added to thicken it; when it was cold, it could then be cut into slices and served as *Ugali-Posho* with a meal.

Luombo was meat or fish stewed with mushrooms and steamed in a banana leaf.

Mugali-Naamaggi was dough, made into pancakes. A savory mixture bound together with raw egg was then placed in the middle of each pancake, folded over it to form a little sealed package, then fried in a skillet. Isaiah was very creative with his *mugali;* they could contain mixtures of minced meat or fish, onions, cabbage and tomatoes—each version a mouth-watering creation. As side dishes, there were starches like cassava (American sweet potatoes or yams) or sometimes white potatoes when they were available. Plenty of leafy vegetables were to be had, as well as bamboo shoots and fried green bananas. Sauces were made with meat or fish, mashed ground-nuts (peanuts) and beans. Isaiah sometimes surprised us at dessert time with sugar-coated sesame seeds, candied ginger, and sugary desiccated coconut served with a bowl of those wonderful tropical fruits.

"One day, Isaiah said, '*Memsahib,* now it is time to try *nsenene.* It is made in a pan with a little oil; cooked with onion and tomato; it tastes lovely; 'specially as a nice snack with sundowners. It tastes like crispy chicken skin; you eat it hot or cold.' It sounded delicious. Flattered to think he would prepare a special treat for us, I asked, 'What *is* that, Isaiah?' 'Oh, *memsahib,*' he replied, that beautiful voice of his almost caressing the words, 'So nice, crunchy and good for you, too, tasty fried grasshoppers! Good too are *mchwa* (termites). I will cook them for you; they are best fried like *nsenene*. The boys catch them when they fly around lights at night.'

"I recoiled in horror; my queasy stomach shivered. 'But, Isaiah, 'I quavered, 'they are *dudus!*' (insects). Isaiah gave me one of his film-star smiles. He insisted, 'But *memsahib,* they taste wonderful, and Isaiah will wash them and take away the wings before he cooks them!'

"I summoned all the charm I could, to tell him, 'No thank-you, Isaiah!'

"Mother agreed with me in her next letter, 'Good for you, Ida, I'm glad you didn't attempt to try them in your *delicate condition*!' (I hadn't heard that expression since I left England, so I tucked it away for future use, thinking it might come in handy.)

"Determined not to let Isaiah have the last word, I tried to be as tactful as possible, especially since he was quite serious in proposing that the seasonal opportunity for his special delicacies was not to be missed. When he mentioned them again I said firmly, 'Maybe some other time, Isaiah, *bado kidogo* (not quite yet).' Isaiah trudged dejectedly back to the kitchen. His cooking continued to be superb. Once in awhile, Jack exploded, 'What the hell is THAT?' when something alien appeared on our plates, but most of the time he would nod his head, and say grudgingly, 'Not bad—not at all bad.' Then I knew I could safely tell Isaiah to try it again. However, I privately decided never again to mention the *nsenene* or the *mchwa* to Isaiah. In the years we were in Africa, neither Jack nor I ever had enough courage to try either one.

BUNTY: Before we leave the subject of termites, let me share some interesting research:

Eating *mchwa* was an obsession with the natives; termites were prized as a delicacy above almost anything else. I read that they were packed high in protein and fat, a good source of nutrition loaded with calories when—pruned of their wings—they were eaten roasted, fried, or even raw.

There was such a good market for *mchwa* that many enterprising natives had created a termite business for themselves. In the rainy season, migrating termites that had developed wings flew out from termite mounds, attracted by lights around which they hovered by the thousands. Professional termite-gatherers hung lights of their own to attract the swarming insects and catch them with nets. It was even common for these professionals to tap on the mounds with sticks and sprinkle water on them to fool the termites into thinking the rainy season had arrived!

***

Mom was still thinking about food:

"Isaiah only tried me out one more time with food that didn't appeal to me when he looked quite excited and announced, "*Memsahib Amiss*, men from some of the villages have worked together to catch a young hippo from river. Meat very good!

"I must have looked interested, because he continued, 'Very dangerous to catch hippo, but one can feed village people for many days. Men from one of villages saw a young hippo sleeping in the sun, so they crept up on him. They put a rope round him while he was still sleepy and pulled it tight. Lots of men are needed to make the rope tight and hold the hippo. Warriors from more than one village came to help, with spears to stab the hippo and kill him. They dragged the hippo up on riverbank and cut him up. It was many hours to cut him up. Women came and helped them take away the meat; it was shared for each village. They put salt on it and it lasts for many days. Good meat—a real treat for the people. People love it and it is so popular that *Muhindis* sell hippo meat at the market. I shall cook some for you and *bwana*, yes?' He looked at me and waited with bated breath.

"Once again, I had to be firm with him and also diplomatic! I replied, in the most polite voice I could muster, '*Sante sana, Isaiah (*thank you very much, Isaiah) I know you are a wonderful cook, and we love your cooking, but I don't think *Bwana Amiss* would like to eat hippopotamus.'

"Crushed, Isaiah never asked us to try out anything new again. I'm sure he must have been sorry for us, thinking how much we were missing out of life!

"Actually, we had quite a lot of variety in our diet, including fresh hen's eggs. Isaiah's helper, Alfred, was the little lad in charge of getting our supply of fresh eggs. His supplier was about the same age as himself, a young boy about 11 or 12 years old, who brought the eggs down from his father's *shamba* in the hills somewhere near Namasagali. Our houseboys sang or chanted as they walked along, or when they were working around the house. I was to learn that this also applied to the rules of meeting and greeting someone on the road. One day, out of curiosity, I watched from the verandah window as Alfred and the egg-boy went through this procedure. Alfred was already expecting him to arrive, and stood in the road to greet him. Fascinated, I watched the next piece of African lore—the 'greeting ceremony'.

"When he caught sight of the egg-boy walking down the dirt road, Alfred began his chant, '*hujambo, hujambo, habari gani, habari gani*' (hello, hello, how are you, how are you?) I couldn't hear what the boy replied, but it was probably a greeting that it was customary to say as he approached on foot. I once read a commentary about this custom, which gave a hypothetical example. I'll number the participants 1 and 2 and not attempt the Swahili. I quote:

'If a friend is expected, the greeting begins when one first sees the other approaching:

1: How are you? (this actually translates: how are *we?*)
2: Who am I, that you care to know?
1: Humble though I be, yet I have dared!
2: But first, say 'How are you?'
1: The better for the honor you do me.

If #2 has come to visit, he concludes:

'The honor is mine, and I shall treasure it.'

"At the end of the visit, there is a long 'A-a-a-h' of satisfaction from both, repeated by each one as they walk away from each other until they can no longer be heard.

"I was told that the custom was also observed whenever a native walking on the road approached someone going in the opposite direction. If the person is a friend, they would stop for a chat. When this was over, or when a stranger had passed by without stopping, courtesy demanded a farewell to be chanted by each of them over and over again (*kwaheri, kwaheri)* lapsing into a series of grunts as the distance between them grew, until they had both walked out of earshot.

"Alfred welcomed the egg-boy with a much-shortened version of this lengthy performance. He sat on the ground with the little fellow who produced the eggs from a basket he was carrying. Between them stood a bucket of cold water that had been provided by Isaiah. One by one, the egg-boy carefully lowered an egg into the water. If it sank, Alfred took it and put it carefully into his own basket next to him on the ground. If the egg floated, he sprang to his feet and shouted at the boy, '*Yai mbaya sana*' (egg very bad). The egg-boy was all apologies and scooped up the egg, sheepishly putting it back in his basket—presumably to dispose of it later or maybe to try it out on the next customer! When the egg-boy had filled Isaiah's order, Alfred took him to be paid. Isaiah gave the boy a few coins, with a little more than the asking price as a reward.

"Speaking of rewards, sometimes Jack brought home a slab of rock salt, which he cut up into smaller pieces. He gave a few each to Isaiah, Obonyo and Omolo. They treated them like prize candy, and sometimes shared them with some houseboy to whom they owed a favor.

On this occasion, Isaiah must have been feeling particularly charitable; when he paid the egg-boy, he popped a small chunk of salt into his egg basket. The little fellow said, *'Asante, asante, bwana* (thank you, thank you, boss) and scurried away as if he were afraid that Isaiah might change his mind and take back his reward. In the absence of refrigeration, I wondered how Isaiah would keep the eggs fresh, and I was surprised to see that he greased them and put them in the meat safe! He also had ways of preserving meat, salting and spicing it, then soaking it in vinegar and drying it over his charcoal fire in the backyard. He brought it indoors at night, or it would have disappeared by morning!

"Isaiah served honey with our breakfast. Jack and I used it in our coffee and tea instead of sugar; it tasted wonderful. We used it on our *ugali*, which actually made it palatable to our unseasoned taste buds. We used it spread on toast; in fact it was delicious any way it was used! I asked Isaiah where it came from, not expecting his reply, which turned out to be a lengthy story:

"'Yes, *Memsahib* and *Bwana* Amiss, I will tell you.' Isaiah sat down heavily on one of the verandah chairs, and treated us to a veritable lecture on the seasonal production of wild honey, unwittingly demonstrating the depth of his own knowledge and education:

'Best wild honey comes from Uganda; tourists buy it to take home with them. It's good to eat, to make beer, to heal wounds, fix tummy upsets and lots of other things. Makes sick and skinny children grow strong. It was used in Egypt long ago in ladies' makeup, also when they preserved bodies. Very old tradition in Uganda. Pictures showing honey-gathering painted on walls of caves, thousands of years ago. In some African countries, they use honey to pay the dowry for a wife.

'Honey-gathering is an ancient skill—not written, passed from father to son. Women now do most of the beekeeping. Bees are very dangerous. Some poor people in Uganda countryside are still honey-gatherers. They know all about bees and where they go to find flowers. Honey-gatherers make it easy for lots of bees to make honey. They cut a piece off a big tree branch and clean it out inside so bees can come in and make a nest. Make lots of logs this way. Then they climb up tall ladders, and put the logs tight in the tree branches. Bees come and make beehives in the logs. When honeycombs are ready, honey-gatherers go up the ladders to the logs—they have to get the honey before animals and insects find it. Honey-gatherers put a damp leaf each end of the hollow logs and light them to make smoke and chase the bees out. Honey-gatherers take out the honeycombs and let honey drip into a bucket. They pour some into bottles to sell. Honey-gatherers keep some honey for themselves, for food and making beer, but they sell most of it to make a living. In past times it was not known what to do with the empty honeycombs, so they were thrown away. But now they sell them to make beeswax for candles. Professional beekeepers are coming to Uganda, so old traditions are going away. But there are still some honey-gatherers left in villages in the mountains.'

"Jack and I were astounded at the story and how well Isaiah had told it. We knew that we now had a wonderful source of answers to our questions about African traditions right in our midst; from then on, we often invited Isaiah to join us after breakfast to listen to his knowledge and stories"

***

Tribes in our Household

It was Dad's turn for the microphone:

"In those days, many of our houseboys clung to their tribal practices and taboos. These sometimes amused or horrified our Western thinkin'. Some of the boys had attended mission schools and converted to Christianity, abandonin' the practices that were most cruel. Over the years that have gone by since we were in Africa, a lot of the old practices and superstitions have died out."

BUNTY: Let me interrupt with more research:

As in some other cultures in our world, the rites of puberty are still performed in Africa for both boys and girls. The one I heard about that shocked me as the most brutal to Western thinking is female genital mutilation (FGM) or female circumcision, which means the ritual cutting and removal of some (or all), of the external female genitalia. This is carried out on little girls usually before the age of five, but sometimes at puberty, allowed by their families as a duty honor. Mothers and grandmothers have their daughters and grand-daughters cut, fearing that failing to do so would cause the girls social persecution later in their lives (at one time, uncircumcised Kikuyu women were treated as outcasts).

I read that that there are no known health benefits from this custom but many unwanted side effects: the procedure can cause difficulty in urinating and menstruating, chronic pain, plus difficulty in childbirth: hemorrhaging and even death. In the year 2016, United Nations' UNICEF reported that 200 million girls in 30 third world countries (27 million of them in Africa) were then currently victims of the procedure. Hopefully, at this writing, the statistics have de-creased, or vanished.

***

After a short break, Dad was eager to continue with his commentary:

"Oh aye, loyalty to their tribal and family ties—and to the vil-lages where they were born—was very strong with our native lads. There was some tribal rivalry—even a traditional hatred (for instance, between the Kikuyu and Maasai) but our house-boys got along well together and respected one another's tribal traditions. As head houseboy, Obonyo's position was well acknowledged; he had inborn qualities of good leadership. We noticed that he avoided possible conflict when he encouraged a houseboy who had seniority to choose a younger member of the same tribe to work as his subordinate. We seldom heard major disagreements between them or any fightin' (with one exception, yet to come.) On the whole, we were very lucky.

"We began to know how to recognize the tribes by their tribal marks. Tattooin' on the face and body was common; it was believed to drive away evil spirits. Many of the accepted tribal marks would be seen nowadays to be a cruel disfigure-ment of the human body. One custom struck me as particularly outlandish: old photos show Kikuyu and Nandi men whose ear lobes were slit when they were very young. A small object was inserted in the slit in each ear lobe, to be replaced by a larger one as the boys grew to men, stretchin' the slits to become longer as they accommodated each new, larger object. In the old photos, some of the slits were so large that the ear lobes hung down onto the men's shoulders and could hold as large an item as a tin of tobacco! It's hard to imagine, but when the slits were empty, would you believe it, the men slung their ear lobes over their shoulders to get 'em out of the way! Some of the old photos also show long-necked women who wore ring upon ring of metal neckbands to stretch 'em. 'How could this be called a beauty mark?' I wondered. I'll be damned if *I'd* be attracted to a long-necked woman!

"Some of our houseboys had tribal marks; usually cuts or deep scratches on the face or tops of their arms, done when they were young adolescents as part of the ritual of passin' into manhood at puberty. The marks became permanent scar tissue that stretched with their skin as the boys grew older. Our houseboys belonged to the Kikuyu, Kavirondo and JaLuo tribes. We were told that the JaLuo didn't practice circumcision.

However, a mark of tribal identification was to extract several of the lower permanent teeth of a son, in the belief that if the teeth were kept he would be killed in a war. It also served as proof of his ability to withstand pain (the teeth were usually extracted with a fish hook, without anesthetic). I thought of Omolo with his lisp and missin' teeth and couldn't help wonderin' if he was proud to have been given this tribal mark or if he had grown to resent bein' so disfigured.

"Each tribe had its own dietary taboos, many of which prohibited them from eatin' a particular animal product—usually lamb or poultry and eggs. Another taboo said that you're allowed to kill somethin', but don't touch it after it's dead. We saw this happen in our own household with the incident of the black mamba, when the houseboys with this taboo left it to the others to cart the carcass away.

"Now I'll let Sunshine do the talking while I take 'forty winks'; just to rest me eyes, of course."

Native family on a tender

UGANDA THE BEAUTIFUL

MOM HAD BEEN chomping at the bit to talk again. She eagerly picked up the microphone:

The Mountains of the Moon

"We had only been in Namasagali a short time when Davey and Meg Griffith decided that we should see some of Uganda's beauty spots. 'You know, Ida,' Meg exclaimed, 'indeed, we ought to take you and Jack to see the *Mountains of the Moon.* I've heard that there's a new branch railway going there from Namasagali.'

"My ears pricked up. Back in England, I had heard talk of *The Mountains of the Moon,* but in my ignorance of Central East Africa I had no idea where or what they were. I said quickly, 'Oh, Meg, I've always been curious about those mysterious mountains; I'd love to go, if it could be arranged and if Jack's willing.'"

BUNTY: Questions ran around in my mind. Where are these mysterious mountains? And how did they get their name? I spent hours and days researching and finding fascinating stories that have been passed down from time immemorial about the *Mountains of the Moon.*

Located in southwest Uganda, the *Mountains of the Moon* are a group of jagged, snow-covered peaks rising to 17,000 feet; part of the Rwenzori

Mountain Range. There is a fascination and mystique about them to this day, ever since they were shrouded in legend and superstition in pre-recorded history when they were believed to be the home of a god.

Back in 500 BC, the ancient Greek dramatist Aeschylus wrote about "Egypt, nurtured by the snows." This is thought to be the earliest known reference to the snow-covered mountains of the Great Rift Valley and the inference that the run-off from their glaciers flows into the River Nile.

But how did the *Mountains of the Moon* get their name? In 110 AD, the Greek traveling merchant Diogenes made a map when he crossed Africa and stumbled upon an ice-topped mountain range. He asserted that he believed the Nile originated from the melting snow that ran off the mountains and created lakes that fed the river. He referred to them as *"The Moon Mountains"* because when light shone on their glaciers it made reflections on them that looked like crescent moons, which could be seen for miles.

In 150 AD, Greek historian Ptolemy adapted an account from the atlas map made by Diogenes in 110 AD. For centuries, the location of these mountains was disputed. The name *Mountains of the Moon* appeared on maps when the earliest exploration began in the interior of Africa, but map makers began omitting it from maps in the 1700s. Nevertheless, tradition won out and today some of our maps still carry that mysterious name.

In the 1920s, these mountains were already attracting tourists and mountain climbers; trekking parties were organized during the months when the climate was suitable for their expeditions.

In 1940, Mount Kilimanjaro is reputed to have been called "The Mountain of the Moon." The movie *Mountains of the Moon* tells a somewhat fictionalized tale of explorers Burton and Speke trying to find the source of the River Nile in part of the Great Rift Valley. And at one time it was thought that the mountains contained diamonds! When Mom was growing up, their existence and whereabouts were still controversial and a favorite topic of conversation.

Rising just north of the equator, higher than the Alps and capped with ice, the Rwenzori mountain range containing the *Mountains of the Moon* in southwest Uganda is now a National Park. Established in 1991, it became an official UNESCO World Heritage Site. At 8,200 feet above sea level, the park contains the third highest mountain in Uganda and many waterfalls, lakes and glaciers.

But time marches on, and unfortunately the 1920s railway extension line from Namasagali was discontinued—replaced by better highways and other forms of transportation. Nowadays, the effects of global warming have been noted as the cause of a new influx of chameleons moving into the area. Also, it is estimated that due to global warming the *Mountains of the Moon* have lost 84 per cent of their ice. The fact that climate change is accelerating the melting of the glaciers is confirmed by comparing records dating back to late 1800s and early 1900s. It is feared that the moonshine on the ice-covered peaks and once visible for miles will soon disappear, and maybe with it the name *Mountains of the Moon.*

Mom's original account of their trip to the *Mountains of the Moon* was sketchy, to say the least. To make it a good story attributed to her, I have taken the liberty of embellishing the core of what she remembered, helped by intensive research. I hope you will find it to be as fascinating as I did.

Note: At this writing, with the Harry Potter stories still fresh in our minds, it would be worth mentioning that in the book *Harry Potter and the Goblet of Fire,* the *Mountains of the Moon* are mentioned as the location for the *Uagadou School of Magic,* located in Uganda, where it was home to the fictional African community of wizardry. The book states that this imaginary Ugandan community was the largest of the eleven schools of wizardry; it accepted students from all over Africa! Hm-mm!

***

Mom was itching to get on with her story:

"I was so excited when Meg suggested a trip to the *Mountains of the Moon,* that I was almost breathless when I remarked, 'They don't look very far away on the map, Meg, and when I go back to England I'd love to report that I've seen those mysterious mountains I've have heard talked about for so many years. I'm just afraid that after the baby comes I'll never get there!'

"Meg exclaimed, 'By golly, Ida, I've always wanted to see them, too. Look you, now there's a branch of the railway going there from Namasagali station. It's an overnight trip, but I'll talk to Davey and see what he says.'

"On her next visit, my new friend lost no time in following up on our conversation. She wasn't smiling as she reported glumly that Davey had asked, 'Honest to goodness, Meg, why do you want to go *there*? You know that would have to be an overnight trip on the train, don't you?' Meg continued, indignantly, 'And to add insult to injury, Ida, he remarked (no doubt referring to *your* expanding middle and *my* round figure) that in his opinion neither one of us is in good enough condition to do any climbing! He added that we would only see the mountains at their base, from the train or from a viewing platform (if there was one). And to top it all off, he said that after spending all that time and effort, we might not be able to see the peaks at all because of the mists that usually hang around them.'

"Meg was well wound-up, 'But I was determined, Ida, look you! I shrugged my shoulders at him and told him that we just wanted to look at as much of the mountains as we could see; we wouldn't be doing any climbing and I didn't think that the mists would put us off. I said that you and I are so keen on seeing the *Mountains of the Moon* that we've thought of going on the trip by ourselves, if he and Jack didn't want to go!'

"The disappointment showed on my face, but Meg put her arm around my shoulder as she hastened to say, 'Dear Ida, that was the bad news—I didn't mean to depress you! But my good news will cheer you up! I explained to Davey that this has been a lifelong ambition of yours, and that I had always been curious about the mysterious *Mountains of the Moon*, too. When I said that we two had even thought of trying it alone, if he and Jack weren't interested, he looked quite alarmed and muttered darkly that two women traveling alone on an overnight train journey might be asking for big trouble. To make a long story short, in the end he grumbled that if Jack agreed, he would book the four of us overnight compartments on the train!' Meg's Welsh accent showed again when she added, 'And look you, Ida, indeed to goodness it has been well worth the try. Fed up I am, with these men! Now we'll have to convince Jack!'

"Jack took some convincing, but not wanting to be a spoil-sport he grudgingly agreed, so it was decided. Davey reserved overnight accommodations for us on the train. A week later, we packed our thermos flasks and some biscuits (cookies), and Davey drove us to Namasagali station.

"The train was a relatively short one with only a few carriages, one of which was a dining car with small tables. We parked our overnight bags in our reserved compartments and then sat down at a table for four in the dining car where we could unpack our thermos flasks and have a cool drink and a biscuit or two while we waited for the train to start.

"Tourists swarmed onto the train, lugging their heavy supplies on their backs; their hiking boots clanking on the metal steps as they boarded. In the dining car, two young men were already sitting at the table across the aisle from ours. They both rose to their feet in deference to Megan and me until we had seated ourselves. Introductions revealed their American accents. The taller of the two rumbled in his deep voice, 'Howdy, folks. Nice ta meetcha. I'm Bob and this bozo here is my buddy, Charlie, from the good ole U.S.A.' Are you folks goin' to give the mountain a try tomorrow? We're hopin' to get to the top of the son of a gun this time around!'

"Both Meg and I sensed their infectious spirit of adventure as we heard the two Americans' excited chatter. Next morning they would embark on the first stage of a perilous journey which would take them to their intended destination: the top of one of the *Mountains of the Moon.* When the last passenger had clambered aboard, the guard blew his whistle and the train began to pull out of the station. We rode through a variety of spectacular scenery, always with snow-capped mountains in the far distance. Gradually they loomed closer, and our anticipation mounted.

"When dinner time came, a quick 'wash and brush up' in our compartments was adequate for the four of us before the meal was announced by the attendant. It was a simple meal, compared to the one we had on the trip from Mombasa to Kisumu when I first arrived in Africa. We didn't change our clothes for dinner; everyone on this train was in hiking clothes, making it blissfully unnecessary for us to dress up. Bob and Charlie came and planted themselves across from us again, greeting us like long-lost friends. We lingered on with them after the meal as they joined Jack and Davey in a drink of Tusker beer and lit up their cigarettes. Knowing that I would never have the experience myself, I couldn't resist asking the two lads about the adventure that waited for them at the *Mountains of the Moon.*

"Bob seemed pleased to be asked. 'Sure, I'd be tickled to talk about it. Shucks, this isn't my first time on these lower slopes—I've done some climbing here once before with some of my buddies.' He looked across the table at his friend. 'Charlie, here, hasn't been on this mountain yet, but he's gotten a helluva lot more climbing experience under his belt than me, in other places. Both of us want to get to the top of this one. It will take us days, but we're joining up with a group of guys who plan on going all the way to the summit—God willin'!'

"I ventured, 'Bob, we won't be climbing. We'll just be admiring the mountains from the train, or—better still—from the bottom of the mountain if we can get off and find a place for viewing. Back in England, I've been hearing about the

Mountains of the Moon all my life, and I'm dying to hear about them from someone who actually climbed on one of them. Could you tell us about your past experience on the mountain?'

"Bob smiled and said, 'Well, if you can stand it, sure, I'll tell you my story.' He took a swig of Tusker beer and leaned back in his seat as if to organize his thoughts, then he began:

'Well, folks, I'd be right glad to tell y'all about my previous trip here. First off, let me say that this place has to be seen to be believed; everything here grows *BIG!* It wasn't dubbed *Africa's Botanical Big Game* for nothin', and I sure found out why!

'I joined up with the guys in my group and we started off. As we began the trek, we hiked single-file through a tropical forest trail with vines twined around the tree trunks; huge, wild fig trees—the likes of which I'd never seen—that dwarfed everything around them. I was lucky enough to see blue-faced monkeys swingin' in the trees to eat the figs. They chattered to one another continually; it was good to hear a cheerful sound to break that otherwise uncanny silence. I suddenly noticed a movement on one of the branches in front of me— could hardly believe it when I saw—a chameleon! I'd read somewhere that fossils of chameleons prove that they were in existence since prehistoric times. Wow! They're 'most never seen, but here was this little bugger lookin' at me with its long tail wound around and around the branch to hold it on. I crept a little closer to get a better look at it: an ugly little bastard if ever I saw one—it looked like a lizard with kind of a horn on its face. It was just about invisible, camouflaged to be about the same color as the tree branch itself. I watched and hardly dared to breathe in case I spooked it. It rolled its big round eyes around. I was told later that a chameleon rotates its eyes so it can see out the back of its head without moving it. Pretty neat, huh? It must have seen a juicy insect for an appetizer; it was focusin' its eyes, which can zoom in on its prey like a pair of binoculars. As I watched, the little critter lashed out with its incredibly long tongue that curled around the unsuspecting insect. It popped its catch into its mouth like a flash and swallowed it in one gulp!

'There were all kinds of exotic birds and colorful butterflies in the forest—geez, I could have watched them forever—but there was no time to linger; I had to run to catch up with the rest of the guys on the trail as we trekked onward and upward on the mountain.

'Next we came to a bamboo forest; skinny bamboo tree-stalks risin' 'way above our heads, so close together that they looked like jailhouse bars. They rattled in the wind; an eerie sound if ever I heard one! It's almost impossible to hack a way through 'em, but lucky for us the trekkers ahead of us had made a path through the bamboo. It was very narrow and my backpack kept hittin' the tree-stalks as I trudged along, but that path sure was a real godsend!

'The next part of the trek was through moorland, where the vegetation began to look really weird. It was a little misty here, and through the gloom we could see long strands of grey moss hangin' on the trees near the path, like the stuff you see in Florida. The scrubby ground was covered with super-sized, dark-yellowish, mossy heather—some of it 6 feet tall! It had already started to grow back over the trail that was hacked through it by previous trekkers. Believe it or not, that heather stretched almost as far as we could see.

'We climbed higher and passed into what scientist call a *tropical alpine environment*. We saw plants that looked like they'd been invented for a science fiction story! Dozens of these strange-shaped suckers rose out of the ground. Some of 'em are called giant groundsel. Each plant resembled a huge cactus; I swear to God, some were taller than either Charlie or me—as much as 20 feet high! Each giant ground-sel plant had a big woody trunk with several huge branches; they all grew straight up, topped with an enormous rosette of green leaves and green spiky flowers. I was told that they collect and store water in their stems from the short bursts of rain in the desert atmosphere. Good to know if your water bottle runs dry!

'God help us, equally as fantastic were the giant lobelias! You wouldn't believe those suckers. Each one rose up grotesquely above the ground—a gigantic cluster of green, spiky leaves, big as cabbages. In each leaf cluster was an enormous, fat 'flower'; big around as a tree-trunk, 10 feet high and honeycombed with big indentations. It looked like a huge, punched-up, prickly needle. This plant, too, stores a reservoir of water, which forms ice cubes when it freezes at night. It's known as *the gin and tonic lobelia!* I was kinda sorry that we never needed to try it out! Some of the giant trunks of the lobelias were covered with hangin' moss and orange-colored lichens, making the landscape even more unreal and prehistoric-lookin'. We almost felt like we'd traveled on a time machine to another planet! The cliffs on the mountain were covered with orange colored lichens—they looked unreal, too. The only thing that looked halfway normal about the whole scene was a bunch of little sunbirds that flitted around on their bright, multi-colored wings. They brought us back into our own familiar world. At least we'd seen *birds* before!'

"Bob paused and took a long swig of Tusker. Charlie was listening intently. Even Jack and Davey were intrigued by all he had to say; Meg and I were spellbound. Bob continued:

'We trekked upward toward jagged, snow-covered peaks that were almost invisible in the misty clouds. Little perpendicular waterfalls trickled here and there down the steep slopes ahead of us. It was gettin' dark, so we pitched our tents and we were soon *dead to the world,* as they say. We were awakened suddenly in the middle of the night by loud, God-awful cries that I never imagined could exist; they were so long and persistent. I'd never heard any sounds like 'em—honest to God, it sounded like someone bein' murdered! We listened in shock, but we didn't dare go outside the tent to see what it was in the pitch blackness around us. The howls and screeches went on at intervals all night. It wasn't until much later that we found out that it wasn't some crazy trekker gone nuts on the mountain, but a nocturnal hyrax!'

***

BUNTY: Time out: What on earth is a nocturnal hyrax? It sounds like a disease that strikes in the night—it wasn't far off! The author of the article I found describes what hyraxes look like:

> ". . . furry little animals resembling a cross between a large mouse or guinea pig and a small, short-eared rabbit, equipped with big, round eyes that don't move (in order to focus on anything, the hyrax has to move its whole head!). Hyraxes have oddly-shaped paws and a short, stubby tail. They live in burrows during the day."

So far, the description makes them sound like cute little friendly animals, but apparently they have a downside! They spend 95 per cent of their time resting, but at night the male hyraxes become banshees! They send out a series of hair-raising noises intruding into the night air. First, they emit a prolonged series of loud, frog-like croaks and a high-pitched series of sounds like "wow", "wew" and "woof". Then comes a howling screech, enough to turn the listener's blood cold as it rises to a deafening crescendo and ends with a "whoop:" They repeat this performance over and over; sleep is impossible for anyone within earshot while the yips, grunts, wails, snorts and tweets go on, leaving the listener wide awake with jangled nerves and praying for daylight to come. I read that the noises are made to send a warning or danger signal if the male hyrax is threatened, angry or frightened, or merely defending its territory. How about that for going overboard to make a point? But I'll bet it works!

I had presumed that these creatures are rodents, but it astonished me to read that they are distant relatives (from prehistoric times) of the elephant! They surely did shrink in size, or maybe the elephants simply got bigger! There's only one remnant left in the resemblance, on a much smaller scale: the hyrax's canine teeth are curved, long and pointed like an elephant's tusks. How amazing nature in Africa can be!

***

Let's go back to the train on the way to the *Mountains of the Moon.* Mom reported the conclusion of Bob's story:

"Bob stretched his long legs under the table, shifting them to find a comfortable position. We were all beginning to feel drowsy from our dinner and from the day's traveling. Bob took another long swallow of his Tusker beer. His speech slowed down; we knew he was near the end of his long story. He concluded, 'We'd climbed up to well above ten thousand feet, and I was gettin' more and more exhausted from the altitude. In fact, after another hour I was so feelin' so rotten and fed up that I decided to go back down the mountain with another guy from the outfit and try again some other time. So here I am, today—tarrah! Back again to do just that.' He finished off the rest of his Tusker beer to recover from talking so long.

"Jack exclaimed, 'Well, Bob, me lad, you know how to spin a good yarn! You've told us a marvelous tale, and I know I speak for all four of us when I thank you. We wish you and Charlie the best of luck when you begin your attempt at the summit tomorrow. I'll bet me boots that you'll climb the bastard this time! We'll all be thinkin' of you, and thanks so much for takin' us on that trek up one of the *Mountains of the Moon* with your wonderful descriptions. Bob, me lad, you should write a book!'

"We never found out if he did!

"Meg still looked dazed as she added her compliments to

Bob, 'Oh indeed to goodness, Bob; you painted such a graphic word-picture of your experiences—we almost felt that we were living them with you, even though we won't *see* much ourselves from the bottom of the mountain!' Her tone became motherly, 'Now, off with you both—you two boys get a good night's rest; indeed you're going to need it!'

"Bob said, 'Thanks for the compliments, folks. It's been mighty nice knowin' you.'

"We all stood up and stretched. The two young men gave each of us an American bear hug and wandered off back down the corridor to their compartment. We weren't far behind them, and I'll bet we all fell into our bunks that night and slept soundly, too tired even to have nightmares about those nocturnal hyraxes!

"At daybreak next morning, as if grateful to be taking a rest, the train sat patiently at its terminus at the foot of the mountain. It would begin its return journey back to Namasagali in another hour or two. As we watched, newly-awakened hikers and would-be mountaineers streamed off it to pick up their equipment from the baggage car, to be replaced immediately by trekkers returning from their mountain adventures in various stages of exhilaration and exhaustion. After a quick breakfast, we left the train to stretch our legs and fill our lungs with the refreshing mountain air, as we gazed up at the awesome sight of the snow-covered peaks towering above our heads. As the sun came up, we watched its shafts of light—like bright moonlight—reflecting crescent shapes on the glaciers; the sight that had given the mountains their name. Even Davey and Jack commented that it had been well worth the trip to experience this once-in-a-lifetime sight and to listen to Bob's story. When the train gave a toot to warn us to board it for our return journey, I thought happily, 'Now, someday I'll be able to go back to Sunderland and say I've really BEEN to the *Mountains of the Moon*!' "

***

BUNTY: I would have to wait until my next visit to England to record more about my parents' life in Africa. Time went by, and once again I packed my tape recorder and a good supply of tapes in my luggage.

Mom had worked on her notes; by this time she had made enough to fill a book of her own, but she never wrote one. Once we were all set to do more recording, she gleefully picked up the microphone and her notebook:

A Furry Present

"One afternoon, I was sitting on the verandah reading a book when Omolo came padding in from outdoors. He gave me a smile (almost full of white teeth) as he said, '*Memthahib*, I bring you prethent.' There was a small bulge on a shoulder under his *kanzu* and it was moving! Omolo plunged one hand into his *kanzu* and fished out what looked like a ball of grey fur. '*Memthahib, iko huko* (Ma'am, here it is), he declared trium-phantly, 'buth baby—very tame; he like people; make good pet.' He cradled the little animal in his hands.

"I must admit, it was the cuddliest-looking little ball of fur that I had ever seen. Although I had heard of bush babies and that some people had them as pets, I had never seen one. The little creature looked like a small squirrel, with a bushy tail much longer than its body. It had enormous brown eyes set in the black fur on its attractive little face; its paws were like tiny hands. I was curious, 'Omolo, why is it called a bush baby?' Omolo looked smug as he replied, 'Becauth *m'toto* have buthy tail, sound like baby crying, *memthahib.* '

"I put my hand out to touch the little creature, half

expecting to have to draw it back quickly when a bite was coming, but it licked my finger adoringly. I was captivated. Omolo had brought with him a ping-pong ball, which he put down on the floor. He then deposited the bush baby and rolled the ball away. We watched with great amusement as the tiny creature leaped after the ball, its long, furry tail flying up in the air behind it as it bounded with several long jumps. The ball rolled along the floor of the veranda with the bush baby in hot pursuit. With the final pounce, the ball squeaked to a halt. The bush baby tried to bite it and recoiled in fright when the smooth surface of the ball made it slip away from its mouth. We were both in stiches from laughing. Omolo asked, '*Memthahib* like *m'toto* for pet?'"

"I thought for a minute before I said, 'Well, Omolo, you keep it until I ask *Bwana Amiss* what he thinks about that!' I wasn't at all sure that Jack would appreciate a little furry animal leaping around the house. Shortly after Omolo left, Meg arrived for a visit. I told her about the bush baby.

"Meg didn't hesitate, 'Oh, Ida,' she cried, 'I wouldn't keep it if I were you. I've heard that bush babies can be dangerous to your health. Indeed to goodness, they say they sometimes carry salmonella and other parasitic diseases that can be transmitted to humans—even yellow fever. Especially with your baby on the way, you don't want to risk it!'

"I was almost relieved, 'Thanks for warning me, Meg; it was very tempting to have it around the house. I was almost ready to persuade Jack to let me keep it. What a delightful little creature it was! But now I'm glad I washed my hands after Omolo took it away! I'll tell him what you said, in case he's tempted to bring it back again! Poor lad, I know he meant well; he thinks I'm lonely with Jack away so much, but It won't be too long now before the baby comes, and I wouldn't need anything more to look after, even if there weren't the risk of disease. If I ever do have a pet, I wouldn't mind having a parrot. At least I could keep that under control a lot better in its cage.'

"I never did mention the bush baby to Jack; he would probably have had the whole house fumigated!

***

Ripon Falls

"Meg and I sat in the sunny verandah one afternoon, each with
a glass of Isaiah's cool lemonade to sip. After a few moments,
she burst out, 'I say, Ida, while you're still in pretty good traveling shape, how about all of us going to see Ripon Falls on the
train? That's a short trip—only about an hour's journey—and
there's a good train service from here to Jinja. The falls are
already a tourist attraction—it's been established that they
are the main source of the great River Nile itself.'

"I thought it over. It took me less than a minute to respond,
'That sounds great, Meg. I'm still feeling up to traveling and
it sounds like a good opportunity. I'll ask Jack next time he's
home; I'm sure he would enjoy seeing the falls close-up!' That
will be an easy day trip—I like to sleep in our own bed, these
days.' The next time Jack was home he agreed, and we set the
date for Davey to make our train reservations.

BUNTY: Time out for some background on Ripon Falls in 1925:
In 1862, British explorer John Hanning Speke set out for Africa with
a mission to discover the source of the great River Nile. Flowing for
4,132 miles, (the longest river in the world) it travels downhill from
south to north through central Africa before eventually emptying into
the Mediterranean Sea at the coast of Egypt. So far, explorers had
come up with some good guesses, but nothing really definitive about
its true source. Speke traced the river's true source to the northern

shore of Lake Victoria near the centre of the continent. At Jinja, he discovered a vast, gushing waterfall feeding simultaneously through several channels, falling into a pool the size of a lake to create a wide river which flowed northward. He declared that he had found the true source of the Nile, naming the waterfall Ripon Falls in honor of the First Marquis of Ripon, Lord George Robinson: president of the British Royal Geographic Society which had sponsored and funded Speke's expedition. Speke recorded the measurements of the water-fall by guesswork, but he wasn't too far off. He described the falls in his notes with words tumbling over one another:

"The falls—about 12 feet high and as much as 400 or 500 feet from side to side—were broken by outcrops of rock. It was a sight that had the hypnotic effect of wanting to watch it for hours. The roar of the water; the sight of thousands of passenger-fish leaping up the falls with all their might; the fishermen coming out in boats to stand on the flat rocks with rod and hook; hippopotamus and crocodile driven down to drink at the margin of the lake below; made in all, with the pretty nature of the country—small, grassy-topped hills with trees in the intervening valleys on the lower slopes—as interesting a picture as one could wish to see."

The Ripon Falls were later officially measured more accurately as 16 feet high and 900 feet across. They became a great tourist attrac-tion as the years went by until 1954, when they were submerged by the building of the nearby Owens Falls Dam to create much-needed hydro-electric power for the surrounding area.

Mom adjusted her glasses and continued the story:

"Davey made all the arrangements for our trip to Ripon Falls. Shortly afterwards, early one morning the four of us boarded a first-class carriage on the earliest train out of Namasagali railway station for Jinja, starting our day in the dining car with cups of coffee from our thermos flasks. The passing scenery began as scrubby grassland, spotted with short trees and bushes similar to the ones seen on our journey to Kenya on the *Lunatic Express.*

Here and there, we saw a few impalas and giraffes through the carriage windows. The wide Victoria Nile was always within sight; occasionally we passed natives—standing on the riverbank and some in boats in the river with their fishing rods cast—hoping to haul in a good catch of fish. With a couple of stops along the way, it took the train a little less than two hours to arrive at Jinja."

***

BUNTY: Before our foursome get off the train, here are a few words about Jinja:

Jinja town and port are situated at the head of a bay on the north shore Lake Victoria. It was originally a small fishing village; its name in Swahili meant "the rock," and it was known in the area as "the place of flat rocks." Located at the source of the River Nile, Jinja town stood astride the now-submerged Ripon Falls. When we visited the falls, Jinja had already became a popular destination, gaining prosperity from the tourist trade. As well as its establishment as an important lake, river and railway junction, in the 1920s Jinja also boasted a new European hospital.

There is an interesting aside about the name of the town of Jinja, recorded by Winston Churchill in his diary after going there to see Ripon Falls, ". . . it is a pity to handicap the town with such an outlandish name—better to have named it Ripon Falls, after the beautiful cascade which lies beneath It."

This time, for a change, Mr. Churchill didn't have the last word.

***

Mom described her experience of seeing the falls:

"When we stepped off the train at Jinja, we found the station bustling with activity. Tourists assembled on the station platform to join their tour groups, with cameras slung around their necks and wearing safari-like shirts and pants, their heads topped with new-ly-bought pith helmets. We milled around with them to get to the station exit. There was a row of rickshaws outside on the street, so we rode from the station to the little guest house already familiar to the Griffiths. After a light breakfast, we made a reservation for lunch so that we could eat and be ready in good time catch the train back to Namasagali in the daylight. A small tourist bus was waiting for passengers, so we signed up to be taken out to Ripon Falls on its next run.

"The bus jolted and shuddered along the rutted, dirt road skirting the river, emptying its passengers out at the entrance to the path-way leading to Ripon Falls. We could hear the falls long before we saw them; their presence announced by the roaring and pounding in our ears as they came into sight, and what a feast it was for the eyes! We sat down on a bench and watched, hypnotized. The water feeding the falls became swirls of green which turned into a torrent of white foam. Fussing and fuming, it divided itself to tumble down through spaces between several small islands of flat rock, to join again into one giant flow. Once over the falls, the white water soon subsided to form a lake, from which the river—now a hundred feet wide—flowed north as the Victoria Nile.

"Winston Churchill's diary also had something to say about the width of the Ripon Falls with its separate cascades. He character-ized each one as being '. . . nearly as wide as the River Thames at Westminster Bridge!'

"'The four of us sat in mesmerized silence for awhile. 'Well, Sunshine, what do you think?' Jack's voice struggled to penetrate above the thundering of the falls. I moved over on the bench, closer to his ear. My enthusiasm knew no bounds. 'Oh, I'll never forget this as long as I live,' I shouted; 'what a spectacular sight!' I turned to our friends on the bench next to me, leaning in toward them and speaking as loudly as I knew how, 'And thank you so much, Meg and Davey, for suggesting that we come. I wouldn't have missed this for all the tea in China!'

"Meg screamed back, 'Honest to goodness, Ida—indeed, I'm glad we came, too.'

"Hundreds of fish flashed in the sunlight as they leaped up the falling water. We watched Ripon Falls in enforced silence, walking the length of the well-worn footpath and stopping frequently along the way to view the awe-inspiring sight. Conversation was out of the question, and I giggled to myself as I watched our fellow waterfall-watchers yelling comments at one another above the roar of the water, or maintaining a stoic silence, overcome by the sight and sound of that booming flow. I couldn't help thinking to myself, 'I must be walking on thousands of invisible footsteps! Countless pairs of feet have carried people over this same ground, before and since the white man discovered Africa—I wonder how many other travelers like ourselves have gazed in awe at the source of the River Nile?'

"Sadly for this great landmark, in 1954 the fabulous Ripon Falls would disappear when they were submerged by the building of the much-needed hydro-electric dam at nearby Owens Falls. But I was so glad to have seen Ripon Falls before that happened, and even more so that Jack had captured the sight on our camera as a reminder.

"I was glad to sit down and take my growing weight off my feet on the bus ride back to the guest house, where we hungrily devoured a delicious late lunch. All four of us were weary on the train ride back to Namasagali, listlessly watching the lush scenery bordering the falls, undulating hills, sugar cane and tea plantations that slid by the train window. We arrived home in time for dinner, but I was almost too tired to eat Isaiah's usual tasty meal. I tumbled gratefully into bed and fell asleep almost immediately. Next day, I wrote home to Sunderland with great enthusiasm to tell the family about our day's excursion. But now I had to admit that I wasn't too comfortable traveling distances any longer, as my pregnancy was advancing."

BUNTY: Mom's voice was getting tired. She turned off the tape recorder and said, "I think it's time we had lunch, so I'll put the kettle on for some tea with our sandwiches. After lunch, Dad can continue awhile and I'll rest *my* eyes for a change!"

***

After our lunch break, Dad switched the tape recorder on and picked up their story:

Obonyo's Cow

"Sunshine's Indian Doctor Singh had told her that she should drink fresh milk (boiled, of course). I thought to meself, 'Well, Jack, me lad, we'll just have to get a cow! There isn't a milkman here like the daily one in Sunderland. I remember him as clearly as yesterday! He came down the street early in the mornin', with a horse that pulled a cart with a big milk churn on the back of it keepin' the milk cool. He called out, 'Milk-ho, Milk-ho,' and the housewives dashed out into the street with a jug and asked him for a gill or two (a small measure) of milk. The horse stood patiently while the milkman reached into the milk churn with a long ladle and filled the jug—I think it only cost two or three pennies! Then the customer paid him and he'd climb back up on the cart and click his tongue for the horse to start again. I can still remember them amblin' away down the street, with his cries of 'Milk-ho, Milk-ho' gettin' fainter as they went on to their next customers. O by gum, those were the days alright, and how things have changed!

"But now we had to figure out what to do about gettin' fresh milk at Namasagali. I thought to meself, 'I'll ask Obonyo—he knows everythin' about everythin'. Obonyo lit up when I asked him where we could get a cow. He was always on the lookout for business; here he saw a perfect opportunity.

"We invited him to sit out on the verandah with us, so we could talk it over. He began, in his 'pidgin English': 'Happy you ask me, *bwana*. Now that *piki-piki* paid for, I look for bride. I see lovely girl in next village, so I have to save money to buy cows; bride price asked by father. She cost a lot. At first, her father want ten cows, four goats! She beautiful girl, but I bargain with him; we agree six cows, two goats. I have to work hard to get cows, goats easy to pay. I get cow for you, *Bwana Amiss*, maybe two. I will keep in *boma* until I can buy six I need. You pay me for milk. All of us happy. What you think?'

"I slapped him gratefully on the back, 'Good for you, Obonyo; that sounds like a great idea.' We solemnly shook hands on the deal.

"I took Obonyo with me to the dock at Namasagali port to watch his cow bein' unloaded from a tender and to help bring her safely to the *boma* down the hill. Ida named her Daisy, as she didn't know anyone by that name who might resent having a cow named after her. Daisy's milk was as fresh as her name! She was sleek and fat, just as a good dairy cow should be, and she produced a seemin'ly endless supply of milk, which Ida drank by the glassful (after it was boiled) every day. Omolo had soon learned how to milk her, and the good lad always remembered to wash his hands before he did so."

BUNTY: Fascinated by the story of Obonyo'a cow, I did some research on tribal marriage customs:

When Mom and Dad were in Africa, tribal laws still dictated the greater proportion of the natives' actions, although by the time of this writing many of them have been discarded or rescinded by updated legislation. Back in the 1920s, most native women had virtually no control over their lives, and in areas away from cities and large towns this might still be the case.

In the early days, a girl would often be promised in marriage at age five or six (marriage by eleven years old was usually normal). She was expected to have sex after her first menstrual period, also after being widowed or having had an abortion. Not all tribes circumcise their boys, but circumcision for girls (now called female mutilation) is still common in many countries, including Africa, leaving a little girl in continual pain and open to infection.

A daughter was totally under the control of her father before marriage. At puberty, she was judged as ready to be bartered to a husband, to be virtually in bondage to him for the rest of her life. A man could have as many wives as he could afford. Marriages were arranged by the girls' parents; the father dominated all the arrangements—even the wedding feast was celebrated in his home. He would dictate a price for his daughter, according to her age and her beauty; the price was set by the value of a cow, sheep or goat. A cow could be quite expensive, representing several months of work for the prospective bridegroom. Haggling over the bride price was taken for granted, so the father would usually set the amount much higher than he hoped to get. Polygamy was traditional; in a man's lifetime, to have five or six wives was common.

A new husband took it for granted that his bride price payment gave him the right to abuse his wife (wife-beating was not uncommon). If he found her unsatisfactory, he also had the right to reject his wife and demand a refund of the bride price from his father-in-law! If the wife died in childbirth without children, the bride price was refundable to her father, unless the husband decided to replace her with one of her sisters. It is hoped that new legislation will rescind this kind of tradition.

***

Back to Mom and Dad! Refreshed from a brief nap, Mom took out her notebook and read the next chapter of her life into the tape recorder:

> "After our full social life at Kisumu, I had bouts of boredom when we first moved to Namasagali. The solution, much like that in Kisumu, was to make one's own entertainment. The Griffiths were adept at doing this, and they invited us to join

with their circle of railway employee couples and their families in sharing dinners and picnics at one another's homes.

"I took it upon myself to teach the Railway Girls how to play mahjong. We had some pretty good games, once they got the hang of it. I also took my turn to invite them for luncheons and teas. Jack called these occasions 'hen parties' (while the 'roosters' were all out at work).

"Isaiah loved to help fill the menus for the hen parties. We worked together to make little meat pies and salads for lunch to go along with his crunchy bread, followed by some of his newly-learned English dessert pastries. I was never quite sure what kind of meat Isaiah put in his meat pies; when it was cut up in small pieces and cooked, it was impossible to identify it. I had a sneaking suspicion that it might have been something he picked up in the market, so one day I got up enough courage to ask him. He beamed and announced with pride, 'Oh, yes, *memsahib*, I use goat meat—fresh and delicious.' And, by golly, it was! Nobody was ever the wiser—they never asked, in fact they usually came back for a second helping of Isaiah's meat pies at my luncheons.

"At my teas, we would serve dainty tea sandwiches and little English pastries, warm buttered scones and sometimes that spectacular dessert: an English cream trifle. Truly dedicated to his cooking skill, Isaiah was pleased to be learning something new and to show off his English recipes, just as I was enjoying learning some of the local cuisine from him.

"These activities made a welcome break in the monotony of an otherwise isolated existence. When it was my turn to entertain for a dinner, Isaiah proved himself to be the master chef that I knew he was. He produced a roast chicken dinner that could compete with the best restaurants in London!

"I still I mourned the loss of the social life that Jack and I had enjoyed in Kisumu; I missed the club and the company of friends we had made there. Especially, I missed Effie and Ted. But it was too far and too inconvenient for us to travel back and forth from our new outpost on the Nile to attend club activities in Kisumu or even to drop in for a visit once in awhile. Visiting was even quite a challenge with the new, far-flung Namasagali neighbors; without Meg's driving, it would have been impossible for me.

"Davey's new car was his pride and joy. I remember how careful Meg was, the first day she drove it to take us both shopping, testing its shock absorbers as it bumped along to the market on the rutted road which covered it with red dust. She always remembered to dust it off before driving to the railway station to pick Davey up from work, to make sure she could ask for it again!

"When I began to feel bored, I learned to keep myself busy sewing and writing letters or playing the gramophone. Also, there were always out-of-date newspapers and magazines to read. In those days, the method of delivering mail to our remote location was sporadic, to say the least; it was mostly accomplished by train and from Namasagali station by the road which was uncertain at best and was inclined to disap-pear altogether in the rainy season. The natives were more efficient with news; they used relays of runners, also drums that communicated messages from one village to another, rain or shine.

"Meg's companionship was invaluable, but much as I valued her friendship, I found myself beginning to yearn for the daily companionship of a baby son or daughter of my very own. It wouldn't be too long, now.

***

Christmas with the "Commish"

"In Namasagali, it felt even less like Christmas than it had in Kisumu, with the sunny climate producing flowers in full bloom. Possibly with a pang of conscience regarding his duty toward the scattered British residents in the area, our genial District Commissioner, 'Reg', traditionally gave a Christmas buffet 'high tea' for all of us outpost-dwellers at his magnificent home on the outskirts of Jinja. This Christmas was no exception. As soon as the Griffiths received the invitation, Davey offered to drive Jack and me to the affair. This time, I didn't have to wonder what to wear—I only had one decent maternity dress that fit me! Jack protested as usual about his cummerbund, and, as usual, it remained where it had always been—neatly folded in his drawer.

"On Christmas Day, we bumped our way in Davey's car over the dirt road at Namasagali until it reached the smoother highway to Jinja , finally coming to a halt in the 'Commish's' driveway at his front door, where it was whisked away and parked by a liveried attendant. What a relief it was to get out of the car after that bumpy ride! I seemed to be feeling it more than usual, with my baby's arrival only a few more weeks away. With all the jolting on the journey, by the time we stopped I was convinced that my teeth had been shaken loose and that the baby-to-be had been sloshing about, thinking that it was rainy season on the ocean.

"The Commissioner's house was lit up like a beacon and decorated lavishly for the occasion. The front door, sporting a large cardboard Santa Claus, was opened by a pretty maid in uniform. Indoors, the house was decorated to the hilt. Rooms were hung with garlands of multicolored paper chains strung across the ceilings, and in the grand front hall stood a large Christmas tree, its branches looped with strands of silver tinsel mingled with dozens of hanging glass ornaments of all colors and sizes.

"In the big sitting room, the carpets had been rolled back to transform the wooden parquet under them into a smooth dance floor. Couples were already dancing to gramophone records playing somewhat dated dance music hits from Britain. I envied the couples dancing and I but felt sorry for Jack, who loved to dance but was dutifully staying by my side. 'Why don't you go and dance, love,' I said charitably, 'maybe you could bring a little pleasure to one of the ladies in that row of unclaimed treasures sitting over there by the wall.' Jack, of course, couldn't resist, and I sat morosely with my bulk wedged on a straight-backed wooden chair, watching his expert steps steering one of the 'wallflowers'—and what's more, *enjoying it!*

"After what seemed like ages, a butler came into the room with his little gong to summon us to the dining room. The non-dancers among the men had been in the smoking room for a glass or two of wine and a smoke. When they emerged, I was horrified to see Algie! When he caught sight of me, he gave me a conspiratorial wink and waved. Dreading a repeat of his unwelcome attentions, I ignored him. I could feel many eyes following his, to look me up and down. Algie charged across the room and seized my hand. He gushed, 'Aw, Ida ewld deer, it's been simply *ages* since I've seen yew. Yew certinly look bloomin'—how *are* yew?'

"'Aha,' I thought, 'this is the perfect opportunity for me to discourage him'. Jack had finished his dance and was standing with a surprised look on his face. I said, 'Oh, hello, Algie. Yes, I *am* blooming—I'm expecting a baby and I feel just fine. I'd like you to meet my husband, Jack Amiss,' adding firmly, 'well, it *was* nice to see you again.' The men nodded rather abruptly to each other. I had meant my '*was*' to sound dismissive, but Algie's hand was still clinging tightly to mine. I dropped it as quickly as I could twist it free so that Jack and I could escape and head for the buffet table in the dining room. Jack said, in an undertone, 'That cheeky sod! He acted as if a juicy young lass like you was more than he could resist! You'd better steer clear of that one, Sunshine.' Wisely, I didn't reply!

"The buffet table was a sight to see! There were platters of smoked fish and sliced meats, salads, vegetables of all kinds, crispy bread rolls, fancy sandwiches, an enormous fruitcake, little mince pies. Dishes of fresh fruit made a colorful touch, and tea was ready for self-service in large silver urns. Jack and I filled our plates, and he carried them into the gracious, wood-paneled dining room. We found our places marked with little engraved name cards. Again, Jack was seated across from me, and I found my place next to a woman whom I recognized as one of the 'wallflowers' with whom Jack had danced earlier. Her name was Mildred. She was somewhat hesitant and soft-spoken. I introduced myself, and we chatted quietly with each other. I heard the chair next to mine being pulled out for someone to sit down. Glancing to see who it was, I saw—who else? Algie! He said brightly, 'Well, well, well, we meet again, my deah!' I thought it best to say nothing and hope he got the message.

"At each place-setting around the table, lay a Christmas cracker: a cylinder of cardboard about 6 inches long covered with red crepe paper. At each end of the cracker, the crepe paper was gathered into a red ribbon tied tightly with a bow. The tip of a small gunpowder fuse could be seen protruding out of the cracker at each end.

"An English Christmas tradition followed. Gripping the end of the fuse between finger and thumb, the owner of the cracker invited a partner to take hold of the other end and pull it at the count of three. Both ends of the fuse were pulled simultaneously, each making a loud 'crack' (which gave the cracker its name). The cracker-owner would then do the same for the partner with his (or her) cracker. I turned quickly to my new friend Mildred and offered her my cracker before Algie could offer his cracker to me. Mildred timidly took hold of her end of the fuse with finger and thumb, and I did the same with the other end. She closed her eyes tightly and at the count of three we both pulled. Mildred cried, 'OOOh!' and I thought she would fall off her chair from the shock. The cracker had erupted with a small explosion, leaving a smell of gunpowder in the air. We did the same for hers. There were similar 'cracks' going off all over the dining room, and the butler quickly opened both doors to let the fumes escape. Everyone opened his (or her) cracker. The cardboard cylinder contained a folded paper hat and a small piece of white paper with a 'fortune' written on it, also a tiny noise-maker. We tested out toots on the noise-makers and then the table sprang into bloom as we put on our paper hats in all their colors, shapes and sizes, to be worn for the remainder of the meal. After all the hubbub had quieted down, we took turns around the table to stand and read our fortunes aloud, chuckling over the silly things they said. When it was my turn, I hoisted my bulk to my feet and read, '*You will meet a tall, dark stranger.*' I couldn't resist looking down at my large bulge with a theatrical grimace and adding, '*But you're a bit late!*' The 'fortunes' were a great ice-breaker, and by the time we began to attack our plates of food, our famous English reserve had disappeared. Sitting around the table wearing our outlandish hats, the roomful of strangers suddenly became friends laughing together.

"Leaving the dining room after the meal, we trooped into the sitting room where tradition dictated that coffee would be served, along with a buffet selection of English cheeses and 'water biscuits' (crisp, salted crackers). There was more dancing in the sitting room for those who wanted to work off all the food they had eaten. Meantime, the sun had set and the equatorial night had descended like a pitch-black blanket. Indoors, we didn't care; the candlelight from several candelabra made the room even more festive. At last, Meg and I said our thanks and farewells to Reg and his wife, making a swift detour to the posh indoor *choo* before getting into the waiting car. On our way home, Meg said, 'I say, Ida, I noticed how annoying Algie was with you; he's quite cheeky (nervy), you know. You were wise to discourage him; he does this with all the new female arrivals, and the rest of us just take no notice.' I had never told Meg or Jack that Algie had groped me at the welcoming dinner—that fact is just getting made public now, on this recording! Fortunately, Algie never followed up, much to my relief!

"The ride home was a slow one as Davey steered the car along the unlit road. Despite his car headlights being on their high beam, he had to lower his speed and strain his eyes to stay on the road to avoid going off it altogether or hitting some creature wandering across it. After more bumping along, Davey carefully delivered us to our front door. Jack thanked the Griffiths, and I could hardly wait to dash into the bedroom, strip off and get into my night clothes. I can't remember— either before or since—when I've felt more relieved to hop into bed!

"I envied Meg's ability to drive their car and its convenience for getting around in a place with non-existent local transportation facilities. In those days in England, it was rare for women to drive cars (there were very few cars to drive, anyway!) In Jack's world of male chauvinism and dominance, a wife's place was in the home; probably females were widely considered not to have enough mechanical ability (or enough sense) to cope with a car!

"I could never understand why Jack didn't buy a car of our own. He seemed to regard the internal combustion engine with great suspicion, and to believe that cars in general were dangerous and unreliable. While we were in Africa, I complained bitterly in a letter to Mother about the absence of a car. Although she wouldn't have dreamed of riding in a car herself, she retorted in her reply to my letter of complaint, 'I can't understand an engineer not wanting a car, Ida! I suppose that Jack knows all about a ship's engine but nothing about a motor car's. Maybe he's worried about losing control of a car or not being able to fix one like he could with one of his turbines—or maybe he's just too stubborn to learn how to drive! To be honest with you, dear, I can't see much sense to those nasty, noisy, smelly things myself!'

"My next adventure would cure me of wanting a car! In the meantime, life went along pleasantly at Namasagali as Jack and I came closer to the next big event in our lives."

"Jack woke up here and said, 'Did I hear you talking about me, Sunshine?' I didn't answer.

***

Ripon Falls

Dad meets Daisy

NOW WE ARE THREE

BUNTY: There was another long interval between my visits to England, but when Mom saw the tape recorder, she whipped out her notes:

Doctor Singh to the Rescue

"We had already begun to make preparations for the coming baby. When we first arrived in Namasagali, we decided, well ahead of time, to mail-order the equipment we would need: a cradle on wheels (bassinette), a tall, wicker pram (baby carriage), a child's cot (crib), a playpen, high chair and a large canvas washbowl suspended on a stand (bathinette). Shortly after our trip to Ripon Falls, Meg took me on a shopping trip to Jinja. In one of the *dukas* in the big market, I had found some beautiful, cream-colored pure silk and soft, white, cotton-lawn fabric. I had the turbaned proprietor cut me a few yards of each. My sewing machine worked diligently to convert the soft cotton into baby dresses and nightgowns (worn both by baby boys and girls, in those days). The silk was reserved to make a christening gown, which I lovingly hand-crafted with rows of tiny tucks on the bodice and above the hem.

"It took several weeks for the cradle and baby-bath to arrive; both were stashed away in the master bedroom, ready and waiting. The playpen, high chair and cot arrived a little later and were stored to have on hand when the baby was older (realizing how long it would take for the items to come through, we had decided to order them all at one time, ready to have on hand before the baby was too old to use them!).

"Dr. Singh had insisted that I should come to the hospital two weeks before my due date, in case the baby decided to arrive early. The nearest European hospital was about 55 miles away at Jinja, and the good doctor had offered to solve my problem of how to get there. 'Mrs. Amiss,' he said, in his rapid, clipped, sing-song English, 'my brother will be driving his car to Kampala on business at about that time. I have arranged so that you will accompany him as far as Jinja, if you agree. I shall be at Jinja hospital to make sure you are well received.'

"I could hardly believe my ears! My words fell over one another as I hastily replied, 'Oh, thank you, Dr. Singh, you have taken such a weight off my mind!' Now almost at the end of my pregnancy, I had been dreading the thought of climbing on and off a train—or worse, a river steamer—to get transportation to Jinja. Davey had offered to drive me to the hospital, but Jack and I felt that the 100-mile-plus round trip would be an imposition on him to be avoided if possible. Doctor Singh's arrangement was a solution straight from Heaven!

"It should take less than two hours by road from Namasagali to Jinja, and I was thrilled at the welcome prospect of getting a comfortable ride to the hospital, where I would stay in plenty of time before I was due to go into labor.

"My suitcase was packed, and the date to leave soon rolled around. I was ready at daybreak, and shortly afterward we heard a car's horn tooting outside the front door. A large touring car with a canvas roof was waiting. To my astonishment, it was already full to overflowing with passengers! Dr. Singh hadn't mentioned that his brother was bringing his wife, her brother, sister-in-law and two children! However, the car was wide enough to allow me to squeeze into the front seat next to the driver.

"When Omolo carried my suitcase out to the car, he stowed it away somewhere in the back. As I was squeezing myself into the front seat, I had noticed that the dickey (rumble seat) was open, and that several sheets of corrugated iron had been stacked across it. For a brief moment, I wondered what they could be doing in there, but this was interrupted as Dr. Singh's brother introduced his wife, her brother, sister-in-law and two children, all of whom *salaamed* politely. In a matter of minutes, the car was in motion and we jolted off on the packed red dirt road which would hopefully take us to a smoother one going to Jinja.

"Once on the road, the driver drove slowly with his heavy load. Everything went fine until the sun came up in full force and began to beat down on the canvas roof of the car. Air conditioning hadn't yet been invented for cars and I felt as if I'd been trapped in a greenhouse! As the perspiration started to run down my back, I became aware of something else in the car. In the days before the more universal use of deodorants, the passengers were exuding a distinctive and objectionable odor! Any other time, this wouldn't have bothered me as much as it did, but in that confined space it made me dread taking my next breath! Later, when I told Jack, he rightly or wrongly blamed it on the fact that the Indians cooked with ghee, which, in those days before deodorants, could be detected in sweat. This refined butter came in tins. It was readily available at the markets, or it could be made by clarifying butter to obtain the butter fat (ghee). Ghee was favored for its convenience in keeping fresh longer than regular butter, and it had a pleasant, nutty, buttery flavor. However, like any other butter, if kept too long without refrigeration (of which there was none in those days) it developed a rancid smell which, when mixed with even a short time's worth of perspiration, was inescapable in a closed car in tropical heat! I furtively reached for the knob on the side door of the car to wind the window down, but as I did, a mixture of hot air and red dust rushed in on me. The driver clicked his tongue at me and shook his head. I hastily closed the window again, and resigned myself to remembering not to inhale too deeply!

"I still couldn't figure out what those sheets of corrugated iron in the dickey seat were for. As the car bumped and lurched along on the rutted road, they caused a deafening clatter with every bump or lurch—but at least this was a change from the non-stop Punjabi conversation in the shrill voice of the driver's sister-in-law. I thought to myself, 'That corrugated iron must weigh a ton! I wonder why they're bringing it with us? I hope the car can hold up under the weight it already has, now that I've added another body and a half, and my suitcase!' Little did I guess that I would find out soon enough!

"There were dried-out patches in the road, hardened by the sun into hard baked clay ruts that ox-carts had made in the mud after the last rainstorm. The car jolted over them, tossing all of us up and down like eggs in a crate (seat belts had not yet been invented). At every bump, the children bounced up and hit their heads on the canvas roof, generating delighted shrieks. I wondered how my baby must be weathering what must have felt like a storm at sea!

"There was virtually no traffic to be seen for miles. As we began to come nearer to the coast of Lake Victoria, there was marshy ground on either side of the road. At a low point on the road, we saw what looked like a long puddle that had been too deep for it to dry out completely after that last heavy rain. The driver came to a halt at the edge of the quagmire, and the men scrambled out of the car. Taking one of the corrugated iron sheets from the dickey seat, they placed it lengthwise on the ground over the wet mud. Next, they carried a second sheet and placed it end to end with sheet number one. The driver hopped back in the car and drove it slowly ahead. It inched across corrugated iron sheet number one and onto sheet number two, where it stopped again, leaving number one free. The men heaved up sheet number one and laid it lengthwise against the front end of end of sheet number two. The car jerked and groaned across sheet number two and onto sheet number one again, in order to leave number two clear. The men then picked up number two and placed it end to end in front of number one, and so on, until the car could be driven safely on to firm, dry road. We came to several more drying puddles of unknown depth. For a longer puddle, the sweating men needed to employ corrugated iron sheet number three, but happily this only happened once. After they had laboriously restored all the muddy corrugated iron sheets back into the dickey seat, we continued on our way with very mud-stained men. Fortunately, the car never got stuck in any mud—with no other vehicle on the road with anyone in it to help us, we could have been there forever! I tried to squeeze further away from the driver, so that I wouldn't be mud-stained, too.

"Because the corrugated iron performance had to be repeated several times more, it lengthened the time it took to get to Jinja. I was grateful to Isaiah for filling a thermos with cool lemonade, and that I had remembered to bring it with me into the front seat. After extracting it from its tightly wedged spot between my thigh and the door of the car, the sips of cool liquid helped me endure the heat and the bouncing vehicle with its load of smelly passengers. At one point, the car had to be stopped for the children to get out and relieve themselves by the side of the road, so the rest of us got out, too. With no convenient bush in sight, and with modesty thrown to the winds, we all followed the children's example, glad of the opportunity and also to be able to stretch our cramped legs (I thought mine would never function normally again). I also began to wonder if we would ever reach our destination, but eventually we pulled in to the driveway at Jinja hospital.

"As the driver slowed the car, Dr. Singh ran out of the hospital, waving his hands in the air for us to stop. The driver stood on the brake, and the car screeched to a halt, flinging its passengers forward and jolting us back again like human eggs. I said a silent prayer of relief, now that the torture of the drive was over.

"I prayed too soon! The doctor rushed up to the stopped car and gabbled something to his brother in Punjabi. Still breathless and very agitated, he turned to me and gasped, '*Memsahib Amiss,* I fear you cannot come into the hospital! Man came to hospital this morning mauled by leopard—his wounds septic. Alas, I cannot have maternity patient here with septic man! My brother is going on to Kampala on business, so I have arranged with him. He will take you there where is good hospital and you will have nice baby. I will send telegraph to tell them you are on the way.'

"My spirits hit rock bottom with shock. In panic, I thought, 'Oh, no! It's at least another hour's drive to Kampala!' Normally, this would have devastated me, but I was too numb to do anything but accept the situation for what it was. I rationalized that I should be grateful that the good doctor had acted to protect the health of myself and the baby. We used the opportunity to get out of the car to stretch our legs while staff at the hospital worked to provide us with sandwiches and fill our thermos bottles with cool drinks, ready for the next 53 miles to Kampala.

"The road was well paved leaving Jinja, making traveling much more comfortable than it had been up to now, and the rest of the trip was also made more bearable by a cool breeze blowing in off the lake. When I cracked my window open an inch, this time there was no scowl on the driver's face. The smooth road, lined with palm trees, wound along the shore of Lake Victoria where the views of the great lake were breathtaking. I had to remember that it was the size of Scotland when I gazed across it and couldn't see any land, even on the horizon. The blue water was dotted with small islands and boats of all shapes and sizes, a soothing sight for my weary eyes. I don't remember much of the fifty-plus-mile drive to Kampala; the smooth road and soothing glimpses of the water allowed me to doze off from time to time.

"I didn't know how exhausted I was until, at long last, the car pulled into the driveway at Kampala hospital. A nurse came to help me out of the car. I was glad she did, otherwise I would probably have fallen out! My legs almost refused to unlock from their cramped position to hold me up. However, the good manners my mother had taught me reminded me to thank the driver, who touched his hand to his turban and with a little bow said gruffly, 'I was coming to Kampala, anyway, *memsahib.* Good luck with baby!'

***

BUNTY: This is a good time to put in a few words about Kampala—after all, it was going to be my birthplace, and each of these African cities had such differing histories:

With an elevation of 3,900 feet above sea level, Kampala sits near the shore of Lake Victoria, straddling the equator. Not far north from there, rolling hills form the lowlands of the Great Rift. Like ancient Rome, Kampala was built on seven hills! It is the capital of Uganda and its largest city (at this writing, it stretches over fifty hills!). The thirteenth- fastest-growing city in today's world, it now boasts its share of skyscrapers and over a million tourists per year.

Before the British arrived in the 1800s, Kampala was capital of the ancient native kingdom of Buganda. The earliest history of Uganda states that the *kabaka* (king) had declared the area surrounding it to be a hunting preserve, particularly for impala. In the Luganda language, Kampala means 'hill of the impala'. The earliest known historical record of Uganda estimates the date of King Kato Kintu as king of Buganda to be about 1300 AD. A descendant of Kintu still reigns in the kingdom of Buganda.

Note: Back in 1926, my birth certificate was written in the Luganda language. In 1946, I had to get it translated into English in order to get a passport to enter the United States!

In 1880, the British East Africa Company built a fort at the site, and in 1894 the British Government incorporated Uganda as a British Protectorate. By the 1920s, it was dominated by British colonialists and Indian merchants. In 1926, to Mom and Dad's eyes, Kampala must have looked very sophisticated in comparison with Kisumu, and even more so with Namasagali!

***

Mom went on with the rest of her story:

"Those few steps to the hospital door at Kampala felt to me like a few miles, stiff and sore as I was from that awful day in the car: a prisoner cramped up in the in the heat, the smells and all that bumping along on those miserable roads. I had to keep telling myself that I had been lucky to get a ride! And it could have been much worse; the ultimate calamity hadn't happened. The baby could have decided to be shaken loose, and then what would I have done, giving premature birth in a hot, smelly car without a doctor? I shrugged off the nightmarish thought.

"Now, here at last I was safe and made comfortable in a hospital bed with white, downy sheets. When a nurse came into the room with a light meal, I thought—somewhat skittishly, 'There can only one explanation: I've died and gone to heaven!'
"It was almost dark by the time the doctor on duty came in to examine me. I slept that night as I had never slept before; in fact, I slept until mid-morning the next day! I was awakened by a nurse, 'Time to wake up, Mrs. Amiss; there's someone outside who wants to see you.' Jack erupted into the room. He took my hand and held it so tightly that I thought it would be compressed into three fingers. His voice was husky with

emotion, 'Good mornin', Sunshine, thank goodness you're alright.'

"I thought I was dreaming. How could Jack possibly know where to find me? He explained, 'On the ship, word was telegraphed to me from Jinja that you were bein' taken to the European Hospital at Kampala, but no details. I was worried stiff! I contacted me friend, Jim Hollingsworth, the stationmaster at Kampala, who in turn contacted his wife, Mary. She'll be comin' to visit you this afternoon to offer you their hospitality and make you comfortable while you're in Kampala.'

"I was so overcome with relief that I broke down and howled with pent-up tears. Jack put his arms around me. 'There, there, Sunshine,' he comforted me, patting my shoulder, 'you've had an anxious time worryin' about what could happen next, but everythin's goin' to be just fine from now on. You'll love Mary when you meet her.'

"Jack stayed and shared my coffee while I ate a late breakfast, then he said reluctantly, 'Well, Sunshine, you're in the best of hands now and I must get back to my ship. I'll be seein' you again very soon—maybe by that time our baby will be here. I'll be able to get a couple of weeks off to take you and the little one back to Namasagali and get you settled; I want to be on hand to help with whatever I can when we get home, just so I can rest easy before I go back to the ship again.'

"We had a long hug, kissed, and he was gone. I settled back on my pillow and drifted off into sleep again, my mind clear of all worry. Later that afternoon, there was a knock on the door and in walked a tall, beautifully dressed, aristocratic-looking woman. All I could think of was that the Governor of Uganda's wife must have come to call on me!

'Hello, Mrs. Amiss; I'm Mary Hollingsworth.' The lovely arrival spoke in a cultured voice. She glided into the room and sat by my bed; I caught a faint whiff of perfume. She continued, 'I have a proposition for you. You won't want to be cooped up in this hospital until the baby comes; you'll see enough of it afterwards when the doctor keeps you here for some time after you have the baby! So, Jim and I would like to invite you to stay with us until you begin your labor and also when you come out of the hospital with the baby. What do you think?'

"What did I think? I was so moved by this act of friendship that I wiped away a tear that had crept out of my eye and was on its way down my cheek. I was so touched that I almost began to sob again, but I realized that she needed a response, so I dabbed my eyes dry and replied, 'Oh, Mrs. Hollingsworth, how very kind of you—I would love to come and stay with you.' She leaned over and gave me a hug. 'Well, I think it's time for 'Ida' and 'Mary', don't you; no more formal surnames?' And so began a friendship that lasted for the rest of our lives.

"The doctor kept me in the hospital until he was satisfied that I had recovered from the stress of the car trip following my being rejected at the Jinja hospital. Jim Hollingsworth collected me in his car and brought me to their beautiful home. Such luxury I had never seen: perfectly-kept antique furniture; a dining room with walls paneled in lustrous, imported wood; beautifully-furnished bedrooms, and a verandah with views of the lake rivaling those of the Victoria Nile at Namasagali. My bedroom was spacious and comfortable with flowered chintz curtains to complement a matching overstuffed chair and footstool. I thought to myself, 'Ida, you'd better make some notes; you can pick up some great interior decorating ideas from all of this!'

"The Hollingsworths made me feel at home from the minute I arrived. Tall and slender, Mary was the epitome of English dignity, and wore clothes that made me feel envious. She seemed to be unaware of her lovely appearance instead of flaunting it, which endeared her all the more to me. Her husband, Jim, was a big, raw-boned man with dark, wavy hair and bright blue eyes; his jaunty air and jovial manner offset and complemented Mary's quieter personality. Their teenaged daughter, Helen, bounced up to me and gave me a hug when I arrived; her eyes glancing over my bulky figure with the typical curiosity of her age. She had obviously been told about the expected arrival of a new little life—I'm not sure whether or not she knew all the details—but she was probably storing up a whole list of questions to ask Mary when I was out of earshot.

"Mary knocked on the door and came in while I was still admiring the pleasant room. 'It's only me, Ida,' she said, 'why don't you lie down for awhile, and I'll call you when dinner's ready? We're here to take care of you for the next few weeks, you know, and we want to do our very best to make you comfortable.' Her sweetness made me dissolve into grateful tears again, meriting another hug and little comforting pats on the back of my shoulders. When Mary had left, I lost no time in shedding my tent-like dress and lying down on the bed. Sleep overtook me. I awoke refreshed, and after a thorough visit with the washbasin I was ready when Helen knocked on the door to announce that sundowners were being served on the verandah. The candles on the dining room table were softly gleaming when the Hollingsworth's cook announced that dinner was ready; he proved himself a good second to my prized Isaiah with his handiwork.

"The next days with the Hollingsworths sped by. There were excursions to Kampala town with Mary. It had a magnificent shopping centre compared with the pitiful *dukas* at Namasagali or even with the shops at Jinja. Mary borrowed the car with regularity, and we had rides through the beautiful countryside on roads that were much better than those on the banks of the Nile. Dominating the view of the entire area atop one of the hills was the red-brick Namirembe Cathedral, presided over by the Anglican Bishop of Uganda.

"At the Hollingsworths', I slept under my mosquito net with feelings of relief and comfort. Then, one night, the first impact of dull pain woke me. I waited until there was another pain before calling Mary. She came hurrying into the room, and we wasted no time in checking to make sure everything I needed was packed in my suitcase before she roused Jim.

"We drove to the hospital as the first blush of sunrise appeared in the sky. It was as if giant fingers were guiding a celestial paintbrush to trail color across a pale blue background. It had been rightly dubbed 'the golden hour', imprinting wide streaks of gold, orange, melon-pink and pale-yellow light on the new day to chase away the black shadows of the night. I had never seen such a spellbinding sight before, and the image of it has stayed with me all my life.

"Mary and Jim helped me up the steps at the front of the hospital to the reception desk. The building was silent, as if sleeping along with its occupants. The nurse on duty was engrossed in reading a book. A few strands of bright auburn hair had escaped from under her starched white cap to fall onto her forehead. Pushing them back, she looked up when we arrived, and said cheerily with a distinctly Irish brogue, 'Well look ay here! Saints be praised, Mrs. Amiss, 'tis you after all! To be sure, we were beginnin' to wonder when you would be comin' for a visit. We're all that excited at the prospect of a new baby arrivin'. We don't get many childbirth cases—begorra, this is a real treat for us! Your room's all ready and waitin' for you. We'll be seein' a lot of each other, you and me, so just call me Norah. You come along now, there's a fine gurrul.'

"Mary and Jim stayed long enough to make sure I was comfortable in my hospital room. Mary said, 'Well, Ida, my dear, next time I see you there will be a new little one for Jim and me to welcome. You're in good hands, love, so *chin up!* Jim will get word to Jack as soon as possible.' She bent over me with a quick hug and kiss. Jim took my hand and squeezed it. Then they were gone, just as another wave of pain washed over me.

"I said to myself, 'Well, Ida, now it's up to you: you'd better pay attention and get on with the job!' A nurse came to time my pulse, then to take my blood pressure. Wave after wave of pain engulfed me as the contractions got closer together.

Even the pictures in Dr. Singh's medical encyclopedia hadn't prepared me for this, although I remembered listening to the stories when my mother invited her friends to tea. At some point, the conversation inevitably included an exchange of their experiences of childbirth—outdoing one another with the agonizing details.

"I remember feeling that I had completely lost control of my own body. There was a vague impression of a second nurse, who mopped my perspiring forehead, and a doctor who gave me a whiff of something as the pains got harder and harder. I must have drifted in and out of consciousness, but I recollect pushing obliging when they told me to. After that, my impressions ended with crescendos of pain blurring into one long agony. What felt like endless hours crawled slowly by. At last, I heard a baby's tiny wail.

"A man's voice broke into my stupor, 'You have a lovely little girl, Mrs. Amiss—6 pounds, 2 ounces.' Just turn your head, and here she is.' A tiny, pink human being was being held up for me to view. My eyes reflected wonderment at what I was convinced was the most beautiful baby I had ever seen. Tears of relief streamed down my cheeks. The doctor bent over me again, 'Congratulations! Mr. Amiss has been reached and he's on his way here.'

"Back in my room, how thankful I was to feel the luxury of release from pain as I drifted off into an exhausted sleep! After what seemed like only a few minutes later, I awoke to hear Jack's voice. He gently shook my arm. Hardly able to suppress the excitement he was feeling, he bent over and kissed me. 'Hello, there, Sunshine, 'he whispered. 'Well, well, look what YOU'VE done!' He pointed to a cradle on legs, which had been wheeled alongside the bed. I was sure it hadn't been there when I fell asleep. Snuggled under a soft blanket, the baby was stirring. As if on cue when I leaned over to look more closely, our daughter's face puckered. Her serene little features reddened as her face contorted into a demanding howl. I recoiled in dismay; what to do? Just then, Norah popped her head around the door. 'Well, the good Lord be praised, Mrs. Amiss, you're awake—and by the sound of her, so's the baby! Begorra, she's got a good pair o' lungs! Ah well, let's get you propped up; now's a good time to meet that new daughter of yours!'

"And so our new family life began; as Jack said, 'Just think, Sunshine, now we are three!'

"My stay in the hospital kept me busy night and day. Never having been around babies, I didn't know that they took up so much of one's time. I almost forgot what a good night's sleep was; it seemed that no sooner had the baby enjoyed one feeding than she was ready for the next! Norah was right, she *did* have a good pair of lungs and she wasted no time in letting me know she was hungry again—her appetite seemed endless!

"I realized that I knew virtually nothing about how to take care of a baby. In addition to the arrival of the cradle, a changing-table stood against the wall of my room. When bath time came, Norah brought in a collapsible stand. Opening it up, she firmly inserted a large canvas washbasin in the top, into which she poured warm water. From my perch among the bed pillows, I watched while she tested the water with a bent elbow, undressed the baby and carefully held her in the water, sponging her gently all over. Lifting her out of the water, Norah expertly flipped her onto a waiting towel on the changing table, wrapping it around her and patting her dry. Taking out a container of sweet-smelling baby powder, she smoothed it all over the little body to complete the process.

The next flip involved depositing the baby onto a waiting terry cloth 'nappy' (diaper), folded into a triangle. The point of the nappy's triangle was brought up between her legs, to be joined with the other two points around her waist. Norah held the three points together, securing them with a huge safety pin to make the nappy into a neat pair of terry cloth panties. Rubber baby pants were then slipped over the nappy to complete the operation. (Lucky mothers nowadays don't have to go through all of this, with the advent of disposable diapers that come already as waterproof panties!) Now that she was securely pinned and waterproof, my baby was ready to be dressed for the day. Lifting the tiny head with one hand, Norah slipped it through the open neckline of one of the soft white cotton nightgowns that I had made during my plentiful free time, BB (Before Baby). Suitably impressed, I realized that this was a procedure that needed practice. I groaned, 'Oh, Lord, I'm all thumbs and I'll never remember all of this stuff!' But before I left the hospital, I had become quite adept at flipping and patting, and the baby didn't object to being slid by me into the warm water for her bath or shoe-horned into her nightgown.

"I was kept at the hospital for almost three weeks for a 'postpartum confinement' period. Statistics show that back then, one in every ten women died from the aftereffects of childbirth, before modern antiseptics and antibiotics were invented to control infection. The traditional lying-in period, as it was commonly called, was to allow the new mother's body to heal and recover itself from the ordeal of childbirth; it usually lasted from ten to twenty days. During that time, the new mother was not allowed to get out of bed until the doctor was satisfied that everything was back in place, and that the few cuts that he may have had to make to ease the birth were completely healed.

"To my great joy, the baby was a good snuggler. I enjoyed feeding times to the hilt, when she snuggled in the crook of my arm while devouring her liquid meal. Luckily, I was able to supply enough of this to keep her happy, and before I left the hospital she was allowing me to sleep through the night. My own meals at the hospital were delicious, prepared carefully and tastily, and served to me in bed on a lap tray.

"Jack had sent a telegram to the families in England telling them the good news, and already I had received a telegram from the Ditchfields in response, saying how thrilled they

were. The baby was the third grandchild for Mother and Father
Ditchfield, but she was the first girl. My sisters Hilda and Millie
each had a little boy, so there was great celebration in the
family when the first granddaughter made her appearance.

"I was getting used to the fact that motherhood meant
that my time was no longer my own; the baby kept me fully
occupied. In between her naps I sometimes sneaked one for
myself, to be ready for a bumpy night. Norah was good company, often sitting on the end of my bed and reading to me
tales in her family's letters about their goings-on in Ireland.
She usually ended with, 'As God's me judge, Mrs. Amiss, to be
sure they're a rare lot!'

"The doctor came to give the baby and me checkups each
day for the first few days, feeling my stomach and nodding his
head with an affirmative-sounding grunt or two. I interpreted
the nods and grunts as his idea of giving me encouragement,
which he confirmed when he said, "Oh, yes, you're making
good progress, Mrs. Amiss, and the baby is very healthy.' Other
than these few words, he floated in and out again in his white
coat without further comment. Looking at my flabby middle,
I despaired of ever being normal again. But my recovery was
evidently satisfying the doctor; after a week, he allowed me
to put my feet down and to walk a few tottery steps with
Norah's strong arm supporting me. Soon, Norah and I were
walking the entire length of the hospital corridors.

"Next came short walks outdoors, always with someone
whose arm was there for support when needed. Mary was
happy to come and walk with me as I graduated to strolls
on the hospital grounds; we shared each other's news and
thoughts in the cool morning air. The 360- degree view from
the hospital was spectacular: mountain ranges in one direction, the blue expanse of Lake Victoria in another, and the
fast-growing city of Kampala spread out beneath us, with
the great cathedral always in sight atop Namirembe Hill
(the word 'namirembe' means 'full of peace' in the Luganda

language). I often wondered what it must look like inside that huge church dedicated to the memory of the Christian martyr, Bishop Hannington. In my overactive imagination, I dreamed the impossible: that our daughter could be christened in that beautiful building. I put the thought out of my mind. 'After all,' I said to myself, 'in England, only people such as royalty are christened in a cathedral!'

"Mary and Jim Hollingsworth were adamant that the baby and I would stay with them as long as I wished, before returning to Namasagali. It seemed to me as if I had lived a lifetime since that day when I had staggered up the hospital steps in labor, but on his final visit, the doctor said the baby and I could leave. Jim and Mary picked us up. I found to my surprise that Mary had outfitted my bedroom with Helen's baby cradle on legs and a table which I could use for the flipping and patting routine after bath time. She had also installed a portable canvas basin which they used periodically when they went on picnics. What a wonderful friend! More days of recuperation saw me regaining strength, culminating in the unforgettable experience of our daughter's christening.

***

BUNTY: Mom's awe of Namirembe Cathedral was impressive to hear. I must digress here to tell the story of the man whose memory it honors, Bishop James Hannington, without whom it wouldn't exist:

James Hannington was born at Hove on the south coast of England in 1847. Educated in the ministry, he became a cleric in the Anglican Church with a calling to become a missionary. After the necessary preparation, in 1884 he was appointed by the church hierarchy to become the missionary Bishop of Eastern Equatorial Africa in Uganda. A Christian mission had begun in Uganda in the 1870s, with the endorsement of *Kabaka* Mutesa, native ruler of a large area of Uganda.

However, this king died in 1884, and was succeeded by his son, *Kabaka* Mwanga, who violently opposed any foreign presence in Uganda, including the missionaries.

In 1885, Hannington and his companions were making their way to their new destination at Kampala, where they hoped to build a church. Before they could reach their goal, they were attacked by native warriors sent by *Kabaka* Mwanga. Most of them were tortured and killed, including Bishop James Hannington. Historical records state that the dying Hannington cried to his attackers, "Tell your master that I have purchased the road to Uganda with my blood." Mwanga was later exiled, but returned—having been converted to Christianity—to grant land in 1890 for the building of an Anglican church on Namirembe Hill in Kampala.

Somehow, Hannington's remains were retrieved and brought to be buried at the site of the first Namirembe Cathedral in Kampala , the church which he had hoped to build as his life's goal, but which he never lived to see. The cathedral was rebuilt four times; each time, Bishop Hannington's remains were exhumed and buried at the new church. The present immense brick cathedral, containing his tomb, was dedicated to his memory. On a stone memorial tablet on the outside wall of the cathedral is carved a paraphrase of Hannington's reputed last words to his attackers as he lay dying: 'Tell the *Kabaka* that I die for Uganda'. Namirembe Cathedral is an enduring, thriving testimony to his sacrifice. The story of its tempestuous history follows later.

***

Mom told her next story with a nostalgic smile:

"Early in my pregnancy, Jack and I had discussed names for the baby. Our choice was simple: a girl would be named Ida after me, and a boy would be named John after Jack. We deliberated about a middle name. Although it was customary in England for children to be baptized with more than one name (a tradition originating in the Middle Ages, having been handed down centuries earlier from the Roman nobility) the Ditchfields had chosen not to give an extra one to me, so I was just plain Ida Ditchfield. However, the Amisses gave each of their children a middle name. Jack said, 'Well, Sunshine, *me* Mam and Dad gave me the middle name Heywood, carrying it with me to the fourth generation. It was the surname of a distant grandmother and had become an Amiss tradition. Since you don't have a middle name, dear, let's keep the tradition going and name the baby Ida Heywood Amiss if it's a little girl, or John Heywood Amiss if it's a little boy.' And so it was decided, now that she had arrived, to name our baby girl Ida Heywood Amiss, carrying the name Heywood to the fifth generation.

"Next time Jack came to see me at the Hollingsworths', I shared with him a lofty ambition. 'Jack,' I began, 'I would really like to have the baby christened here in Kampala. I don't like the looks of that little run-down, corrugated iron church with its tin roof near the marketplace in Namasagali, when we have this beautiful Anglican cathedral right here in Kampala, almost on our doorstep. What do you think?

'Well, blow me down, Sunshine!' he exclaimed, I've been thinkin' along the same lines: 'While we're at it, let's try to aim for Namirembe Cathedral for our baby's christening!' I remember that me Dad always used to say, ALWAYS TRY FOR THE TOP, LAD; THERE'S MORE ROOM UP THERE THAN THERE IS AT THE BOTTOM! Wouldn't it be a great honor for our daughter to be christened in a *cathedral?* She would be proud of it for the rest of her life.'

BUNTY: And she is! Also, Mom and Dad's grandson's middle name is Heywood, carrying it to the sixth generation.

Mom continued:

"I still had rather important questions for Jack, 'By the way, dear, I thought I'd ask Mary Hollingsworth to be godmother; after all, she's been so kind to me and the baby, before and since Little Ida was born. Have you anyone in mind to ask to be her godfather? Jack didn't hesitate, 'Oh aye, I'd like to name me best friend, John Ryles. We know he won't be able to attend because he's back in England, but I know he would be honored to be asked. I'm sure Jim Hollingsworth wouldn't mind standin' in as proxy for John'.

"I was excited, 'Oh yes, Jack, by all means let's ask John Ryles to be godfather; he's been such a good friend to you since you were boys together in Sunderland. And I'll ask Mary to be godmother; I'm sure she would be thrilled to hold Little Ida at the christening. I have a feeling that Mary will always stay in touch with her afterwards, too'.

"Sitting at breakfast next morning with Mary, I said, 'Mary, my dear, I can't begin to tell you how happy you've made me, inviting the baby and me to stay with you like this—someone you didn't even know! Jack and I would love to have the baby christened here in Kampala, before we go back to Namasagali. Mary, will you be her godmother?' Mary didn't hesitate. She replied, 'Oh, Ida, I'd consider it an honor; of course I will be her godmother! And we'll never know if she can be christened in Namirembe Cathedral unless we go and find out—let's make a trip to try to see the bishop.'

***

Namirembe Cathedral

BUNTY: But first, a word or two about the history of Namirembe Cathedral seems appropriate. The story sounds like a bad movie, but it has a happy ending:

Namirembe Cathedral is the oldest church in Uganda. The first time the cathedral was built, in 1890, it was on land granted by the *kabaka* at the foot of one of the seven hills of Kampala; Namirembe Hill. It was constructed in native fashion, with tree-poles supporting its woven reed walls and a thatched roof. It was built to seat eight hundred worshippers. However, it had been built on swampy ground, which caused it to be abandoned a year later to be rebuilt on higher ground; the rebuilding was also needed to accommodate its growing congregation. Between 1891 and 1892, the second cathedral was built, to seat three thousand. Nature intervened; in 1894, a high wind in a tropical storm blew the roof off. The interior was ruined by the torrential rain pouring into the building, so the cathedral had to be rebuilt once more. The third building was completed in 1895. It seated four thousand. Constructed with local wood, it was abandoned because of serious termite damage which threatened to weaken, and eventually destroy, the structure.

The fourth cathedral was constructed between 1900 and 1904, with an estimated ten thousand people attending the opening cere-mony. Sadly, in 1910 this church also fell victim to the power of Nature; it was gutted by fire caused by a lightning strike in a tropical storm, and had to be totally rebuilt once more.

Erected between 1915 and 1919, the fifth and present huge Namirembe Cathedral of Saint Paul was constructed atop Namirembe Hill with earthen bricks and earthen roof-tiles. At this writing, it boasts five hundred pupils in its Sunday school classes for toddlers through 13 -year-olds, and has a very active adult congregation of over four thousand.

***

After a short break, Mom was anxious to continue her story:

"Jack and I had decided that as soon as possible after the christening we would return to Namasagali. We had inconvenienced Mary and Jim long enough—as we used to say in England, we didn't want to wear out our welcome.

"So we began with our first step; to see if we could hold the christening in Namirembe Cathedral! When Jim handed over the car to Mary a few days later, she dropped him off at his railway station and Helen at her school, before picking up the baby and me to drive us to the cathedral, hopefully to see the bishop and ask if we could arrange for him to perform the ceremony. We entered by the carved front door and I achieved my ambition to set foot in this magnificent building. Our destination was the vestry; a small room off a hallway at the end of the nave, used by the bishop as an office. As we walked down the long, central aisle of the nave, I was aware of the enormity of the cathedral with its soaring arches and raftered ceiling far above our heads. There were stained-glass windows on both sides of the nave, depicting scenes from the Bible. The light streaming through them dropped pools of color on the flagstone floor which echoed our footsteps. We lowered our voices almost to a whisper to speak the words of reverence that we felt; but they still echoed through the empty nave, leaving behind them an awe-filled silence.

"We walked slowly toward the chancel and found the vestry with its door open. As luck would have it, the bishop was sitting behind his desk. I had been nervous about meeting a real bishop, but he turned out to be a pleasant fellow, with the professional manner of a seasoned church dignitary balanced with a knack of putting people at ease. He admired the baby, who blinked at him obligingly, and told us what to expect at the traditional Anglican Service of Infant Baptism. Mary listened intently. As the godmother, she would be required to hold the baby in her arms at the font and hand her to the bishop for him to baptize at the appropriate time. The words of the service sounded vaguely familiar to me, having attended the christening of Bryan, my younger brother, long ago in Sunderland. My nervousness gradually melted away as we chatted with the bishop, and we parted after filling out the information needed for the baptismal certificate. The date for the christening was set for the following week.

"The christening day dawned bright and calm. Jim, Mary, Helen, Jack and myself, with the star participant (the baby) arrived half an hour before the ceremony so as not to risk being late for such an important occasion. The empty cathedral looked even larger to me than before. Sunlight poured in through the stained-glass windows, slanting across the rows of pews. Our footsteps echoed, as an elderly usher in his black robe escorted us to sit in the front pew in front of which stretched the chancel and the altar. The carved, stone christening font was waiting, partially filled with what I hoped would be warm water. The organist played quietly as we settled ourselves in the pew. Sleeping blissfully, the baby looked beautiful in her christening gown. I took private satisfaction in knowing that I had been instrumental in making two such lovely products!

"I was nervous, to say the least—too nervous to move in case I woke the baby. I was vaguely aware that there were some people in the front pew across the aisle, but dismissed the notion that we would know them, thinking that they were probably visiting tourists who were sitting quietly to witness the glory of the cathedral with a christening ceremony as a bonus. The baby didn't stir; I began to relax. I looked across the aisle again more carefully. I was glad I was sitting down or I would surely have collapsed with astonishment—I could hardly believe my eyes! The two couples sitting there were none other than Effie and Ted McTavish and Meg and Davey Griffith! I could scarcely adjust to the reality of their being in Kampala or that they were here to share this wonderful moment with us! How did they find out where and when the christening was going to take place? Or that it was going to take place at all? It had seemed unfair to ask them to travel so far to join us at such short notice, so we hadn't told them about it. Later, we learned that news of the christening-place, date and time had been communicated to both husbands by Jim Hollingsworth the previous week through the railway stationmasters' network, and he had sworn them to secrecy to surprise us! That turned out to be the understatement of the year! We were stunned! It had been a true labor of love for both couples to travel such distances from two different places to surprise Jack and me. I thought my mind was playing tricks on me! We smiled and waved but didn't venture out of our seats to greet one another; the bishop was expected to arrive at any minute. McTavishes had come from Kisumu by train, the day before; Davey and Meg Griffith had driven all the way from Namasgali, bringing the offer to drive us back with them on the following day.

"Right on time, the bishop appeared. He walked slowly down the aisle in his heavily embroidered ceremonial regalia, flanked by two altar boys looking like cherubs in their flowing, white surplices. They came to a halt by the font. The bishop handed one of the boys his ceremonial staff; the other boy stood in front of him to hold his prayer book open so that he could read the words of the baptismal service with his hands free. The bishop motioned to Jack, Jim, Mary, Helen and me to come and stand beside the font. I carefully placed the baby in Mary's arms and said a fervent prayer that the water would be warm; I had one horrible moment visualizing the alternative: my daughter feeling ice-cold water on her forehead and letting out an out-raged howl from the shock! She was still sleeping peacefully.

I had taken off her shawl so that the skirt of her christening gown cascaded down over her little legs, falling gracefully into folds to show the tiny tucks near its hem that I had sewn so laboriously. I indulged in a moment of pride to admire my eye-straining work which had paid off so handsomely, before paying full attention to the words of the baptismal service being read by the bishop from the Anglican Book of Prayer.

"Jack and I made our promises to bring up our daughter as a Christian in the Anglican Church—-promises which she would confirm when she was old enough to do so—and then it was time for Mary to step forward with the baby in her arms. Jim stood next to her as proxy for the real godfather, John Ryles, in England. He made the promise, on John's behalf, to see that the baby would receive a Christian upbringing if any tragedy happened to prevent Jack from doing so. As godmother, Mary made the same promise, on my behalf. The bishop asked Mary what the name of the baby was to be, taking the tiny bundle into the crook of his arm. He dipped his free hand into the water in the font. I silently prayed that the water was warm! The bishop made the sign of the cross on the little forehead and laid his hand gently on the baby as he intoned, 'I baptize thee Ida Heywood Amiss, in the name of the Father, Son and Holy Spirit.' As I watched, Little Ida suddenly opened her eyes. 'Here it comes, Ida,' I thought, 'I wonder what it will sound like when that howl reverberates through this huge building?' I held my breath and was rewarded with—silence! The bishop handed Little Ida back to me and I breathed a sigh of thankfulness; she was gazing up at the soaring ceiling above us with wide open eyes, not uttering one peep!

"The altar boy holding the ceremonial staff put it in the bishop's hand, while the other altar boy closed the bishop's prayer book with a firm 'clap'. We went with the bishop to the vestry where Jack and I signed the baptismal certificate. The bishop then signed it and gave it to Jack. He shook our hands, and we felt that we had been dismissed.

***

BUNTY: With a lifetime to look back on, I have now realized that my life has been directed by a series of preplanned coincidences beyond my control. Before we leave Namirembe Cathedral, let me fill you in on my surprising connection with the man it honors: Bishop James Hannington:

Could it have been only a coincidence that in 1926, because a man had been bitten by a leopard, I was not born at Jinja after all the arrangements had been made, but at the next hospital at Kampala—another 50-plus miles away, where my father happened to have a friend?

And when I was a few weeks old, was it a coincidence that at Kampala the bishop was in his study for Mom to see him without a pre-arranged appointment, and that he agreed to conduct my christening in his cathedral—beyond all my parents' dreams? And was it a coincidence that this was Namirembe Cathedral, the church dedicated to the memory of martyred Bishop Hannington? The series of coincidences continues:

I returned with my parents to live in England when was two years old. Fast-forward to 1939: By now, I was a young teenager at our home in a London suburb, when Hitler broke a treaty with Britain promising that he would not invade Poland. Drunk with conquest as he gobbled up Europe and ignoring his treaty with Britain, Hitler ordered his vicious Nazi storm troopers and Luftwaffe to attack ill-prepared and ill-equipped Poland. Despite a heroic effort to defend itself, Poland succumbed to the overwhelming German odds. Because of Hitler's breach of promise and its brutal results, the outraged British declared war on Germany, endangering London as a prime target for Nazi bombers. In accordance with carefully pre-planned voluntary arrangements with their parents and with hosts and hostesses in the reception areas, London's schoolchildren were immediately evacuated to towns a safe distance away from the endangered city and its surrounding suburbs.

With my girls' prep school, I was evacuated from London by train to an unannounced destination 60 miles away, which turned out to be a town on the south coast of England. Of all places, could it be a coincidence that this town happened to be Hove—Bishop Hannington's birthplace? And was it another coincidence that the newly-built church in the Anglican diocese where I happened to be billeted in Hove was named The Bishop Hannington Memorial Church? And was it yet another coincidence that this was the year when I would study to confirm the promises made by my parents, at my christening in Namirembe Cathedral, Bishop Hannington's memorial church in East Africa? And because of the string of circumstances caused by a war, was it only coincidence that my confirmation ceremony took place in the Bishop Hannington Memorial Church in Hove, England,—6,500 miles away from his cathedral in Kampala, Uganda where I had ben christened?

I wonder if Bishop Hannington's ghost recognized me?

Coincidences? There have been so many more in my life—I believe otherwise!

**

But now, let's go back to 1926 in Uganda, where more coincidences followed the christening day of Ida Heywood Amiss. Mom was impatient to continue:

"Outside the cathedral door, there was a great 'meet and greet' celebration going on between the McTavishes, the Griffiths and the Hollingsworths, with introductions, hugs and kisses, followed by a rush by our friends to admire the baby, contentedly slumbering in Helen Hollingsworth's long-outgrown carry-cot. We now had a special name to call our daughter: Little Ida. I was so thankful that she had been so contented all through the ceremony. Could it be that she was already waiting for the next coincidence?

"Jack insisted on treating everyone to a substantial lunch at one of the hotels in Kampala. We lingered over our hearty, cooked meal, chattering and bringing one another up-to-date on our news. I felt enfolded by the warmth of such good friends on a day I shall never forget. Little Ida slept contentedly after having had her lunch when I excused myself and took her into the lady's restroom to give us some privacy.

"The McTavishes and Griffiths had made overnight hotel reservations, so they decided to do some sightseeing together in and around Kampala while the daylight lasted. Davey was briefed with directions to the Hollingsworths' address, ready for the following morning when he and Meg would pick up Jack, Little Ida and me for the trip back to Namasagali. After exchanging goodbyes and hugs with Effie and Ted, we were taken home for the night with Jim and Mary Hollingsworth. I was glad to get into bed for a rest after all the festivities and excitement. Jack packed up my belongings ready for the following day.

"Davey was tooting the horn at the front door at daybreak next morning, as arranged. Before we left, Mary held Little Ida in her arms and gave her a kiss on the forehead; Helen bent over her and planted another kiss next to her mother's. Davey remarked that Meg couldn't wait to get her hands on the baby! She begged, 'Oh, Ida, may I hold her?' She held Little Ida on her lap for most of the journey back to Namasagali, reluctantly giving her up when we had a rest stop and I took the opportunity to care for Little Ida's needs again in the ladies'restroom.

"The car traveled smoothly at a good speed on the road from Kampala to Jinja, but it slowed down on the dusty, rutted one as we approached Namasagali. Little Ida slept peacefully through all the bumping and jostling (I speculated on whether she could have remembered it from the drive from Namasagali to Kampala before she was born!) At the end of the long day, we pulled into our own driveway a short time before dark. Davey tooted outside our front door and Obonyo and Omolo burst out of the house, their smiles wide in welcome. Jack got out of the car and gave my suitcase to Omolo. I handed Little Ida over to her father so I could get out of the car. A look of panic flitted over his face but he took the little bundle carefully into his arms, remembering to put his hand under her head to support it. I hugged Meg and Davey, thanking them for their thoughtfulness in coming to the christening and bringing us home. Jack handed the baby back to me with obvious relief. 'You'll have to get used to this, Jack,' I teased. He sounded defensive, 'Well, blow me down, Sunshine, give me time to get used to the idea. I'll soon get the knack of it, just you wait and see—If I can steer a ship, I can navigate a baby!'

"Next morning, after one of Isaiah's superb English breakfasts, Jack and I were sitting on the verandah enjoying the view. Omolo came timidly to the verandah. I beckoned him in. He asked, shyly, '*Memthahib Amith*, pleathe could Omolo thee *m'toto*?' 'Of course, Omolo,' I replied, I'll let you know next time she's awake.'

"From the moment he saw her, Omolo hardly let Little Ida out of his sight. He would probably have been the most faithful nursemaid anyone could wish for, but Jack and I decided that we would hire a professional *ayah* (nanny) as all the European women in the area did for their children.

Ayisha—Crisis in Paradise

"The ayah duly arrived—a Kikuyu beauty who looked to be in her late teens. Her name was Ayisha. She was tall and willowy, with the body and face of a model, and with the grace when she walked that I had always admired in the native women. I introduced her to the houseboys and heard them mutter appreciatively among themselves, '*Ayisha msichana mzuri sana*' (Ayisha's a very beautiful girl.) She spoke English very well, and had a sophistication about her that commanded respect. What was most important, she knew all about babies and discharged her duties with professionalism. She announced, '*Memsahib Amiss*, I also make beds and do baby's washing.' I wondered, 'How lucky can I get?'

"Ayisha was given the large guest bedroom next to ours to be near Little Ida, and she soon settled in. I supervised the first few times when she gave Little Ida her bath and learned the patting, flipping, nappy-folding-and-pinning drill, all of which she did flawlessly. I hovered over her the first few times that she dressed the baby for the day and put her in the pram which stood ready on the airy verandah with its hood up. Precautionary mosquito netting would be securely tucked in, as soon as Little Ida was safely aboard.

"Omolo tried not to show his jealousy of Ayisha. This was an emotion that I had never seen in him, but now his normally happy face wore a frown when he watched her with the baby.

"But Omolo's were not the only emotions to be affected by Ayisha! One day, when Jack was home, there was an unusual commotion in the backyard. Jack went out to see what was happening, and came back almost at once to the verandah where I was relaxing while Little Ida napped in her pram. He looked worried, and said quietly, 'Sunshine, they're fightin' over Ayisha. I want you to take the baby, go into our bedroom and close the door, to be away from all this upset.' I wheeled the baby in her pram into the bedroom with me and actually locked the door behind me. I was terrified for Jack's safety. I had heard what sounded like a vicious fistfight going on outside the back door among the houseboys, with a lot of shouting. Then I heard Jack roar at them, '*Shari gani? Kwacha kelele, mara moja.*' (What's all this? Stop the noise, immediately.) Thankfully, I heard the noise die away. After what seemed like a lifetime, Jack came back. He said, 'You know, Sunshine, they must have been workin' up to this ever since Ayisha arrived! I'll pay her, then we'll have to let her go, I'm sorry to say.'

"Sad as I was to see Ayisha depart, I realized that this could be the only solution. On the other hand, Omolo was elated. 'Now I take care of *m'toto, Memthahib Amith''*, he exulted. I told him that although Ayisha was gone, we would have to get another *ayah* to take her place. I couldn't resist teasing him with a conspiratorial smile when I added, 'but this one will be old and ugly!' I never knew whether Omolo believed that I was serious, but if he did, he kept it to himself!

"It was several more weeks before we found a replacement for the departed Ayisha. During this time, Omolo insisted that he would do the baby's laundry, resulting in a row of blindingly white nappies, small sheets and towels flapping in the breeze on the outside clothesline. He watched for them dry, and then snatched them off the line before the red dust could get at them. Omolo became quite adept at ironing, too, and seemed to take pride in heating the iron on Isaiah's grill to the perfect temperature for pressing the tiny garments on the ironing board in the kitchen. He kept a wary eye on every movement Little Ida made. When she finally mastered the art of rolling over, Omolo watched her closely, sharing with her each triumphant smile she gave him after she successfully completed the maneuver.

"When the new *ayah* arrived, she wasn't old or ugly, but short and sturdy—a nice, plain-looking girl who didn't have Ayisha's provocative wiggle or those beautiful eyes that could melt any man who looked her way. Her name was Rachel.

"Rachel made life so much easier for me! She even earned Omolo's grudging approval when she frequently enlisted his help. She was very competent, and had the loving way of a true nanny with Little Ida. I was soon able to leave her to do the daily washing-flipping-patting and dressing routine. As Little Ida grew older, Rachel became adept at bottle-sterilizing, also. Because there was no refrigeration, Daisy had to be milked every day. Rachel always made sure that enough milk was boiled, cooled and strained daily, to fill the sterilized baby bottles. Omolo was proud to milk Daisy himself. He and Daisy became good friends; I think she knew that he always made sure to wash his hands before beginning. On his part, he made sure that Daisy was always comfortable in the *boma* down the hill.

"My life took on an extra dimension after the arrival of Rachel. She was tolerant of Omolo's insistence on helping with Little Ida, and especially welcomed his help in things like carrying the cumbersome pram and playpen up and down the verandah steps to give the baby an airing out of doors in the cool of the morning. Omolo never minded carrying her used bathwater outside to dump it on the flowerbed. His ever-present vigilance gave me an extra feeling of confidence in leaving Little Ida in Rachel's competent hands. Meg and I could go on a trip to the market together without my worrying about exposing the baby to the noise, smells, dust and heat that went along with it.

"As Namasagali expanded as a railway depot and river port, it also was also developing other industries. Not least of these was the tourist industry, bringing in an influx of visitors to establish it as a popular new centre for safaris. The train connection could now bring would-be-explorer tourists to the town, where they could join organized safaris in many different directions. Realizing the need for the protection of game and natural beauty in East Africa, the British Government had begun to designate large tracts of land in Kenya and Uganda. These reserves would later be conserved as national parks. After they were established, their guides helped the tourist industry to thrive on resulting safari trips to view and photograph the wildlife and flora, under safe supervision.

"With Rachel's arrival, I was free again to join with Meg's cluster of friends who traveled to one another's homes to play cards or to share luncheons and teas, or both. A new friendship developed between myself and one of the other Namasagali wives, Cynthia Smith: a pretty, blue-eyed blonde from the south of England who spoke with an accent that pronounced vowels softly instead of the hard ones heard in my native north. When I first met her, she said, 'Ow, Ida, pleez call me 'Thia. Cynthia sounds sew formal, yew knew. And Cyn sounds as if I need the help of a priest in the confessional! That's why I use the end of my name instead of the beginning. '

"Thia's fun-loving husband, Tony, came from east London. Bronzed and muscular, he loved the outdoors. He had been leader of a Boy Scout troop in England, becoming attracted to Uganda after hearing about the budding tourist industry that was developing there. A born entrepreneur, he was now the owner of a small safari company. Acting as a trail guide himself, he had already taken several tourist groups into the Mabira forest near Jinja on mini-safaris; he took particular care to train the trail guides he employed to create interesting and informative nature walks for the tourists. Tony was a great entertainer—the 'life and soul of the party' type. He loved to put on a cockney accent, embracing the notorious rhyming slang for which cockneys are famous. Tony tried this out on us the first time we were invited, with the Griffiths, to the Smiths' house for dinner. He stood at the front door to greet us as we puffed up the last one of the twelve steps to the verandah, ''Ello, 'ello, 'ello, congrats on climbing them *apples and pears* (stairs) safe an' sound. 'Ow 'bout a little *kitchen sink?'* (drink). By then, we were certainly ready for one!

"Thia and Tony had a two-year-old daughter, Rosemary, and they were trying hard to conquer the challenges and pitfalls of bringing up a child in 1920s central Africa with its climate, different food and lifestyle, to say nothing of the local fauna. Together with Meg and Davey, the six of us became a close-ly-knit group of friends. We shared dinners at one another's homes and picnics on our big back lawn, much to Isaiah's delight, giving him the opportunity to show off his culinary talents. I felt a close bond with Thia; now that I had a child of my own we had a bottomless topic of conversation! She proved to be a priceless source of information about how to bring up a child in these frontier-type surroundings. We both dreamed of the day when our little girls would form a friendship of their own.

"Little Ida had grown out of needing me to supply her nutrition, so Jack and I were able to go out to occasional neighborhood events and dinner parties with no worries about leaving her with her adoring and capable *ayah*. Rachel had settled into the job like a duck takes to water. Thrilled to have her own room, she had added to it tastefully with her own touches, topping the curtains with colorful valances and dressing up the furniture with matching pillows. Her good taste also showed when she dressed herself up in a flowing sari and native jewelry on her days off, often being picked up for an outing with some of the other *ayahs* in the town. Whether the houseboys had learned their lesson from *Bwana* Amiss' wrath when they had their fistfight over Ayisha, or if they were simply 'turned off' by Rachel, they never fought over her or even (to our knowledge) took her out on dates; if she had a boyfriend, nobody knew. For whatever reason, peace prevailed once more in our household."

***

BUNTY: The tourist industry was beginning to boom in Uganda, a country rich in untapped business opportunities with its wealth of natural beauty. Mom's next notes reflected how Tony Smith provided another experience for herself and Dad. At Namasagali, it was quality and not quantity that prevailed in Mom and Dad's social life. They missed the busy time they had in Kisumu (probably Mom did, more so than Dad), but with a baby to absorb much of their time and interest, and particularly for Mom, the ingenuity-testing experience of bringing up a child in these alien surroundings more than compensated.

The close friendships of the Smiths and the Griffiths were about all they could handle in the way of social life, but Mom also welcomed the ladies who came regularly to play her beloved mahjong.

Mom positioned the tape recorder to suit herself and began:

The Enchanted Forest

"It was our turn to invite the Smiths and the Griffiths over for dinner. Tony had us all in stitches as usual with his rhyming cockney slang. He suddenly became serious, and said in a more natural, cultured accent, 'I say, how would you like me to take you on a nature walk in the Mabira Forest? I've done it a few times now with clients, like a mini-safari, and they have loved it. I've been researching a lot lately, so now I know quite a bit to tell them that's authentic about the flora and fauna in the forest as we walk in it. I predict that Mabira will become one of the top attractions for tourists as time goes by; it's quite breathtaking. I can get all six of us in my car, and if we start off early in the morning we can safely leave the kiddies with their *ayahs* for the day and be back before dark. What do you think of that idea?'

"Caught up in Tony's enthusiasm, Davey replied, 'Well, Tony, I'm game. How about the rest of you? Meg and I nodded vigorously.

"Thia remarked, 'Well, I've been on one of Tony's walks, and it's really an experience not to be missed. I shall never forget that magical place; I'm ready to go again!'

"I knew this wasn't exactly Jack's cup of tea, but when he saw my excitement he nodded his head, much to my surprise. We all agreed that Tony should plan a special bonus trip for us, as he had offered to do. So, very early one morning, Jack and I were up and dressed, with Isaiah's sandwiches and two large thermos bottles of his special lemonade packed in a canvas shoulder bag to share with the others. Tony had admonished us in his best cockney accent, 'Now, folks, for our *bottle and cork* (walk), you'll need your *tit for tat* (hat) on your *loaf of bread* (head), and good, waterproof hiking shoes on your *plates of meat* (feet)!'

"How could we forget what to wear?

"We were ready when Tony tooted outside the front door at sunrise, with Meg and Davey already in the car. Tony shouted: 'Alright, you two Amisses, let's get on the *frog and toad* (road).' We were soon bumping along our local track toward the smoother road to Jinja, accompanied by good-natured laughter with each bump.

"A little over an hour later, we arrived at the entrance to Mabira rain forest, which was a short distance off the road, just outside Jinja town. Tony parked alongside the two cars already there, and we began the experience of a lifetime—one that I can still close my eyes and live all over again. A tropical rain forest has been described as an underwater cathedral, and I was soon to agree. We eased our cramped legs out of the car, walked over a stretch of grass, and there was the forest, right ahead of us.

***

BUNTY: It's time for me to elaborate about Mabira (the word for forest in the Luganda language). This rain forest has now become a top tourist destination in Uganda. At this writing, so many decades after Mom and Dad walked down that dirt path in the forest, there are now ten networks of well-groomed walking trails. Mabira Forest's large Eco-Tourism Centre now exists: a large visitor centre with *bandas*—unique accommodations for the tourists, where they can enjoy living surrounded by the undisturbed glory of a natural rain forest. In the present-day forest there is a picnic trail, with others for cycling, bird and butterfly-watching or viewing the native flora. In addition, the forest now has a paved tarmac road running through it, where it can be observed from buses or cars.

Mom relished her memories of this memorable day:

"The crunch of dry grass underfoot and the smell of red dust from the road were forgotten as we saw the rain forest spreading out like a jungle before us. It was as if we had stepped out of our familiar world into an entirely different one. The short trail that led us into the forest had been cut through 15 foot high elephant grass that towered on both sides. Emerging from this dramatic entrance, Tony led us onto a footpath that had been cleared and packed hard to support nature walks. Putting on his best cockney accent that made us smile, Tony said, "Once we're in this 'ere forest you won't need yer sunglarsses. Yer *mince pies* (eyes) will 'ave to adjust to the gloom inside. And watch yer feet, folks—you'll see creepy-crawlies like millipedes and lots of beetles; these are 'armless, but some are fierce-lookin', fer sure! He dropped the cockney vernacular and became serious, 'I hope not, but there may be snakes and fire ants. Most of all, watch out for safari ants. For God's sake don't step on any!' I noticed a little shudder in Meg's shoulders.

"And so began an adventure into a place that would excite our senses and try our muscles. As someone once observed, 'A nature walk in Mabira is better than going to the gym!'

"The first two impressions I had of the forest were its sudden tranquility and the immensity of the trees, some of which had several feet of grey moss hanging down from their branches. In this haven of peace, Tony told us that Mabira has over two hundred different species of trees, many of them with functions ranging from providing food and making cloth, to generating medicinal properties in their bark (a tree called the *moringa* is called the 'miracle tree' for its healing qualities). There are also special trees regarded by native tradition to have unique magic properties; one of them is said to make warriors invisible—others are thought to make lovers lucky in love.

"Our rubber-soled shoes squelched as we began to walk on the trail. At the beginning, sunlight slanted through the treetops, dappling the footpath with patches of light. Someone had written '. . . it was like the light in a beautiful cathedral. . .' but it soon darkened as the canopy of treetops closed far above our heads to create an eerie half-light. The forest smelled damp, and the trail was damp underfoot, but there was a soothing, refreshing breeze to save the air from becoming too humid or stagnant.

"Tony told us that only 2 per cent of sunlight can penetrate the thick tree-canopy, making the trail a bit chilly. I was glad he had warned us to make sure that our walking shoes were waterproof, and to bring a jacket! If there were other humans in the forest, they had already been swallowed up in its immensity; there was no sight or sound of them. The quiet was broken only by the hum of insects and the calling of birds, invisible in the high branches above us, ranging from deep-throated bell tones to high-pitched tweets.

"Our eyes gradually adjusted to the filtered light. It cast a strange, greenish glow across the tangled ropes of lianas and vines that wound around tree trunks to climb upward in their search for light and sunshine. I almost expected to see a pixie or a hobgoblin peering out at us from the base of some of the trees that towered hundreds of feet above us. Tony told us that the tallest ones were probably more than a hundred years old! Some had enormous roots above the ground, forming living arches so high and wide that we could actually walk under them. If there were any animals prowling in the forest we didn't see them, for which I was grateful; it had been reported that charging wild pigs, leaping gazelles, and even an occasional skulking leopard had been sighted at Mabira. I was glad to hear that Tony carried a pistol on these treks!

"After we had walked for awhile, murmuring to one another our impressions about this strange other world, Tony suddenly stopped in front of one of the lower branches of a tree growing near the side of the footpath, holding out his arms in a gesture for us to halt. He put his finger to his lips to silence our chatter. In the quiet, we heard sounds in the tree above us. Without a word, Tony pointed up into the tree. Out came our binoculars, and we followed the sounds to reveal a sight for our surprised eyes that we never expected. Spread out among the leaves on a large horizontal branch was a cluster of monkeys. They had yellow-brown coats, black cheeks and white noses. Entranced, we watched as what looked like an entire family gathered on the branch to greet one another with a nose-rub, and paired off to groom each other with comic concentration. There were youngsters and adults, some with babies clinging to their mothers' fur. Their long tails (about twice the length of their bodies) were rusty red, and hung down over the branch. I thought, 'Aha, so these are the red-tailed monkeys I've heard people talk about!' We stood, mesmerized, absorbing into our memories the once-in-a-lifetime scene and not wanting to take our eyes off it.

"Meg couldn't contain herself any longer. She whispered loudly, 'Ooh! Indeed to goodness, I never thought I'd ever see anything like this!'

"Tony gave her a withering look and put his finger to his lips.

"We might still be watching the monkeys! But, at last, our legs told us we should move on after standing still so long. We reluctantly tiptoed away to continue on down the path. We had been so engrossed in watching the monkeys that we had hardly noticed the beautiful flowering plants growing along the way. Stopping to peer into the forest from the footpath, our eyes adjusted to its depth to let us see lush, green ferns and brown, decaying leaves covering most of the forest floor, but in the occasional bare patches were scattered bright red flowers looking like tiny pineapples. Tony told us that these were called ground pineapples—parasitic plants that grew almost entirely underground. We also noticed some strange-looking orchids growing in the forest with grotesque, umbrella-shaped fungi springing up among them. The orchids would have been prize exhibits in the front windows of flower shops back in England, but the mushroom-shaped fungi looked suspiciously dangerous to eat.

"Mabira Forest has been described by an ornithologist as 'a hidden Eden and wonderland for birds'. Along the way, we stopped again as we glimpsed some of the birds. A flash of blue attracted our eyes to a large, spectacular bird with bright blue plumage, which flew down from the canopy to perch in a tree above our heads. Its tail was as long as its body, helping it to balance its weight as it came to rest on the branch. Tony stood in front of us on the path with arms outstretched to stop us in our tracks so as not to scare it. He reverted again to his cockney accent in a loud whisper, 'Crikey, it's a Great Blue Turaco! 'E's got a body almost a foot long, and take a look at them skinny black legs, and that crest of tall black feathers on 'is 'ead. Wot a sight! We've probably 'eard 'is voice already: a deep, gutt'ral tone like a rusty bell, so diff'rent from the twitterin's and chirpin's of the other birds. You can't miss them gawjus bright blue feathers—and jest look at 'is big yeller beak!'

"We were surprised and impressed, never having expected to see such a bird, let alone to see one at such close quarters. As if it had heard us, it spread its spectacular blue wings and flapped its way back up into the forest canopy—having shown itself off to an admiring fan-club as if to say to us, 'Alright, you humans, you've had your ration of my time for one day! Now I'll go and relax for awhile until it's time to impress somebody else.'

"Trees gave way to a grassy clearing with sunlight pouring through the break in the canopy. Blinking at the unaccustomed brightness, we whipped out our sunglasses to look at the birds in the trees at the edge of the grass. In his 'experienced guide' voice, Tony told us, 'There are over three hundred different species of native birds in the forest, and a whole bunch more if you count those from colder countries that migrate to spend the winter here. His cockney accent crept through again, 'You wuddent b'lieve some of the queer names of these 'ere birds. Let's just stop 'ere awhile and see wot's over there in them trees. Look over to yer left, and you'll see a Forest Wood Hoopoe. Crikey, wot a name! See it? It's blue, with a brown 'ead and a long, thin, curved beak. Its blue tail is about twice as long as the rest of it, like the Turaco we just saw. It 'elps 'em keep their balance when they perch on a branch!'

'I can see it!' shouted Jack, triumphantly, craning his neck and pointing upward. I had never heard him so enthusiastic about finding a bird!

'Good for you, Jack. Now, look over to your right, folks,' continued Tony, 'and you'll see a Sooty Boubou—'ow about *that* fer a name? Sounds a bit naughty!'

"We put our binoculars to our eyes to search the branches over our heads. Thia squeaked, 'Oh, is it that little black bird on that low branch?'

Tony grinned, 'Yes, you've 'it the nail on the 'ead, me luv, as you always do!'

"Hearing such praise from her husband, Thia looked like the proverbial cat that swallowed the canary—oops, I shouldn't have said that, now that we had become bird lovers! I'd better get back to the story of our safari!"

BUNTY: A small digression here, to interrupt Mom with another quotation from Churchill's trip to Africa (a fitting description of the flying fauna, as he may have experienced them on a walk in Mabira) ". . . birds as bright as butterflies; butterflies as big as birds . . ."

I read that Churchill had neglected to bring his butterfly net with him to Africa on his famous trip. With no butterfly nets available to buy, he regretfully had to leave his love of butterfly-collecting behind him in England as an unfulfilled, wistful dream.

***

But let's get back to Mom's description of the hike in Mabira Forest:

"While we were in the forest, we had developed a habit of
dividing our attention from looking up in the trees for birds
to looking down on the trail for insects, avoiding stepping
on caterpillars and weaver ants, centipedes and at one point
a huge stag beetle with its ferocious-looking head and pincers. When we arrived at a patch of sunlight under another
break in the canopy, our eyes had to adjust once more to the
bright light. In the clearing, flowering plants flourished in
the sunshine, their fragrance perfuming the air. Bees buzzed
busily as they flew from flower to flower to bring their load of
nectar back to the hive. We stopped to watch the spell-binding
sight of brilliant little sunbirds with breasts of red and yellow.
Their wings flashed iridescent blue and green as they darted
back and forth, pausing to hover like hummingbirds over the
flowers to sip nectar with their curved beaks, before hurrying
away again to revel in the sunshine. They were joined by the
hundreds of butterflies which flitted from flower to flower in
such great numbers that it looked as if some of the plants grew
butterflies instead of blossoms, covering them completely
with pulsing, multicolored wings.

"The forest had taken on a new sound: the muted roar
of falling water. Not realizing how far we'd walked, we had
reached beautiful little Griffin Falls, gurgling and roaring as it
gushed hungrily over outcrops of rock into a pool below. Near
the waterfall, *lantana camara* plants grew with their fragrant
pink and yellow flowers. These plants were literally covered
with butterflies feeding on the nectar of their blossoms. A
wheeling circle of butterflies fluttered in the air around them,
as if awaiting their turn. Tony told us that there were more

than two hundred species of butterflies in Uganda, to say nothing of the moths that fed on night-blooming flowers.

"I was beginning to feel tired. I thought, 'Oh, I'd give anything to be able to take off my shoes, sit awhile to watch the butterflies and the waterfall—and rest my poor feet!' As if it had heard me, I spotted a huge fallen log lying on the grass nearby. I sat down gratefully, followed by my companions. Realizing how hungry we were, we decided that this would be a good time and place for lunch. Each of the three couples had brought something different, so we pooled everything and had a varied feast while we spread ourselves out on the log and rested our tired feet. Conversation died while we munched contentedly and surrendered ourselves to our fairytale surroundings, caught up in the music of the forest.

"We could hear birds singing all around us, but, being inexperienced bird-watchers, we couldn't identify their songs in the high branches of the tree canopy. No conversation was necessary as we ate our sandwiches to the sound of the waterfall, splashing over the rocks below it. A little kingfisher with rainbow feathers sat on one of the rocks, patiently waiting for a fish to come within sight. Suddenly, it dived like a flash into the water for its catch, taking it back to perch on the rock and swallow it whole.

"Tony looked at his watch and lapsed back into his beloved cockney accent, 'Look 'ere, yew intrepid trotters,' he quipped, 'we'd better get 'ome before sundown, or we'll be gettin' lorst in the *wot a lark* (dark) on the *frog and toad!*'

"We packed up our picnic and headed back along the path, with Tony in the lead and the rest of us panting along behind him. On the way, we stopped again for one more surprise. For the first time, we saw another group of walkers. They were standing immobile, staring down at the path. As we came closer, we saw that they had had come across some grey-cheeked mangabey monkeys in a tree, and had enticed them with pieces of sandwich to come down onto the footpath.

Tony's voice dropped almost to a whisper as he said, in his best safari-leader tone, 'This type of mangabey is found only in Uganda; they live in family groups of as many as thirty. They eat well from the fruit trees in the forest, but they aren't afraid of humans, having discovered that people are strange animals who usually mean delicious handouts. They realize that humans will do them no harm, and often venture down to the path to eat the treats left for them, as long as the folks stay to watch at a comfortable distance.'

"We tiptoed to join the little group of hikers, who were obviously proud to have been successful in getting a good look at this second variety of monkeys in the forest. The grey-cheeked mangabeys have long black hair and resemble a small version of baboon. We could get a good look at them, and noticed a crest of greyish fur on top of their heads and their grey, furry cheeks (bulging with food they were storing) which gave them their name. Their tails stood erect, ending in a jaunty-looking curl which gave them a look of always being in a hurry as they ran to and fro picking up the pieces of bread and stuffing them into their cheek pouches. All too soon, the feast was over and they decided to go off with their loot. We watched them leaping up into the trees until they were out of sight.

"Heading back to the forest entrance, Tony—in his practiced guide voice—reminded us, 'Now, be sure to watch your feet, so you don't tread on any safari ants on the move. If you step on their column, the soldier ants will probably attack you. Don't forget, there's only one of *you,* but there's thousands of *them*!' Sobered by the thought, we trudged in silence—with our eyes on the path all the way back to its beginning. And so we came to the close of our memorable trip to Mabira, which has been rightly called Nature's Wonder Forest.

"The car was quiet on our way home; five drowsy people and an alert driver. It was still daylight when Tony stopped the car at our front steps. Jack and I got out stiffly after the long drive, and we were thrilled to be welcomed at the front door of the verandah by an excited Little Ida with a small grey parrot at her heels. But that's the next story.

***

Joey

"Even with all his self-assumed duties for Little Ida, Omolo still had *my* welfare uppermost in his generous young heart. He must have been concerned that the baby wasn't enough company for me—I was still without a pet. One morning, he appeared on the verandah with a dome-shaped bamboo bird-cage in his hand and something peeking out of the pocket of his *kanzu*. It turned out to be a baby African Grey parrot! When I offered the ball of grey feathers my hand, it immediately came out and perched on it. The orange-colored eyes looked up at me trustingly as the little black beak gently felt my finger. I melted, much to Omolo's satisfaction. Yes, we now had a parrot!

BUNTY: A word or two about African Greys:

African Grey parrots are reputed to have been one of the oldest-known pets kept by humans; records date back to biblical times. Acknowledged as the top talkers in the parrot world, they are also known for their talent for mimicry. Renowned for their intelligence, they can understand the meaning of words, be taught to identify objects and count in numbers. They have been dubbed "The Einsteins of the Bird World."

The African Grey has a black beak and orange eyes with a patch of white feathers around its eyes and head. It has red tail feathers.

The grey feathers covering most of its body are scalloped with thin white edges, and it has a white breast. Although it has been dubbed as the most drab of all the parrots, it makes up for it in character!

***

Mom continued with her story:

"Omolo hung up the cage on the inside wall in the corner of the verandah and popped the little parrot inside. It sat contentedly on the perch and Omolo, proud of his knowledge of parrots, announced that they love fruit and also eat nuts, seeds and a variety of raw vegetables. He offered the little bird a piece of melon; it pecked off small chunks as if it had never seen a square meal, washing them down from the little water bowl that Omolo had placed on the floor of the cage. Omolo declared it was a male parrot, and next time Jack was home we decided on a name for him: 'Joey.' Joey became a member of the family very quickly. Soon, he began to mutter to himself, repeating things he heard us say like a little echo.

"We had heard that African Greys were the top talkers in the parrot world; it wasn't long before we could believe it! As Joey grew, so did his vocabulary. He seemed to be proud of his command of the English language! At first, it consisted of single words like 'hello, hello, hello', graduating to 'Hello, Joey' and then to repeating short sentences. We only had to repeat something two or three times for him to learn to say it. And by the time he was a year old, his memory seemed to tell him exactly what he was saying!

"Jack was noted for singing sea shanties handed down from past generations of seafaring relatives; songs that he had learned when he was a boy in Sunderland. In his resonant baritone voice, the rolling lyrics of the shanty songs echoed throughout the house. Joey must have been listening—he would sit on his perch with his head cocked to one side—but he remained silent. One day, he caught sight of Jack and suddenly warbled (on key), '*Wey, hey, blow the man down.*' Jack was amazed! He shouted to me, 'Sunshine, come and listen—Joey remembered one of the sea shanties!' He began to sing, '*Blow the man down, bullies, blow the man down*', and Joey promptly joined in to sing a duet with his squawky soprano, '*Wey, hey, blow the man down*'! After that, Joey continually astonished us with his intelligence and memory.

"I usually let Joey out of his cage when I saw him working at the latch with his beak, and he fluttered down to the verandah floor. As he began to walk along it, I would tell him to go back to his cage, 'Go on, Joey, get back.' Later, I would see him walking in his pigeon-toed steps along the verandah saying, in a voice that mimicked my own, 'Go on, Joey, get back; go on, get back,' as he kept on walking away from his cage. To guard against his slipping out of the door when it was opened, and flying away, I clipped his wings as I had been shown by another parrot owner - just enough for him to flutter but not to fly. Sometimes he would lapse into Swahili and say,'*Kwenda nyuma,kwenda nyuma,*'(go back, go back)—just to let us know how talented he was! And when the local ladies arrived for an afternoon mahjong session, Joey would welcome them with, 'Hello, hello, let's have a cup of tea!'

"I used to call him 'Little Joey'. He had trouble pronouncing his 'Ls', so the mimic of my name for him came out 'ickle Joey'. He must have been listening when the boys were cleaning up the verandah. They paid particular attention to the corners when they chattered about sweeping out any *kwecha kufa du-dus* (dead insects) that may have accumulated. Joey always made a point of inspecting the corners when he was out of his cage. After the boys had done their usual sweeping, I once heard him say, 'Joey's an ickle *du-du*'! Whether he thought he had been an insect in a previous life, or that he morphed into one periodically, or whether he just said it as a joke to amuse us, I never could figure out. Once he could say it, he made it one of his favorite remarks.

"I tried him out with, 'Here's Amiss', when the river steamer bringing Jack home hooted three times—the signal that he was on board. Joey's intelligence and memory would always tell him when this was happening, and he never missed. Whenever he heard those three hoots, he loudly responded, 'Here's Amiss, here's Amiss,' as he walked down the verandah in typical parrot-fashion—one foot in front of the other with toes turned inward—to the front door where he knew he could meet Jack and flutter at his heels when he came in. One day, he surprised me by adding 'Ahoy, mate" to the 'Here's Amiss' and I knew that Jack must have been coaching him when I wasn't around.

"When Joey was trying to take a nap on his perch one afternoon, I decided to cover his cage with a cloth to darken the strong light coming in through the verandah windows. I rummaged in my bedroom drawer and found a large piece of black material that I hadn't used since we came to Africa; I'd even forgotten what I had intended to make with it. I draped it over Joey's cage and said as I did so, 'Joey wants his blanket.' Evidently, this went over well with him, because after that—when he wanted to go to sleep—he would say, 'Joey wants his blanket,' and whoever was nearest the cage would have to do the honors. Very often, when he saw his blanket coming, he would stand on his perch on one leg, tuck his head under his wing, and mutter, "Joey's an ickle *du-du.*" We never discovered why he associated his blanket with its power to turn him into a little insect for his siesta. We decided that it must be parrot logic, and therefore too advanced for us humans to understand.

"Shortly after Joey had mastered many phrases, we invited the Griffiths and another couple in for dinner. When they arrived, Joey announced: 'Let's have a cup of tea.' Our guests looked at me anxiously, as if I'd forgotten it was dinner time. Once they were introduced to Joey, however, we all had a good laugh. Just before sundowner time, we were all out on the verandah. A little voice said, 'Joey wants his blanket'. Meg and Davey sat with mouths open when he saw me coming, stood on one leg on his perch and tucked his head under his wing. Jack said, 'Sunshine, you'll have to teach him to say thank you when he gets his blanket.'

"Joey liked to have the last word. From the cage came a muffled, 'Thank you, Joey.'

***

Namirembe Cathedral

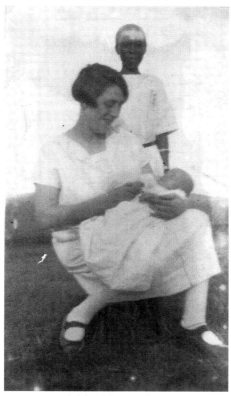

Ayisha, Mom and me

DANGER IN PARADISE

Terror of the Nile

BUNTY: Now that Mom and Dad were living on the riverbank over-looking the White Nile, they recalled some not-so-nice memories of the Nile crocodiles. But first, a few words about these creatures that I learned from several research articles:

The second-largest reptiles in the world (after the common variety of salt-water crocodiles), Nile crocodiles have always had the reputation of being man-eaters; they are accused of bringing death and destruction to Africa. It is estimated that two hundred people each year are killed by Nile crocodiles. Reports abound of children who were sent to the river to get water and were snatched by 'crocs'. Out of the water, they have been known to run quickly for some distance to grab a zebra while its attention was focused on grazing. Moving with lightning speed, they clamp down on their prey with their huge jaws to hold it while they take it into the water, tossing it from side to side or spinning it over and over (called 'the death roll') under the water to drown it. The victim is swallowed almost whole.

A female Nile crocodile can lay up to 80 eggs, in a hole dug about 18 inches deep near the water. The mother and father crocodile both ferociously guard the nesting burrow containing her eggs, but it is estimated that only 10 per cent of the hatchlings will survive. When the eggs are ready to hatch, the baby crocodiles make a peeping noise and tap on the inside of the eggshell with their egg-tooth to crack it open. Crocodile parents have been known to roll the hatching eggs around in their mouths to help the babies out! They also are known to take the hatchlings into their mouths to bring them to the water in safety, but they don't feed them—junior is now on his own! Even so, the female has been known to carry the small fry on her back in the water, to keep them safe from predators. Crocodile life prognosis is dubious; It is estimated that only one out of a hundred hatchlings survives to maturity, and in modern times adult crocodiles have been hunted mercilessly for their hides to make leather items such as shoes, wallets, handbags and luggage.

***

Dad showed no sign of finishing his 'forty winks', so Mom was soon well on her way with another story:

"One day, when Jack was away, Rachel had retired to her room to rest and I was peacefully reading on the verandah where Little Ida was sound asleep in her pram, when Obonyo suddenly appeared and knocked on the verandah door. There was urgency in his voice when he spoke, '*Memsahib Amiss,* put on topee quick; I have something to show you.' Thinking there must be some kind of crisis in the backyard, I grabbed my topee and told Rachel I was going out. Too surprised to ask questions, she rushed onto the verandah and sat down to watch over the baby.

"Obonyo held the verandah door open and said, 'Come, *memsahib,* we go on *piki-piki.'* I was consumed with curiosity mixed with worry as I climbed into the sidecar. Obonyo didn't look at all distressed, so I calmed down. He handed me something to hold, and when I put it on my lap I saw it was a folding camp stool like the ones people took on safari. We started off down the hill toward the river on the well-trodden, sunbaked track through the *shamba.* I could understand how Alice in

Wonderland must have felt as I she remarked, 'Curiouser and curiouser! ' I could hardly contain my excitement. The *piki-piki* jolted to a stop on the path, a few feet back from the river's edge. Obonyo said, '*iko huko, memsahib*' (there it is, ma'am) and got off the motocycle. Obonyo took the stool, opened it up, and set it down on the path in front of us, before helping me out of the sidecar. I was glad that I had grabbed my topee, as there was no shade in sight and the afternoon sun was beating down mercilessly.

"I sat down on the stool, and Obonyo put his finger to his lips to warn me not to make a sound. It was very quiet at the spot where he had parked—some girls and children were further down the riverbank, doing the family wash and taking a quick bath in the process, but they were all out of earshot. Obonyo pointed to the path in front of the stool. My eyes widened with astonishment when I heard a faint tapping noise coming from under the path. A crack appeared, and through it came the tiny head of a baby crocodile! The little creature wriggled its way through the crack and scurried down to the river's edge, using its legs for the first time. We both watched it slither into the water and swim away!

"Obonyo took out a small shovel from his toolbag on the *piki-piki* and quickly dug around the crack to make it wider, uncovering a large, deep hole. I peered into the hole, and at the bottom of it I could just about recognize a pile of oversized eggs. The tapping sounds were more easily heard now, as the unborn baby crocodiles tapped their way to crack their shells open and follow their brother (or sister). I was still sitting there with my mouth open, when Obonyo said, with some urgency, '*Pesi-pesi* (hurry, hurry), *memsahib*. We go now, quick, before *bwana* and m*emsahib croc* come back!' He started up the engine of the *piki-piki* and you never saw a human being fling herself and her stool into a sidecar as quickly as I did! I had heard enough about crocs to speed up the process!"On our way back to the house, I marveled again that I had observed one more of Africa's wonders to write home about and to keep in my memory forever. We were living *so* close to the miracles of nature in this astounding new world! I felt touched that Obonyo and Omolo held us in such esteem that it enabled them to share these wonders with us."

***

Dad woke up from his 'forty winks' and said to Mom, "You seem to have been talkin' for a long time, now, Sunshine, tellin' us about Joey and now about the crocs. I was wonderin' whether I was hearin' your voice or just dreamin', but of course I wasn't asleep; just restin' me eyes. How about lettin' *me* talk for awhile?"

Mom looked rather relieved. "Oh, Jack," she said, "I'm so glad you're back with us again. I sneaked a look at your notes, and I know you have more tales to tell.' Having found the right page in his note-book, Dad took the microphone and began to read:

"Oh aye, there are crocs all up and down the riverbanks; I could spot 'em from the deck of the river steamers. They were in groups, almost invisible with their protective coloration until one of 'em moved, and then I could spot 'em all. They look sluggish, but when alarmed they can move like greased lightnin', slidin' into the river and under the water to become completely invisible. They say that a croc can hold its breath under water for up to two hours! When the bastards were out of the water, they'd all be lined up baskin' in the sun on the riverbank, some of 'em stacked up on top of each other in a pile on a warm, flat rock. They're cold-blooded, so they sun themselves when they're out of the water to stay warm. They lie there motionless with their jaws wide open as if caught in the middle of a toothy yawn. In their open mouths, little black and white 'crocodile birds' hop about, pickin' out bits of food from their teeth—cheeky little devils! Sounds a bit foolhardy of them, but those little birds are servin' two purposes, one to feed themselves, and the other to keep the croc's teeth clean—and the croc knows better than to close its mouth, because each bird is performin' a valuable service for it as a livin' toothbrush!

"Water is vital for all of us, as we know, but the natives had to find a safe place on the riverbank where there were no crocs in order to wash clothes, take a bath, or fill buckets to carry back to their *shamba* and also to our house. The water-carriers were often young children. Someone told me that women and girls often spend up to 36 hours a week walkin' to the river and back, collectin' water in buckets and heavy water jerries (large bowls). Water is so important that the children are sometimes pulled out of school to help carry it!

"As beautiful and innocent the river looked, it hid its own terrors. When I was home for the weekend one time, Ida and I had just settled down to lunch on the verandah. Obonyo burst in on us lookin' very upset, which wasn't like him. I asked him, '*Kwa nini, Obonyo?* (what's happened, Obonyo?) He actually looked pale—-his normally shiny black face had a greyish pallor about it. 'Oh *Bwana Amiss,*' he faltered, 'something bad happen. Small *m'toto* from *shamba* run away down to river, girl run after him, but not catch him before croc rise up out of water, run up on bank quick and catch *m'toto* in mouth. She watch while croc shake poor *m'toto*', pull him under water. Drown him. Him *kwesha kufa kabisa* (made completely dead).'

"Obonyo's voice shook, '*I* see *m'toto* when he run away from *shamba*, so I run all way down to river to help, but too late, *m'toto* gone. Mother crying, she lie down, want to die too.'

"Ida dissolved into tears. Now that we had a baby of our own, we could both feel that poor woman's loss and that of her husband who was one of our houseboys, but our hands were tied. We could do nothin' to comfort her. It was best for us not to interfere anyway; she would be well supported by her neighbors down in the little village in our backyard; they could think we were interferin' in their affairs. I just said helplessly to Obonyo, 'Well, Obonyo, we know how badly you must feel. You did your best to try to save the *m'toto*. But if you know what we can do to help the poor parents, please let us know.' I had to let it go at that. I gave some money to the houseboy whose child it was, to let him know how I felt his sorrow, but otherwise I knew that danger and loss was part and parcel of life in this unforgivin' , cruel country. The natives were very resilient, helped by the support of close family and friends in dealin' with all kinds of circumstances in times of trouble. However, neither Ida nor I slept very well that night."

***

Dad was on a roll. He continued with what became a family classic:

Lion on our Doorstep

"This reminds me of another tale; our own experience of how cruel nature can be:

"Little Omolo came onto the verandah one mornin' when I was home for a few days, lookin' very agitated. I asked, '*Habari gani, Omolo?*' (What's the news, Omolo)? He lisped, '*Habari baya thana, bwana* (the news is very bad, boss). I am much worried. Friend from next village thay to me, '*hatari*' (danger!). He tell about old *thimba* (simba—lion) who come his village and carry off *m'toto*. Friend thay lion comin' our way.'

"I had heard that when a male lion became too old and too slow to hunt with the rest of the pride, they ostracized him and sent him away, reinforced by the belligerence of the young male that had displaced him as its leader. As the old lion wandered away, gettin' desperate from hunger, he would find less and less game that he was quick enough to catch and eat, so he had to turn to easier prey—humans. I said, 'Well, Omolo, go and find Obonyo and tell him I want to see him, *pesi, pesi!*' (be quick).

"Ida and I quickly talked the situation over and made a decision. Just then, Obonyo came in. I said to him, 'Obonyo, *bado kudago*' (wait a minute). He stopped to listen to me. I said firmly, 'Omolo has told us about the lion. You can tell the people in the *shamba* that they can come and spend the night here in safety, locked in on our verandah. And tell them, *hapana chukula kupikia* (no cooking allowed), and to come here before it gets dark.'

"One by one, the houseboys came in to thank us for offerin' shelter and safety for their families. They cleared all the stuff out of the verandah and put it outside or in other rooms in the house. As a precaution, they closed all the heavy wooden storm shutters on the doors and windows, and brought all the oil lamps they could find to light the verandah when darkness fell. Poor Joey looked a bit flustered from all the activity, but stayed glued to his perch and waited while his cage was put in the kitchen before he asked for his blanket.

"Just before sunset, a procession of men and women with children of all ages straggled its way up the hill from the *shamba*, carryin' their belongin's in bags and tied up in blankets. The verandah soon looked like a Boy Scout camp-out. I was glad we'd said that they should come *after* their evenin' meal—Obonyo had told them sternly, '*hapana kupikia*' (no cooking!). Heaven knows what would have happened to the verandah, otherwise! They'd also brought buckets for their own sanitation, thank goodness! It was chaos for awhile, with babies cryin' and small children runnin' around, but they eventually settled down on their sleepin' mats. The house grew quiet as our guests adjusted to their temporary beds, with an occasional snore or two and a tired wail from some of the babies. Ida and I 'battened down the hatches' in our bedroom with Little Ida, and slept.

"It was dark outside except for the oil lamps on the verandah, when suddenly Ida and I, and the members of the verandah's sleepin' human cargo were jolted awake. We could hear our visitors murmurin' anxiously. This stopped after awhile and a hush fell over the house, as we heard more of the dreaded sounds that had awakened us. Now fully awake and paralyzed with fear, we listened silently and held our breath. Little Ida slept peacefully in her cot; I quietly rolled it closer to our bed.

"In the African night, even small noises are magnified. A series of loud grunts, growls and snufflin' sounds outside the house came closer and closer. Then we heard the terrifyin' snarlin' sound of an animal on our front steps. Clawin' at the storm shutters on the front door and windows of the verandah was the old male lion; he was so driven to desperation by hunger that the smell of human flesh overcame his fear of the lighted lanterns burnin' on the verandah to scare him off. Ida clung to me; we held each other without speakin'. Only a few feet separated us from the front steps, where the sounds went on for what seemed like a lifetime. We hardly dared to breathe while we listened to the hungry lion frantically clawin' to get into the verandah. Thankfully, the shuttered door held fast throughout the onslaught. At last, the snarlin' and growlin' slowly began to fade as the old *simba's* strength ran out and he gave up tryin' to tear his way into the house. The shutters on the verandah door and windows had mercifully been too sturdy for the weakened animal to claw them down. Minutes extended into what seemed like hours before he retreated down the steps—presumably to find easier prey. The grunts and wheezin' became slower and fainter as the beast moved away. I murmured a quick prayer of thanks. The almost palpable fear of the people out in the verandah gradually grew less; their murmurin' began again, this time in relief.

"It took us all awhile for our nerves to calm down after we realized that the danger was over. Daylight returned with no sign of the lion. Later that mornin', we heard that he'd been found a few hundred yards away, 'simba quenda kufa' (the lion went away to die). He had died outside one of the other European houses. What we had experienced, unknown to us, had been his last attempt to find food in his old age; weakened from starvation and exhaustion, he had been unable to reach his next intended prey after tryin' to attack us. If he'd been younger and stronger, he could easily have mounted our front steps and clawed open one of the doors or windows to get onto the verandah—I didn't want to imagine the terror of the massacre that would have followed.

"Next mornin', some lion droppin's on our top step and deep claw scratches on the door and window shutters were the only reminders of our unwelcome guest's visit; proof that he hadn't merely been a nightmare or a figment of our imagination. One of the boys rushed up with a shovel to remove the lion's 'callin' card' and with it the reminder of a terrifyin' experience that would remain etched in our memories for the rest of our lives. The natives would probably tell or sing about it at their next village ngoma, durin' their evenin' of dancin', singin' and tellin' stories.

"When her nerves had returned her to her normal cheery self, Ida neatly wrapped up the episode when she said, 'Just think, Jack, we can write home and tell the family that we had a lion on our doorstep, but he decided not to come in! I wonder what the neighbors would say to that?"

BUNTY: Dad ran out of breath after this long stretch of talking. He relinquished the microphone and we gave up recording until my next visit to England.

Dad would never admit that he felt ill. He didn't discuss his bouts of malaria, but I gathered that there had been more than one of them. Mom didn't mention having malaria again after her illness in Kisumu. If she had, I'm sure we would have heard about it. The rest of their story would have to wait until my next trip!

Each time I returned to America from one of my trips to England, I took time to catalog and file the tapes that were completed. Listening to the tapes many years later, after Mom and Dad were both gone, I kicked myself mentally to think that I had neglected to ask them more questions. But back then, I had no idea that I'd be putting the stories into this book!

***

On my next visit, the stories of my parents' experiences in Africa were coming to a close. Mom had been working on her script in my absence between visits and she was anxious to begin:

Little Ida

"Time went by in Namasagali much more quickly now that Little Ida had come on the scene. She was the daily companion that I had longed for in those first years in Africa. She brought with her a new dimension to my life, full of learning experiences for this inexperienced mother. The instructional baby book I'd ordered before she was born was now getting quite dog-eared; it was our bible, preparing us for every stage of her development and reassuring us as we made the inevitable mistakes. We depended upon it so much that we referred to it as 'THE BOOK'. However, no book could ever express the human emotions we went through. I'll never forget the relief we felt when we saw Little Ida's first tooth appear, after mentally suffering with her through the misery of cutting it!

"The pram we had ordered was proving to be a good invest-ment. Omolo was in seventh heaven when Rachel asked his help to carry it down the front steps for Little Ida's morning nap in the fresh air, safe under the netting from any stray mosquitoes or biting flies. If Rachel had to leave temporarily for a short time, she left Omolo in charge. He bent over the pram and chatted softly to Little Ida in Swahili, and he always seemed disappointed when Rachel came back sooner than he had hoped. Little Ida loved him, and lifted her arms for him to pick her up, which he never had the courage to do.

"Then came the day when Little Ida could sit up without being propped with pillows, bringing her into a whole new upright world to look at instead of a horizontal one. As time progressed, her triumph at being able to roll over, sit up—and later to crawl, stand up and walk—could be compared to that of a gold medal winner at the Olympic Games! The day she decided to get up on hands and knees and scoot around on the verandah floor, we knew it was time to bring out the playpen! I made a soft playpen pad on my sewing machine with material from the *duka* in the market that sold fabrics, and the pad became an asset, sometimes making the playpen an inviting place for her to take a nap. We watched with a mixture of pride and amusement when Little Ida first hoisted herself up to a standing position in the playpen. After many attempts ending in a plop back down again onto the pad, she eventually got the hang of it by holding on to the rail to for balance. One day, there arrived her crowning achievement—those first stagger-ing steps before the plop. By a happy coincidence, Jack was home when it happened; he was so tickled that you'd think *he* was the one who had learned how to walk!

"Mealtimes with Little Ida were an adventure of discovery for her and challenge for us. She graduated from food that had been pureed to a new kind with little lumps to be chewed (not as easy for her to spit out all over us if she didn't like the taste; the usual fate of pureed peas). The first time she encountered the lumps, she gave me a dirty look as if to say, 'Oh you've just spoiled all my fun!' However, she soon mastered the art of chewing before swallowing them. The next milestone came when she learned how to hold a little cup in both hands and sip the sweet, warm, boiled milk without spilling it.

"From the day when we came home from Kampala, Meg was an ardent member of Little Ida's fan club. She was a regular visitor and didn't miss one stage in the baby's development. When Little Ida was an infant, Rachel sometimes left Meg in charge outdoors while she and I had a break. One day, I watched from the verandah window while Meg spread a blanket on the short grass under the eucalyptus tree, then plucked Little Ida from her pram and put her down on it on her stomach, turning her over when she was tired of one position and letting her lie on her back, little legs kicking. Meg took great pride in having introduced the growing baby to her own tiny bare feet! Little Ida was fascinated with these strange objects, and became a contortionist, grabbing hold of them during a kicking session to taste her toes. This became her favorite occupation for awhile, much to Meg's satisfaction and amusement.

"As time went by, Little Ida began to roll around and off the blanket. Whenever Meg patiently restored her onto the blanket, the performance promptly happened all over again. Meg rose to the occasion and became retriever-in-chief a few times, before giving up and putting Little Ida in her pram, where she could communicate with her safely and distract her with her toys. Omolo found an excuse to linger by the pram when Meg was absorbed in reading a magazine while she baby-sat. He always stayed awhile to talk to Little Ida and share her toys. I was never quite sure which he enjoyed more: playing with her toys, or playing with her!

"One day, I found a knitting pattern in one of the month-old magazines that arrived from England, showing how to knit a toy 'monkey sock' (the directions began with the monkey's body, which looked like a fat, knitted knee-sock.) Scanning the directions, I thought they looked easy enough. Curiosity got the better of me, and I thought I would try making a monkey sock. It took me several months in what spare time I had, to knit all the separate pieces. To describe it kindly, when all the parts had been knitted, pressed, sewn together and stuffed, the result was a rather ugly-looking monkey! After numerous attempts at trying to make its face more appealing, I still couldn't get the expression on its mouth embroidered just right; it looked more like a misplaced grimace than a sweet smile! I finally gave up and decided to show it to Little Ida anyway, to see her reaction.

"By now, our daughter had developed by leaps and bounds. She had recently begun to repeat the last word that Jack or I spoke, sounding like a little echo just like Joey. I held my grinning handiwork in front of her and said,' monkey sock.' I was fully prepared to see her face pucker up and let out a howl of terror! Instead, she looked inquiringly at the monkey and because she had trouble in pronouncing 's', she pointed to it and said firmly, 'Jock'. Much to my surprise, she didn't recoil in tears of fright but held out welcoming arms and clasped the monkey tightly to her chest, as if to say, 'Just don't try to take him away from me!' From that moment on, she and Jock became inseparable.

"A great milestone in her little life (and ours) was when Little Ida began to walk. After she had mastered the first tottery steps, she usually started off down the verandah at a run. The first time she tried it she quickly lost her balance and sat down suddenly on her bottom. Instead of crying, she cheerfully picked herself up and tried again. Jack was sometimes "in charge" while I had a rest or did some urgent chore somewhere else in the house. I had to smile to myself when I heard him roar, 'Steady on lass, steady on, there!' Lapsing into Swahili, he added, '*poli-poli*, (slow down) there's a good girl.' Once Little Ida gained confidence and good balance, the monkey sock (Jock) became her constant companion. She dragged him around with her all day by one leg and cradled him fondly when she went to bed. I had to wash him when she was asleep—he spent time regularly swinging from the outdoor clothesline.

"Once Little Ida found her speaking voice, she graduated from repeating our last word to repeating the last half of a sentence, then a full sentence. Jack and I had to be careful what we *did* say, after that! "

BUNTY: Comment: Maybe this was the time when I began to hear my parents lapse into Swahili when they didn't want me to know what they were saying—a habit that they continued for as long as I can remember!

***

Mom took a well-earned break for a cup of tea, but she was anxious to get back to her notes:

"All too soon, Little Ida had come to the end of her babyhood. Her first birthday party, in February 1927, was a gala occasion. It was held—like all the European children's birthday parties in the area—at the imposing, white brick headquarters of the "Super" (Marine Superintendent) which was situated at a convenient, central point for families of men like Jack, who ran the ships and docks on the local waterways. I had invited Meg, Thia and Rosemary to the party, and we were picked up by a wheezy little bus sent by the "Super" which was crammed full of ayahs and children by the time it reached its destination.

"The seat of honor was reserved for the birthday girl at the head of the long, beautifully decorated dining table. Poor Little Ida! I don't believe that she understood what all the commotion was about. She was accustomed to being on our quiet verandah with Jock; her closest relationships were with Jack and me, Joey, Meg, Rachel and Omolo. Upon occasion, there were visits from Thia and Rosemary. As her birthday party continued noisily, with children she had never met, Little Ida cried in alarm and clung to me when the little girl sitting next to her burst a balloon by mistake, with a loud 'pop". She recovered when her birthday cake was served; attacking it with delight and getting white icing all over her chin—a better fate than the large white glops of it that were accidentally dropped by the guests and ended up on the floor around the table. What she enjoyed the most was ripping the paper off her presents, squealing with joy after each rip. The following year, by the time she was two years old she had attended birthday parties for several other children in the Namasagali enclave and had become quite a veteran; when her turn came around this time, she enjoyed all the fuss to the hilt.

"Our daughter had grown from a baby into a toddler with all its challenges. Having gone through something similar with Rosemary, my friend Thia was of no comfort when she said, 'Oh, they call that age Terrible Two. She'll grow out of it, but you may get a few grey hairs before she does!' Although Little Ida was a strong-willed Terrible Two, she had a charm that would melt the hardest heart, so she got away with quite a lot! However, she had developed a delight for running, as if she had to hurry to get from Point A to Point B to outdistance something imaginary that was chasing her. We all had trouble keeping up with her, and I worried about her safety. When he was home, Jack's 'forty winks' increased in frequency—he said, for him to recover.

"Knowing how long it took for anything to arrive from England in the mail, I was glad that we'd had the foresight to order a child's walking-harness from England ahead of time, to be ready for the day that Little Ida found the way to manipulate her legs and take off on them outside the house. When the contraption arrived—months after it was ordered, but luckily in time to avoid disaster—it turned out to be a masterpiece of invention. The small, leather harness had a wide waistband decorated with three little silver bells stapled on the front that tinkled loudly whenever the harness moved—at least we could locate Little Ida if she decided to hide under something! Leather straps attached to the waistband could be buckled onto a pair of leather reins to complete the harness, so that the adult holding them (with our squirming toddler firmly strapped into the harness) could guide her in the right direction or heave her upright to save a fall.

"One day, Meg drove Little Ida and me on a trip to the market in Namasagali. Thanks to the harness, I wouldn't have to worry if Little Ida tried to play her favorite game of running in the opposite direction, squealing with delight when we chased her. There were no complaints when I strapped her into the harness, although we did have a few differences of opinion when we got to the market and she became determined go off on her own. There followed a few embarrassing moments, including the one when she suddenly tried to dive under a pile of melons. To placate the native woman sitting cross-legged alongside them on the market street, I quickly bought one, leaving the poor vendor to rescue the rest as they rolled all over the road.

***

Dad intervened:

"Oh aye, I remember that whenever I came back for a few days off, Little Ida with Jock and Joey were always there at the front door to welcome me. When the steamer sounded its three toots, she and Joey knew that Amiss was almost home. Before she could walk, Little Ida would scoot like mad on hands and knees down the verandah to meet me, followed closely by Joey who was let out of his cage for the occasion. On the days when Rachel carried her outdoors to put her in the playpen, as they passed a flowerbed she would pick a little flower to give to me when I came home. She would always want to show me her toys that were kept in her playpen. After she could walk, it didn't take her long to discover that if she piled them up in a corner of it, she could stand on them and climb out! A 'Terrible Two' she was, by gum! We learned not to leave 'climbin' toys' in the playpen; one or two nice, flat, thin children's books had to be found to take their place. There was a routine at the front door: I had to make sure that I first said 'hello' to Jock, then Little Ida would seize me hand and take me to admire her latest toy. Oh aye, and after she could walk, Sunshine and I got our exercise, just keepin' up with her! Blow me down if she couldn't run faster than we could! We often complained to each other: 'THE BOOK didn't tell us that they had so much energy at this age, or such good legs!'

"By this time, Sunshine had established us in the European society of Namasagali (such as it was). We took our turn at havin' other couples over for dinners and card parties and we shared birthday celebrations with the other government employees in the district. Ida was always sayin' she wished we had a car, but it didn't make much sense to me. It was about 55 miles to Jinja port. I'd have to leave the car standin' idle in the blazin' sun at Jija port for 14 or more days while I was away on the lake—no good for the car, or Ida, or me! The Griffiths almost always attended the same social affairs as ourselves, and good old Davey always offered to pick us up for these. Davey had no use for his car durin' his workin' hours. His railway station was only a few minutes away, makin' it easy for him to be taken to work and picked up again, so once Meg learned how to drive she took him to work and made good use of the car durin' the day. She enjoyed takin','Ida with her, but they always got back in time for Meg to go and pick Davey up from work and bring him home. The two of them always polished the dust off the car before Meg took it to pick him up!"

***

BUNTY: Before Mom had time to comment, Dad scrutinized his notes and hurried on to the next chapter in their life. His face clouded over, as if he felt the pain of telling such an event:

A Hideous Tragedy

"Well, this one's a difficult story for me to tell, but tell it I must, as it impacted our lives mightily.

"From time to time, Omolo, who must have been about 14 or 15 years old by now, had been askin' if I would take him with me on the ship so he could see Lake Victoria. I hadn't the heart to keep puttin' him off. He'd been so good to Sunshine and was so devoted to Little Ida—I often wondered what I could do for him, to reward the loyalty that he'd shown us ever since he came to work for me in Africa. This wish of his seemed to me to be the perfect solution. So, one bright mornin' when I was goin' back to work after a few days off, Omolo and I set off together. Accordin' to the rules in those days, he was expected to travel to Jinja with the natives on the tender that was pushed ahead by the river steamer. I bent the rules a little to take him aboard the steamer and show him how the stern-wheeler's engine worked.

"After showin' him the engine, I took him up onto the steamer's deck, where he was wide-eyed with wonder at all he saw. From high up on the deck, he could see for the first time the sweepin' grandeur of the Victoria Nile. He had been able to see only a small stretch of it from the riverbank at Namasagali. I had to send him back onto the tender to avoid criticism from the steamer's crew. I waited for him when he got off the tender at Jinja port, sensing his excitement as we boarded my ship. Just seein' and hearin' him react to every new experience was refreshin' for me, too—it was like takin' the young lad on his first Sunday school picnic!

"To justify bringin' him with me, I had to put Omolo to work on board my ship. He couldn't have been a more dedicated addition to the ship's crew! At Jinja and at the succeedin' ports, we stopped to take on passengers, cargo and the Royal Mail. One time, I brought Omolo up on the bridge for a special treat so he could see, from that high vantage point, the workin's of trade and commerce as we proceeded to each port. He watched the comin's and goin's of passengers, and marveled at the big nets carryin' crates of exports and imports as they were lifted in and out of the hold. He put his hands over his ears when the ship's whistle sounded, so much louder than the toots he'd heard from the river steamers. He was a willin' helper for the natives in the crew, and he obeyed every word of command from his superiors with speed and good humor. Never havin' slept in a bunk before, he was thrilled to tell me how he'd been given the honor of a top one, and how he actually had to climb up a ladder to get into it!

"We completed the voyage around the lake, transferrin' on our return at Jinja port to a river steamer for the last leg of the journey up the Victoria Nile to Namasagali. Omolo traveled on the tender, as was expected. On this trip, it was particularly heavy—loaded with freight and packed tightly with dozens of natives ridin' free of charge. When we were about half-way up the river on our way back to Namasagali, there was a loud commotion among the natives on the tender. They could be heard shoutin', screamin' and wailin'. One of the men broke loose from the crowd and jumped across onto the steamer. He shouted somethin' in Swahili to one of the deck hands, who pointed in me direction. 'Oh, Lord, 'I groaned, 'not another woman in labor!' I always carried me first-aid kit with me, so I knew just where to put me hands on it. I grabbed it when the man came and sought me out. His face was grey, showin' great distress. He cried, *'Bwana, bwana, Omolo kuanguka katika— mamba ya maji ya mto akamwua!'*

"I reeled with shock. He had said that Omolo had fallen off the tender into the river and that a crocodile had killed him! The commotion I had heard must have been the natives on the tender as they saw the terrible thing happenin', yet they were helpless to do anythin' to rescue him. In disbelief, I searched frantically all over the tender for Omolo, and then I looked all over the deck of the steamer. There was no sign of the little chap anywhere. My mind still refused to accept the man's message. I thought, 'Oh, he must be mistaken—it was just a boy that looked like Omolo. I'll bet Omolo is tucked away somewhere out of sight takin' a nap; he'll show up when it's time for us to get off at Namasagali'.

"After what seemed an interminable time, we reached Namasagali. I had often seen those crocs from the deck of the steamer—ugly bastards—some of 'em baskin' on the riverbank and others barely breakin' the surface of the water as they swam in the river alongside the tender, hopin' for discarded food to be thrown overboard by the travelin' natives. I had a prickly feelin' of anxiety at the back of me neck as I stepped off the steamer's deck onto the wharf at Namasagali, still vainly hopin' that momentarily I would see Omolo trottin' behind me, but there was no sign of him. With the horror that had taken place slowly sinkin' in, I went home to the house.

"Little Ida was there at the door to greet me with Jock, followed by Joey as usual. Mechanically, I picked up Little Ida in me arms and kissed her as I always did, settin' her down to let her scamper ahead of me across the verandah, followed by the flutterin' little parrot. Me feet dragged as I walked down the verandah and saw Sunshine come out of the dinin' room, smilin' to welcome me home."I didn't know what to say to Ida or how to broach the news to her. She looked at me, saw the distress on me face, and said, 'Jack, what's the matter; what has happened? You're as white as a sheet!' Where's Omolo? I replied, 'Sunshine, sit down, I want to talk to you.'

"I put me arms around her and took her hand in mine. As I talked, I tried to soften the story as much as I could, but the raw truth had to surface. When Sunshine grasped the reality of what had happened, she gave a heart-wrenchin' cry. She collapsed in me arms, sobbin' her heart out as she suffered the pain of visualizin' the terror and agony that must have been experienced by that poor lad before death mercifully claimed him. Obonyo came runnin' in when he heard Ida scream, and I had to repeat the grisly story again for him. He was stoic as the truth penetrated his mind, but then he turned quickly on his heel and padded away to his room without a word, where he could express his grief in privacy."

***

BUNTY: While he was telling this story, Dad had become quite teary-eyed. Temporarily overcome, he gave up the microphone to Mom, as this terrible memory was refreshed in his mind. She dabbed at a tear that had run down her own cheek, but she gallantly went on with the tape recording:

"Omolo and I had become very close in the years we had been in Africa. I almost felt like his mother, but sometimes he showed me wisdom far beyond his age. Jack held me in his arms for a long time after he had told me the news, but I had nightmares for weeks afterwards. In my imagination I re-lived over and over again what must have been Omolo's last minutes, and what he must have gone through: slipping on the wet deck of the tender and unable to save himself from falling into the river; the shock of the impact as the water closed around him; the rush of crocodiles to reach him; the frightful jaws and teeth grabbing him; the agony as the animal closed its mouth over him, its death rolls shaking him like a rag doll beneath the water; and, at last, the merciful loss of consciousness and the finality of darkness.

"It was a sad house, to say the least, in the following days. The shocking news was passed from one houseboy to another, resulting in their usual exuberance being respectfully subdued. We heard none of the singing that usually accompanied their chores, or Isaiah's rich laughter that echoed through the house, lifting my spirits when Jack was away. In the next days, the blissfully unaware antics of Little Ida and Joey kept us afloat, or it would have been a house of morbid quiet. The hardest thing of all was to try to comfort Obonyo. He mourned the loss of his little tribal brother with whom he had shared so many experiences, including their long, exciting trip on the train to Mombasa to meet me off the ship when I first arrived in Africa. Then there was their voluntary decision to travel the considerable distance from Kisumu to Namasagali out of loyalty to their *Memsahib* and *Bwana Amiss*, to an unfamiliar place and a house where they would live and work among houseboys who were strangers belonging to tribes other than the JaLuo.

"No, Omolo would never be forgotten; he would be remembered as the endearing, happy little soul that he was. I don't know of anyone who had not liked him.

"Obonyo had the sad task of gathering up Omolo's pitifully few belongings from his room and packing them up to take back to Omolo's native village to give them to his family. It was fitting that Jack would tell Obonyo to take as many days off as he needed to make the journey on his *pikki-pikki* , with the only tangible memories of Omolo packed into the otherwise empty sidecar. Later, Jack asked me what I thought we should do to replace Omolo as my personal houseboy. I thought about it for awhile and replied, "Well, dear, we have Rachel with us now, so I won't really need a personal boy for myself just yet. I'm sure that I would be comparing a new one with Omolo— and he would always fall short! Anyway, it won't be long now until we'll be getting ready to go on leave to England. Let's wait until we come back."

ENGLAND BECKONS

Pack Up Your Troubles!

BUNTY: "Pack up your troubles in your old kit bag, and smile, smile, smile . . ."; so goes the song that was a standard in England both in World War One and again in World War Two.

Mom and Dad had now been in Africa for four years. The British Colonial Government advised British subjects to return to England for several months' leave after they had been in Africa for three years, and to have a thorough medical examination while they were there. Mom and Dad were already overdue. Early in 1928, they began to pack in preparation for their leave. They had accumulated an odd assortment of items, some they had bought from the local market and the shops in Jinja, others had been given to them by friends to keep for themselves as souvenirs, and some to take with them to England as gifts. Nowadays, many of the items would be frowned upon, but in those days the awareness of the need for reverence of wild life and its conservation had not fully dawned on the British "ex-pats". Values were somewhat different then, and the use of animal souvenirs for decorative purposes was an accepted practice.

***

Mom was ready with her notes :

"Leopards were valuable for their skins to satisfy the fashion in Europe for women's fur coats, muffs, hats and handbags. When we were in Kisumu, someone gave Jack a leopard skin, dried and stretched, which he had folded up into a manageable bundle, disguised as a bulging package. He deposited it in my lap, and said, 'A surprise for you, Sunshine.' Not suspecting its contents, I opened the mysterious package and I almost dropped it with the shock of discovering what it contained. My hand instinctively reached out to feel the fur. It was short, soft and thick. I couldn't help admiring its bold patterns of protective coloration, which I had never before seen up close (thank goodness)! In addition to its desirability for making clothing and accessories, it was the fashion in those days to display a mounted leopard skin as a rug or wall hanging. I had admired the mounted skin that hung on the wall in Effie's dining room as a status symbol, and we decided to use ours as a decoration in our own home. First of all, it would have to be mounted on some kind of backing, so I bought what I estimated would be enough thick dark green felt material from one of the shops in Kisumu town. Next, Effie took me to the shop where she'd had her leopard skin mounted, and we left mine there to be mounted on the felt, with enough to be left around the edges as a border. In a week or two, the result was a beautifully mounted leopard skin, and a good excuse for another trip into Kisumu town with Effie to pick it up and treat ourselves to a nice lunch at one of the tea-rooms. After I had scalloped the edge of the felt backing, the leopard skin was eventually installed as an elegant wall-hanging in our dining room and admired by all our visitors. I decided to bring it home with us to show to the family. Along with the leopard's skin, Jack's benefactor had also included one of its claws! I would have to think it over before deciding to show them that!

"Although some restrictions and penalties had been imposed, a considerable number of African animals were hunted—predominantly elephants—by poachers. The poachers killed healthy elephants for no other reason than to extract their ivory tusks and sell them to be used in a variety of ways. Poaching was officially prohibited by the authorities, but illegal poaching was nevertheless a thriving industry in Africa. Although elephants were killed for their ivory, it was common practice for some of the natives (upon finding an elephant's body that had recently been abandoned after being killed for its tusks) to sever its feet at the ankle, in order it to have them hollowed out, dried and stuffed to become footstools for the souvenir market. Nowadays, the use of such objects would be abhorrent; in those days it was not given much thought. Jack was given an elephant's foot footstool by one of his ship's crew as a present to bring home with us. I never heard any adverse criticism of the footstool in England; in fact, it became a conversation topic on many an occasion. It left our house when I gave it as a gift to an English friend who admired it. Frankly, I was relieved to see it go, taking my pangs of reflected guilt with it as it went.

"From somewhere, we had acquired the tooth of a hippopotamus! It had probably been brought to Jack or me by one of the houseboys, to add to our collection. Obonyo contributed a beautiful little native drum covered with goatskin, which was his parting gift to us. In one of the shops in Jinja town, we found exquisite families of little elephants, expertly carved out of ebony wood with its black surface polished until it shone. The elephants had small pieces of ivory inserted to form their tusks and toenails. In each family grouping, there was a father elephant with upraised trunk and tusks, a mother with trunk and tusks down, and a baby with little tusks to match its size. We bought two of these families of elephants to take back to England.

"We gradually accumulated gifts to take home with us for the family in England. I was constantly impressed by the beautiful workmanship in native jewelry. The shops in Jinja town carried a variety of it, among which was one novelty piece that I saved to give to Little Ida when she was older: a bracelet fashioned from a thick, black hair plucked from an elephant's tail. This long, single hair had been wound around several times to make an ingenious little bracelet of hair which had a catch that could be slid back or forth, making the bracelet larger or smaller to fit the wrist of its wearer. It was said to bring good luck to anyone who wore it. Glass beads they could get in England, so for the women of the family, I accumulated necklaces made with oval ivory beads and others made with dark orange amber ones from neighboring Tanganyka (now called Tanzania). We decided to give to my father and Jack's a set of cufflinks fashioned from black volcanic stone, each inlaid with a tiny silver elephant.

***

BUNTY: While we're still thinking about elephants, I had been wondering why the demand for ivory was so great, so I did a bit of research. I was fascinated by its history:

Ivory from India and Africa has been used extensively since prehistoric times for its ease in carving; in China, it is estimated that it has been carved since 6,000 BC! Imported ivory was also carved and prized by all the early civilizations around the Mediterranean. The ancient Egyptians used it to carve decorative objects ; the ancient Greeks beautified a life-sized statue of one of their gods with inlaid ivory and gold. The Romans used ivory on items of war to make spear tips and decorate sword hilts. They also used it to decorate furniture and to make jewelry, plaques and boxes, some of which still exist.

Present-day ivory carving is practiced in China, India, Thailand, Vietnam, the Philippines, Japan and North America, used as an inlay and also to make decorative objects. Cut from the elephant tusk in spirals, it could be used as a veneer for furniture. In modern times it has been used to make piano keys, billiard balls, handles for walking canes and countless ornaments. It is also used in modern industry in the manufacture of specialized electrical equipment for airplanes and radar. In centuries past and until recent decades, to own ivory quickly became a "must have" status symbol for wealthy and upper middle class consumers all over the world.

In recent times, in response to the growing concern of conservationists, China is winding down its market by closing ivory-carving facilities; however, at this writing, China and the U.S. still allow domestic sales of ivory. It is estimated that thirty thousand elephants are killed worldwide for ivory each year, threatening their extinction within the foreseeable future in Africa. Documented research declares that 30 per cent of all the elephants then in Africa were killed between 2007 and 2014. I pray that concern for our wildlife will win out over some of humanity's baser instincts.

***

Standing on the Equator

Mom continued with her description of preparations prior to our family's leave in England, back in 1928:

"Meg and Thia were envious about the news of our leave. Meg said wistfully, 'It seems like ages since I saw the mountains of Wales; indeed to goodness, they are 'the hills of home.' She added, with a mischievous smile, 'I was hoping there might be room in your luggage, look you, Ida, for a homesick Welsh woman! But it won't be too long before you're back again; Davey and I will miss you until then.' "Thia was on the verge of tears. She wailed, 'How I wish we could go with you, Ida. Rosemary was just an infant when we went on leave to London more than two years ago; I get upset when I think of her growing up not knowing her Grandma and Grandpa, and with them not getting to know her, either, but maybe next year Tony can tear himself away from his business long enough for us to take a break and go home for a visit. How I envy you!'

"We all promised to write, but with the postal system in its current condition, we would probably arrive back in Africa before our letters could reach one another!

"We wrote to Effie and Ted in Kisumu, and Mary and Jim in Kampala, with the news that we would be going on leave, offering to give our mutual homeland their regards. We received cheery letters in response, saying they wished they were coming with us and promising to be in touch more often after we came back. The Hollingsworth's letter invited us to spend a few days with them in Kampala before we sailed for home. It was so nice of them to offer their hospitality once more, and we accepted. It took a whole day for us to make the trip, but Little Ida survived it even better than we did!

"Jim, Mary and Helen met our train with the three weary travelers. Little Ida and Helen bonded immediately, to their mutual delight. Although we had corresponded to keep in touch, we hadn't seen the Hollingsworths since Little Ida had been christened, so it was somewhat of a reunion. They were astonished at how she had grown into a toddler from the tiny baby they remembered in Namirembe Cathedral. Jim said, 'I'm taking the next few days off from work, and before you go to England I want all of us to step on the equator! Kayabwe is only a little less than an hours' drive from here, where they have a place for the tourists to stand on the equator! If we leave here early in the morning it shouldn't be too hot by the time we get there.' "

BUNTY: Let me interrupt here for a few words about Mom and Dad's next destination, the equator. Mom had already crossed it by sea at King Neptune's Court, on her way to Africa; now she would experience it on land. The simplest dictionary definition of the equator that I could find is "an imaginary circle around the middle of the earth at zero degrees latitude, marking the centre of the earth halfway between the North Pole and the South Pole."

Further research revealed that the equator's location had been calculated by means of a complicated formula to measure the earth's surface, involving the earth's axis. Invented to divide the world on maps into north and south for the purpose of showing longitude and latitude, the imaginary line of the equator passes through land in 11 countries, and in Uganda it is only a 20-mile drive from Kampala. At the equator, the year is divided equally into two seasons with no variations from each other. Day and night are divided into two equal twelve-hour stretches. And, on a useful (?) note for weight-watchers, I learned that on the equator people weigh 3 per cent lighter because gravity is less—it's a bit far to travel, though, to avoid going on a diet!

***

After a break for tea, we're back with Mom's adventures in Africa, as she continued her story of the trip from Kampala to the equator:

> "The three of us piled into the car with Mary and Helen; Jim was already at the wheel. The condition of the road out of Kampala was again a welcome change from the ones around Namasagali. On our way out of Kampala, we waved affectionately to Namirembe Cathedral crowning one of its hills, while through the car window we caught exciting glimpses of the great Victoria Nyanza. It seemed like no time at all after we had left suburban Kampala behind that we saw a sign on the side of the road which read 'WELCOME TO KAYABWE—EQUATOR STRAIGHT AHEAD'.

"Jim parked the car at a small building with a restaurant attached, where we ate a late breakfast (or early lunch). Some enterprising individual had seen the tourist possibilities of the location and had built a little souvenir shop next to the restaurant. At this writing, it has mushroomed into an elaborate visitor centre, where tourists line up to wait patiently for their turn to experience standing at the middle of the world.

"Outside the restaurant was the destination that we had been seeking: a sign printed EQUATOR on the paving in large letters, with a colorful, hoop-like arrangement arching above it. Jack realized that he had left our camera behind in Namasagali, so Jim gallantly took a photo of the three of us. We posed under the arch, standing across the equator line with a foot planted on each side of it. In large letters on one side, painted on the paving, was written NORTHERN HEMISPHERE and on the other side SOUTHERN HEMISPHERE. Then Jack did the honors for the three Hollingsworths, after which he handed Jim's camera back to him. It was some time before Jim had finished the roll of film and sent it in to be developed. When the prints came, I carefully put them away. Whatever happened to those photos remains a mystery. I searched high and low and hunted for them for several months, but I never saw them again. Eventually, realizing that they must have been lost when we packed to return to England, I gave up and wrote to the Hollingsworths for copies, but incredibly, Jim couldn't find his either, and he had thrown away the negatives! Gone was the proof; people would just have to believe my word for it that the Amisses stood on the equator!"

BUNTY: So much for proof that we stood on the equator! While we're on the subject of the equator, thanks to Mom and Dad, they not only took me to stand under that fancy hoop on the equator in Uganda marking zero degrees *latitude*, with one foot in the northern and the other in the southern hemisphere, but many years later they took me to stand on the Prime Meridian line at Greenwich, England. It is a plain metal bar in the paving, below the sign PRIME MERIDIAN, indicating zero degrees *longitude.* I straddled it with one foot in the eastern and the other in the western hemisphere! I can now say that I have stood on the joining places of north, south, east and west of the whole world. Thanks, Mom and Dad!

***

It's time to go back to Mom where we left her at our visit to the equator with the Hollingsworths:

"We rode back to Kampala. Thanks to Jim and his thoughtfulness, we had accomplished an unspoken wish of mine to see the equator, even before we came to Africa. After another day with the Hollingsworths, Mary and Jim drove us back as far as Jinja, where we took a train to Namasagali to resume packing for our journey home to England.

"Mary Hollingsworth stayed in touch with us throughout the following years. She was a faithful godmother, remembering 'Little Ida's' birthday and the day she was christened, never forgetting to send her a card and a little gift. When Jim died, years later, she and Helen moved back to England to live in a beautiful house not too far from our suburb south of London. Helen never married. Bunty and I went to visit them frequently as the years went by, in fact right up to the week before Bunty left England to live in America. There was always a warm, loving reception from the two lonely women."

Mom sounded tired, so Dad continued the narrative from his notes:

"Sunshine and I weren't quite prepared for all the 'goodbyes' we would be sayin' at Namasagali. They sounded so final!

After all, we'd only be gone for a few months—you'd think we were goin' forever! Reggie, the DC, gave us a surprise 'Bon Voyage' party with some of our neighbors invited for an informal dinner and a bit of dancin', but I did think that Reg held Ida's hand a bit too long when he said goodbye. That rascal, Algie Bloomsbury, was nowhere in sight. I'm glad—after a few drinks, I'd have bopped him one!

"Before we left, we invited the Griffiths and the Smiths over for dinner, and Isaiah did himself proud again. He would have to find work while we were away. I found meself envyin' the people that might inherit him while we were on leave and hoped that we could coax him back again when we returned. Rachel was obviously overcome by our leavin' and hugged Little Ida over and over again.

"I'd agreed to pay Obonyo to look after the house while we were away; his room was already there, and it should be an easy task for him. To my amazement, I saw tears in his eyes when he gravely shook Little Ida's hand, then Sunshine's, then mine, bendin' deferentially over each one. I'd only seen him show such emotion once before, when he heard the news of Omolo's terrible fate. He insisted, 'I come to railway station with you, *Memsahib and Bwana.* I see you off.'

"As the train pulled out of Namasagali station, we both waved to Obonyo until we could see him no longer. I watched his shoulders slump as if he thought he wouldn't see us again. I felt me own eyes mistin' over. I turned to Ida, 'Why Sunshine, you're cryin', too!' I exclaimed. She looked at me with a tearstained face, 'Oh, Jack,' she said, 'I am going to miss this beautiful country and our friends, and Obonyo, every minute we're gone.' (I didn't mention missing the *choo* or our tin bathtub, however).

"The branch railway line from Namasagali soon joined the main *Lunatic Express* line, which we now traveled in reverse back to Mombasa to board the ship home to England.

"From our previous experience, we knew what to expect from the splendid scenery that we saw from the window of our first-class train compartment. This time, it was complicated by havin' a busy little girl with us. Little Ida didn't complain, except on the first night in a strange bunk bed, but she quieted down as soon as she had Jock to snuggle with her. Keepin' her occupied during the daylight hours, with only one fitful nap to give us a break when she took one, was a superhuman effort for both of us. She adamantly refused to wear her harness on the train. The other passengers must have found it entertainin' to see us dashin' up and down the corridor trying to keep up with an active two-year-old as she squealed with delight throughout the chase. I remember shoutin' to her what we said on the ships when the sea was rough, 'Steady as she goes, girl,' but she was too busy to listen. Sometimes, she tripped and fell with the motion of the train, but she was soon picked up and easily distracted by the ever-changin' panorama outside the window, especially when it contained the sight of so many animals grazin' and gallopin' on the plains.

***

Starboard, Home

"Embarkin' on the ship at Mombasa, the next challenge was the long, slow sea voyage, retracin' that outward-bound journey with an active toddler. We were now completin' the last two letters in the acronym POSH—**S**tarboard, **H**ome. Strangely enough, each of us had excellent accommodation on the port side of the ship on our separate outward voyages, and I noticed that our well-appointed stateroom for the trip home was on the starboard side—it was, in fact, posh!

"We gave King Neptune's Court a miss this time when we re-crossed the equator. After all, both Ida and I were now officially Shellbacks; only Little Ida was still a Pollywog, but we didn't think she would appreciate her initiation at her tender age. I'll bet her outraged shrieks of protest would've been heard all the way back to Sunderland! On the ship, her harness was mandatory and invaluable; without it we might've heard someone shout, 'Child Overboard'!

"As we sailed further north, the air became a lot cooler than Sunshine and I had been used to for the past four years. When we got as far as the Mediterranean, we realized that we had no winter clothes with us, so we went ashore at the stopover in Marseilles and bought ourselves warm sweaters, hats and coats for the rest of the journey. Sunderland wasn't very warm even in summer, let alone in the frigid winters, and central heatin' in average, middle class homes was unheard-of, back in those days. We would need more warm clothes, but we could stock up after we arrived.

"As usual, Sunshine was seasick. She was at her worst after we left the calm Mediterranean, comin' down with it like a ton o' bricks after we started north up the choppy Atlantic coast and into the Bay of Biscay for our stopover at Lisbon. It was a good thing she had me there to take care of Little Ida. Poor lass, she was so sick that she lived on dry biscuits (crackers) and ginger ale for the last part of the voyage."

***

Dad said Mom always had the last word, so he handed the microphone over to her:

"I wasn't feeling very perky after my bout of seasickness, lack of sleep and starvation diet. How I got through the next ordeal

I'll never know. The ship docked early in the morning at the London docks, and we had to go through customs. Jack went off somewhere to arrange for the two trunks and several large packing boxes to be shipped to Sunderland, leaving Little Ida and me with the entire pile of luggage to be examined before we could leave the customs shed. I had made a list of the odd assortment of souvenirs, and when I handed it to the customs inspector he looked at it in disbelief!

"'AN ELEPHANT'S FOOT, MADAM?' He looked at me with a raised eyebrow. 'Yes,' I said, brightly, 'it's in one of these boxes. It was given to my husband as a footstool. I can unpack it to let you see it; would you like me to?' He didn't reply, just looked at me in despair, viewing me intently. I thought I detected wary suspicion in his eyes. Did he think I was a professional smuggler, or a subversive disguised as a tired, distracted mother? I was glad that I hadn't mentioned the leopard's claw on my list; he might have thought that I was carrying a secret weapon!

"Little Ida began straining at her harness, trying to wriggle out of it. I wondered when Jack would come back and help me.

"The customs inspector looked over the list of things that I had declared and gave me another piercing look. I held my breath. Was he going to make me rummage through those boxes and trunks to produce my trophies? I thought, somewhat resentfully, 'Oh, dear, where on earth can Jack be—just when I need him the most? This customs man might yet have me ending up in jail if I have to show him all those new, unused souvenirs and the jewelry that we bought. And I don't have enough money on me to pay the duty on them!'

"My examiner looked over the pile of trunks and boxes which were thoroughly tied up with rope reinforced every few inches with a nautical knot, as Jack always did when he packed anything. Little Ida whimpered and tried to wriggle out of her harness. I felt more and more stress mounting in me. The customs officer's shoulders sagged visibly. Again, there came that piercing look, but this time I thought I detected a hint of resignation on his face. He growled, 'Madam, that will be all,' and, whipping out a worn-down piece of chalk, he put a large 'X' on each piece of luggage and bellowed, 'NEXT, PLEASE.'

"Standing there on the pier, in my mind's eye I remembered seeing Obonyo and Omolo standing on a different pier at Mombasa waiting to greet me four years ago. The memory burst like a bubble as Jack appeared. He looked as if a weight had been lifted off his shoulders as he said cheerfully, 'Well, Sunshine, I've arranged for the trunks and boxes to be sent by Carter Paterson and delivered to the Ditchfields'. I sent your father a wire to tell them that we're on our way. Our two suitcases and Little Ida will be as much as we can manage to wrestle with when we change trains in the Midlands and when we arrive at Sunderland. Oh, I see you got through customs with no trouble at all. Good for you!' I was too exhausted by that time to think of a reply, so I just smiled weakly and Jack called for a porter to take our luggage to the appropriate places: the trunks and boxes to be transported, and the suitcases to go with us on the train.'

"Jack picked up Little Ida, squirming in her harness, and added, 'Let's head for the dinin' car as soon as we get on the train, Sunshine; me stomach's growlin' for somethin' to eat!' I replied, 'All I want to do is to sit down—I feel as if I've been standing up for days in that customs shed; but (triumphantly) just think, Jack—we had no customs duty to pay!

"Looking as fresh as a daisy, Jack hailed a taxi outside the docks. It took us to King's Cross station, the London terminus for trains bound for the northeast of England on the LNER (London and North Eastern Railway). While he stood in line for tickets, Little Ida took me for a gallop around the platform, pretending to be a horse in her harness. I thought, hopefully, 'Great! This ought to tire her out and she should sleep while we're on the train. Maybe I can, too, I hope!'

"Our train was already waiting at the terminus, and we headed straight for a carriage. Luck was with us; we found seats just before the guard shouted, 'All aboard.' He blew his whistle and waved his flag at the train driver. Jack heaved our suitcases onto the overhead luggage rack. The train gave a piercing hoot, followed by a loud belch of sooty steam, and slowly pulled out of King's Cross Station. The carriage was now full with its six passengers. The crowded train had people standing in the corridor outside. Asking the man in the next seat to ours to save our seats, we left our overcoats on them and wobbled along the corridor to the dining car. It was packed; it looked as if most of the passengers on the train had the same idea! Probably looking as disheveled as I felt, I must have touched the heartstrings of a nice elderly man seated with a woman at a table for four. He rose gallantly to his feet and said, 'Sit down here, my dear; I'll move over and we can share a seat. My wife will move over and make room for your hubby.' The wife gave him an 'I don't think that's funny' look. She was a lot thinner than her paunchy husband, so Jack managed to wedge himself and Little Ida into the seat alongside her. A steward came down the aisle taking orders. Eventually, we were served our lunch—sandwiches and sausage rolls, little tea-cakes, tea in thick china cups and milk for Little Ida. With this familiar food, at last I knew that we were home again in England. I was curious to see what our daughter would do with her sausage roll (they had not been in Isaiah's repertoire). She systematically unrolled it and ate the pastry and the sausage separately, finishing them to the last crumb, and drinking a cup full of milk like water in the desert.

"Leaving the dining car, we headed back to our carriage to prepare for the long journey north. I confided to Jack, 'You know, Jack, when we got off the ship, I had the strangest experience when I stepped onto the pier. As if it had been yesterday, the memory of landing at Mombasa all that time ago came back to me and I thought I could see Obonyo and Omolo standing there with their lovely white smiles of welcome. I almost felt that I could put my hand out and touch them. I know it was silly of me, but I will never forget that moment, nor will I forget either one of them.'

"Ever practical, Jack snorted, 'Oh, Sunshine, stop being so sentimental! You're talkin' as if we'll never be goin' back to Africa!' Temporarily crushed, I rationalized silently, 'At least he could have said something comforting, but I suppose that if he had, it might have made me cry, so that's probably why he didn't.'

"Back in our carriage, I maintained a stony silence before relaxing in my seat. It had already been an exhausting day, but when we eventually sat down in the train, that upholstered seat felt so comfortable! I had forgotten that each one was equipped with a headrest covered with a white linen doily to prevent the men's hair oil from staining the upholstery. For me, the headrest encouraged long-awaited relaxation. Mercifully, Little Ida took a long nap, which let Jack and me have some well-deserved rest to gear up for when she re-awakened.

"The train headed north as it pulled out of London, leaving the suburbs behind to emerge into the fresh green scenery of the south of England—so sharply different from the landscape we had seen from our window on the *Lunatic Express!* Sleepily, I remembered the palm-tree-studded Mombasa coastline and lush coastal meadows, followed by mile upon mile of barren plains filled with herds of wild animals. In contrast, we now looked out on tidy, hedge-enclosed fields, some of them edged with deciduous trees doggedly holding on to the last few leaves of summer. The green, rolling countryside slowly gave way to the Midlands, with towns huddled under grey skies and smoking factory chimneys.

"Here, we had to change trains for the northeast coast. Loaded down with our suitcases, Jack hailed a porter to help us get from one platform to another at the large railway junction. Another scramble for seats in the next train yielded three, in a carriage already occupied by three other passengers. Jack prepared to hoist our suitcases onto the luggage rack above our heads. Before he did so, I opened them and took out the sweaters we had bought in Marseilles on our voyage home. The weather in Sunderland would be cold by this time of year, with that cutting north wind from Denmark gusting across the North Sea. We were already feeling the chill, after living in Africa's warm climate. We all put on our sweaters, and Jack had barely stashed the suitcases on the luggage rack before the train lurched into motion in obedience to the conductor's whistle.

**

Bunty Gets Her Nickname

"The scenery outside our carriage window became more and more familiar as the train traveled north through craggy hillsides, eventually swerving eastward to cling to the edge of high cliffs on the North Sea shoreline. We stepped off the train at Sunderland station, awkward on our cramped legs, to be greeted by Mother, Father and my two unmarried sisters, Lily and Nell (Eleanor). Such a welcoming committee I hadn't expected! Tears and laughter mingled with greetings as the Ditchfields enfolded us with family hugs. Little Ida was shy, and hid behind the skirt on my coat when Mother bent down and exclaimed, 'I can see you! There you are, my lovely little Bunty!' This was a north-of-England nickname of endearment, often given to little girls.

"Father, the family patriarch, took one of the suitcases and Jack took the other. We marched out of the station to board one of Sunderland's double-decker trams (street cars) attached to a network of overhead wires on routes crisscrossing the town, enabling it to run on electrically-generated power. After another short walk, we were at the stately old Victorian house of my childhood. It looked exactly the same as I remembered it when we left, four years ago. My older sister, Hilda, came to open the front door with its stained-glass panel, in response to our 'rat-tat-tat' on the bright brass knocker, and we stepped over the newly-polished brass doorstep into the front hall. My oldest sister Lily ran into the hall for another round of hugs and teary greetings. The front hall was just as I remembered it with the carved, dark-oak chest standing against the wall where it had always stood, with its seat for travelers to sit on to take off wet or snowy boots before going further. The favorite gathering place for the family was the breakfast room. I could see it ahead of us down the hall, with a welcoming fire burning in the grate. The table was already set for high tea. A lingering aroma of baking was still in the air, bringing back childhood memories of my old home.

"Mother hung her hat and coat in the hall, on the oak 'clothes tree' stand, in the same place as it had always been. She looked as if she hadn't aged at all since I last saw her, except for the little grey bun of hair on top of her head which was now pure white. Tears of joy trickled down her cheeks as she opened her arms wide to embrace me again. I couldn't stem back a tear or two, myself. Mother recovered in record time. 'Now, Ida,' she said, I'm giving you and Jack the back bedroom, so you'll be near the 'lav' (short for lavatory—a toilet) in case you need it during the night. We still have the old one outside in the backyard, but Father decided we needed an indoor one, now that they have become the fashion.'

"Looking down at Little Ida who was shyly peering out at her while hanging on to my coat, she exclaimed, 'Why, there's my lovely little Bunty again, hello, Bunty! What a *canny bairn* (nice child) she is, Ida. Come back downstairs as soon as you can, and we'll have something to eat. You must be starving!' Jack and Father toiled up the staircase with the suitcases. Little

Ida and I followed them and visited the small room occupied by the lav in the nick of time before she had an embarrassing accident. After our experience with a *choo* in Africa, an indoor toilet that flushed seemed heaven-sent. For Little Ida, it was a heaven-sent toy! I practically had to tear her away from flushing the lav one time after another, by pulling on the long chain hanging from the water tank on the wall above it. A visit to the washbasin in the adjacent bathroom followed, to wash away the grime of the long train journey from our hands and faces, leaving us presentable to go downstairs and join the family. Oh, what luxury it was to have indoor plumbing again! A newly-refreshed Jack joined us, and the three of us went down the carpeted staircase together.

"In the toasty-warm breakfast room, Mother and my sisters Hilda, Lily and Nell were waiting for us. Little Ida stared at the open fireplace—the first she had seen. Looking at the flames beyond the protecting metal fire screen, she observed, 'Fire hot, Mam,' calling me by the north-country name she had been taught (in the south of England it became 'Mum', and in America it is 'Mom'). Her doting relatives smiled fondly at her, as if she had just imparted the wisdom of the ages, 'Oh, Ida,' my schoolteacher sister Lily cried, 'she talks!' I hadn't realized that ever since we had arrived at Sunderland station, my daughter had been too overcome to utter a word until now. Once unleashed, I was sure her powers of speech had returned with a vengeance!

"Sister Nell, who loved children, was awaiting news of her application for a job as nanny and housekeeper to a wealthy family in the south of England. She applauded, 'Just wait! Our little girl will soon be talking sixty to the dozen! I'll bet she'll be a good match for her two boy cousins when she meets them.' She added,' you know, Ida, we call our Hilda's boy *Little Lewis* and his father *Big Lewis,* but our Millie's little Alan wasn't named after Tommy, his Dad, so each kept his own identity. It seems to me that somehow the two Lewises sound as if they've lost their individuality, and I wonder if that will happen if we start calling the two of you *Big Ida* and *Little Ida?* Mother just called her 'a lovely little Bunty,' so why don't we call her *Bunty*? By the way, I've lost *my* proper name with the two little boys—they both call me '*Nantie',* but I rather like it!'

"Jack and Father occupied the soft armchairs on each side of the fireplace. They were waited on like royalty while the rest of us had our meal at the table.

"Over the teacups, we resumed our conversation where we had left off. Surprised and pleased not to be *Big Ida,* I agreed with Nell, 'Oh yes, Nell, I think *Bunty* is a great idea instead of 'Little Ida'—don't you agree, Jack? I know I've put on some weight since we've been in Africa—although I DO intend to go on a diet—but if you called me *Big* Ida, I would feel like a circus freak advertised as *The Fattest Woman in the World!* Everyone laughed, and Jack said, '*Bunty* sounds like a good idea to me, too, Sunshine. I wonder what Little Ida will think?' Surprising us all, Little Ida pointed to herself, smiled and said, 'I'm Bunty'. 'Well, that settles it,' said Jack, 'She seems to like it, so Bunty it is'"

Bunty, 2 years old

HOME TO STAY

It was Dad's turn again for the tape recorder. He cleared his throat, 'Sunshine, how about a nice cup of tea to help me along for the next chapter?'

Mom trotted off to put the tea kettle on while Dad sat back and began:

Doctor's Verdict

"I didn't waste any time, once we were installed at the Ditchfields. I said to Ida, 'Well, Sunshine, the first thing we have to do is to make an appointment with the Ditchfield family doctor for our medical checkups—after all, that's what brought us back to England!' I made the appointment, and Ida passed the doctor's examination with flyin' colors, as did Bunty. When it came to me turn, he listened with his stethoscope—several times in the same places—me heart and lungs. He asked, 'Jack, have you been well during your years in Africa?' I replied, 'Yes, I've been strong as a horse, except for a few bouts of malaria in spite of taking me quinine regularly.' 'Aha,' he said quietly, 'I thought so. Your heart is beginning to be affected. Well, I'll give it to you straight. I can tell you now that if you go back to Africa and have another attack of malaria it could develop into blackwater fever. To put it bluntly, your heart might not be able to stand it. You could come back to England in a wooden box.'

"The shock of what he said took a minute or two for me to absorb. I'd never had a sick day in me life, other than comin' down with malaria, and I was completely taken off-balance. After a minute or two of silence, I asked, 'What's me chances if I stay here in England, doctor?' He smiled and said, 'Then you'll probably live to a ripe old age, me lad, if you watch your health.'

BUNTY: Note: Dad did OK. He lived to be 92. He had what he would have called "a good innings".

Let me add a word about blackwater fever. Research told me that this is a complication which can happen when several attacks of malaria have become progressively more severe. The victim's temperature has been known to rocket up to 107 degrees F., destroying the red blood cells in the organs of the body. It is signaled by a discharge of dark red or black urine, giving it the name *blackwater fever,* and is usually fatal.

***

Dad shuddered slightly, as he continued:

"When I told Sunshine what the doctor told me, she burst into tears. 'Oh, Jack,' she sobbed, 'these are tears of fear for your life, but even more—although I grew to love Africa—they are tears of relief that we'll not be trying to bring up Bunty in the harsh living conditions we had there. Let's just leave everything out there and start fresh with a new home here in Sunderland. I can always make new curtains!' She stopped when a new thought struck her. 'But what do you have in mind for a job, though, Jack?' "

BUNTY: Here's where I butt in again with a bit more research:

Conditions in Britain at that time were far from the best. To quote one source, an observation of a professor of economics at a British university:

"It is well-known that World War One was expensive for Britain, to say nothing of the cost in British lives (36 per cent of the men in Britain were sacrificed—dead or wounded). Among other considerations, the economic costs were astronomical, due to post-war damage to employment and trade throughout the 1920s. Other countries had been able to replace Britain in world markets during the war; in the mid-1920s Britain's exports were only 75 per cent of previous levels."

In the north of England, Sunderland had been the world's leading shipbuilding city, and coal mines in the region were flourishing. By the mid to end of the 1920s, 19 shipyards had closed in the region and coal mining was in decline. Unemployment in some towns had reached 45 to 80 per cent by 1930. It was called The Great Depression.

***

This was the economic climate facing Dad when he decided not to return to Africa. He spoke slowly into the tape recorder with the memory of hard times in his voice:

"After I made the decision not to return to Africa, I wrote to the Crown Agents for the Colonies, regretfully tenderin' me resignation for health reasons. That wasn't an easy letter to write, but all me life I'd been taught to look forward, not back, so I prepared me résumés again and began to send 'em out. I would have to go back to sea, but it was what I was qualified for and the only kind of employment I'd ever known. I was now able to add to the résumés not only me qualifications as a certified Chief Engineer, but also me service as captain of a ship for the British Board of Trade. In addition, I could also throw in me shore experience supervisin' at Namasgali's marshalin' yards. A couple of good offers came back, and I chose the one from a passenger steamship line traveling to and from the Far East: P&O, the Pacific and Orient line. I would go to sea as a Chief Engineer once more.

"I tried me best to reassure Ida and she took the news better than I'd expected. 'Look Sunshine,' I pointed out, 'although I'll have to be away from home a lot, we'll have a good income. Now, me lass, with economic conditions as bad as they are in Sunderland and spreadin' throughout most of England, aren't you glad I didn't buy a car in when we were in Africa? The money we saved by not having one will help us to buy a nice house in a good neighborhood! While I'm away, I want you to start lookin'".

***

BUNTY: Dad trotted off to have 'forty winks' and Mom remarked to me, "I couldn't quite understand your Dad's justification for not having a car in Africa in order to save up for a house in England, but I let it go without any comment. It was 'water under the bridge', anyway. As you know, Bunty, he never did buy a car for the rest of his life!"

Mom opened her notes to where she had left off, and began recording:

"I was feeling more relaxed in my family home than I had felt for quite some time in Africa. How comforting it was to have both parents and my sisters in the house. And no other luxury could compare with turning on a tap to get purified water— already cool—for drinking and washing, without having to boil it first to kill parasites. Oh, and that wonderful hot water, too, coming out of another tap—without having to get someone to heat it outside over a charcoal fire in the backyard! I saw with new eyes that beautiful tub in the bathroom that could be drained by just removing the plug—instead of a tin one with handles that had to be carried outdoors to be emptied! And what a blessing it was to turn on a wall switch and get a whole room to light up, without relying on a temperamental generator!

"I think the best thing of all was the indoor lav! Posh people called it a WC (Water Closet). The rest of us called it a lav. Mother and Father had kept their outdoor *choo* down the backyard for emergencies, but now a shiny, white enamel toilet stood enthroned alone in its own small room with a door that we could lock for privacy. To be able to pull the chain and have it flush water from the tank above it on the wall was pure heaven! I had to be careful not to let Bunty get into the lav by herself; she would usually forget why she went in and amuse herself by flushing the toilet over and over, ending each achievement with a burst of giggling. Between flushes—if we didn't catch her in time—she amused herself further with the novelty of unrolling yards and yards of toilet paper into a pile on the floor. Yes, she was still a Terrible Two!

"In a separate, slightly larger room next to the lav was a white, enameled washbasin on a pedestal, accompanied by a white, enameled bathtub supported by four short legs, each one of which stood on a clawed foot of white-painted steel. The tub was too high off the ground for Bunty to step into it, but once she had been lifted in, it was always a challenge to get her out. I had to resort to pulling the tub's plug and leaving her sitting in a drained bathtub without the warm water surrounding her. As soon as she began to shiver, she gave up and allowed herself to be lifted out and toweled dry.

"Bunty had her own corner of our bedroom, with a growing family of new toys. Jock had stood the trials of the past weeks very well—I had even been able to pry him loose from her long enough to wash him, when she wasn't looking! New experiences seemed to energize her more than ever. She soon became acquainted with the milkman with his cart, and was so fascinated by his horse that he invited her (with my permission) to ride with him perched on the seat next to him while he drove the cart to his next stop down the street. He and Bunty walked back to the house hand in hand, and he promised her another ride some other time. I had never seen her so excited; she couldn't wait to tell the family all about her adventure.

"By African standards, the weather had turned frigid by mid-autumn. Bunty received her first set of 'combs'; a winter undergarment called 'combinations' (long underwear). The lower part had leggings with a trap door type of opening in back of the waist, held up with two buttons. I soon learned to be expert at unbuttoning it very quickly to avoid accidents! The cooler climate had us bundling up in sweaters indoors, which the family thought was hilarious while they were all still running around in short-sleeves."

***

A Home of our Own

Mom paused for a cup of tea, then she continued:

"All too soon, Jack went off to join a P&O ship which was bound for Japan. Jokingly, I said ,'Ooh! What some people will do to avoid the English winter!' He wasn't amused! He changed the subject, 'Sunshine, while I'm away, how about looking for a house of our own?' After he left, I decided to contact a real-estate agent before the weather closed in for the winter. Taking the advice of the family, I chose the agent they thought best. Mr. Finch was a small-boned, dour, thin-faced man with a deep voice that took me by surprise when he boomed, 'Oh, yes, Mrs. Amiss, I have some choice houses available now in Sunderland; we can start as soon as you're ready.'

"So the house hunt began. My sister Nell had gone off to her new job many miles away near London, leaving Mother feeling rather lonely without her, so she was always available as a baby sitter who was ready and willing to have Bunty's company while I spent time looking at houses. On her part, Bunty basked in the attention of her doting grandmother, so we were all happy.

"There was a long list of available properties within our price range, and I was pleasantly surprised by the good quality of the houses that Mr. Finch showed me. One house particularly appealed to me, on a quiet street in a desirable neighborhood. It was standing empty. I realized that the price had been reduced considerably by the owners—they had put it up for sale and moved out because of the economic downturn and their need for ready cash from the mortgage payments they had already invested in it. I had to tell Mr. Finch that I couldn't commit to anything without my husband's having seen it and if he agreed to the price. I explained that he was a seagoing engineer and that he would not be home for several weeks. As I expected, Mr. Finch frowned and said, 'Well, of course, Mrs. Amiss, you will understand that there is no guarantee it won't be sold before that.' I replied, 'I'll just have to take that chance, Mr. Finch'—and we left it at that. The more I thought about the house, the more passionate I was to own it, but In those days, traditional, stay-at-home wives depended upon their husbands to hold the purse strings as head of the household, and to make all the major decisions—so I just had to wait and hope!

"When Jack came home, we went to see Mr. Finch together, and to my relief he was still able to show us the house I had spotted as being a good investment and a wonderful home. In these difficult economic times, it was still on the market! Jack grilled poor Mr. Finch about costs including 'rates' (charges for water, etcetera, imposed upon home owners by the local authorities), and whether the house was 'freehold' or 'leasehold'. This is a peculiarity of British real-estate. If a house is freehold, its purchase includes the land on which it stands, whereas one that is leasehold must be bought with a lease, which does not include the land!

"Jack was adamant, 'Well, Mr. Finch,' he began, looking rather belligerent, 'I wouldn't *consider* buyin' a house that wasn't freehold.' I held my breath. Jack had been very enthused about the house, strolling from room to room and nodding his head, poking into the attic space and coming back down the disappearing staircase with an approving look. I was walking on air—feeling that a weight had been lifted off me to think that our owning the house was a foregone conclusion—until he asked Mr. Finch the question about something that I hadn't even known existed: who owned the land?

"For me, the next minute stretched out forever! While I quivered inside with foreboding, Mr. Finch straightened up, squared his shoulders, and affirmed, 'Oh, Mr. Amiss, yes, of course it's freehold.' That clinched the matter. I was so relieved that I thought I was going to collapse! Once this hurdle had been overcome, Jack agreed that the house would be a good buy for us. He and Mr. Finch went into a huddle about a reduction in the price, and when both were satisfied Jack told a beaming Mr. Finch to have the necessary papers drawn up. I was overjoyed! 'Tarrah'—we had a new home! My feet felt as if they hardly touched the ground as we walked through the Ditchfields' front door with the news. Before Jack went back to sea, the signed agreement of sale was in our hands. The house was almost ours!

"Our new home-to-be was a pleasant, brick, two-storey house, standing behind a low brick wall with a black wrought iron gate. The wall had a privet hedge that shielded the house from the sidewalk and the road. Between the hedge and the

house was a small lawn and flower borders that were overgrown through neglect. My hands itched to do the weeding! The house had a lounge, dining room and kitchen on the
ground floor. Upstairs were three bedrooms, a bathroom and
lavatory. There was also a loft (attic for storage) accessed
by a disappearing staircase which appeared and unfolded
when it was let down through a moveable access panel in
the ceiling. The fenced backyard had obviously been owned
by a gardening couple. It had three small apple trees and an
almond tree. Closer to the house was a lilac tree with spreading branches. Flower beds encircled the lawn, and a concrete
path led from the back door to the back fence. In this fence
was a door leading to a rather unkempt grass alleyway where
the dustmen (garbage collectors) could function when the
dustbins (garbage cans) were put out once a week.

"I couldn't wait to begin measuring for curtains, but Jack
(the logical engineer) cautioned, 'Now, Sunshine, this is all
goin' to take some time. The house isn't legally ours until we
have the deed in our hot little hands! Don't go jumpin' the gun,
dear—you're inclined to do that, you know! After we have the
deed, it's goin' to take us awhile to fix up the house so that we
don't have to do it after we move in. Luckily, we don't have
to wait for anyone to move out! His words of wisdom calmed
me, and I said grudgingly to myself, 'Gan canny, (go easy), Ida,
you know he's always right!'

"The deed seemed to take ages, but it clinched our ownership of the house. Actually, I was glad of the time lapse. We
had arrived on leave from Africa leaving behind all the furnishings and kitchen utensils that had come with the house in
Namasagali. Shopping for them was going to be exciting—just
like being newlyweds!

"Shopping for household items in department stores was, for
me, a new adventure, as we didn't have our own home before
going to Africa. I had great fun, parking Bunty with Mother while
I took the tram into Sunderland's busy shopping district to look

for what I needed to fill the kitchen drawers in our new house and get ideas for what kind of furniture to buy. I even had time to relax over lunch and a cup of tea in a department store's little restaurant. Taking time to rest my aching feet and luxuriate in the wonderful sensation of freedom, I enjoyed every minute.

"I had time to browse the stores' furniture departments and pick out pieces to show to Jack for his approval on his next leave from the ship. I asked him what he thought about having the sewing machine, as well as the gramophone and its records, crated and sent to us from Africa. He said it would probably cost as much, if not less, to buy new ones which would be the latest models. He also added that they might be damaged in transit from Namasagali, so—all things considered—it would be best to leave them for the next tenants. The two items were added to my shopping list, and when I mentioned the gramophone to my sister Lily, she surprised me by saying that the Ditchfields would buy us some records for it as soon as we had our new one, as a 'Welcome Home' present.

"I still could hardly believe that we had the deed, at last. The house was really ours! I thought about what was needed to refresh it before we moved in. While Jack was away, I spent time in a flurry of choosing wallpapers for the bedrooms to replace the existing ones with their overpowering, leafy patterns, and deciding on colors to brighten the tired paint in the other rooms. The lounge and dining room were wood-paneled in beautiful, dark oak, so they were no problem, but the kitchen would need a new coat of paint and the bathroom could do with a facelift for its walls. There was plenty for us to do next time Jack was home, and by the time he left again the house was ready for us to move in. Moving day went off smoothly. No moving truck was needed; the furnishings had been paid for and stowed away in warehouses until the stores delivered them. When everything was installed, at last, I put my new sewing machine to work making curtains.

"It was almost Christmas. It would be a challenge for me to

find a present for Jack, because he was in uniform on board ship most of the time, and we had already bought all the winter clothes he needed to keep him warm after we came back to chilly Sunderland from Africa. What to get us for Christmas? Then I had a brilliant idea! We had all missed Joey so much since we were back in England; I thought it would be nice if I used my meagre savings to treat us all to a parrot for Christmas. I knew that one of Sunderland's pet shops had a good selection in preparation for the usual holiday pet rush, so Bunty and I took the tram downtown.

***

Polly

"At the pet shop, I asked the girl at the desk if they had any parrots. She looked up from the book she was reading and said rather impatiently, 'The birds are at the back of the shop, madam.'

"Bunty had headed straight for the puppies and kittens, and I pried her away from them to tell her I needed her help to find a parrot like Joey. She took off at a trot for the back of the shop with me in hot pursuit. There wasn't an African Grey in sight, but in one of the bird cages was a beautiful young Amazon parrot, named after its river home in South America. It was a brilliant green and it had a yellow topknot. Just as we arrived, as if on key it spread its wings and tail, which flashed color with long, red and blue feathers. Joey had been handsome, but rather drab in his grey feathers compared with this parrot, which had been pacing back and forth on its perch as we came close to the cage. It stopped and stared us through the bars with head cocked to one side; then it surprised us by saying, very distinctly, 'Hello, Polly'. Next, it made a quick turn on its perch as if to show us how beautiful its green plumage looked from the back. I presumed it was a female, with a name like Polly! I asked Bunty, 'How do you like her, Bunty?' Bunty responded very firmly, 'Polly's a nice parrot, Mam.' That clinched the matter; we now had a new (female) parrot!

"Polly became a wonderful companion and a fast learner, although she didn't quite come up to Joey in intelligence. After we brought her home, I clipped her wings as the owner of the pet store recommended, so that she could still flutter but to make it clear to her that flying away was taboo. She and the cage took up residence in the dining room where she could look out of the window and see the pleasant back garden (backyard). As I had done with Joey, I opened the door of the cage to give her some freedom, once she became used to her new surroundings and whenever we were spending time at home. Polly hopped out of her cage and climbed on top of it whenever the door was open, but as soon as she saw me sit down she hopped down into my lap. I offered her my arm to let her hop onto it and from there she hopped up to perch on my shoulder, where she would talk to herself and to anyone else who wanted to listen. She clamped her feet tightly onto my shoulder to ride on it when I stood up and walked out (slowly) into the kitchen to get tea ready, seeming to enjoy a little safari into unexplored territory.

"Jack lost no time in teaching Polly a sea shanty or two; he was happy for the challenge, now that a new parrot had joined the family. However, he was never able to coax her up onto his shoulder and he was obviously envious that she preferred mine to his. Like Joey, Polly seemed to crave the comfort of something over her head at dusk, before she went to sleep for the night—possibly some primitive, instinctive desire for safety from night predators. She soon learned to ask for her blanket, after which the cage went silent until morning.

"Bunty was almost three years old, and she was becoming aware of the fact that there was a Santa Claus (known as 'Father Christmas' in England). Jack and I prepared for Santa as we usually did, and she was thrilled with her first doll in a little wicker pram. The doll had come from the department store in a white dress; within minutes Bunty had named her Snowdrop. Knowing that the dress wouldn't stay white for long, my fingers were soon busy making doll's clothes and wishing Snowdrop had been a few sizes larger, as I worked my sewing machine for hours making her eye-straining wardrobe. My reward was that Snowdrop always looked presentable whenever Bunty and I took her visiting.

"That winter was long, dreary and cold; it seemed endless in a house with no central heating or tropical sunshine. On scarce, sunny days, Bunty and I bundled up and made short trips, often walking to the baker's shop on the corner of the street to buy raisin-rich teacakes and toast them on the dining room fire with our long, brass toasting fork. Split and buttered when they were hot so that the butter disappeared into the nooks and crannies, teacakes were the greatest favorite at teatime."

"That winter, we wore underclothes day and night. Electric washers and dryers hadn't yet been invented, so washing and drying the clothes was an upward battle, especially for me, who hadn't done any of this in Africa. Weekends were supposedly used by British housewives for relaxation, but I soon discovered that (in my case) their main purpose was to give me strength for the weekly laundry onslaught that followed the day after. Monday was known as "Wash Day", and it usually *did* take all day! I washed the laundry in a moveable washtub on wheels. It stood on legs at about waist height and had a wringer attached. It was kept in the kitchen. A hose hitched it up to the water tap in the kitchen sink, so that it could be filled and emptied. After being washed and rinsed, the dripping clothes had to be heaved up out of the water and fed into the hand-cranked wringer with one hand while the other operated the handle. My goodness, what a test it was for my aching biceps! I developed arm muscles that I never knew I had! The used water had to be drained into the sink, and by then it was almost lunchtime! Before that much-needed luxury, however, there remained the exercise of using wooden pegs to hang up washed clothes and bedding on the outdoor clothesline. The afternoon was spent in running out to feel them to see if they were dry. All went well until winter came. I was shocked that first winter, when I looked out of the window and saw the clothes and bedding hanging there, frozen stiff as boards, bumping against each other with little thuds in the frigid breeze. In those days, there was no simple way to dry clothes indoors. In Mother's house, damp clothes and bedding were hung in a special room—an ice-cold 'scullery', a few steps down from the kitchen—on racks strung from the ceiling with ropes and pulleys. The wash sometimes took a week or more to dry! Central heating in those days was to be found only in large buildings: flats (apartment houses), large stores, municipal offices, etc. In our house, we had a small open fireplace in every room except the kitchen and bathroom. Much of the heat went up the open chimney; cold drafts came down. We virtually lived in the dining room in winter, where there was always a fire in the fireplace. I hung up our damp clothes on the 'clothes horse' (a folding rack that stood almost perpetually in the dining room) in front of the metal fireguard; on Mondays the rack stood there all night. We went to bed before the fire gradually died out, to sleep with hot water bottles under piles of woolen blankets. The dining room fire was re-built and lit again next morning before breakfast, after the residue left by the fire the night before had been cleaned out. It took another decade before most private homes could get hot-water radiators!

***

BUNTY: After Christmas, Polly had settled in with us and formed a great attachment to Mom. She seemed quite at home in her cage in our dining room. When warmer weather finally arrived, she permitted Mom to let her enjoy flapping her wings in an inch or two of warm water in the roomy kitchen sink. When Polly shook herself dry, Mom had to dry herself off as well, and clean up the splashes in the kitchen after each session. She must have seen Mom smile tolerantly and say, "Go on, splash, Polly". Polly loved her baths, and if too much time elapsed between them she would remind Mom when she squawked, "Polly wants a splash."

Polly the Prankster

And now, it's my turn to tell a story about Polly that I remembered from my childhood—when Mom almost got arrested!

By the end of May, Mom announced to Dad—after he had taken a liking to Polly when she sang his sea-shanties—that it might be a good idea to put Polly outside on warm days to give her some fresh air. Dad obligingly decided to try her out by standing the cage (with Polly in it) on the lawn. The first time this happened, a dog could be heard barking in the neighborhood. Delightedly, Polly mimicked the bark. Then another dog joined in, and another and another, until it sounded as if all the dogs in the neighborhood were barking. Polly stopped barking and uttered a peal of laughter, as if to say, 'look what I can do!'

Obviously, Polly enjoyed being outdoors and there were no ill effects, so it was time for the next step in her semi-emancipation.

There was a large lilac tree in the back garden that had come into bloom, gifting us with fragrant purple blossoms hanging from its branches. Dad bought a long chain from the pet shop with a metal ring at one end to attach to Polly's ankle. He secured one end of the chain to the lowest branch. At the other end, the ankle ring was hinged and closed with a metal screw so that Polly's foot couldn't slip through it. With her clipped wings, we knew that she couldn't fly far if she did escape, but it is a fact that if an escaped domestic bird encounters wild birds they may peck it to death, and we didn't want that to happen to Polly! When the day of Polly's emancipation came, Dad carried her out in her cage to where the chain was secured on the tree branch. He attached the anklet to Polly's leg and lifted the cage up so Polly could hop out on to the branch, which she did after careful consideration. The anklet ring fitted comfortably around Polly's ankle, and Dad had used all his strength to tighten the screw with a pair of pliers to keep it closed. She sat on the branch for awhile, adjusting to this strange new environment. Becoming aware of the alien metal ring, she lifted her ankle as if wanting to rid herself of such a nuisance. She then figured out that the screw held the key to her freedom, and began to work at it with her beak. Satisfied that she would never be able to loosen the screw that he had tightened with all his strength, Dad took her empty cage back into the house and left Polly to enjoy her new surroundings.

Mom went about her housework while Dad had 'forty winks'. The windows, as well as the outside doors, had been left open to catch the warm, spring air wafting through from the outdoors, carrying the perfume of lilacs with it. Mom checked on Polly after about an hour to see if she was enjoying her "airing". She gasped in horror; there was the chain, hanging from the tree with the ankle ring wide open, and there was no sign of Polly. Panic-stricken, she searched under bushes and plants in the backyard, with no success. In desperation, she went into the lounge and gazed through the front big bay window to see if Polly could possibly have found her way into the front yard. There was still no sign of her, but all at once Mom noticed a movement near the brick wall that separated the front yard from the sidewalk. In the dark shade under the hedge, there, to her relief, was Polly—who must have walked through the house when both back and front doors were open. She had ended up wandering contentedly under the gloomy protection of the hedge. Mom didn't want to scare Polly, so she pondered what to do next.

Just then, a woman came walking down the sidewalk with a wicker shopping basket over her arm. As she came abreast of the wall, a loud voice said, "Hello, Polly." The woman stopped in her tracks and looked through the gate at the house. The voice said again, insistently, "Hello, Polly." This time, while Mom watched from behind the window, the woman looked in her direction then took to her heels and ran as fast as she could away from the voice, her shopping basket gyrating wildly on her arm as she fled. By this time, Dad had joined Mom at the front window. He roared with laughter. Lapsing into his favorite dialect, he said, "Before she took to her heels, I'll bet she asked herself, '*Why, whee is 't?*'" (Sunderland dialect for 'Well, who is it?'). He added, "Ida, I'm goin' to get Polly's cage and we'll entice her into it, before she gets any more ideas!" Polly went into the cage like a lamb, and that was the first and last time that she was "aired" on the lilac tree.

Mom and Dad thought no more of it. They closed the doors and windows before the sun went down. Polly was talking quietly to herself, perfectly content on the perch in her cage. Mom was preparing to serve supper when a knock came on the front door. Dad opened it to see a policeman standing there. Surprised, Dad said, "What can we do for you, sir?" The policeman looked stern, "Well, a woman has complained that your wife shouted her name out of the window—twice—but she doesn't know your wife or what she wanted. Hearing her name from a stranger, in a silly kind of voice, she became annoyed and came to report it to us as a public nuisance. That's a punishable offense, you know."

Mom was scared to death. Dad stifled a smile, "Well, sir, your 'public nuisance' is right here in her cage. Our parrot's name is 'Polly,' and she escaped and ended up under the front hedge. It was her voice that the woman heard!" The policeman looked unbelievingly at Polly, a picture of innocence on her perch. As if she had understood the conversation, she broke the silence with, "Hello, Polly." The policeman looked shocked, then he grinned and said,

"Oh, please excuse my visit, sir. They are never going to believe me at the station when I tell them this story, but it's going to be good for a laugh!"

***

Let's go back to Mom, who was itching to tell an anecdote about my first meeting with my cousin Alan after coming home from Africa. She gathered up her notes and began:

"When we first arrived back from Africa, I took Bunty to visit my sister Mildred. A pretty woman, sophisticated and always impeccably dressed, Millie had accomplished what Mother described as 'marrying well' and was the lady of the Ditchfield family. Through connections at her millinery shop, she had met the son of the prosperous owner of the foremost funeral business in Sunderland. The Weston family owned stables housing teams of matched black horses, tossing their feathered headdresses as they drew the casket and mourners in elegant black funeral carriages through town to the cemetery. The Westons were what Jack called 'in the money'.

"With her charm and good looks, Millie had bowled Tommy Weston over, and within a year she was Mrs. Thomas Weston. A son followed in due time after the marriage; Young Alan was five years old by the time we returned to England. He had been looking forward to meeting his little cousin from Africa.

"Millie said, 'Oh, Alan's having a bath, but I'll take Bunty up to meet him.'

"I thought I'd better go with them! So we trooped upstairs to the steam-filled bathroom. Alan was sitting in the tall, white bath tub, playing with a flotilla of toy boats. Millie said, "Alan, this is Bunty, your little cousin from Africa." Alan's head appeared through the steam. He looked over the edge of the tub, took one look at Bunty and burst into tears. 'Whatever's the matter, dear?' inquired Millie. Alan howled through his tears, 'But, Mam, she's not black—she's *white!*'

BUNTY: I don't think Alan ever liked me after disappointing him. I couldn't understand it—after all, I couldn't help being white! He struck terror into my heart every time he was at Gram Ditchfield's when we were visiting, chasing me all over the house with his water pistol. I thought it must be his revenge. Happily, I was usually rescued by my older cousin, 'Little Lewis', who remained my favorite and my hero.

But, let's get back to Mom's notes:

"Well, that ended our visit to Millie! Now, I'll tell you about more of Polly's misadventures:

"With the return of warmer weather, Mother liked to walk the couple of blocks to our new home for the afternoon, staying for tea and a chat. As always, she wore a dress that she considered to be appropriately modest for her age, with its Victorian skirt covering her ankles.

"I had forgotten that Polly was out of her cage. She had crept into one of her favorite spots under the tea wagon, which stood by the serve-through hatch in the wall between the dining room and the kitchen. Polly loved the feeling of the dining room carpeting under her feet and the darkness of the wagon above her head. She was so quiet that I had completely forgotten she was there. I suppose she may have drowsed off for a nap; there was total silence from under the tea wagon.

"Mother had made herself comfortable in the dining room on one of the upholstered chairs by the fireplace, her teacup on her lap. She had been bringing me up to date on the latest neighborhood gossip when she suddenly let out a blood-curdling screech. The teacup flew through the air, and she bent down to the floor, yelling at me, 'Help, Ida; something just bit me on the ankle!' I lifted the folds of her skirt, and there was Polly, looking wounded by all the fuss. She had walked silently on the carpet from under the tea wagon and found in her path another promising shelter to explore: Mother's skirt! Why she decided to give the intruding ankle a peck, I'll never know—maybe it was some territorial instinct and Polly was staking her claim! I retrieved her and put her back in her cage. Upon examining Mother's ankle, I found nothing to indicate it had been bitten (Polly had probably only tried to taste it) so I rubbed it firmly with my hand, which seemed to calm Mother down. After another strong cup of tea and a piece of warm, toasted teacake, she was back to normal.

"Polly got into trouble again, not long after that:

"Jack was home. He was always astonished (and probably frustrated) when an angelic Polly let me give her a bath in warm water in the kitchen sink. He also seemed envious that she would sit on my shoulder for hours, all the while ignoring his attempts to entice her to do the same with him. On this occasion, he seemed to have resolved in his mind that this was an achievement he was entitled to share as master of the household. He moved his chair close to Polly's corner, where she was preening her feathers on top of the cage. Cutting a slice of apple, Jack enticed Polly to come down to his hand to retrieve the treat she adored. Like clockwork, Polly clambered down and fluttered over to his hand, took the apple slice in her beak, climbed up his arm and perched on his shoulder. She stood on one foot and held the apple with the other, nibbling on it with obvious relish. Success, at long last! Jack looked as if he had just conquered the world! He sat bolt upright in his chair, not wanting to dislodge her from his shoulder while he wallowed in his victory. The triumphant smile on his face suddenly disappeared when, after a few minutes, he gave a yelp of pain. I ran in from the kitchen to see if he was alright, and saw him sitting in the chair, his face flushed with rage and indignation, while Polly sat on the floor calmly eating the apple slice where it had landed. Jack shouted, 'Ida, come and take this bloodthirsty beast and put her back in her cage! She just bit me on the ear!'

"I had to stay in the kitchen until I had stopped giggling! Whether this was Polly's idea of retribution or whether she had fancied tasting Jack's ear will remain a mystery! I examined Jack's 'wound' but couldn't see where her beak had made contact—no treatment needed! So, I made him a cup of tea to soothe his indignation and his wounded pride. He never tried to coax Polly onto his shoulder again, and it was several months before he forgave her enough to teach her a new sea shanty!"

***

BUNTY: Mom went off to stretch her legs and make lunch. Dad awoke from resting his eyes. We munched our sandwiches together, having a good laugh now that time had diluted Dad's indignation over Polly's betrayal. Although he was far from being amused at the time, this story became one of the favorites in Mom and Dad's repertoire. I thought to myself, 'These are such precious moments to remember—each one of us enjoys these trips down memory lane. I suppose I should be writing these stories down'. Little did I know how long it would be, until this would happen!

It was Dad's turn with the microphone, but he was getting older and his emotions were closer to the surface as he re-lived memories from the past. Very much unlike his old self, he was becoming more easily moved to tears. He replayed Mom's last contribution on the tape, and I saw a tear or two in his eyes. He said, 'Bunty, let your Mam go on with the stories; I don't quite feel up to it today.'

***

Mom gently took the microphone from his hands and picked up her notes. She began a new chapter in their lives:

"Meantime, in Sunderland, a new era had arrived and the dawn of the 1930s saw big changes in our family life. To make it more viable, Jack finally gave up the sea, accepting employment as chief erection engineer for a large water filtration and purification company, which installed water purification plants in cities and towns all over Britain and also in other countries in the world. The work was never boring, which suited Jack's restless nature and his 'take control' personality. He hired contractors and local labor to build filter beds and to install turbines and other equipment for large waterworks, providing pure drinking water for thousands of people in cities. His jobs ranged from these to installing purified water for community swimming pools or supplying drinking water for military camps. After the filtration plant was in operation, Jack stayed on while tests were run to ensure the success of the job and safety of the water. Upon occasion, the jobs involved travel overseas. The last of these was in 1938, when he was sent to supervise the installation of the first comprehensive, purified drinking water supply for the city of Baghdad, which kept him away from home for nine months. But when the job was in Britain, Jack was always near enough to come home for weekends and holidays.

"Before Bunty was school age, we sometimes traveled with Jack to his jobs around Britain, using our house in Sunderland as a home base. We left Polly with a somewhat reluctant Mother and Father Ditchfield while we were away, but happily there were never any disasters to report. However, when it was time for Bunty's education to begin, I decided that she and I should stop wandering and settle down.

***

Moving South

"After suffering through a second winter in Sunderland, I decided that my body, having become so thoroughly accustomed to the warm climate in Africa, would never tolerate the frigid northeast coast weather indefinitely, especially as I grew older. Even in summer, its main attraction, the sea, seldom became warm enough for more than a quick dip before we had to run back to the beach-tent shivering, to change into warm, dry clothing. I had come to dread the cold weather. Bunty and I developed colds with bronchial coughs that lasted for weeks, and she suffered from bouts of childhood diseases.

"One day, Jack put into words what I had been hoping to hear, 'Sunshine, why don't we move to the south and give up this blasted cold climate? There's a nice suburb just outside London near the headquarters office of me company. Movin' there would put us in easy reach of good train service for commutin' to me jobs, and excellent schools would be available for Bunty's education.'

"I needed no urging!

"We had a nice 'town house' built in a pleasant London suburb and our health improved in the balmy southern weather. Polly lived with us until 1939 when war became inevitable, making London a prime target for Hitler's bombers. The children in the city's schools and its suburbs were to be evacuated immediately to a safer area. I volunteered to go with Bunty's prep school as a liaison person between the students' needs and the school authorities, which meant closing up the house. But what could we do with Polly? We couldn't leave her behind in an empty house, and we certainly couldn't take her with us! I found the address of a man living in the country, far enough away from the danger in London. This man had an aviary with parrots, and in response to my letter he agreed to take Polly for the duration of the war.

"When the war ended, we didn't reclaim Polly. The 'parrot man' and his family had taken her to their hearts in the six years of the war. She had settled happily into their lives, just as she had into ours so long ago."

BUNTY: Mom laid down the microphone and I turned off the tape recorder. Dad was enjoying his usual 'forty winks' in his favorite arm-chair. They had both come to the end of their notes, leaving me with a treasury of tape recordings collected on my visits to England over the years. Little did they (or I) dream that their words would one day become a book!

EPILOGUE

MOM UNKNOWINGLY WROTE the Epilogue of this book for me. After I had packed up the tape recorder, with tears in her eyes, she read some of the thoughts that she had jotted down.

"Thank you, Bunty, for making these tape recordings possible so that we could tell the story of such memorable times in our lives and the beginning of yours. They have made Dad and me look back on our brief years in Africa with humility and gratitude. I treasure the memory of generous, caring and loyal friends, both African and British, who were our faithful companions sharing those difficult living conditions in which we found ourselves. Effie and Ted, Meg and Davey, Thia and Tony, Mary and Jim, all shared with us the challenges of every-day living, taking time to laugh at its incongruities.

Mom paused to turn the page in her notebook:

"Unlike your new country, America, the black people we met in Uganda did not carry the bitter stigma imposed by past years of slavery, so our own experience with the natives was without the lingering memory of years of hurt, subjugation and prejudice. Even now, I see a black person without thinking of his or her color; I see only another human being like myself.

"I shall never forget the loyal devotion of Obonyo and poor little Omolo, and the other Africans who were so important to our lives in their country: Rachel, with her loving care of Little Ida; Isaiah, who labored proudly to keep us well-fed and taught us so much about Africa; the houseboys who sang as they worked. I cherish the memory of the shy women who came up from the *shamba* to admire my lampshades, and also Albert, Isaiah's helper, and the little egg-boy who watched his profits slip away as some of his eggs rose to the top of the water in Isaiah's bucket. In our memories, the native people we knew were sweet and innocent in their ways—in some respects like unspoiled, happy children in their own environment— untouched by the nerve-wracking challenges outside in the sophistication of the Western world. Separated from such distractions, they counted their world of friends and family as treasure above all other. As the years have passed, it almost seems a shame that the intrusion of Western scientific logic has spoiled their faith in such things as nature's spirits which inhabited a tree, stream, mountain or thunder shower.

"For me, Uganda is—and always will be—'The Pearl', despite the fact that some things have changed so radically since we were there; some for the better and others for much worse. It was like watching beloved children being whipped, to see how the people suffered after *Uhuru* (freedom) when the European nations so abruptly pulled out of most of the African countries. Strife and bloodshed were Uganda's inheritance; the result of being torn apart by native dictatorships and brutal political rival groups. One writer has called Uganda 'The Tarnished Pearl'.

"But fortunately, conditions seem to the getting better in Uganda. To quote a recent BBC Profile: 'Landlocked Uganda has transformed itself from a country with a troubled past to one with relative stability and prosperity.' After such a beautiful place and its people could have been so brutally treated in the past few decades, may conditions continue to improve. Amen to that!

Mom concluded:

"I used to think to myself, 'I must somehow get our memories written down', but I never did. Now I'm going to challenge you, Bunty, to do it for me."

***

BUNTY: Well, how could I refuse?

As it is well known, Winston Churchill always liked to have the last word. He called Uganda "a land of infinite possibilities." What could be a better ending for *Bunty's Beginnings* than to borrow a quote from his book, *My African Journey,* written after he visited Uganda in 1907?

"My journey is over and my tale is told. What message do I bring back? What is least worth having is most difficult to hold; what is most worth having is the easiest. Concentrate upon Uganda."

And with this book goes my fervent hope that Churchill's vision for the people of Uganda will be fully realized in that beautiful country where my life began. Amen to that!

REFERENCES

Barnes, Juliet: *The Ghosts of Happy Valley* (2013): Arum Press, Ltd.

Best, Nicholas: *Happy Valley* (2013): Thistle Publishing

Byrne, J.P., Editor: *Encyclopedia of Pestilence and Plagues* (2008): Greenwood Press

Carberry, Juanita,: *Child of Happy Valley* (1999): Random House, UK

Churchill, Winston: *My African Journey* (1908): Holder & Stoughton, London

Dinesen, Isak (a.k.a. Karen Blixen): *Out of Africa* (1937): Putnam, UK; Gyldendal, Denmark

Fox, James: *White Mischief* (1988): Vintage Press

Grant, Ian H.: *Nyanza Watering Place—The Remarkable Story of the S.S. William McKinnon:* The British Empire Magazine (no date)

Hemingway, Ernest: *The Green Hills of Africa* (1935): Charles Scribner & Sons, Inc.

Houston, Dick : *Safari Adventure* (1991): Cobblehill Books, Penguin Books, USA

Huxley, Elspeth: *The Flame Trees of Thika; Memories of an African Childhood (1959):* William Morrow & Co. .

Huxley, Elspeth: *Out in the Midday Sun* (2011): Random House

Johnston, Harry, Russell E: *A History of the Colonization of Africa by Alien Races, (1913):* Smithsonian Libraries, University Press, Cambridge

Lorimer, Norma: *By the Waters of Africa, British East Africa, Uganda and the Great Lakes(2019):* Forgotten Books

Markham, Beryl: *West With the Night* (2002): North Point Press, New York

Miller, Charles: *The Lunatic Express, an Entertainment in Imperialism* (1971): Ballantine Books

Nicholls, Christine: *Elspeth Huxley, a Biography* (2002): Harper Collins

Osborne, Frances : *The Bolter (2009):* Knopf, Doubleday *Publishing Group*

Parke, Thomas Heazle: *My Personal Experiences as a Medical Officer in Equatorial Africa* (1887): Sampson Lowe & Co., Marston & Co. London, Good War Diaries

Patterson, J.H.: *The Man Eaters of Tsavo* (1907): Oxford India Paperbacks

Ploth, David : *Uganda Rwenzori, A Range of Images* (1996): Little Wolf Press, Switzerland

Rowling, J.K.: *Harry Potter and the Goblet of Fire* (2000): Scholastic

Riddell, Florence: *Kenya Mist* (1924): Henry Holt & Co.

Roscoe, John: *The Baganda* (2011): Cambridge University Press

Scott, Nick: *Altitude Sickness; The Happy Valley Set* (2016): Magazine Feature Article, The Rake Magazine

Sheldrick, Dame Daphne (2012): *An African Love Story; Love, Life and Elephants* (2012): Farrar, Straus and Giraud; New York; Penguin Books, Great Britain

Todd, Marjorie: *Winnie - Her Life in Kenya 1927-1945* (2010): In pdf. online

Trzebinski, Errol: *The Life and Death of Lord Erroll* (2011): Harper Collins Publishers, UK

Werner, Susan: *National Wonders of the World* (1980): US Reader's Digest Association

Wheeler, Sara: *Too Close to the Sun - The Audacious and Adventurous Life and Times of Denys Finch-Hatton* (2007): Random Press

In addition: verification, where necessary, of information and historical data via countless articles and reference links on the Internet.

Printed in Great Britain
by Amazon